Small Business Solutions

for Networking

Alan Neibauer

PUBLISHED BY
Microsoft Press
A Division of Microsoft Corporation
One Microsoft Way
Redmond, Washington 98052-6399

Copyright © 2000 by Alan R. Neibauer

All rights reserved. No part of the contents of this book may be reproduced or transmitted in any form or by any means without the written permission of the publisher.

Library of Congress Cataloging-in-Publication Data
Neibauer, Alan R.
  Small Business Solutions for Networking / Alan Neibauer.
    p. cm.
  Includes index.
  ISBN 0-7356-0685-4
   1. Local area networks (Computer networks)   2. Small business--Computer networks.
  I. Title.
  TK5105.7.N443 2000
  658'.0546--dc21
                                                         99-057856

Printed and bound in the United States of America.

1 2 3 4 5 6 7 8 9 QMQM 5 4 3 2 1 0

Distributed in Canada by Penguin Books Canada Limited.

A CIP catalogue record for this book is available from the British Library.

Microsoft Press books are available through booksellers and distributors worldwide. For further information about international editions, contact your local Microsoft Corporation office or contact Microsoft Press International directly at fax (425) 936-7329. Visit our Web site at mspress.microsoft.com.

Intel is a registered trademark of Intel Corporation. BackOffice, FrontPage, IntelliMirror, Microsoft, Microsoft Press, MS-DOS, MSN, NetMeeting, Outlook, PowerPoint, Windows, and Windows NT are either registered trademarks or trademarks of Microsoft Corporation in the United States and/or other countries. Other product and company names mentioned herein may be the trademarks of their respective owners.

The example companies, organizations, products, people, and events depicted herein are fictitious. No association with any real company, organization, product, person, or event is intended or should be inferred.

Acquisitions Editor: Christey Bahn
Project Editor: Kim Fryer
Technical Editor: Dail Magee, Jr.

To Barbara,
One millennium is not enough.

Contents at a Glance

Part 1
Choosing Among Network Options
1 Why It Pays to Network 3
2 Making Basic Network Decisions 17
3 Ethernet Networks 37
4 Alternatives to Ethernet 47
5 Networking with Thin Servers 61
6 Client/Server Networking with
  Microsoft BackOffice Small Business Server 75
7 When Does Your Business
  Need Microsoft Exchange Server? 93
8 Does Your Office Need Microsoft Windows 2000? 103

Part 2
Installing Hardware, Cards, and Cables
9 Installing Network Interface Cards 119
10 Cabling Your Network 137
11 Hardware for Thin Servers 159
12 Hardware for Client/Server Networks 167

Part 3
Setting Up Computers on a Network
13 Installing Software on Network Workstations 185
14 Configuring Personal Profiles 215
15 Setting Up a Microsoft
   Windows–Based Server Appliance 231
16 Setting Up Clients on Microsoft
   BackOffice Small Business Server 245

Contents at a Glance

Part 4
Running Your Office on a Network

17	Learning to Share	259
18	Printing Anywhere on the Network	301
19	Communicating over Your Peer-to-Peer Network	317
20	Client/Server Communications with Exchange Server	345
21	Sharing Modems and Internet Accounts	371
22	Setting Up Servers for an Office Intranet	393
23	Networking for Road Warriors	421

Table of Contents

Acknowledgments xix
Introduction xxi

Part 1
Choosing Among Network Options

1 Why It Pays to Network 3
   Sharing Files and Folders 4
      Avoiding the Floppy Shuffle 4
      Making Files Easy to Find 5
      Keeping Documents Current 5
      Safeguarding Important Documents 6
   Sharing CDs and Removable-Media Drives 6
      Escaping the CD Shuffle 6
      Sharing Removable Disks 7
   Sharing Printers 8
      Avoiding Parallel Overload 10
   Sharing the Internet 10
      Don't Worry If the Line Is Busy 12
      Getting the Most from Your Monthly Bill 13
   Managing the Workgroup 13
      Fostering Communication 14
      Coordinating Schedules 14
      Collaborating 14
   Maximizing Your Investment 16

2 Making Basic Network Decisions 17
   Start by Planning Your Network 17
      Planning for Hardware 18
      Planning for Information 19

Table of Contents

    Determining Network Control 24
        Setting Up a Level Playing Field 25
        Putting Someone in Charge 27
        Thin Servers 30
        Combination Networks 32
        Selecting the Network for You 33
    Determining the Connection 34

3 Ethernet Networks 37
    Types of Cables 38
        Twisted-Pair Cable 38
        Coaxial Cable 41
        Fiberoptic Cable 43

4 Alternatives to Ethernet 47
    Weighing the Pros and Cons 47
    Using Wireless Network Devices 49
        The Pros and Cons of Wireless Networks 50
        Choosing a Wireless System 54
    Setting Up a Phone Line Network 56
        Pros and Cons of Phone Line Networks 56
        Choosing a Phone Line System 57
    Setting Up a Power Line Network 58
        The Pros and Cons of Power Line Networks 59

5 Networking with Thin Servers 61
    The Downside of Peer-to-Peer Networks 61
    Filling a Need for Small Business 63
    Types of Thin Servers 64
        Network-Attached Storage 65
        Print Servers 67
        Modem Servers 68
        Remote Access Servers 69
        Time Servers 70

Internet Servers 71
Universal Serial Servers 72
Network Appliances 72

6 Client/Server Networking with Microsoft BackOffice Small Business Server 75

Levels of Expertise 76
Network Operating System Security 77
Multiple Platforms 80
Microsoft BackOffice Small Business Server 81
   Microsoft Windows NT 82
   Microsoft Internet Information Server 83
   Microsoft Transaction Server 84
   Microsoft Index Server 84
   Microsoft Exchange Server 85
   Microsoft Outlook 86
   Microsoft FrontPage 86
   Microsoft SQL Server 86
   Microsoft Modem Sharing Service 86
   Microsoft Proxy Server 87
   Microsoft Fax Service 87
   Microsoft Office 88
   SBS Console 88
SBS Varieties 90

7 When Does Your Business Need Microsoft Exchange Server? 93

How Exchange Server Works 95
   Public Folders 97
   Directory Access 98
   Client and Server 98
   Microsoft Exchange Client 99
   Microsoft Outlook 100

Table of Contents

8 Does Your Office Need Microsoft Windows 2000? 103
  Ease of Installation 104
    Shared Files 105
    New Hardware Support 106
  Accessibility Features 107
  Security 109
    User-Level Permissions 109
    File Encryption 110
  Working Remotely 111
  IntelliMirror 114

Part 2
Installing Hardware, Cards, and Cables

9 Installing Network Interface Cards 119
  Are You Network-Ready? 119
  Working Without Cards 120
  Can You Do It Yourself? 121
    Installing an NIC Yourself 122
    Finding Someone Else to Do It 122
  Buying and Installing an NIC 123
    Selecting the Card 123
    Fitting Your Computer's Bus 124
    Using Network Starter Kits 126
    Where to Shop? 127
    Preparing for the Installation 129
    Installing NICs 130

10 Cabling Your Network 137
  Before Proceeding 137
    Patch Cables 138
    Premises Wiring 139

Planning for Network Hubs 139
    Hubless Networks 139
    Getting to the Hub of the Matter 141
    Placing Hubs 144
    Alternatives to Hubs 145
Running the Cables 147
    Running Cables Within a Room 148
    Running Cables Between Rooms 148
Using Twisted-Pair Cable 149
    Making the Grade 149
    Making Your Own Network Cables 150
Using ThinNet Coaxial Cable 151
    Making Your Own Coaxial Cable 154
Using Fiberoptic Cable 154
Good Cables Equal Good Networking 155
    Use Continuous Lengths 155
    Prevent Bends at Sharp Angles 155
    Keep a Tidy Appearance 156
    Don't Force Cables 156
    Use a Fish 156
Expanding Your Network 157

11 Hardware for Thin Servers 159
Choosing a Thin Server 159
Connecting Thin Servers 160
The Microsoft Windows–Based
Server Appliance 161
Network-Attached Storage 163

12 Hardware for Client/Server Networks 167
Using Domain Controllers 168
    Domain Controllers in Windows NT 168
    Domain Controllers in Windows 2000 170
    Domain Administration 171

Table of Contents

Selecting Client/Server Hardware 171
    Servers and Thin Servers 174
Setting Up Client/Server Hardware 175
    The Computer Room 175
    Racks, Panels, and Blocks 176
Using Thin Clients 179
    Windows-Based Terminals 180

Part 3
Setting Up Computers on a Network

13 Installing Software on Network Workstations 185
Installing Network Drivers 186
    Loading Drivers Automatically 186
    Installing Drivers Manually 188
    Installing Drivers for Non–Plug-and-Play NICs 190
    Checking Hardware Conflicts 192
Configuring Windows for Networking 193
    Adding the Network Client 194
    Installing Protocols 196
    Selecting Network Services 200
    Identifying Your Computer on the Network 201
    Configuring TCP/IP 204
    Using Server-Assigned IP Addresses 208
Welcome to the Neighborhood! 209
Troubleshooting 211
    Accessing the Network 211
    Checking Network Settings 211
    Diagnosing Hardware Conflicts 212

14 Configuring Personal Profiles 215
What's in a Profile? 216
Turning On Profiles 217

Adding Users 218
    Adding Users When You Log On 218
    Adding Users Through Control Panel 219
    Changing User Settings 220
Logging On as a Different User 221
Using the Microsoft Family Logon 222
Locating Your Folders 222
Changing Passwords 223
    Surviving Password Forgetfulness 224
    Deleting All Profiles 224
Microsoft Windows 2000 Profiles 226

15 Setting Up a Microsoft Windows–Based Server Appliance 231

Assigning IP Addresses 231
Using a Microsoft Windows–Based
Server Appliance 233
    Installing the Appliance 233
    Setting Up an Internet Connection 236
    Setting Up Printer Sharing 237
    Setting Up Security 239
Setting Up Clients 241
    Manually Setting Up a Client 242

16 Setting Up Clients on Microsoft BackOffice Small Business Server 245

User Accounts 246
    Types of Accounts 246
    Creating a User Account 247
    User Manager For Domains 252
Configuring Client Computers 255

Part 4
Running Your Office on a Network

17 Learning to Share 259
- Turning On File Sharing 259
- Sharing and Accessing Network Resources 260
- Types of Access Controls 262
  - Share-Level Access 263
  - User-Level Access 267
- Accessing Shared Disks and Folders 268
  - Accessing Resources with the Run and Find Commands 270
  - Accessing Resources with Passwords 271
  - Making Sharing Easier 271
  - Working with Remote Files 275
- Sharing with Microsoft Windows 2000 Professional 284
  - Turning On File Sharing 285
  - Sharing Drives 286
  - Sharing Folders 288
- Sharing Programs 289
  - What Can Be Shared? 289
  - Running a Program Remotely 290
  - Sharing a Data File 290
- Backing Up Important Files 292
  - Using Removable Disks 293
  - Storing Files Remotely 293
  - Using Tape Storage 294
  - Using RAID 294
  - Using Microsoft Backup 296

18 Printing Anywhere on the Network 301
Sharing Printers 302
Let the Printer Beware! 302
Setting Up Printer Sharing 303
Installing a Printer 303
Handling Problem Printers 306
Enabling Printer Sharing 307
Separating Print Jobs 308
Accessing a Shared Printer 310
Selecting a Different Printer on the Network 311
Using Printer Shortcuts 311
Connecting Printers Directly to the Network 312
Setting Up a Pocket Print Server 313
Setting Up an External Print Server 315

19 Communicating over Your Peer-to-Peer Network ...317
Sending and Receiving Pop-Up Messages 318
Starting WinPopup 318
Installing WinPopup 319
Using WinPopup 320
Creating Your Own Post Office 322
Using Mail Servers and E-Mail Clients 322
Using Microsoft Post Office 324
Setting Up Windows Messaging 328
Setting Up Microsoft Outlook 334
Selecting the Mail Service 335
Working with Profiles 336
Using the Microsoft Outlook Address Book 338

20 Client/Server Communications with Exchange Server 345

Creating Mailboxes 346
Offline Address Book 347
Security 348
Setting Up Exchange Clients 350
   Setting the Delivery Point 351
Communicating with Microsoft Outlook 353
   Using Exchange Security 354
   Getting a Digital Certificate 355
   Changing Security Settings 356
   Securing Contents 357
   Using Security 358
Coordinating Calendars on Your Network 359
   The Calendar Folder 360
   Setting Up an Appointment 362
Setting Up a Meeting 364
   Including but Not Inviting Others 367
   Inviting Resources to Your Meeting 368
   Receiving and Responding to a Meeting Request .. 368
   Checking Attendees 369

21 Sharing Modems and Internet Accounts 371

Internet Sharing Alternatives 372
   Getting Ready to Share a Modem 374
   Making Sure TCP/IP Is Installed 374
Using Modem-Sharing Software 375
   Installing Windows Internet Connection Sharing 375
   Internet Connection Sharing with Microsoft Windows 2000 382
   Using Microsoft BackOffice Small Business Server 382

Using Modem Sharing Service 383
Using Microsoft Proxy Server 384
Other Software Solutions for
Internet Connection Sharing 385
Using Internet Routers 386
Sharing Fax Modems 387
Sharing Faxes Peer to Peer 388
Using SBS Fax Service 391

22 Setting Up Servers for an Office Intranet 393
Creating a Web Site
with Microsoft Windows 98 395
Installing PWS 395
Using the Personal Web Manager 397
Creating Your Home Page 399
Accessing Your Home Page 401
Using Your Guest Book and Drop Box 402
Publishing Documents on Your Site 403
Creating a Web Site
with Microsoft Windows 2000 405
Creating a Web Site
with Small Business Server 406
Creating a Web Site
with Microsoft Office 408
Creating Web Pages with Microsoft Word 408
Creating Web Pages with Microsoft Excel 416
Creating Web Pages with Microsoft Access 417
Creating Web Pages with Microsoft PowerPoint ... 419

23 Networking for Road Warriors 421
Packing for the Road 422
Dialing In to Your ISP 424
Creating an Additional
Dial-Up Networking Connection 425

Table of Contents

Dialing In to Your Network 429
    Preparing Your Laptop 429
    Using Dial-Up Server 432
    Using Remote Access Service 436
    Accessing an Office Computer Remotely 441
Keeping in Touch
Using Microsoft NetMeeting 443
    Starting a Meeting 446
    NetMeeting on a Network 446
    Using the Microsoft Internet Directory 448
    Chatting in NetMeeting 449
    Using the Whiteboard 450
    Working Together on Programs 453
    Sending and Receiving Files 455
Controlling an Office Computer Remotely 455

Index *457*

Acknowledgments

Many people deserve my thanks and appreciation for making this book a reality. My thanks to Kim Fryer, who served as project editor, coordinating everyone's efforts and keeping the entire process on track. I wish to thank Dail Magee Jr., technical editor, for his attention to details, and Kristen Weatherby, who acted superbly as the copy editor. My appreciation to Barbara Ellsworth, who guided the book through development, and to Barb Runyan, Carl Diltz, Barbara Norfleet, and Dan Latimer, compositors, for their work in creating the attractive pages that you will soon be reading.

My thanks to Christey Bahn, acquisitions editor, who brought me on board; to Claudette Moore, my agent, for knocking on the right doors and calling the right numbers; and to Lucinda Rowley, editorial director.

I could not have completed this, or any, book, without the devoted love and support of the remarkable woman I am blessed to call my wife, Barbara. Since we walked down the aisle in 1966, she has managed to charm me with her smile and take my breath away with her beauty.

Introduction

If you have a small business, you're no doubt concerned about the bottom line. Expenditures must be less than income, with a comfortable margin for profit, and capital investments must be aimed at producing income or lowering expenses. Increased efficiency reduces costs and boosts production.

Creating a network can provide increased efficiency, giving you a better return on investment for your technology budget. The expense of setting up a network can be minimal, and it'll have an immediate impact on your office efficiency and levels of production.

In this book, you'll learn how to create a network for your small business using the Microsoft Windows family of products and a wide range of readily available hardware. If you already have Microsoft Windows 95, Microsoft Windows 98, Microsoft Windows NT Workstation, or Microsoft Windows 2000 Professional, you already have the software you need for a basic network. With a small investment in hardware, you can get your network up and running in a short time.

If you need more features than a basic network offers, you can use Microsoft Windows NT Server, Microsoft Windows 2000 Server, or Microsoft BackOffice Small Business Server to operate your network. These products let you perform mission-critical business tasks and host your own e-mail system and Web server with all of the security features your business requires.

You can use this book whether you are just thinking about setting up a network or you already have a network and want to get the most out of it. You'll learn how to plan your network and how to select, purchase, and

Introduction

install network hardware. You'll also learn how to set up and configure your hardware and software and how to share files, printers, and modems with other members of your office.

Part 1 of this book covers the benefits of setting up a network. You'll learn that you can share files and documents, use any printer in the office, and save money by sharing one Internet account and phone line to access the Web. This section of the book also guides you through the process of making basic decisions about your network. You'll learn about the various types of networks and how to determine which is best for your business. I discuss the types of hardware and software you'll need for the type of network you choose.

In Part 2, you'll find out how to select, purchase, and install the hardware you need to create a network, including network interface cards, cables, and hubs. You'll also learn about hardware for thin servers and client/server networks for more sophisticated small business networks.

Installing and configuring network software is covered in Part 3. You'll find chapters on installing software for network computers, configuring profiles for network users, and setting up workstations.

Using and getting the most from your network is covered in Part 4. You'll learn how to share files, printers, and Internet accounts. You'll also learn how to set up an office e-mail system and intranet and how to access your network from the road.

Creating a network for your office will help bring your business into the new millennium, and this book shows you how. If you have any questions about setting up your network, you can contact me at alan@neibauer.net.

Part 1

Choosing Among Network Options

1. Why It Pays to Network
2. Making Basic Network Decisions
3. Ethernet Networks
4. Alternatives to Ethernet Networks
5. Networking with Thin Servers
6. Client/Server Networking with Microsoft BackOffice Small Business Server
7. When Does Your Business Need Microsoft Exchange Server?
8. Does Your Office Need Microsoft Windows 2000?

Chapter 1

Why It Pays to Network

Some businesses are like a golf course fairway—healthy and green—while others die like grass without water. To keep your business green, you have to run your office efficiently, respond to clients and changing markets, and ensure that your team works together smoothly. In essence, you have to keep your business healthy for it to have a good bottom line.

Networking—connecting two or more computers together—is about the bottom line. Networking provides work efficiencies that can increase a company's *return on investment* (ROI) in computers, software, and computer training. While the network itself might not be a profit center, it contributes to the efficiency and effectiveness of your office by saving you time and money and by aiding the decision-making process.

Communication is often the key element in any decision-making process, and its presence or absence can lead to the success or failure of a project. If a staff member is out of the office, a memo is lost on someone's desk, or people are too busy to meet and exchange information, communication can break down and a poor business decision might be made. By linking computers together, you are also linking the staff members who sit in front of the computer screens. The computer monitor and keyboard (as well as the microphone, speakers, and video-conferencing camera, if you have them) become an extension of the staff member's eyes and ears, making communication among staff much easier.

Part 1: Choosing Among Network Options

Let's take a look at some of the efficiencies that networking with Microsoft products on PCs can bring to your business, contribute to your bottom line, and facilitate communication within your office.

Sharing Files and Folders

When you have more than one computer in the office, sooner or later you'll need to share files between them. For instance, your assistant might be using one computer to write a letter when you'd like to work on a document that exists on only that computer's hard disk drive. If you're not on a network, here's what you have to do before you can begin working on the document:

1. Ask your assistant to stop working for a moment.
2. Copy the file from the assistant's computer to a floppy disk—assuming it fits on one.
3. Go to another computer in the office and copy the file from the floppy disk onto that computer.

Avoiding the Floppy Shuffle

When your computers are on a network, you can grant other users on your network permission to access files and folders located on your computer. If others have granted you access, you can get to files that are on their hard disk drives, too. Accessing the files is as simple as if they were on your own hard disk drive. You can copy or move files from one computer to another, as shown in Figure 1-1, and even delete files on other computers. Not only can you avoid shuffling floppy disks, you can move files that are too large to fit on a floppy disk.

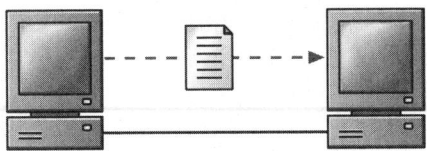

Figure 1-1
You can move files between computers on a network.

Does this mean that all of your personal files are available for everyone to read? Not at all. You can control who has access to your files and whether others can just read them or also change and delete them.

Making Files Easy to Find

Because files don't have to be physically moved from one computer to another, you can designate set locations for certain types of documents. You can store all of your company's billing information on one computer, save project files on a second, and put other business documents on a third. This way, when you need a certain type of document, you'll know exactly where to find it. And if you can't remember on which computer the file is stored, you can search for the file on the network using the Find or Search command on the Start menu.

Keeping Documents Current

Copying a file to a floppy is no big deal, you might be thinking. Maybe not. The inconvenience of copying the file might not bother you, but you can end up with a version nightmare. Here's a familiar scenario:

Your company's budget is on your partner's computer, but you want to work on the budget in your office. So you copy the budget file to a floppy disk and move it onto the hard disk drive of the computer in your office. You make some additions, a few changes, and one or two deletions, and then you save the budget on your computer's hard disk drive. As you're working, your partner decides to make a few changes to the version of the file on her computer. Now you have three versions of the budget: the one on your computer, the one on the floppy, and the one in your partner's computer. And, of course, none of them match.

When your computers are on a network, you can just access the computer in your partner's office and make changes to the budget in its original location. If someone else tries to access the file while you're working on it, that person gets a message saying that the file is in use. Once you've finished working on the file, simply save your changes and close the file, and you can be sure that anyone who uses it after you will have the most recent version.

Safeguarding Important Documents

While you want only one working copy of a file, you can make *backup* copies on other machines. That way, if a hard disk drive goes berserk and the original file is corrupted or lost, you'll always have a safety net.

You should always back up important files. You can copy them to an Iomega Zip disk or, if they're small enough, to a floppy disk. You can also back up to a tape drive, which I'll cover in Chapter 17. If the original file gets damaged, all you have to do is retrieve the backup. When you're on a network, you can also back up files to another hard disk drive on the system, taking advantage of the higher-capacity disk drives found on newer computers. Moving a file from one networked computer to another is faster than making backup copies on a tape or a series of floppy disks. In addition, the backup version is available to everyone on the network.

> **Note**
> You'll learn how to share documents over a network in Chapter 17.

Sharing CDs and Removable-Media Drives

CDs and removable-media drives, such as Iomega Zip drives, are a real boon to computer users. They store vast amounts of information, and they're fast, safe, and convenient. These days, most computers come with CD drives and many also come with removable-media drives.

Escaping the CD Shuffle

A great deal of business information is now available on CD, and you might even store your own office information on CD. Detailed specifications, accounting and engineering data, legal references and citations, and industrial standards are now routinely available on CD as an alternative to stacks of books and printed manuals.

Recordable and even rewritable CDs are also becoming office necessities. You can store the contents of over 50,000 pages of information or about 400 floppy disks on one CD, or you can use CDs for incremental office backups. If you have a scanner, you can scan documents and store them electronically on CDs to cut down on office clutter and manual filing. DVDs can hold even more—the contents of about 300,000 pages of information or 2400 floppy disks.

Chapter 1: Why It Pays to Network

In order for your company to realize the full potential of CDs, you must learn how to use them efficiently. Consider this example: When you need to look up a specification, a citation, or other information, you have to locate the CD in your office and insert it in your CD drive. And since many programs come on multiple CDs, you might have to swap discs to locate just the information you need.

To improve efficiency, you can configure a network so that staff members can access any CD on any computer in the network, as shown in Figure 1-2.

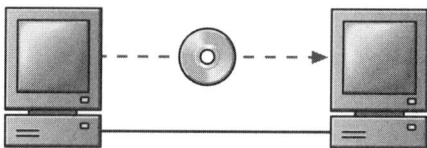

Figure 1-2
You can share CDs on a network.

That means you can leave a particular CD in your computer's CD drive and still access other CDs in the office. You can also set up a *CD server*, which is a special device that holds multiple CDs at one time, making them instantly available to everyone in the office.

Note

The licensing agreements with many programs might prohibit you from sharing a CD with multiple network users at the same time. Check the documentation that came with the program to determine your rights to network the program.

Sharing Removable Disks

Removable disks are great for backups and for transferring files that are too large to fit on a floppy. They're also terrific for storing those files you don't need often but still want to have around. The Zip drive is one of the best add-ons you can get for your computer. The newest Zip disks can store up to 250 MB of information—all on a cartridge small enough to fit in a shirt pocket! But the Zip drive has a lot of excellent competition, including removable disks that can store gigabytes of data, enough to back up an entire hard disk drive. In fact, you can swap some removable hard disk drives from one computer to the next.

Part 1: Choosing Among Network Options

When your computers are part of a network, removable disks and disk drives can provide further advantages to your company. Any staff member who is on the network can access, save files to, and retrieve files from a drive that's attached to any one of the other computers on the network. For more information on how to share removable disks on a network, see Chapter 17.

Note

Some removable drives fit into a slot on the front of the computer, while others are outside of the computer and attached through the parallel port. When the drive is attached to the computer's parallel port, though, you have to be careful. No one can access the drive while that machine is printing.

Sharing Printers

Suppose you have a laser printer connected to your PC and your assistant has a color printer on his machine. If you aren't on a network and want to print a special presentation in color, you'd have to complete the following steps:

1. Save the file on a floppy disk.
2. Take the disk to your assistant's computer.
3. Print the document on your assistant's machine—assuming the computer has the program needed to print.

The other option would include these steps:

1. Unplug the color printer from the assistant's computer.
2. Carry the printer over to your computer.
3. Unplug your printer and plug in the color printer.
4. Print the document.

There must be a better way!

When you've set up a network, anyone on the network can connect to any printer, even if the printer is attached to another computer. No one needs to transfer files or printers manually from computer to computer.

If you have only one printer, everyone on the network can use it, as shown in Figure 1-3.

Chapter 1: Why It Pays to Network

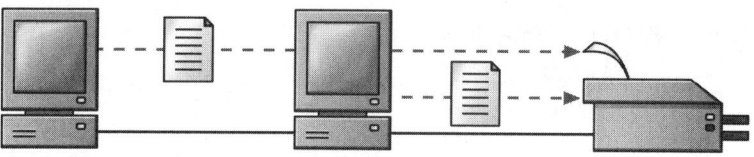

Figure 1-3
You can share printers on a network.

If you have more than one printer on the network, you can pick the one you want to use, as shown in Figure 1-4.

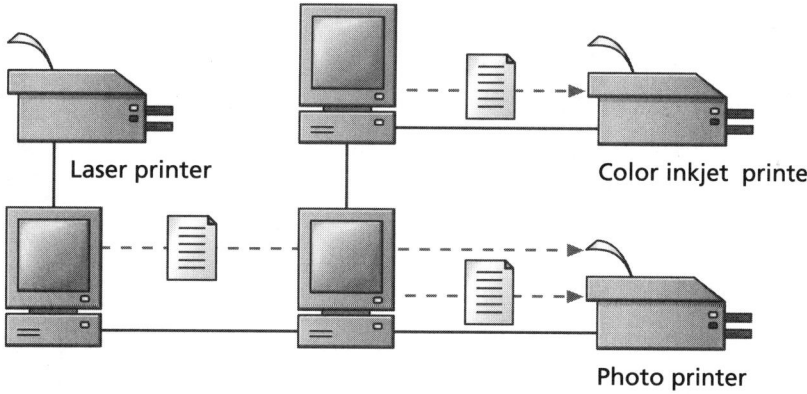

Figure 1-4
Users on this network have three printers from which to choose.

In order to access a printer on the network, you have to install the printer drivers on your computer and tell Windows where to find the printer. You'll learn how to do that in Chapter 18. Once the printer is set up, however, you can print your document on the printer on the network by doing the following:

1. Select Print from the File menu in whatever program you're using.
2. Choose the printer you want to use.
3. Click OK.

It's as simple as that.

If the printer you have chosen is in use, your document just waits in line until the printer is free.

Avoiding Parallel Overload

Normally, a printer is connected to a computer through the printer port, which is usually the parallel port. Connecting a printer to the network instead of the parallel port saves you from dreaded "parallel overload." In addition to a printer, you might have a Zip drive, scanner, or other hardware connected to the parallel port. If you use any of these devices individually, everything should work fine. But if you try to use two devices at the same time, you're asking for trouble. If you print a document while accessing your Zip drive, for example, your system might freeze up. By connecting the printer directly to the network, you don't access it from your parallel port, and you can avoid this problem.

> **Note**
>
> You'll learn how to share printers over a network in Chapter 18.

Sharing the Internet

The Internet is much more than a gathering place in cyberspace—it's an important business tool regardless of the size of your business. The Internet is a:

- Way to buy and sell products and services
- Place to advertise
- Means of communication with clients and vendors
- Method to stay in touch with the office, regardless of your location
- In many ways, the Internet can be considered a virtual extension to your office network. If your office is small, you might have only one Internet account that you share with everyone. However, most *Internet service providers (ISPs)*—the companies through which you connect to the World Wide Web (see "The Buzz on ISPs," following)—let only one person per account log on, regardless of the number of screen names or e-mail accounts you have. You'd need to set up a separate ISP account for each person in your office who needs Internet access, and that starts to get expensive.

Chapter 1: Why It Pays to Network

If you are using Microsoft Small Business Server on a client/server network, however, you can actually host your own Internet site. You can also make arrangements with your ISP for company-wide access to the Internet through full-time broadband services such as ISDN and DSL lines or cable modems.

> ### The Buzz on ISPs
>
> To connect to the Web, you need an ISP, whose phone number your modem dials to access the Internet. There are countless ISPs; some of the largest are America Online, MSN, AT&T WorldNet, and CompuServe.
>
> Most ISPs generally fall into three categories: those that don't require special software, those that do, and those that give you a choice. Some ISPs don't require special software because they use a Microsoft Windows feature called Dial-Up Networking in Microsoft Windows 95 and Windows 98 and Network And Dial-Up Connections in Microsoft Windows 2000. You can connect to a network—in this case, the Internet—by using this feature with Microsoft Internet Explorer and Microsoft Outlook Express, which are included with Windows. Other ISPs make you use their special software and their dial-up services. A few ISPs actually give you a choice of whether to connect through Dial-Up Networking (or Network And Dial-Up Connections) or through their software.

When you connect your office computers to a network, everyone in the office might be able to share a single ISP account. They might also be able to share one modem and one phone line if you have a small home-based business. So everyone in the office can chat online, browse the Web, and even download software—all at the same time.

Unfortunately, sharing has some drawbacks:

Browsing and downloading might be a little slower when more than one person is connected to the Internet. However, at least staff members can go online without waiting all night for the phone to be free.

Sharing an Internet account might not work with some ISPs. Some require that you use their own special software and won't let you connect using the Dial-Up Networking or Network And Dial-Up Connections feature in Windows. Many ISPs also have legal restrictions that allow just one person per account to log on at a time.

You might need to buy special software or hardware to let you share a phone line and Internet account. The good news, however, is that the software is inexpensive and might even be free in some cases.

Note

Windows 98, Second Edition, and Windows 2000 both have modem-sharing features built in. With these programs, you don't have to buy additional software to share a phone line and an Internet account.

Don't Worry If the Line Is Busy

Nearly all new computers come with built-in modems, so you'll probably have a separate modem for each computer in your office. But perhaps you have one phone line that you've designated for Internet access to keep your other lines open for client calls and other business.

To keep staff members from dueling over a dial tone, you can connect your office computers in a network and designate a modem on one of them to be shared—that is, used by staff members on other computers connected to the network. If one modem is faster than the others, such as an ultra-fast cable modem, it makes sense to share the fastest connection. You'll learn how to share modems and Internet accounts over a network in Chapter 21, but for now I'll show you briefly how sharing a modem on a network works.

Suppose your computer has the modem that's being shared. Another staff member working on a computer connected to the network opens a Web browser or uses an e-mail program. The browser or e-mail program actually accesses the Internet through your modem, as shown in Figure 1-5. If your modem isn't connected to the Internet, the modem will dial in and become connected. It's as if the other staff member actually came into your office and dialed the phone with your modem.

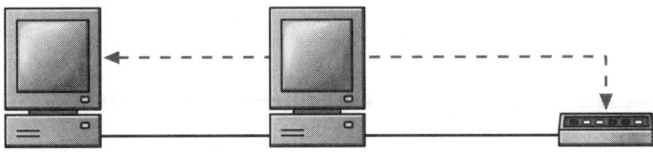

Figure 1-5
Other users on the network can access your modem.

Chapter 1: Why It Pays to Network

If you're already using the shared modem, other staff members on the network just share the ride. They don't have to dial in because the connection to the phone company is already made. When they go online, they won't hear a phone dialing; they'll just connect.

What if your computer is not turned on? No problem. Other staff members can still go online using their own modems, as long as the line is free.

Getting the Most from Your Monthly Bill

Because of the way sharing works, a second or third person connecting to the Internet doesn't even have to log on to the ISP. The person wouldn't have to enter a user name or password and wouldn't have to wait until a connection is made. The browser or e-mail program just joins the connection already made by another computer on the network.

As far as the ISP is concerned, you're using only one account, so you pay for only one account. If your ISP offers unlimited use, you don't have to worry. But if your ISP gives you only so many hours for free and charges for additional time, sharing is an even better idea. If two people are on at the same time for one hour, their use of your ISP account only counts as one hour, not two.

Managing the Workgroup

Every business, no matter how small, must work as a team. If you run a one-person shop, you'll still need to work with clients, bankers, accountants, attorneys, or other professionals to keep your business running smoothly. In larger businesses, from two people to two thousand, teamwork is even more important. Schedules have to be coordinated, progress has to be checked, and individual pieces of a project have to be brought together when the time is right. If the pieces don't fit together, the entire team has a serious problem.

Networking can help teamwork by fostering the workgroup. A workgroup is two or more individuals who are working on the same project or task. When your computers are part of a network, cooperation and collaboration between team members is easier and more efficient.

Fostering Communication

Networking is really all about communication. Not only are the office computers connected, but the team members sitting in front of the computers are also connected. Team members can post "instant messages" on each other's screens to grab attention or to get a quick response. They can also communicate via e-mail. If some members of a team are out of the office, e-mail will be delivered to them when they next turn on their computer to check their mail, even if they are at home or away on vacation.

In fact, you can conduct entire team meetings regardless of where the team members are, as long as each person has access to a computer. Programs such as Microsoft NetMeeting and online chatting software let you communicate in real time. With NetMeeting, you can even collaborate on documents and share programs over your network with each team member working at their own computer.

Important clients, contractors, and associates can be brought into the meeting as well. From their own offices, they can meet with all of the team members across your office network to get project updates and give feedback.

Coordinating Schedules

Your company might use PERT charts or timelines to organize the tasks in a project and conduct periodic team meetings. Or your company might be less structured, with informal meetings around the coffee machine.

Every member of the staff has his or her own appointment schedule. When you need to set up a meeting, you can telephone the other participants to check their schedules or just set the date and time hoping everyone can attend. One method is time-consuming; the other leaves too much to chance.

When you are part of a network, you can check each other's schedules online. You can either send e-mail to each participant confirming the meeting date or, using programs such as Microsoft Outlook, check everyone's schedule for free time when you set up the meeting. Outlook can warn you if an invited participant is busy when you've scheduled the meeting and look for a better time when everyone can attend.

Collaborating

As your project continues, use your network to keep track of progress and to report problems or delays. The instant nature of communicating over a network makes project reports easy.

Chapter 1: Why It Pays to Network

Because networking allows you to share files, you can collaborate with other members of the office. After you make your changes to the budget, for example, your partner can review what you've done. You can take a look at a team member's work to give praise, suggest improvements, or ask for feedback and support from other members of the team.

Most word processing programs, for example, help you collaborate by tracking revisions. Revision marks in the document can show other users which text you think should be deleted, rather than actually deleting it. They can also indicate text you've added through color and formatting. As you can see in Figure 1-6, which shows a document that's been edited with revision marks, changes are easy to see, and they can quickly be incorporated into the final document. You can also add a *comment*, a short note that doesn't appear in the document but is indicated by a color or an abbreviation of the user's name. To display the comment, you simply point to the color or the abbreviation and the comment appears in a small pop-up box.

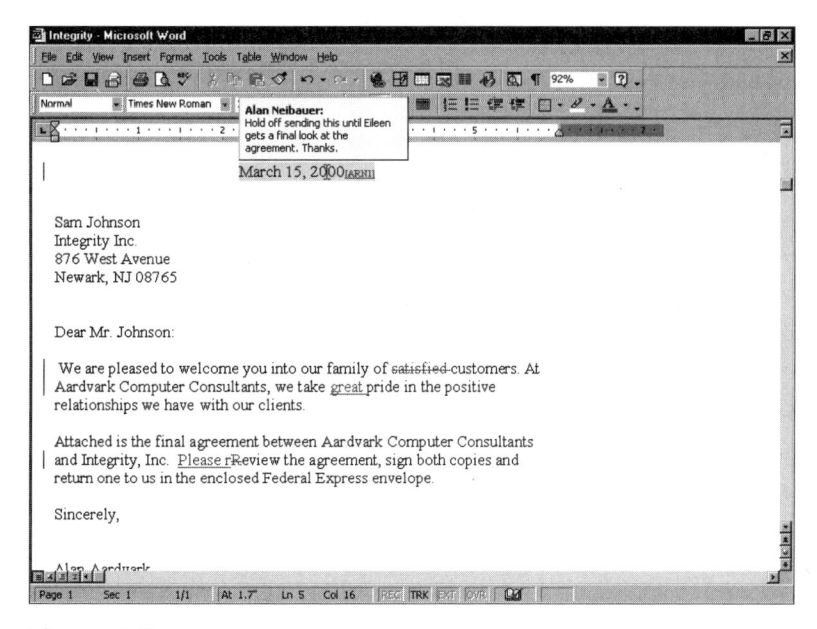

Figure 1-6
Use revision marks to collaborate on a document.

Note

You'll learn how to communicate over the network in Chapter 20 and Chapter 21.

Part 1: Choosing Among Network Options

Maximizing Your Investment

In many ways, creating a network for your office computers is a time-saver, a money-saver, and just a smart thing to do. It requires a small investment in time and money and some planning and foresight, but it is well worth the effort.

Networking will help you maximize the efficiency of your office and get a greater benefit out of your hardware and software investment. Networking will also help staff work more effectively by streamlining office procedures and by sharing resources.

In the next chapter, I'll cover the types of networks and how to pick one that's best for your needs.

Chapter 2

Making Basic Network Decisions

Networking doesn't have to be complex or expensive; you don't have to learn the history of networking or study arcane subjects such as network layers in order to set up a network for your business. Before you run down to the computer store and part with your hard-earned cash, however, take the time to make some basic decisions about your networking needs.

This chapter will help you choose the type of network you want and the best way to connect your computers. You'll learn the difference between a *peer-to-peer* network and a *client/server* network, and you'll learn four ways to move information between the computers on the network.

Start by Planning Your Network

Basically, you can plan your network in two ways. If you have a small, rather straightforward business without a lot of employees and not much inventory, you can plan your network based on the hardware that's needed to connect your computers. If you have a medium-sized business or expect

Part 1: Choosing Among Network Options

your small business to grow in the near future, you should base your network plans on the information your company gathers, stores, and disseminates in the course of doing business.

Planning for Hardware

Some businesses start planning for a network by looking at the hardware they already own or at the physical layout of their office. This method can be shortsighted, however, because it assumes a network is just a physical system.

If you have computers and don't need more, you're probably most concerned with the physical connection between the computers. Read the rest of this chapter as well as Chapters 3 and 4 to learn the most efficient way to connect your computers. To begin, it might help you to draw a floor plan of the office, noting where the computers and printers are located, and plan a wiring scheme. You might want to wire every office in your business even if you currently have computers in just one room, to accommodate growth in your business, such as the addition of new employees. You should also consider enabling remote connections, to accommodate employees who might need to dial in to the network from home or when they are away from the office on business. Even if you don't envision needing to connect to your office network from the road, remote networking is likely to be in your future.

The type of network that you set up for your business should depend on two factors:

- Resources that you have currently or plan to acquire in the near future
- Resources that you might need in the intermediate future

This means if you have only two computers in the office, you can start by creating a network for those two. But you should plan your network so it can eventually accommodate the number of computers, printers, and other resources that you see your business having over the next two years. It doesn't make sense to start with a network that allows little or no growth when the cost differences between networking two and five computers, for example, are negligible—just a few dollars for additional cables.

You should also look about three to five years further into the future of your business. Visualize how you'd like your company to grow and the different things your company might be doing. Plan a network that will grow with your company; this foresight could save you the later expense of scrapping what you have already purchased and starting over. Ideally, your network's infrastructure should be capable of handling your business's expected growth, plus about 20 percent more.

> **Note**
>
> The infrastructure of a network is the basic design of how it works, including hardware issues such as your network cabling; personnel and organizational issues such as network passwords and security; troubleshooting and repair procedures; and computer-use guidelines.

Planning for Information

The best way to plan your office network, however, is to look at the flow of work and information in your office, rather than just considering the hardware you need. The infrastructure of your network should aid in the collection and dissemination of information that supports your business's decision-making processes and goals.

> **Note**
>
> In many medium and large companies, the computer system is part of an overall division called Information Systems. The person in charge of this division might be titled the Chief Information Officer (CIO). These names stress that the computer system is a management tool that helps the company process information.

Consider the task of inventory control as a very simple example of the type of information that a network can process. Analyzing the flow of inventory from your stock can tell you a lot about your business, such as which products sell, when they sell, and who buys them. This information is available individually with every order your company receives, but how fast is the composite analysis of your sales made available to management?

By making the information available over a network, management can get current inventory levels and detect seasonal buying trends, which enables them to react to changing markets and market conditions. The faster a business reacts to the market, the stronger its position in that market.

This type of planning requires a few distinct steps:

1. Analyze your current system.
2. Determine how the system can be improved.
3. Determine the infrastructure needed to support the system.

Analyzing Your Current System

In planning your network, you should be concerned with the following issues, even before thinking about hardware:

- **What information is currently shared within the office?** You need to look at both formal and informal sharing. Formal sharing includes printed documents that all employees need access to such as memos, letters, reports, and calendars. Informal sharing includes ad hoc conversations and other discussions among your staff and those with whom you do business.

- **Who shares information?** Consider the employees who share each type of information. What are their roles in the office and in the decision-making process? Why is the information shared with them?

- **How current is the information when each employee receives it?** Determine when each piece of information flows from one person to the other.

- **How does the information flow?** Look at the direction in which information flows and the form that the information takes.

- **Where is information stored?** Consider where information, both printed and electronic, is currently stored. How long is it retained, and how is it retrieved if needed?

- **What are the deficiencies of the current system?** Identify any obvious problems that you have experienced with the current information system.

Making Desired Improvements

Next, you should determine how your current information system can be improved to support your business goals and the decision-making process.

Look at your responses to the questions in the previous section, and consider these questions:

- **What information needs to be shared?** Identify this information and determine who generates it and where it's located. Look beyond the information you currently generate in the office to what you'll need to make informed decisions and to support your business in the future. Consider administrative data, such as budgets and personnel, as well as client and project information.
- **Who should be sharing the information?** Determine who needs to know each type of information and in what detail. Do other professionals with whom your business is associated, such as accountants and attorneys, need access to certain information? Do you have any exceptions to sharing each type of information, such as for special projects?
- **How current does the information have to be?** Consider the timing of information dissemination to each individual. Who needs current information, and who can use information when it is older?
- **How should the information flow, both within the office and remotely?** Determine the form in which each type of information should be distributed—in hard copy, electronically, or verbally.
- **Where and how should the information be stored?** Consider where information should be stored for reporting, analysis, and archival purposes. What mechanisms—and safeguards—are needed for retrieval?
- **How will your needs change in the near future?** Do you envision any changes to the generation and flow of information that might be required as your business grows, and what is the timeline?

Planning the Infrastructure

You should now be able to plan both your computer network and office infrastructure to support your information system. Working with your office staff—and a network consultant if necessary—look into the following issues. Keep in mind that that your decisions should be equally based on solid business principles and procedures and the technical aspects of networking.

Operating Procedures

What standard operating procedures (SOPs) are needed to ensure the collection, dissemination, and analysis of the information? You should have clearly defined operating procedures for every major office function. Putting the procedures in writing helps you organize the network and account for all types of information.

Before purchasing any new hardware and software, make sure you know the following about your company's SOPs:

- Who should enter data into the information system?
- When and how should it be entered?
- Who should receive the information?
- When should it be distributed?
- Where should the information be archived?
- How should the information be analyzed to help your bottom line?

Chances are you already have SOPs for your current information system. For example, when an order is received in the mail, you have a procedure for putting the order through a manual processing system that might go something like this:

1. Person A in Orders opens the order and records it in the master order book.
2. Person A copies the order, places one copy in the client file, and sends the other two to the shipping floor.
3. Person B in Parts collects all of the items, noting which are back ordered, and sends the items to Shipping.
4. Person B pulls the inventory cards for each item and reduces the number of the stock on hand. If any items have to be reordered, a form is completed and sent to Purchasing.
5. Person C in Shipping packs the order and computes shipping charges.
6. Person C files one copy of the order and forwards the other to Billing.

7. Person D in Billing posts the order to the client's account and notifies Person A that the order has been filled.
8. Person A notes the shipment in the client folder.

The same procedure for this information system when a computer network is used might be similar:

1. Person A in Orders opens the order and keys it into the computer system. The computer checks for available inventory, generates any necessary reorders, and forwards the order to processing.
2. Person B in Parts collects the items, noting any exceptions on the computerized record, and forwards the items to shipping.
3. Person C in Shipping packs the order, computes the shipping charges, and notes it on the computer record, which is forwarded for billing.
4. At the end of each day, the computer generates a summary report of all transactions and forwards it to the company executives.

Networking Scheme

Later in this chapter you will learn about two types of networking—peer-to-peer and client/server. Once you read this chapter and Chapters 3 through 8, you'll be able to determine the network type you need to put the SOPs into operation.

You'll have to determine whether you need a client/server network or whether you can use a peer-to-peer network. You'll be able to determine the number of computers and their placement in the office to handle the input, processing, and output of information.

Personnel

Defining your SOPs, determining the flow of information around the office, and specifying the computer network required to handle your SOPs and the flow of information will tell you the personnel you need to operate the network.

If you use a peer-to-peer network with a small number of computers, for example, you probably won't need to hire a *network administrator*, a person who handles the day-to-day chores of ensuring the network runs smoothly. But if you determine you need a client/server network serving 50 computers performing mission-critical applications, then you might consider either a part-time or full-time administrator.

Security

Your analysis of your information system will also indicate the level of security you require. Certain applications and computer hardware lend themselves to tighter security—control over who has access to the data and the level of that access. You'll need to keep the level of security in mind as you read about the various network types and hardware in the coming chapters.

Evaluation

A thorough evaluation of your office procedures and network shouldn't be considered optional. Only through this evaluation and the flexibility to make necessary changes can a computer system promote your business's goals.

Take the time and make the extra investment to plan thoroughly for your network. You don't need to install the network of your company's future today, but your network should be designed so that you can expand or change aspects of it to accommodate changes in your business.

Determining Network Control

One of the first decisions you have to make when you're deciding how to set up your network is whether or not to give someone control of it. In one type of network called *peer-to-peer*, no one person or computer is in charge and has control of the network. In another type of setup called *client/server*, a computer called a *server* controls access to the network and serves as a central storage area for files and information. Table 2-1 summarizes the features of these two types of networks.

Table 2-1 Peer-to-Peer vs. Client/Server Networks

Peer-to-Peer Network	Client/Server Network
Can share files, printers, and fax/modems	Can share files, printers, and fax/modems
Anyone can connect to the network	Only authorized users have access to the network
No central file storage	Central file storage
Security set by each user	Central security
Easy setup and maintenance	More complicated setup and maintenance
Low cost	Moderate to high cost
Limited expansion	Unlimited expansion

Setting Up a Level Playing Field

Since no single computer acts as the controller in a peer-to-peer network, everyone on the network is equal—all are peers. Any computer on the network can communicate with any other computer on an equal basis. It also means that information flows directly between two computers, as shown in Figure 2-1.

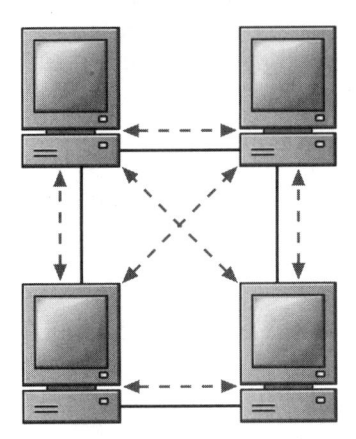

Figure 2-1
Computers on a peer-to-peer network communicate with each other directly.

    A peer-to-peer network, however, does not eliminate all forms of control. Each person on the network can use passwords to protect files and folders. (*See "Accessing Resources with Passwords" on page 271.*) While everyone can connect to the network, you don't have to let everyone share your files or use your printer or modem. How much access to your computer other people have is entirely up to you. You can create a password that controls who has access to your computer, which files they can access, and how they can use them.

    For example, you can allow only certain folders to be shared. In fact, to protect critical Windows files, you always want to prevent the Windows folder from being shared. You can also grant *read-only* rights to a folder. This means that others on the network can look at a file in a shared folder on your computer and copy it to their computers, but they won't be able to change or delete the original file on your computer.

    You can grant full access or *read/write* access to certain folders on your computer, which means that everyone on the network can read, change, and delete files in these folders just as you can. Grant full access only to people you really trust and only to those folders that you want to be totally accessible.

A peer-to-peer network can also have an e-mail system. Staff members will be able to send and receive e-mail messages within the network, just as they can on the Internet. But one person has to set up the e-mail system and control who has access to it. You don't need to hire a network administrator; you can usually set up and maintain a peer-to-peer network yourself or assign the task to someone knowledgeable about computers.

In a peer-to-peer network, if any one computer is down—either turned off or not working—everyone else on the network can still communicate. In Figure 2-2, for example, even though two of the four computers on the network are turned off, the other two computers can still share files and printers. You won't be able to use the printers attached to the computers that are off, but you'll still be able to use the files and resources of those computers that are on.

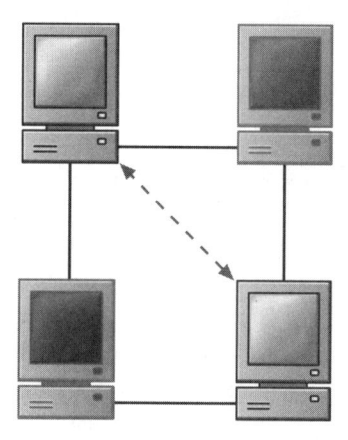

Figure 2-2

Peer-to-peer networked computers can still communicate when other computers are turned off.

If you decide to use a peer-to-peer network, you should also remember that some computers, especially laptops, have a *suspend mode*. After a certain period of inactivity, they save information about all open programs on their hard disks and turn themselves off. When you later turn the computer back on, the screen appears exactly as you left it. If a computer on

Chapter 2: Making Basic Network Decisions

the network goes into suspend mode, its resources won't be available to other users. Other computers have an energy-saving feature that turns off only the display or the disk drive after a period of inactivity. The resources of these types of computers might also be unavailable when they are in energy-saving mode. Because there are so many different kinds of computers, you'll have to experiment to see how a particular computer reacts on your network.

> **Note**
>
> In Chapter 18, you'll learn how to connect printers directly to a peer-to-peer network so any computer can use them at any time.

A peer-to-peer network has no central storage location for everyone's files. If you're looking for a file that is not on your machine, you'll need to know where it is on the network or search all of the computers on the network to locate the file. And if the computer on which the file is located is turned off, you're out of luck. You'll have to wait until it's on to get to the file.

Still, the advantages of peer-to-peer networks—they're inexpensive and easy to set up, run, and maintain—outweigh the disadvantages for very small businesses.

Putting Someone in Charge

When you want tighter control over a network, the solution is a client/server network. The *server* is a single computer equipped with special software that supervises everything on the network. The *clients* are the computers that connect to the server to use its resources. Communication among the clients must go through the server, as shown in Figure 2-3, and clients can use all printers or modems that are attached to the server. The network can be set up so each client must log on to the server before the client can use the resources attached to that server. The server authenticates the clients, verifying that the client computer has permission to log on to the network. It does this by checking the user's logon name against a database of authorized users created by the network administrator. If the user's name isn't in the database, he or she won't be able to access any of the files or other resources on the server.

Part 1: Choosing Among Network Options

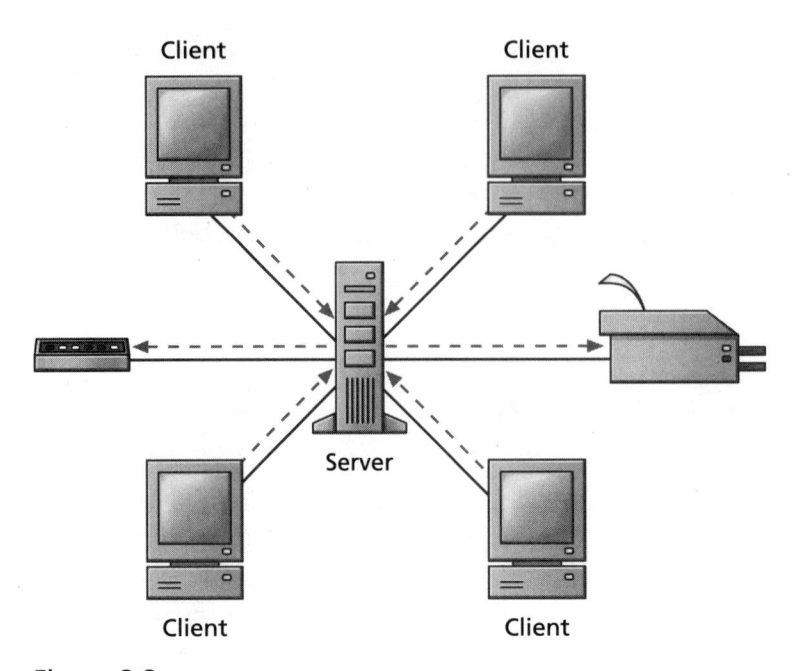

Figure 2-3
Client computers connect through a server in a client/server network.

In addition to the security offered by verifying users of a network, a client/server network offers these benefits:

- The server can act as a central storage location that everyone on the network can reach. Because the server is always on, you can use it to store graphics, downloaded files from the Internet, and other documents that you want everyone to share. The files are always available to everyone who is authenticated by the server.

- You can also password-protect files. Not only must the server authenticate a user before the user can access the server, but the user will also need a password to access the protected file or folder.

- You can load and run applications from the server instead of installing them on every computer. This way, you can be sure that everyone on the network is using the same programs and can easily share files. When you want to update a program—from version 6 to version 7, for example—you need to install the update

Chapter 2: Making Basic Network Decisions

on only the server. However, running applications on a server can seriously degrade the overall network performance, especially if many users try to access the application at the same time.

- The server in a client/server network can act as a central message center for e-mail and discussions. As with an Internet newsgroup or a computer bulletin board, you can leave messages on the server for everyone else on the network to see and respond to.

You'll need either Microsoft Windows NT Server or Microsoft Windows 2000 Server to create a client/server network. The server can't use Microsoft Windows 95 or Microsoft Windows 98, although the clients can. Windows NT and Windows 2000 have both server and client versions; to set up a client/server network, you'll need one of the server versions of the operating system.

If your network is small, you can set up and maintain a Windows NT or Windows 2000–based network yourself. As your network grows and your staff starts utilizing more resources, however, you'll need to spend more time maintaining the network. If your company and network grow even more, you might also need to hire a part-time or full-time network administrator.

Note

You can set up a Windows NT or Windows 2000–based computer so it also has Windows 95 or Windows 98 in a dual-boot configuration. You can then decide which operating system to use when you start your computer. If you start or boot your server in Windows 95 or Windows 98, however, you'll lose the benefits of client/server computing because the server computer will be operating on a peer-to-peer basis.

In most large client/server networks, the server computer is usually dedicated to the task of being the server and isn't used as a regular workstation for everyday jobs. The tasks the server has to do and the information stored in it are extremely important; you don't want to risk losing any information by allowing an employee to use the server computer as his or her personal machine. If the server is down, the network is down, and none of the computers can access any resources on the network or communicate with each other, as shown in Figure 2-4.

Part 1: Choosing Among Network Options

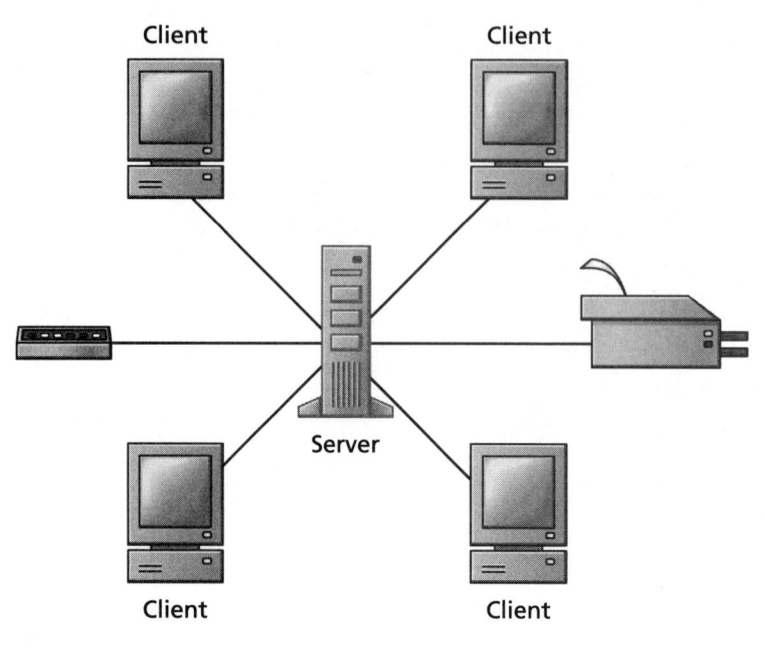

Figure 2-4
When the server is down, the entire network goes down with it.

Tip

You can start with a peer-to-peer network to keep your initial cost and efforts down and expand to a client/server network later by adding a Windows 2000-based server into the configuration when the need arises.

Thin Servers

To keep your maintenance costs down and get some of the benefits of client/server computing while using a peer-to-peer network, consider using a thin server. A *thin server* doesn't have all of the power and capabilities of a full server in a client/server network and can perform only specific functions, such as printer or file sharing.

One type of thin server is a *Windows-based server appliance,* which you'll learn more about in Chapter 11. Available from a number of manufacturers, a Windows-based server appliance is a computer that runs Microsoft Windows for Express Networks and provides centralized file, printer, and Internet sharing for peer-to-peer networks, as shown in Figure 2-5.

Wizards—a series of dialog boxes—take you step-by-step through the process of setting up a Windows-based server appliance and configuring the client computers on the network. This enables you to set up your network without any technical knowledge of networking. Just plug each of your computers into the appliance and insert the setup CD in your computer to configure the network.

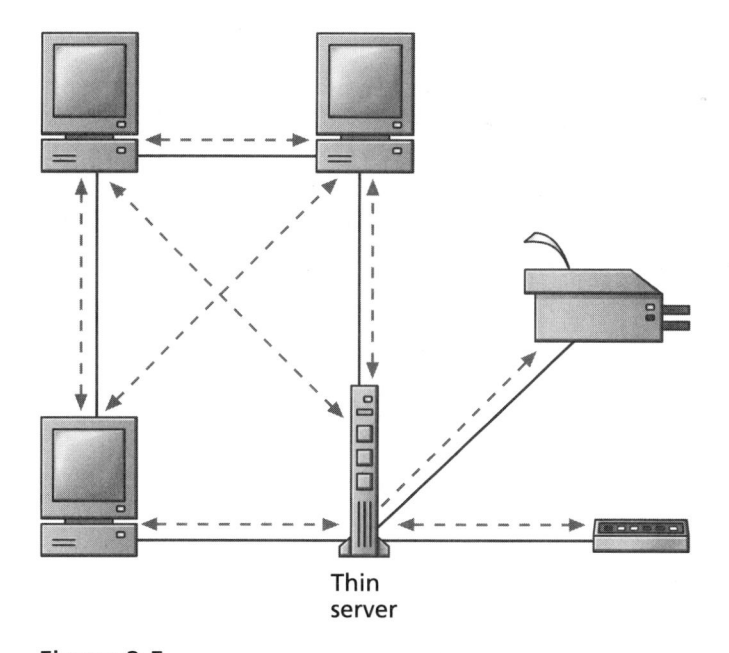

Thin server

Figure 2-5
Add a Windows-based server appliance to a peer-to-peer network to get some of the advantages of a client/server network.

The Windows-based server appliance contains all of the software you need for networking, so you don't need to purchase and install Windows NT Server or Windows 2000 Server. The appliance can even back up your files, making duplicate copies of all files saved on the server in case the primary hard disk drive is damaged.

With the appliance, you don't need to create a peer-to-peer network first and then migrate to the appliance. You can use the appliance to set up your first network because the configuration and setup process is automatic.

Combination Networks

While I distinguished between peer-to-peer and client/server networks in this chapter, many networks are a blend of the two. For example, you can have a client/server network set up so that if the server goes down, the other computers on the network can still communicate on a peer-to-peer basis, as shown in Figure 2-6.

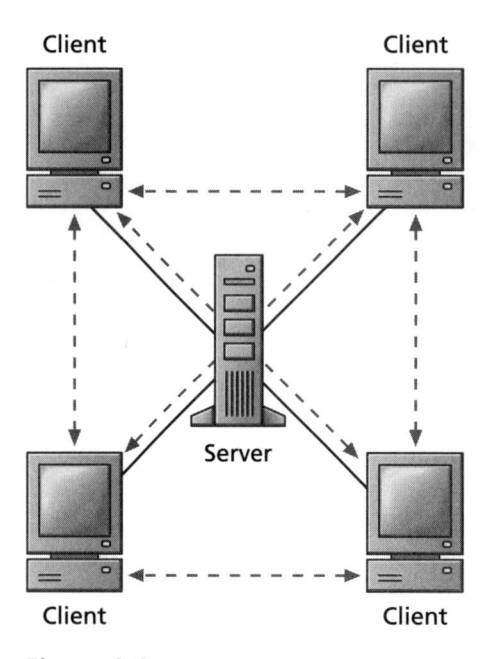

Figure 2-6

Networks can be a combination of peer-to-peer and client/server networks.

In this type of setup, each client computer must log on to the server to use the server's resources. Each client, however, can also communicate directly to the other clients on the network without going through the server. If the server computer is turned off, a client can't access the files or e-mail messages that are stored on the server. The client can, however, access shared files stored on the individual workstations and use printers attached to other computers.

By combining a peer-to-peer and client/server network, you can also have networked computers that aren't authorized to use the server but are still allowed to share files with other workstations on a peer-to-peer basis.

> **Tip**
>
> Most of the software and procedures needed to set up a network are the same whether you're setting up a peer-to-peer network, creating a client/server network, or using a Windows-based server appliance. So you can easily create a peer-to-peer network first and then move to a client/server network as your computing needs increase. None of your effort and none of the hardware or software you use will go to waste if you have to make this transition.

Selecting the Network for You

No hard-and-fast rules exist for deciding which type of network is best for your business. Generally peer-to-peer networks are more suitable for smaller businesses, and client/server networks for larger ones. Some network administrators suggest this classification:

- Peer-to-peer network for up to 10 computers
- Windows-based server appliance for up to 20 computers
- Client/server network for more than 20 computers

You might find that your own situation is different. You can certainly network 20 computers or more in a peer-to-peer configuration or connect just two or three computers to a Windows-based server appliance or a server running Windows NT or Windows 2000. It really all depends on the performance you expect, the features you want to use, and the type of control you want to exercise.

For very small networks that don't need a central location to store files, the choice is easy. If you have Windows 95, Windows 98, or Windows 2000 Professional running, you already have everything available in Windows; you don't need to buy any other software. Windows 98, Second Edition, and Windows 2000 Professional even have a feature that lets you share a modem over a network. You can also download free or inexpensive networking utilities from the Internet.

When you need a central storage location for files and tighter control and security, consider using a Windows-based server appliance or Windows NT or Windows 2000 for a client/server network. The Windows-based server appliance is suggested for up to 25 users, depending on the number of licenses that come with the version of the appliance you purchase.

Network Access Controls

Peer-to-peer networks have *share-level access controls*. This means that you determine what can be shared on the network and set passwords for each resource that you want to share, such as individual drives and printers. If you protect a folder with a password, for example, anyone who logs on to the network and has the password can access the file. Since other unauthorized users can discover passwords, this isn't the most secure type of sharing. The only way to remove a person's permission to access the resources is to change the password and not give him or her the new one. If you decide to change the password for a resource, however, you have to notify all the users who want to access the resource. If you forget to notify someone of the change, he or she will be denied access.

With client/server computing, you can select *user-level access controls*. This means that you can specify which authenticated users have access to a folder. Then a network user must both be on the access list and have the password to access a resource, providing much tighter security. The server maintains the access list. If you want to remove someone's permission to access the resource, you simply remove his or her name from the list of allowed users. You don't have to change the password and notify other users.

Determining the Connection

Your next decision is how to connect computers so that information can flow between them. Your choice depends on several factors:

- Number of computers
- Distance between them
- Speed you want
- Amount of work you want to do
- Amount of money you want to spend

You can generally have four different types of network connections:

- Network cable
- Wireless
- Phone line
- Power line

Table 2-2 summarizes the major differences among network connections. For most businesses, network cable is the preferred choice because of its speed and dependability using what's called an *Ethernet* network. Ethernet is a set of specifications that determine how information is communicated across a network.

Table 2-2 Comparing Network Connections

Network connection	The good	The bad	The ugly
Network cable (Ethernet)	The cheapest, fastest, most flexible, and expandable type of network connection	Requires running cable between computers	Might require running cable through walls, ceilings, and floors; extra jacks and special hardware might also be needed
Wireless	Requires no cables; "broadcasts" network over the air	Might be subject to interference from electrical appliances. Computers might have to be moved to improve performance	Generally more expensive and slower than network cable
Phone line	Requires no cables; plugs into existing telephone wiring	Requires a phone jack in rooms in which you want to connect to the network	Much slower than network cable
Power line	Requires no cables; plugs into a wall outlet	Slower than network cable	Can be subject to electrical interference, which can break contact between network computers and result in data loss

Wireless networks are suitable where cable can't be used. Telephone and power line networks are suitable for very small home-based businesses with a limited number of computers to be networked. Many of these network

Part 1: Choosing Among Network Options

systems don't totally conform to the Ethernet standards because of differences in the way information must be transmitted.

I'll cover Ethernet networks in the next chapter, and phone line, power line, and wireless networking in detail in Chapter 4.

Chapter 3
Ethernet Networks

The most popular type of network today is called Ethernet. Ethernet, which supports both peer-to-peer and client/server networking, was originally developed by Xerox Corporation and further defined by Xerox, Digital Equipment Corporation, and Intel. You'll also see Ethernet referred to as IEEE 802.3, the technical standard on which the current version of Ethernet is based.

In Ethernet networking, information is transmitted in a group of data called a *frame*. A similar group of data transmitted over the Internet is called a *packet,* so sometimes the terms frame and packet are used interchangeably. As shown in Figure 3-1, a frame contains four basic elements: the address of the computer to which the frame is being sent, the address of the computer sending the frame, the size of the frame, and the actual data being transmitted. Up to 1500 bytes of actual data can be contained in a frame. Data larger than 1500 bytes is divided into a series of frames that are sent individually.

| Destination Address | Source Address | Length | Data (up to 1500 bytes) |

Figure 3-1
An Ethernet frame contains four basic elements.

Part 1: Choosing Among Network Options

Types of Cables

Ethernet networks are connected with cables, which transmit information faster than any other type of network connection. As long as the cables are connected, very little can interfere with the flow of information. In office networks, information can travel through the cables at speeds of 10 million bits per second (Mbps), 100 Mbps, or even 1000 Mbps, depending on the speed of the hardware and the cables used.

These numbers might not mean much to you unless you've waited online for a file to download. The fastest telephone modems today can download files at about 53,000 bits per second (bps) if you have a great phone line. A file that takes 10 minutes to download from the Internet takes only a few seconds to transfer from computer to computer on a network.

With Ethernet networks, you have to run cables to each computer. This isn't a problem if the computers are in the same room or in adjacent rooms and you don't mind drilling holes in the walls. When your computers are spread throughout the office, running cable can be a problem unless you're lucky enough to find ways to run the cable without having to pass through too many walls, such as running cable through suspended ceilings or as you build or remodel an office.

The two most common types of cable are twisted-pair—also known as 10Base-T cable—and 10Base2 coaxial cable—also known as ThinNet. Fiberoptic cable isn't as common but is growing in popularity.

Note

10Base-T is named for its original maximum speed of 10 Mbps on twisted-pair cable. 10Base2 is so named because coaxial cable has two parts, an inner core and an outer metal braid.

Twisted-Pair Cable

Twisted-pair cable is a thick, round cable that has two copper wires twisted together in a pair; a cable can have between two and eight pairs. Twisted-pair cable has *connectors* that look like large telephone plugs, as shown in

Chapter 3: Ethernet Networks

Figure 3-2. Network cable connectors, labeled RJ-45 connectors, and telephone connectors, labeled RJ-11 connectors, can't be used interchangeably.

RJ-45 plug (Network cable connector)

RJ-11 plug (Telephone cable connector)

Figure 3-2
Network cable connectors resemble oversized phone connectors.

Twisted-pair cable comes in two types: *unshielded twisted-pair (UTP)* and *shielded twisted-pair (STP)*. As shown in Figure 3-3, UTP cable consists of eight insulated wires, twisted together in pairs within an insulating sheath.

Figure 3-3
Twisted-pair cable contains four pairs of insulated wires that are twisted together.

STP cable is similar to UTP cable but has a layer of woven copper and foil around the wires within the plastic sheath to shield them from extraneous electrical signals. STP cable is more expensive than UTP cable and is more difficult to work with because it's heavier and less flexible. The advantage is that STP cable is resistant to *crosstalk*—when signals from one cable mix with signals in another cable running adjacent to it.

Twisted-pair cable also is available in several grades. The higher the grade, the better and more reliable the cable, but quality comes at a price. For more information about grades of cable, *see "Making the Grade," on page 149.*

Part 1: Choosing Among Network Options

> **Tip**
>
> For speeds up to 100 Mbps, standard UTP cable will usually be sufficient. Consider STP if you have to run "gangs" of wire in a bundle along the same path.

In most cases, when you wire a network with either type of twisted-pair cable, all the cables must converge at a device called a *hub,* as shown in Figure 3-4. The hub acts like a traffic intersection, where all roads come together and traffic can flow in any direction. This means you have to run all of the network cables to a central location in the office, and the hub has to be turned on for any of the computers to communicate. This type of layout is called *star topology* because all of the workstations radiate from the central hub.

> **Tip**
>
> As you'll learn in Chapter 10, several types of hubs are available, and you can use other devices called *switches* as the converging point of the network cables. See "Alternatives to Hubs," on page 145.

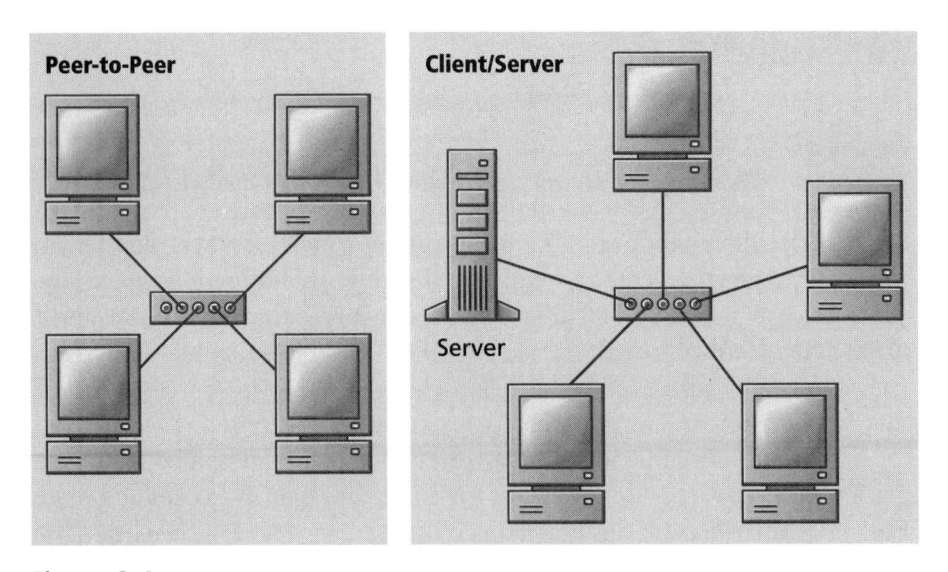

Figure 3-4
In a network wired with twisted-pair cable, all the cables converge at a hub.

Chapter 3: Ethernet Networks

> **Note**
> If you're creating a network with only two computers, you don't need a hub. See "Hubless Networks," on page 139.

When the hub receives a frame of information from a computer, it sends the frame to every other computer connected to it, regardless of which computer is the destination for the frame. Each computer looks at the destination address in the frame and determines whether the frame is intended for it. So all of the computers on the network can see the packet, but only the computer for which the packet is meant acts on the packet. (See Figure 3-5.)

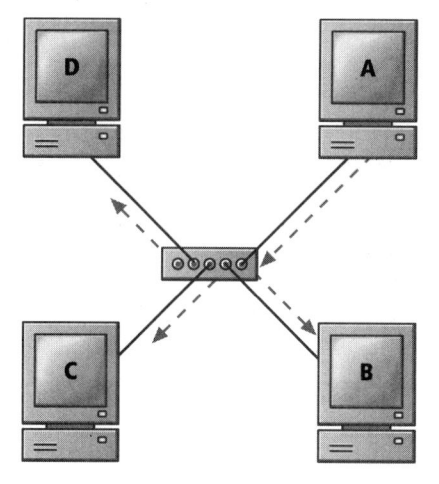

Figure 3-5
All the computers see the message from Computer A, but only Computer B accepts the message.

Coaxial Cable

The 10Base2 coaxial cable is an alternative to twisted-pair cable. It looks like the coaxial cable from your VCR or cable box, only a little thinner, which is why it's also called thin Ethernet, or just ThinNet. As shown in Figure 3-6, coaxial cable is a round cable with a solid insulated wire at its core and a layer of braided metal under its external sheath. Although thinner than other coaxial cables, 10Base2 coaxial cable is thicker than twisted-pair cable, so it's slightly more difficult to fish through walls and lay along baseboards.

Part 1: Choosing Among Network Options

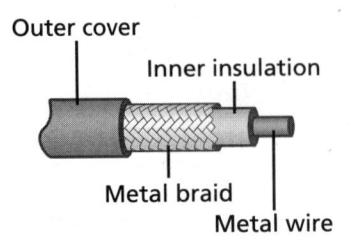

Figure 3-6
10Base2 coaxial cable, or ThinNet, is an alternative to twisted-pair cable.

A coaxial cable network doesn't require a hub. As shown in Figure 3-7, you simply run the cable from one computer to another. The absence of a central hub reduces the amount of cable you need to run from room to room and between floors. This type of layout is called *bus topology*. You can join two lengths of coaxial cable to make a longer cable. Two lengths of coaxial cable joined with a coupler are more reliable than two lengths of twisted-pair cable coupled together.

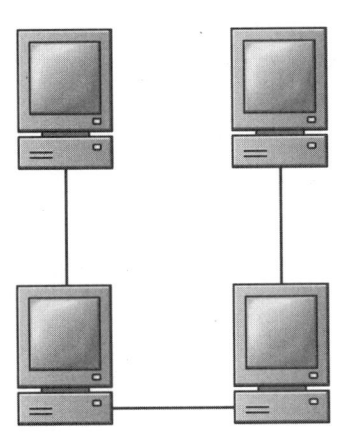

Figure 3-7
Coaxial cable connects computers directly, without a hub.

> **Note**
>
> Before the advent of twisted-pair and 10Base2 coaxial (ThinNet) cable, Ethernet networks used thick coaxial cable, called ThickNet. *ThickNet* is about a half-inch thick, twice as thick as ThinNet, because it has an extra layer of metal braiding and plastic sheathing.

Chapter 3: Ethernet Networks

When a computer sends a frame using coaxial cable, the frame is sent in both directions across the cable, as shown in Figure 3-8. It passes by every computer and is accepted by only the computer to which it was sent.

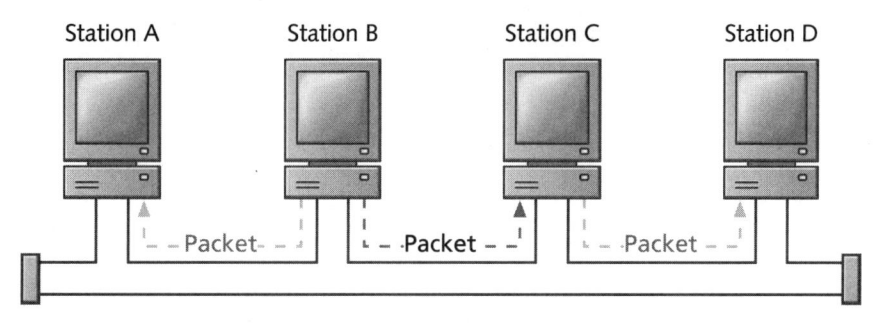

Figure 3-8
The frame is sent in both directions on a coaxial cable.

Fiberoptic Cable

Fiberoptic cable is growing in popularity for larger networks because of its speed and capability to handle large amounts of information. Fiberoptic cable consists of a thin glass fiber through which light passes in pulses. The light pulses represent the digital information being carried over the network.

Fiberoptic cable has a very low error rate and isn't susceptible to electromagnetic interference. The cable can transmit signals in the tens of gigabits per second and can handle several different channels simultaneously, since each channel is on a different wavelength of light.

Gigabit Ethernet

Gigabit (1000 Mbps) speed networks are just emerging, but they're expensive. While some day Gigabit Ethernet will be able to run satisfactorily on twisted-pair cable (perhaps even as you are reading this), it currently requires fiberoptic cable as defined by two gigabit-speed standards, 1000Base-LX and 1000Base-SX. Gigabit Ethernet can run on coaxial cable, but only up to lengths of 25 meters.

The problem with Gigabit Ethernet is that many computers just can't keep up with the network, so you won't see the full benefit of gigabit speeds unless you have very high-end computers.

However, fiberoptic cable costs more than twisted-pair or ThinNet and is more difficult to install. You can't make any sharp bends while installing the cable, and it's less flexible than other types. If you need to install your own connector on the end of a fiberoptic cable, it must be attached with epoxy or by a heat process, although some connectors can be put on the cable by crimping for emergency repairs.

As shown in Figure 3-9, fiberoptic cable contains five parts:

- The glass core that carries the light
- Glass cladding surrounding the core that reflects the light back to the core so it travels without signal loss
- A buffer layer that protects the core and cladding from damage
- A layer of material that strengthens the cable
- An outer jacket, such as PVC plastic (For more information on PVC plastic, see "Making Your Own Network Cables" on page 150.)

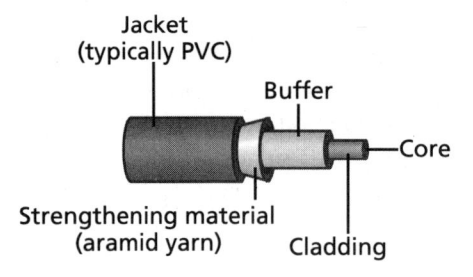

Figure 3-9

Fiberoptic cable has five parts.

Two optical fibers in fiberoptic cable connect the computer to the network hub, as shown in Figure 3-10. Because one fiber carries information to the computer and the other fiber carries information to the hub for distribution to the network, fiberoptic cable is usually purchased with two fibers together in the same outer jacket.

I recommend cable, whether it be twisted-pair, coaxial, or fiberoptic, over the other choices described in Chapter 4 as long as you can physically run the cable between computers. Cable is faster than the alternatives and can connect over almost any distance in an office.

Chapter 3: Ethernet Networks

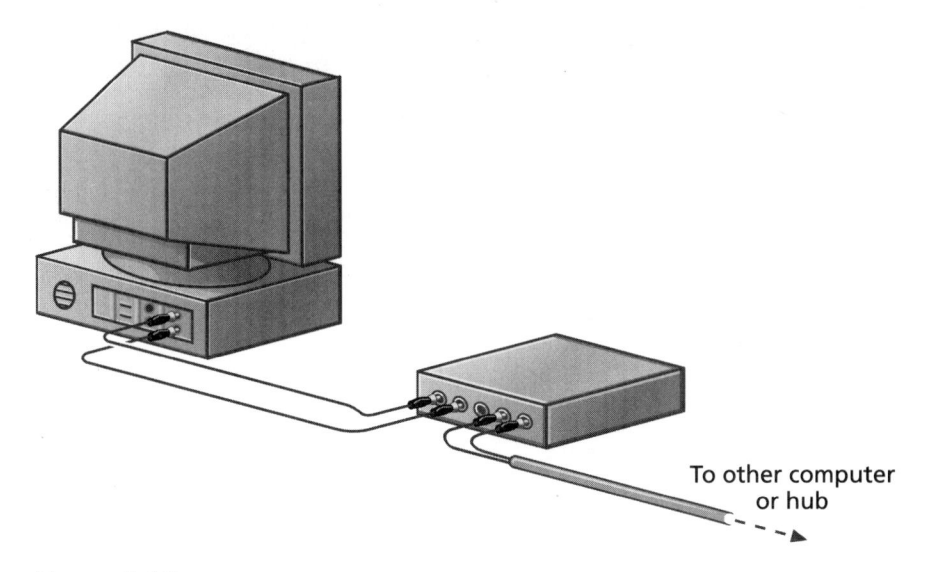

To other computer
or hub

Figure 3-10
You can connect a computer to a network hub with fiberoptic cable.

Note

You can mix twisted-pair, ThinNet, and fiberoptic cables in the same network, but you'll need additional hardware. See "Connecting Hubs," on page 142.

In the next chapter, I'll take a look at some alternatives to Ethernet for a small business.

Chapter 4

Alternatives to Ethernet

This chapter takes a look at alternatives to Ethernet networks for which you don't need to run cable through the office. These alternative networks are completely wireless or run through existing telephone lines or power lines. All of these alternatives to Ethernet, however, use Microsoft Windows, so you can share files using Windows Explorer, My Computer, Network Neighborhood or My Network Places, and other standard Windows techniques.

Weighing the Pros and Cons

Non-Ethernet alternatives are easier to set up and use than Ethernet networks because they don't require you to run any cable or connect to hubs. Either these alternatives use existing wiring, such as your telephone or power lines, or in the case of a wireless network, they use no wiring at all. They are generally slower than Ethernet networks, sometimes about one-tenth the speed or slower, which will affect performance in all but the smallest networks.

While startup kits for these systems, containing all of the hardware you need for networking two computers, might cost about the same as

Part 1: Choosing Among Network Options

Ethernet startup kits, they usually lock you into using proprietary hardware. Network devices on an Ethernet network, such as network interface cards (NICs), don't need to be made by the same company. You can even mix internal and external network devices on the same network, as long as they are designed for Ethernet.

> **Note**
>
> A *network interface card* or *NIC* is a card or similar device that fits inside your computer and handles the flow of information to and from a computer and the rest of the network. For more information on NICs, see Chapter 9. Both Ethernet and non-Ethernet networks can use internal NICs or external network interface devices, sometimes combining both on the same network, depending on the manufacturer.

The network devices that you use on a non-Ethernet network, however, need to be made by the same company. If you purchase a telephone network kit from one company and need to add a computer to the network, you'll have to get the additional hardware to connect the computer to the network from the same company that made your telephone network kit. That could be a problem if the company discontinues the product line or goes out of business. You might need to start over with new network equipment.

Some non-Ethernet kits allow easy migration to an Ethernet network. For example, many wireless systems, especially the more expensive commercial-quality systems, can easily be converted to an Ethernet network. Some telephone line networks have Ethernet connections as well. If you decide to upgrade to the speed of Ethernet, you simply unplug the phone line from the network hardware and plug in your Ethernet cable and hub.

So when should you select a non-Ethernet network? The alternatives to Ethernet covered in this chapter are perfect when you want to avoid cutting holes in walls to run Ethernet cable from room to room or when you need to set up a temporary network such as one to support a conference or special event.

Commercial-quality wireless systems can sometimes achieve Ethernet speeds and can be bridged to connect to a wired Ethernet network. You could use a wireless system, for example, to connect a network in one building with a network in another. To expand the system, simply plug a wireless network device into a computer and install the software.

Chapter 4: Alternatives to Ethernet

While most Ethernet networks require you to have a network device installed in your computer, many of the non-Ethernet systems use an external network device or connection. The external connection kits are especially useful when you don't want to open your computer to add hardware or when you have no space available inside your computer. Telephone line networks that use an external device rather than an internal one offer the most in terms of ease of use and expandability. They're easy to install and can connect a computer to a network in any room where you have a telephone outlet. If you think you might want to upgrade someday to Ethernet and you have space in your computer for a network device, consider a system whose hardware has both a telephone and Ethernet connection.

The focus of the chapter will be on the hardware needed to set up a non-Ethernet network, rather than the software. Everything you'll learn in Chapter 13 about the software side of getting a network up and running applies equally to Ethernet and non-Ethernet networks. All the network kits discussed in this chapter include software that automates the setup and configuration process. The software installs the drivers needed to run the network and configures Windows for the proper protocols. Most of the kits also include software for sharing your Internet connection with other members on the network. For more on sharing modems and Internet accounts, see Chapter 21.

You can choose from many different non-Ethernet hardware combinations when you're setting up a network. With wireless and telephone networks, as with Ethernet networks, you have a choice of using an internal network device, a universal serial bus (USB) device, or a parallel port device, depending on the speed and range desired. Your options are more limited with a power line network. No USB power line network kits are currently on the market, and you probably wouldn't want to connect an internal network device directly to a power line because your computer might be directly exposed to power surges.

Using Wireless Network Devices

Wireless networks (WLANs) are ideal for linking a laptop computer to a desktop because you can situate the laptop anywhere or move it from room to room without worrying about wires. Wireless networks send and receive information as radio waves through the air by means of a device called a *transceiver*. So called because it both transmits and receives radio waves, a transceiver is either installed in or connected to each computer on the network.

Five configurations exist for connecting a computer to a wireless network:

- An internal network device or a NIC that serves as the transceiver
- A PC Card transceiver that plugs into a laptop
- An external transceiver that connects to an existing Ethernet network device
- An external transceiver that connects to the USB port
- An external transceiver that connects to the parallel port

A wireless network device is installed in approximately the same way as an Ethernet network device. The only difference is that the wireless version might have a protrusion in the back that serves as the antenna. You might have to angle the device or card slightly to get the protrusion through the back of the computer before you straighten out the device or card so that it fits in the socket.

The Pros and Cons of Wireless Networks

The least expensive wireless systems are designed for small businesses and offer USB and parallel connection options. They transmit information on a frequency that's picked up by other computers in the office, as shown in Figure 4-1.

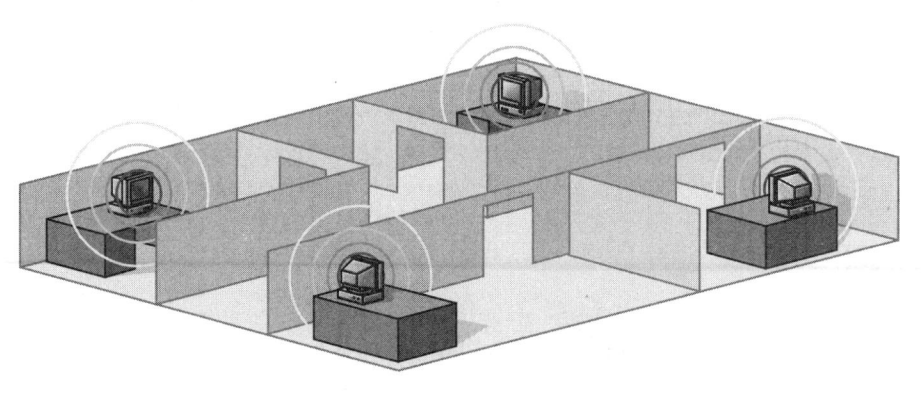

Figure 4-1
Wireless systems send information in radio frequencies through the air.

Chapter 4: Alternatives to Ethernet

The USB versions are the easiest to set up because you don't have to open the computer to install an internal network device or share a parallel port with a printer. These small systems are slower than Ethernet and operate only within a certain distance, which is usually a radius of about 150 feet between the computers. Although that distance should be enough to accommodate the computers in a small office, you should check the documentation that comes with a wireless network kit to ascertain its range. If a computer on the network appears to be turned off when you install a wireless network, the computer might be out of range. Try moving the computer closer to the others. If that fixes the problem, leave the computer in its new location.

A more common problem with wireless networks is interference from walls or large metal objects. If the system unit for a computer on the network is located on the floor under a metal desk, for example, the metal might block incoming and outgoing signals. Try moving the system unit to another location, such as on top of the desk or to one side of it. A wall with metal pipes or studs can also interfere with signal transmission.

Tip

Watch out, too, for interference from cell phones, pagers, and other wireless devices in the office.

If you want to network computers that are more than 150 feet apart, you might want to consider a commercial-quality wireless system. Such systems cost more, but they operate at speeds between 2 Mbps and 10 Mbps and have a wider range than wireless networks designed for the home.

Commercial-quality wireless systems use an *access point,* an external device that acts as a network hub to receive and manage network signals. The access point determines the size of the area in which the computers can communicate, called a *cell* (shown in Figure 4-2). You'll need an access point for each cell and a network device for each computer in the cell. In many cases, you also need to purchase a separate network device that plugs into the access point. To configure the access point, you connect it to a computer through a cable and install the software for a wireless network.

By properly positioning access points, you can overlap cells, as shown in Figure 4-3, to extend the network's coverage area. Because the cells overlap, a user with a notebook computer can move throughout the office

Part 1: Choosing Among Network Options

from cell to cell and stay within range of the network. You can also use an access point to bridge a wireless and wired network by connecting your wired network to a port on the access point.

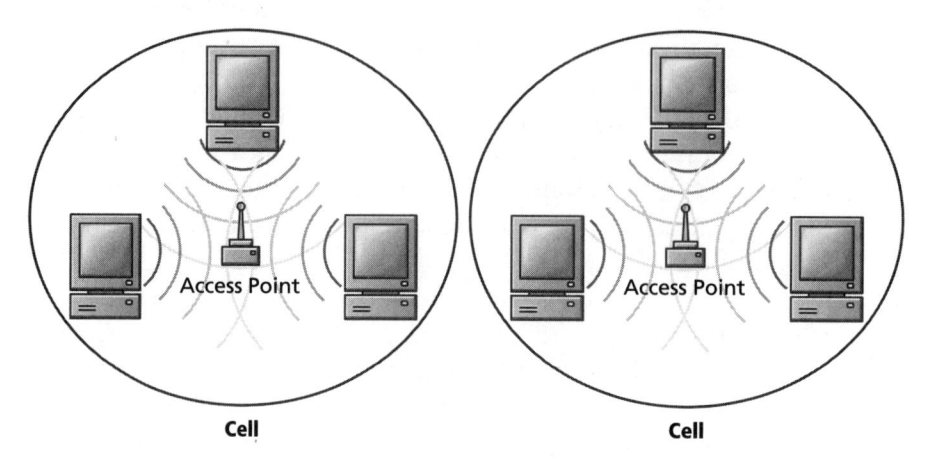

Figure 4-2
A commercial-quality wireless system uses an access point to create a cell.

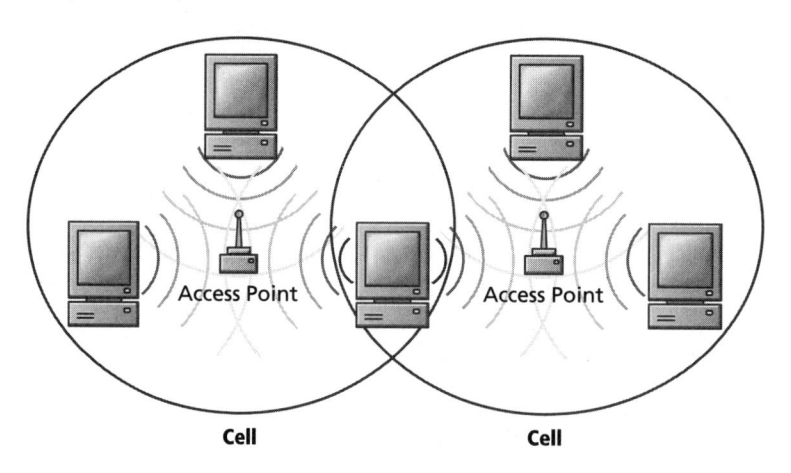

Figure 4-3
Overlapping cells extend a wireless network.

Chapter 4: Alternatives to Ethernet

Many of the commercial-quality wireless systems conform to the Institute of Electrical and Electronics Engineers (IEEE) 802.11 standard, but to varying degrees. The standard specifies a speed of at least between 1 Mbps and 2 Mbps and compatibility or interoperability among manufacturers. *Interoperability* means that a computer with a wireless network device from one company would be able to communicate with a computer that has a wireless network device from another company. Not all wireless systems perfectly conform to that part of the standard, however, so it's best to stay with hardware from one manufacturer or test the interoperability before making a large investment in hardware.

Wireless Technologies

One problem with interoperability is that the IEEE 802.11 standard permits two different spread spectrum radio technologies—direct sequence and frequency hopping. Although the wireless signal is divided into small pieces in both spread spectrum radio technologies, the two technologies aren't compatible.

In *frequency-hopping spread spectrum* radio technologies, signals from the network switch, or hop, between several different frequencies for a specific amount of time. Both the sending device and the receiving device know the pattern for frequency hopping, so the signals are received intact. Frequency-hopping spread spectrum provides some degree of security because other devices won't be able to match the pattern and intercept the communications.

In *direct-sequence spread spectrum*, each signal is encoded with extra redundant bits of information that the receiving device can decode. The redundant bits help ensure that the information is received successfully even if some bits are lost during the transmission.

You can't have a sending device that uses frequency hopping and a receiving device that uses direct sequence on your wireless network or vice versa. All of the network devices on your wireless network need to conform to one of these spread spectrum radio technologies.

Choosing a Wireless System

A number of companies market low-cost wireless network systems for home and small business. Two Aviator network kits from WebGear (*www.webgear.com*), for example, contain either two parallel port or two USB port transceivers, which can be plugged into a desktop or a laptop without opening up the computer. Because the parallel and USB versions are compatible, you can mix both on the same network, with up to 32 computers. The parallel port kit also includes an internal Industry Standard Architecture (ISA) parallel port card that gives you a second parallel port for your computer that you can use for your printer.

Types of Interfaces

As you'll learn in Chapter 9, an internal network device must match the type of interface you have in your computer. Terms such as ISA and PCI refer to the type of interface in which an internal card fits.

Industry Standard Architecture (ISA) devices are designed for an interface found on most earlier computers. The *Peripheral Component Interconnect (PCI)* interface is replacing ISA because PCI devices are easier to install and configure. Both ISA and PCI NICs fit inside of your computer in *slots* in the *motherboard*. The card contains a network connection that is accessible from the back of your computer. Newer computers are designed for mostly PCI devices, with perhaps room for just one ISA device.

Some notebook computers have network devices already built in. Most don't, however, so you have to purchase a network device on a *PC Card*. A PC Card is about the size of a business card, only much thicker, and it slides into an opening on the laptop, so you can insert and remove a PC Card without opening up the computer.

Other network devices connect by a cable to a *Universal Serial Bus (USB)* connection found on most newer desktop and notebook computers or to the *parallel* port to which you normally connect your printer.

Chapter 4: Alternatives to Ethernet

S3, which acquired Diamond Multimedia (*www.diamondmm.com*) in 1999, markets two HomeFree wireless network kits. One kit includes both a PCI NIC and an ISA NIC; another kit includes one ISA card and one PC Card for a laptop. You can purchase additional cards separately, including PC Cards for laptops, if you need them for other computers. The Internet NIC has a small protrusion that sticks out of your computer to serve as an antenna. The HomeFree kits also include the HomeFree Assistant, an easy-to-use program for keeping track of the computers and peripherals being shared on the network.

SOHOware's CableFREE wireless network kits (*www.sohoware.com*) also come in two versions. One version contains two ISA NICs; the other, one ISA and one PC Card. The company also offers a product called EtherBridge that connects a wireless network to an Ethernet network.

If you're interested in a commercial-quality wireless system, then consider any of these alternatives:

- The BreezeNET PRO.11 system (*www.breezecom.com*) transmits data at speeds between 2 Mbps and 3 Mbps and claims to have a range up to 3000 feet in an unobstructed environment and up to 600 feet in an obstructed environment. The access point can accommodate up to 20 users in a cell.

- The AviatorPRO wireless system (*www.webgear.com*) boasts a range of 500 to 1000 feet at 2 Mbps, with up to 61 users per access point.

- Aironet's 4800 Turbo DS (*www.aironet.com*) wireless network supports 1024 users per access point at speeds up to 11 Mbps. Each cell has a range of between 350 and 1800 feet, depending on its speed.

- WaveLAN Turbo (*www.wavelan.com*) operates at 2 Mbps and can accommodate 250 users per access point. Its range is between 375 and 1800 feet.

- RadioLAN (*www.radiolan.com*) can achieve 10 Mbps Ethernet speeds and can link devices up to 300 feet apart. The system can handle up to 128 computers in a peer-to-peer network. You can also purchase a bridge that connects the system to a wired Ethernet network and a bridge (called Campus BridgeLINK) that connects multiple wireless segments between buildings.

Setting Up a Phone Line Network

Phone line networks work on the principle that the phone lines running through your office can be shared. The technical term for this is *frequency-division multiplexing (FDM)*, which simply means that you have separate signals running through your telephone line on different frequencies, as shown in Figure 4-4. Voice, fax, and modem calls use one frequency; your network uses a completely different frequency. As a result, network signals can travel through the phone line at the same time you are using your phone to speak, fax, or surf the Internet.

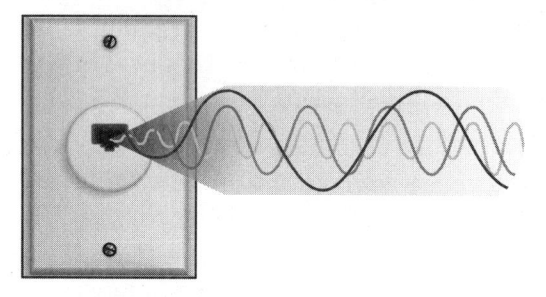

Figure 4-4
Standard telephone lines can carry three separate transmissions on different frequencies.

Pros and Cons of Phone Line Networks

Phone line networks are convenient for two main reasons:

- You don't need to run any special cable.
- You can add a computer to a network in any room that has a phone jack.

With a phone line network, the phone jack serves double-duty by allowing you to connect a computer to the network as well as to the Internet. If you do need another phone jack in your office, your phone company can install it for you, although the company will charge, of course. You can also get an adapter, such as the one shown on the next page, to connect both a phone and an NIC to one jack.

Chapter 4: Alternatives to Ethernet

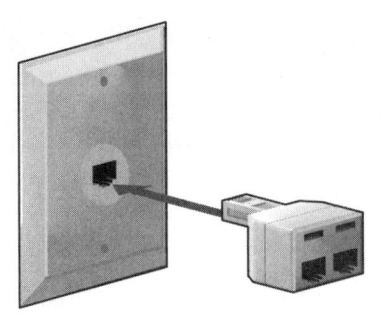

If you have more than one computer in the same room, you can usually connect their NICs with phone cables directly, as shown in Figure 4-5.

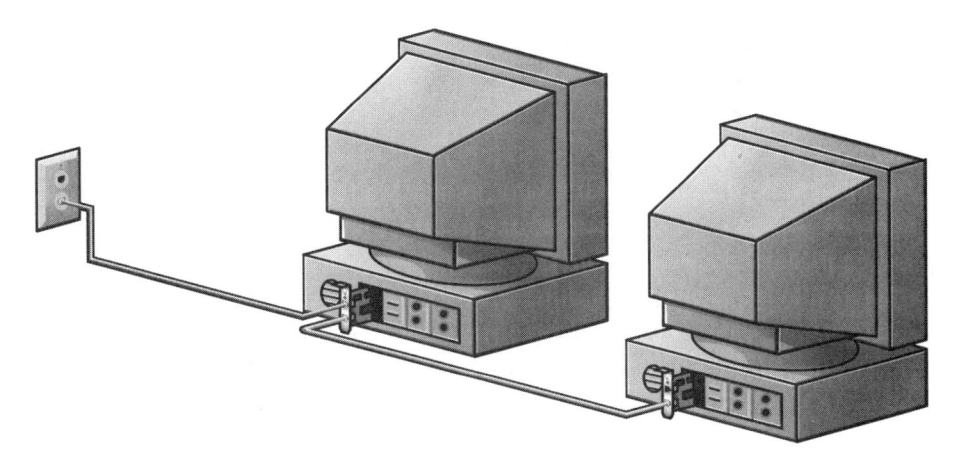

Figure 4-5
Computers can be linked directly with telephone cables.

The main limitation of phone line networks is their lack of speed. Phone line networks typically operate at 1 Mbps, compared to an Ethernet network's speed of 10 Mbps or 100 Mbps, although the speeds are increasing with newer technologies.

Choosing a Phone Line System

Several companies sell phone line network kits. The AnyPoint Home Network kit from Intel (*www.intel.com*) comes in parallel port and USB versions that include a small box for each computer. One end of the box plugs into your computer's printer or USB port through a cable; the other end connects by phone cable to a phone jack.

Other phone line network kits, such as the HomeLink Phoneline Network in a Box from Linksys (*www.linksys.com*), use an internal NIC that connects through a phone cable to a jack. The Linksys PCI cards have both a telephone interface and a twisted-pair Ethernet jack, just in case you want to change later to an Ethernet network by installing twisted-pair cables and a hub.

S3 offers its HomeFree Phoneline Desktop Pac consisting of two ISA phone line cards. You can also purchase PCI cards and a USB device separately to add more computers to the network. All of the devices are compatible with each other.

Setting Up a Power Line Network

In a *power line network,* which is also called a power line cable (PLC) network, your office's existing electrical wiring serves as the network cable, relaying information among the computers. You don't have to run any special cables between computers, and you can connect any computer that's within reach of an electrical outlet to the network. The information traveling to and from computers is added to the electrical waves running through your office wiring. PLC networks are slower than cable and some phone line systems.

Most PLC networks employ a special device that plugs into a wall outlet, as shown in Figure 4-6. A wire from that device connects to a special NIC linked to the computer. Some PLC networks connect directly to a computer's parallel port, which saves you the cost of buying an NIC.

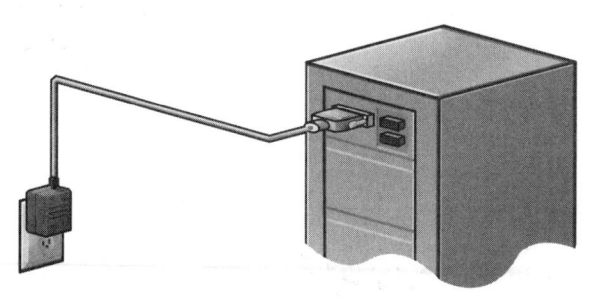

Figure 4-6
Most power line networks require a special NIC and a device that plugs into a wall outlet.

The device sends information through the power lines as a low-frequency radio wave. The frequency of the radio wave prevents the radio wave from interfering with the regular electric current running through the wires or vice versa. The radio wave travels throughout your office until it's "picked up" by a power line device connected to another computer on the network.

The Pros and Cons of Power Line Networks

PLC networks are the newest of the Ethernet alternatives, so the technology still has some drawbacks, especially if you share an electrical transformer with a neighbor.

A *transformer* is a device that reduces the voltage of the current flowing through outside power lines to the level required for interior wiring. In a PLC network, radio waves from a computer on the network travel from the computer's electrical outlet through the wiring to the transformer supplying the current to your office. If, as is often the case, the transformer serves more than one office, your network signals will actually travel through the wires of other offices, houses, or apartments served by the same transformer.

Theoretically, if the office next door shares your transformer and has the same type of PLC network device, they could become part of your network. Some PLC networks, however, include software that lets you create a "secure" network that prevents unauthorized users from accessing your network. This is done through a *firewall*, which is a security system through which all communications to and from the network must go. A firewall prevents computers outside of the network from communicating directly with computers on the network. A firewall limits access to your network to only authorized persons. The secure network setting, however, isn't turned on by default when you install the network software.

The other problems with PLC networks are electrical interference and power line fluctuations. While the radio waves traveling through the power lines are separate from the electric current, interference from other electronic equipment in the house is possible, especially from other power line devices, such as those for telephones and video transmission. Power line fluctuations can be caused when a large electrical appliance, such as an air conditioner, is turned on. These fluctuations can result in a temporary loss of your network connection.

Part 1: Choosing Among Network Options

The PassPort system from Intelogis (*www.intelogis.com*). is a good example of power line technology. The PassPort network kit includes two plug-in computer modules, a plug-in printer module that lets you connect a printer to the network, and a CD containing installation software. Each module is a littler smaller than a paperback novel, and it plugs into a wall outlet. You connect a cable from the module to your computer's parallel port.

> **Note**
>
> Other companies are currently developing power line networks and may even have released their products by the time you are reading this.

The next chapter takes a look at getting some of the benefits of client/server computing on a peer-to-peer network using thin servers.

Chapter 5

Networking with Thin Servers

Client/server networks have definite advantages over peer-to-peer networks for most small businesses. However, the cost of a client/server network might be prohibitive to some smaller businesses. In this chapter, you'll learn how to enjoy some of the advantages of client/server networks for the cost of a workstation by using a thin server.

The Downside of Peer-to-Peer Networks

Sharing resources, such as discs and printers, is one great feature of peer-to-peer networking. Sharing resources does have problems, however.

If you're sharing a folder or a disc that's attached to a network workstation, that resource will be available only when the workstation is turned on and connected to the network. So you might need an important file that's

Part 1: Choosing Among Network Options

on your partner's computer, for example, but be unable to access it on the network because her computer is turned off, as shown here:

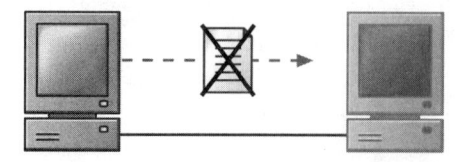

You'd have the same problem if you tried to access a printer or a modem connected to your partner's computer. As long as her computer is turned off, none of its resources are available to anyone on the network.

When network workstations are turned on, their resources can be shared but at a cost. Sharing resources puts a drain on the computer to which the resource is attached. For example, suppose you're working on your computer and another network user accesses a large file on your hard disk. The disk access is using some of your computer's resources, slowing down your own requests to read from or write to the same disk. You might also notice a definite drop in performance when a network user is accessing your CD drive, printer, or modem. Your own computer is doing double duty to satisfy your own tasks as well as those on the network. See Figure 5-1.

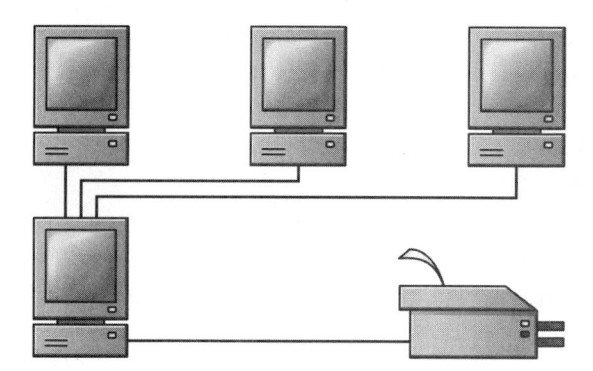

Figure 5-1
When a printer is connected to a computer on a peer-to-peer network, the computer tends to drop in performance when the printer is in use by others on the network.

In addition, you can connect only so many pieces of hardware to your computer's ports. The parallel port, for example, was originally designed to handle a single device such as a printer. If you have a printer, a scanner, and an external Zip drive using the same parallel port, the performance of the individual devices can be affected and you might experience device conflicts and other problems that can bring your entire system to a halt.

Filling a Need for Small Business

Client/server computing can prevent all problems this book has covered. By connecting printers, modems, and other devices to the server, anyone on the network can access the device regardless of who else is connected at the time.

However, many small businesses can't justify the expense of client/server computing or don't want the extra work that is involved in setting up and maintaining a server. Certainly, client/server networks do require some degree of technical expertise that might be beyond a small business manager. In addition, you need individual licenses for each client on the network. If your network operating system includes licenses for five clients, for instance, you'll need to purchase additional licenses to add more clients. And if the server goes down, all of its resources are unavailable to everyone on the network.

These drawbacks to client/server networks are unfortunate because peer-to-peer networks offer limited growth and performance. As your business grows and you add more computers to a peer-to-peer network, network performance can become unsatisfactory and the additional burden placed on each workstation greatly increases.

The solution for these problems is a new technology called appliances, or thin servers. A *thin server* is a special limited-purpose device that can be attached to a network independently of other servers or workstations. The thin server is connected directly to the network by a network hub, for example, so only the hub and the thin server must be turned on for anyone on the network to access the thin server. You can attach a thin server to a peer-to-peer or client/server network without affecting the workstations or general-purpose servers on the network. A thin server can be placed anywhere on the network a workstation can be attached. See Figure 5-2.

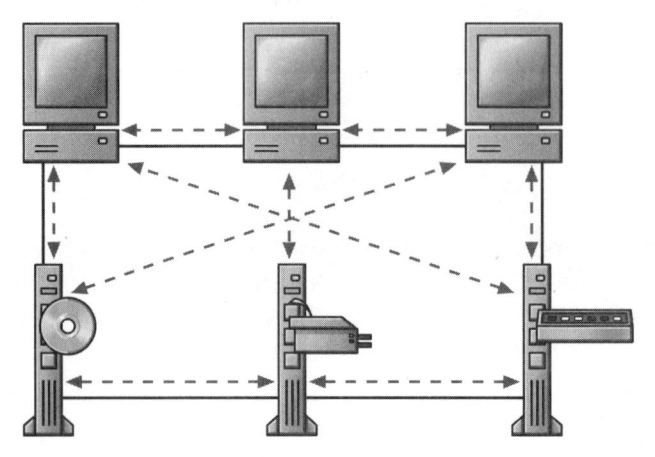

Figure 5-2
Thin servers can be added anywhere on a network that a workstation can be attached.

In addition, thin servers typically require little technical expertise to install and configure. Many thin servers are virtually plug-and-play, with the entire configuration performed by a program supplied by the manufacturer. In fact, many thin servers have a Web-based interface. This means you access their setup and configuration menus using a Web browser, and all information appears as a Web page.

Types of Thin Servers

A variety of thin servers exists, including the following types:

- Network-attached storage servers
- Print servers
- Modem servers
- Remote access servers
- Time servers
- Internet servers
- Universal serial servers
- Network appliances

Chapter 5: Networking with Thin Servers

You can connect as many types of thin servers as you need to your network. If you have several thin servers attached to the network, any one of them can go down without affecting the others, as shown in Figure 5-3.

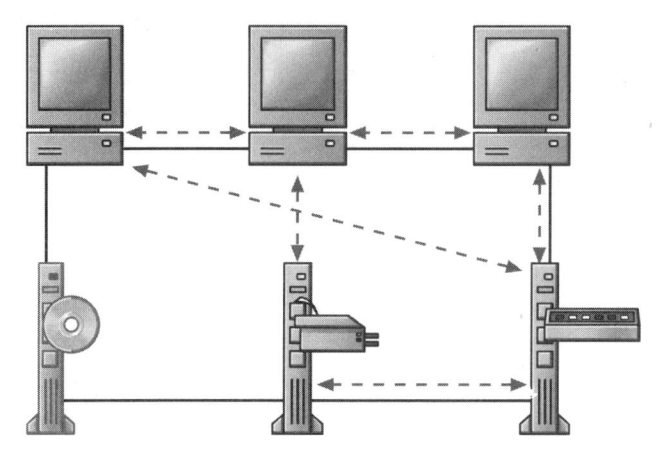

Figure 5-3
Any thin server can go down without affecting other thin servers on the network.

Network-Attached Storage

With *network-attached storage (NAS) servers,* you can store a file in a central location, accessible to every network user who's authorized to access the file. Because the file is on an NAS server, it's available all of the time, even if all of the other workstations are turned off.

One of the simplest NAS servers is a single external hard disk drive or CD drive that connects directly to the network, as shown in Figure 5-4. An external CD drive might be less expensive than purchasing multiple copies of a CD to make it available to all network users. You can purchase a single copy and store it in the external CD drive for network access.

Network hard disk drives are more expensive than simply replacing an internal drive with one having greater capacity. While high performance internal drives cost about $15 to $20 per gigabyte, an external hard disk drive attached directly to the network might run between $50 and $100 per gigabyte. The advantage, however, is that the network-attached hard disk drive is available to everyone on the network, and if the hard disk drive crashes, it doesn't put any workstations out of commission. The network-attached hard disk drive can also serve as a quick backup solution since transmission over a network to a hard disk drive is much faster than backing up to a tape or other device.

Part 1: Choosing Among Network Options

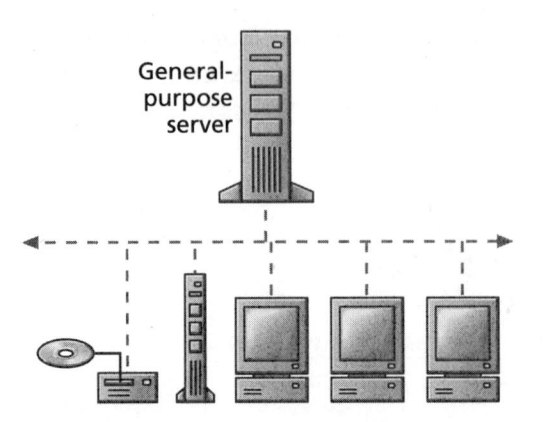

Figure 5-4
A CD drive attached directly to a network is an example of a simple network-attached storage (NAS) server.

You can also purchase NAS servers that store several CDs or DVDs. Some of these servers have multiple CD or DVD drives (see Figure 5-5), which appear to users as individual drives on the network. Other NAS servers contain one CD drive and a large hard disk drive. Special software lets you copy the contents of the CD to a folder on the hard disk drive and makes the folder appear as a separate drive to network users. Because hard disk drives are faster than CD drives, the hard disk drive appears to be a 66X read-speed CD drive to users. Some NAS systems use multiple Jaz cartridges, a removable hard disk storage device. You'll learn more about NAS servers in Chapter 11.

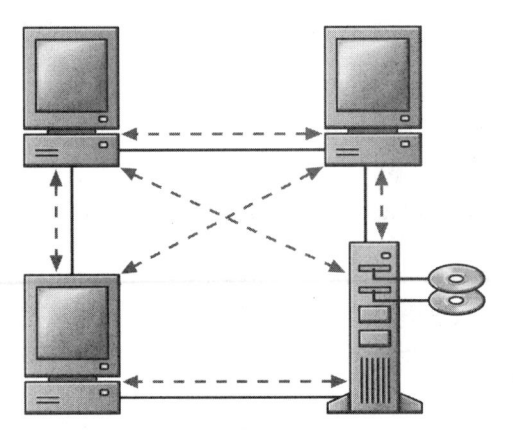

Figure 5-5
Some NAS servers have multiple CD or DVD drives.

Chapter 5: Networking with Thin Servers

Side-Grading

While thin servers are normally viewed as a way to provide features to all network users, you can consider thin servers as a way to upgrade the capabilities of a client computer, often called *side-grading*.

For example, you might have a computer for which upgrading it by adding a larger hard disk drive, faster modem, or DVD drive isn't practical. If the computer is on the network and you're satisfied with the computer, you can install a thin server to provide the extra capabilities.

You might also have a client/server network and want to add network resources without taking the server offline for upgrade. By using a thin server, you can add resources to the network, such as CD drives, DVD drives, and modems, without affecting the general-purpose server, as shown here:

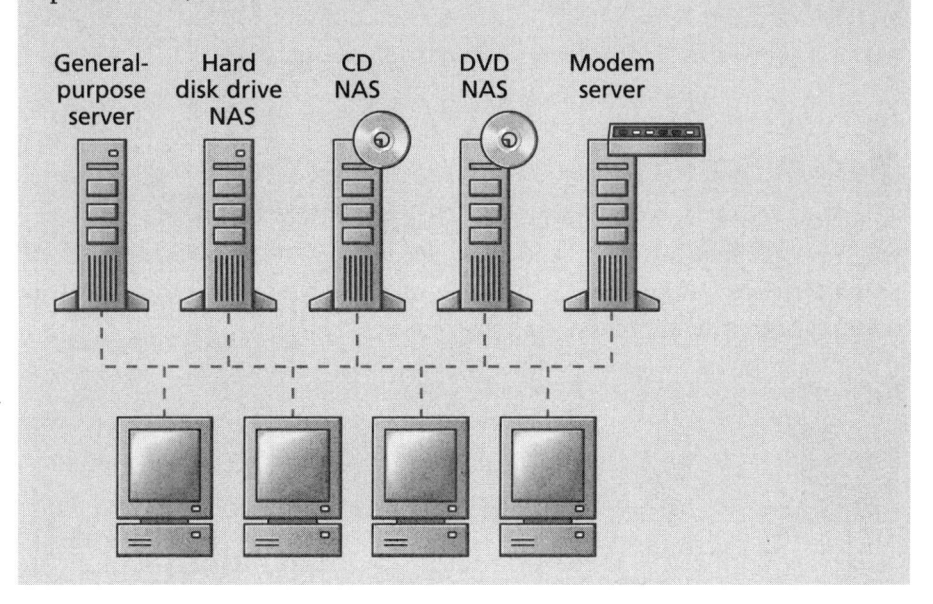

Print Servers

Connecting a printer to the network, rather than to an individual workstation, makes the printer available to everyone on the network. Only the printer and the hub must be on for the printer to be available.

Some printers are *network-ready,* which means they have their own network interface cards (NIC) built in. You plug a cable into the built-in

NIC and then to the network hub. You don't need to connect the printer's parallel port (if it has one) to a specific computer. Network-ready printers, however, don't come in a wide variety of models. Most of them are more costly than non-network-ready printers and are designed for high-speed, heavier-duty operation.

A *print server* is an alternative to a network-ready printer. You plug one end of the print server into your printer's parallel port and the other end into any direct connection on the network, such as the hub or a wall jack. You don't need to plug the printer into a computer's parallel port, but all computers on the network can now access the printer.

The least expensive print servers are called *pocket servers*. About the size of a pack of cigarettes, a pocket server plugs directly into a printer's parallel port. The twisted-pair cable from the network hub or the coaxial cable from another networked device plugs into the other end of the server.

Some external print servers can accommodate one or more printers and one or more network connections. For example, you can use an external print server to connect three printers to the network.

You'll learn more about print servers in Chapter 18.

Modem Servers

A *modem server* connects to the network so all workstations can share a single phone line and Internet account. See Figure 5-6. Some modem servers contain their own analog, ISDN, DSL, or cable modems; others must be connected to a separate external modem.

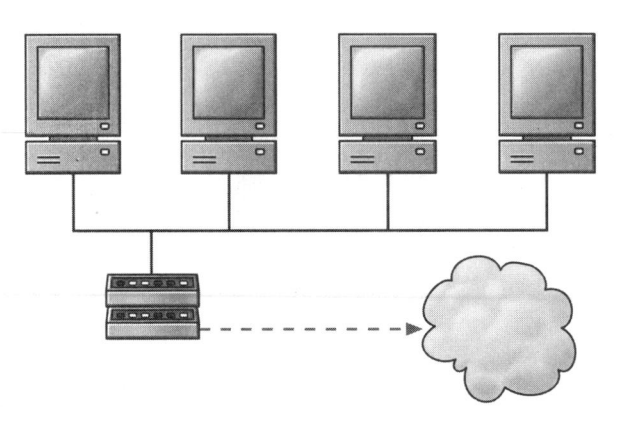

Figure 5-6
Workstations on a network can share a phone line and Internet account through a modem server.

Chapter 5: Networking with Thin Servers

When a modem is shared on a network, only one user—the first to dial in to the ISP—is actually logged on, and that user can be anyone on the network. Other users who want to access the Internet just piggyback onto the existing connection through the network. Their modems don't need to dial in because the first computer has already made the connection. As far as the ISP is concerned, only one person is logged on.

After plugging the modem server into the network, you have to configure it for your network. Most modem servers have Web-based management, which makes configuration easy. You also have to configure each workstation to access the modem server, rather than its own modem, when a user opens a browser or checks for Internet mail. Detailed instructions are included with each server.

You'll learn more about modem servers in Chapter 21.

Remote Access Servers

Remote access servers are similar to modem servers in that they link your network and your phone line, but they also provide a way for users away from the office to dial into your network to share files, print documents, and check for network mail. See Figure 5-7.

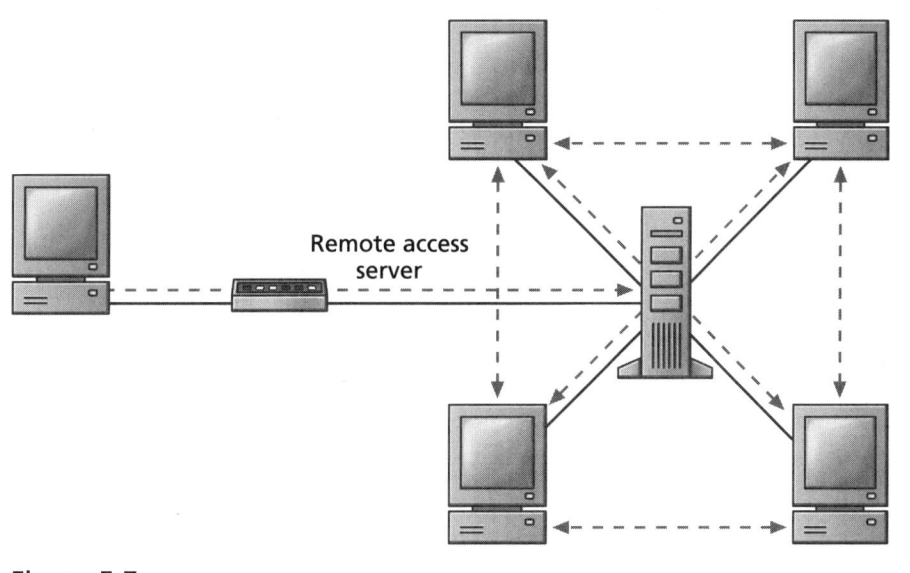

Figure 5-7
Users who are out of the office can dial into the network through a remote access server.

Some remote access servers have one or more serial ports to which you attach external modems. Each modem is connected to a phone line for simultaneous connection to several dial-in users. Other servers have slots in which you can insert internal modems.

Because remote access servers provide a way to dial into your network, they also include security features. Some, for example, offer callback service. The way this generally works is as follows: after a remote user dials into the system and is identified, the call is disconnected and then the server calls the user at a designated phone number authorized by the system administrator. This system doesn't work well for staff members who travel, but it's a good system if staff members tend to telecommute.

Note
Chapter 23 covers remote access servers in more detail.

Other remote access servers support a *virtual private network (VPN)*, a Windows feature that offers secure access to your network over the Internet. For more information on VPN, see the *Microsoft Windows 2000 Professional Resource Kit,* published by Microsoft Press.

Time Servers

A *time server* keeps the on-board clocks of all of the networked computers synchronized so they all have the same time, accurate to the second.

Some time servers obtain the time from Internet sites when users go online. The Coetanian Systems TSS-100 Time Synchronization Server and the Lantronix CoBox Network Time Server, on the other hand, include a Global Positioning System (GPS) receiver that gets the time from GPS satellites, which are in constant orbit around Earth. See Figure 5-8.

All time servers, by the way, operate on the Network Time Protocol (NTP) and the Simple Network Time Protocol (SNTP) standards. They can maintain your computer clocks with a typical accuracy within 1 to 5 milliseconds. For older operating systems that aren't capable of supporting NTP or SNTP, some time servers also provide their own special protocol.

Time servers, however, are among the most expensive thin servers and are used only when time-critical applications are running.

Chapter 5: Networking with Thin Servers

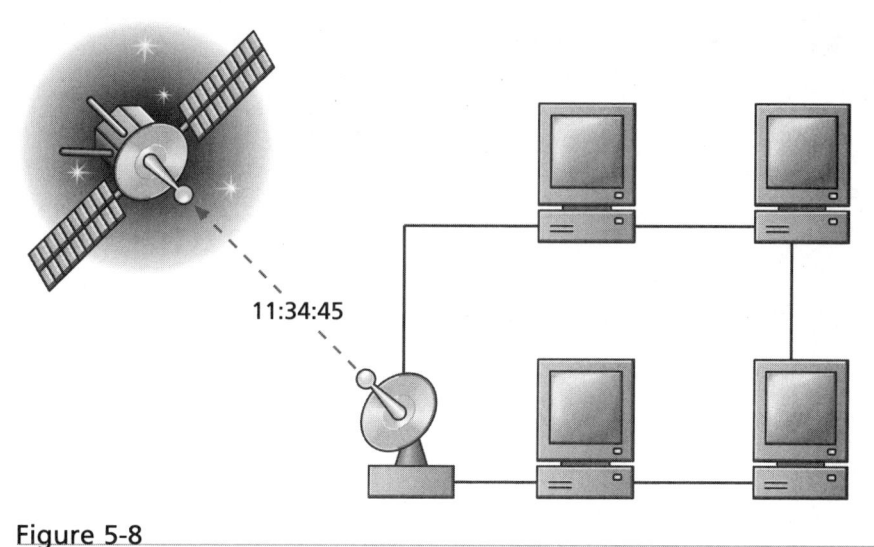

Figure 5-8
Some time servers use GPS satellites to synchronize the computer clocks on a network.

Internet Servers

Internet servers provide a relatively inexpensive and easy-to-use way for a small business to have a presence on the Internet. You connect the server to the Internet either over regular dial-up lines or over a high-speed connection such as DSL or ISDN.

Internet servers can perform these primary functions:

- Publish your Web pages for viewing over the Internet
- Provide e-mail services so office users can send and receive e-mail through the server
- Provide security to prevent unauthorized access to your company data
- Perform as a news server for private or public discussion groups
- Provide a Secure Sockets Layer (SSL) for Internet commerce to sell your products online

More expensive Internet servers can be used to offer actual ISP services to dial-up users.

Part 1: Choosing Among Network Options

Universal Serial Servers

While most computers and other devices can be connected to a network using one of the thin servers already discussed, some devices aren't as easy to connect. You might have a printer, for example, that has a serial port rather than a parallel port. Or you might have a piece of laboratory or industrial equipment that needs to be connected to a PC for users to access its data or controller.

A *universal serial server* lets you connect these devices to your network. Universal serial servers typically have a serial connection on one end and an Ethernet connection on the other. In the case of laboratory or industrial equipment, special software lets you access the device from a workstation on the network.

Network Appliances

While it might seem a contradiction in terms, some thin servers serve several roles on the network. The most popular of these *multipurpose thin servers* are network appliances, which offer network-attached storage, printer sharing, and modem sharing in one box for about the same price as a standalone computer or a network-attached hard disk drive alone.

Network appliances are basically computers without a monitor, keyboard, mouse, floppy drive, CD drive, or graphics board. They contain an embedded operating system that boots up and connects to the network without operator assistance and have a parallel printer port and a modem port. Typically they have a series of LEDs or a small display panel. When you turn on the thin server, you'll hear a series of beeps and see one or more of the LEDs turn on or flash. The pattern of beeps and lights indicates the status of the server. You might also see the word Ready or something similar on the LCD panel. If for some reason the device fails to boot up, your workstations can still communicate and share resources on a peer-to-peer basis.

You can set up most network appliances for either public or private file storage. Public storage folders are available to everyone on the network. Use these for files that you want to share with everyone, such as clip art. Private storage folders require a password to access them so that network users can keep their personal files secure.

Chapter 5: Networking with Thin Servers

Network appliances offer the ease of a peer-to-peer network with many of the features of a client/server network. Because they're basically plug-and-play, they're ideal for small businesses that don't want the administrative overhead of client/server networking but want some of its benefits.

In fact, many of these devices also contain their own network hubs. To create a network, you basically just plug into the network appliance the workstations, printer, and phone line and turn on all the devices.

You perform whatever configuration is necessary by using a Web-based interface from one of the attached workstations. For example, you'll need to create folders on the network appliance drive to store files, configure its dial-up networking to connect to your ISP, and install drivers for the printer you attach to its parallel port.

In the next chapter, I'll cover using Microsoft BackOffice Small Business Server as the network operating system for your network.

Chapter 6

Client/Server Networking with Microsoft BackOffice Small Business Server

While thin servers are great ways to expand a peer-to-peer network, they don't offer all of the benefits of client/server computing. In addition to access to shared resources, client/server networks provide performance, control, security, and centralization features that are necessary for mission-critical applications. One way to get these added benefits is by installing Microsoft BackOffice Small Business Server (SBS). SBS, which was designed specifically for use by small businesses, provides all the software you need for a client/server network in one suite.

This chapter takes a closer look at client/server computing and gives you an overview of how the features in SBS offer you the benefits of client/server networks. You'll learn about the hardware required for client/server computing in Chapter 12.

Levels of Expertise

If you've heard that setting up a client/server network is always difficult, then you're in for a welcome surprise. In reality, the degree of difficulty in setting up a client/server network depends upon the size of the network, the tasks you want the network to perform, and the hardware you're using.

Certainly, many fine points have to be remembered and many settings have to be made to get a client/server network up and running. But you shouldn't avoid client/server computing if you have a small network—say ten or so users—and you want the basic file, modem, and printer sharing that a client/server network provides. Many of the configuration steps are the same for both peer-to-peer and client/server networks. In fact, setting up clients on a client/server network requires little more effort than setting up workstations on a peer-to-peer network.

Setting up the server to provide basic services isn't difficult. Plenty of books, such as the *Microsoft Windows 2000 Server Resource Kit*, published by Microsoft Press, take you through the process step-by-step and explain everything you need to know. You can get a small client/server network up and running with little trouble. As you become comfortable with server software, you can expand the network to perform other services and to accommodate more users.

> **Tip**
>
> Some of the more advanced features of client/server computing, such as hosting a Web site, providing access to the network for remote users, and setting up an Internet firewall, do require more technical knowledge to implement. I strongly recommend that you get professional assistance if you want to run mission-critical applications or host an e-commerce Web site on the Internet or if you have a large number of workstations to support.

Chapter 6: Client/Server Networking with Microsoft BackOffice Small Business Server

Network Operating System Security

To create a client/server network, you need a network operating system (NOS) such as Microsoft Windows NT Server or Microsoft Windows 2000 Server. The NOS provides a mechanism for users to share files, printers, and modems. In addition, it authenticates network users who have permission to log on to the network and access network resources.

> **Note**
>
> Remember, for a peer-to-peer network, you need only Microsoft Windows 95, Microsoft Windows 98, or Microsoft Windows 2000 Professional.

The *network administrator* creates a user account for each person who is authorized to use network resources. The *user accounts* contain the name and password for each user and are stored in an account database maintained on the server. When a user tries to log on to the network or access a file on the server, the operating system checks the account database for the user's name and password, as shown in Figure 6-1.

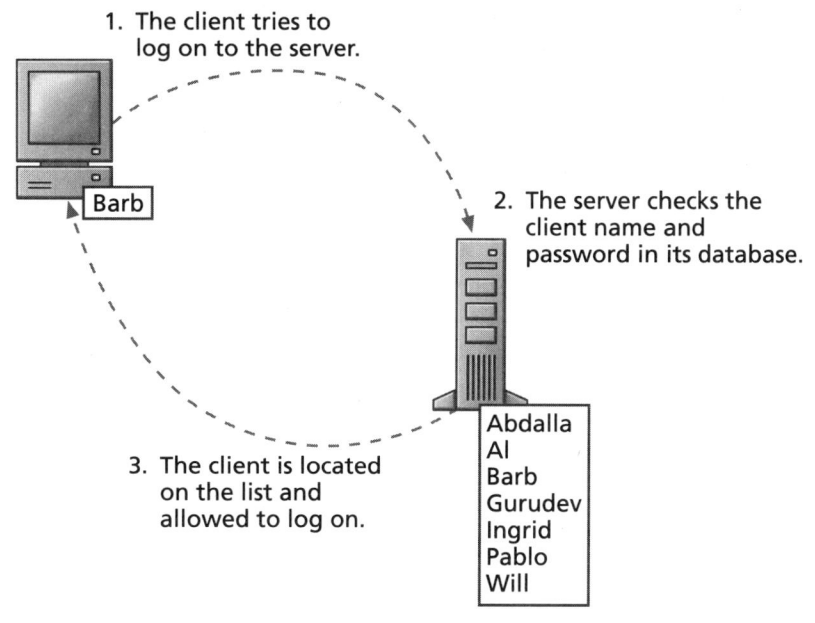

1. The client tries to log on to the server.
2. The server checks the client name and password in its database.
3. The client is located on the list and allowed to log on.

Abdalla
Al
Barb
Gurudev
Ingrid
Pablo
Will

Figure 6-1
The server checks users against its account database.

Part 1: Choosing Among Network Options

If the user's name isn't in the database or if the user didn't log on to the network with the correct password, the user is denied access to the server. If the user information is in the account database, the resources of the server become available to the user.

Windows NT and Windows 2000 let you organize users into groups. Each group has a set of *permissions*—certain tasks that they are able to perform on the server. Groups save you time by letting you define sets of permissions for a class of users, rather than for each individual user. So all you need to do is tell Windows to which groups a user belongs to provide that set of permissions to that user. Figure 6-2 shows some of the groups you can assign to a user as well as which groups are already assigned to a specific user account in Windows NT.

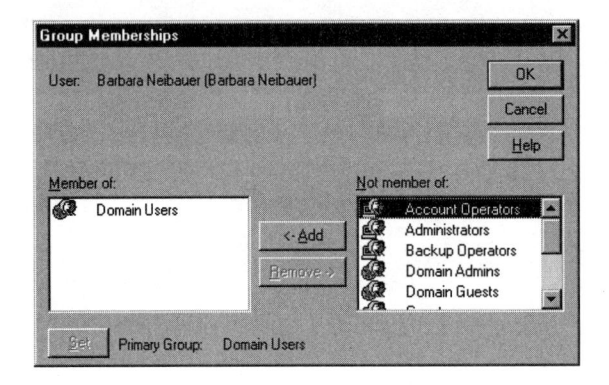

Figure 6-2

You can assign users to groups to help you control permissions.

You can also control when a user is allowed to access the network from a workstation. You might have a part-time employee, for example, who should be on the network only at certain hours of the day. To prevent another user from logging on to the part-timer's workstation during other hours, you can designate specific times that the workstation is authorized to use the network. The dialog box shown in Figure 6-3 is used in Windows NT to designate the hours a user can connect to the network. The bars on the chart in this dialog box indicate that the user is allowed access only on Monday, Wednesday, and Friday mornings.

Client/server computing also provides better security for file access through user-level access controls. You can specify which users have access to a folder, for example, even though all users have access to the network.

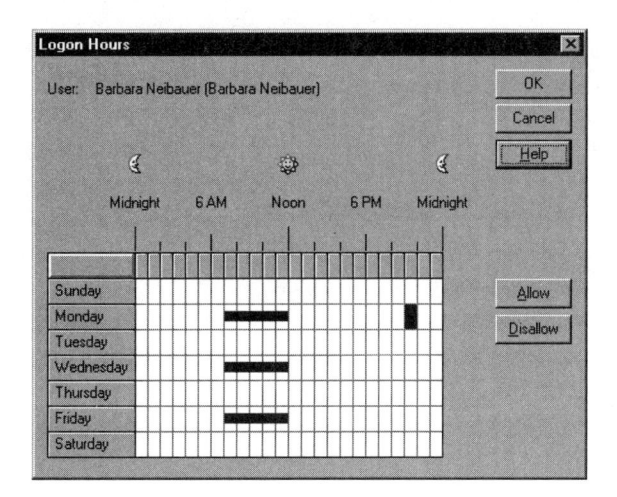

Chapter 6: Client/Server Networking with Microsoft BackOffice Small Business Server

Figure 6-3
You can limit authorized connections to the network to certain times for each user.

Network Licenses

When you purchase a program for your PC, you're purchasing the license to use it on one machine at a time. Whenever you purchase an NOS or other network software, you also purchase the right to have a maximum number of persons use it simultaneously.

Windows NT Server, for example, is packaged in three versions: Windows NT Server, Windows NT Terminal Server, and Windows NT Enterprise Edition. You get the first two versions with up to 25 user licenses; the Enterprise Edition version offers 25 licenses. Separate licenses are sold singly or in packs of 20. This means only a certain number of persons can be logged onto the server at any one time, depending upon the number of licenses you purchase.

The same applies to most programs that are designed for use on a network. If you purchase Microsoft Office 2000, for example, you have the right to use it on only one computer. You can also purchase additional licenses to let you use the same CD to install the program on more than one computer.

Part 1: Choosing Among Network Options

Multiple Platforms

An NOS should also be able to accommodate a variety of *platforms* or types of workstations. Because the Ethernet standard can be used by all types of computer systems, any computer with an Ethernet card will be able to communicate with the network, for example, as shown in Figure 6-4.

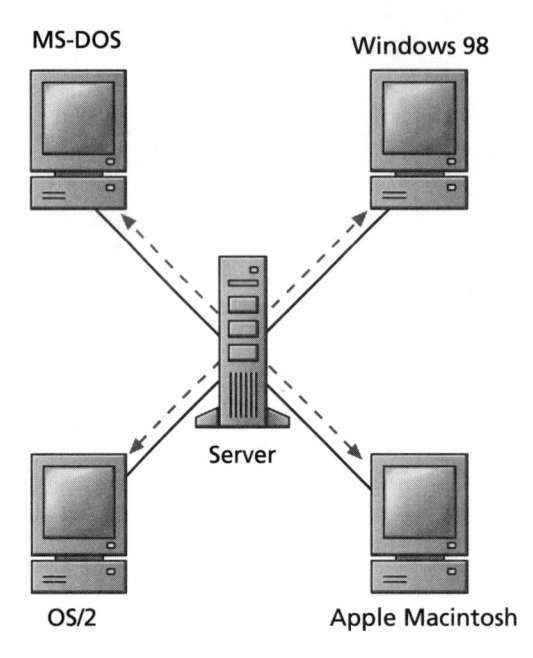

Figure 6-4
You can connect any computer with an Ethernet card to an Ethernet network.

Windows NT allows client computers to log on if they use any of these operating systems:

- Windows 3.1
- Windows for Workgroups
- Windows 95
- Windows 98
- Windows NT Workstation
- Apple Macintosh
- MS-DOS

Chapter 6: Client/Server Networking with Microsoft BackOffice Small Business Server

- OS/2
- UNIX

This means you can combine PC and Apple Macintosh computers on the same network to share files and communicate by network e-mail.

Microsoft BackOffice Small Business Server

You can purchase the NOS by itself. In fact, that's all you need if you want to set up a very minimal client/server network, such as one that shares files and authenticates users.

However, a Windows client/server network can also serve as an e-mail system, host a site on the World Wide Web, manage pools of modems and fax machines for the entire office, and perform other tasks. In all probability, you'll want to expand your network to include some, if not all, of these functions as your office and business grow.

Microsoft has programs that provide these features to your client/server network. But purchasing each program separately and getting enough licenses for all of your workstations can be quite expensive.

To make client/server networks more affordable for the small business, Microsoft has packaged the most popular client/server programs together as Microsoft BackOffice Small Business Server (SBS). SBS enables you to purchase one software package with programs and licenses for your networking, e-mail, and Internet needs. The applications are tightly integrated, reducing the amount of setup and configuration time and the amount of technical expertise needed to set up and maintain the network.

When you install SBS, you have the choice of which components you want added to your system. A number of the components, such as Windows NT Server itself and Microsoft Proxy Server, are required. Other components are optional, and you don't have to install them unless you want to.

The installation of SBS creates three special folders on your system:

- **Company Shared Folders**, which stores documents that you want to share with everyone on the network
- **User Shared Folders**, which includes a subfolder to store documents for each person who has a user account.

- **ClientApps**, which contains Microsoft software that users can access to set up their workstations. This includes software for fax and modem sharing.

Microsoft Windows NT

> ### Note
> At the time of publication of this book, Windows 2000 Server isn't available as part of the SBS package.

The heart of the SBS suite is the Windows NT Server operating system. The package includes a minimum of five client licenses, and you can purchase licenses for up to 50 workstations. Windows NT provides user authentication and file, printer, and modem sharing, as well as Remote Access Service so users can connect to the network when they're away from the office.

> ### Tip
> If you need to accommodate more than 50 workstations on your client/server network, you might need more than one server. See Chapter 12 for more information.

After installing Windows NT Server as part of SBS or as a separate program, you have to take a few steps to get it ready for your network. You need to create a user account for each client computer that you want to access the server's resources. This involves specifying the logon name and password for each user on the server, which you'll learn how to do in Chapter 16. You also have to configure each workstation or client to communicate with the server.

When you use SBS, creating a user account also performs these tasks:

- Creates the user's Microsoft Exchange mailbox
- Adds the user's address to the Global Address List in Exchange
- Creates the user's personal folder on the server
- Helps you configure the client computer to communicate with the server

This means you can specify the client's name and password, designate folders the client is allowed to access on the server, and set up other permissions.

Chapter 6: Client/Server Networking with Microsoft BackOffice Small Business Server

Microsoft Internet Information Server

Microsoft Internet Information Server (IIS) is a full-featured Web server. You can use IIS to create and manage an office Intranet and to host your own Web site on the Internet. IIS also lets you create an FTP site for downloading and uploading files on the Internet or your intranet.

SBS creates two Web-site locations when it installs IIS. One location is a staging area where you can test your Internet Web site before you actually place it on the Web. You design your site using Microsoft FrontPage or any other Web-site development program and then place it in the staging area. You can then access the Web site with a Web browser to see how it'll appear to users and to test it out. When the site is ready, you transfer the files to your Web hosting company to make it available on the Internet.

The other Web-site location is for a local intranet. An *intranet* is a private network that can only be accessed by computers on that network. Use an intranet to share company information with employees and to make files and messages available through a Web browser.

A Web-based interface in SBS, shown in Figure 6-5, lets you manage your Web sites.

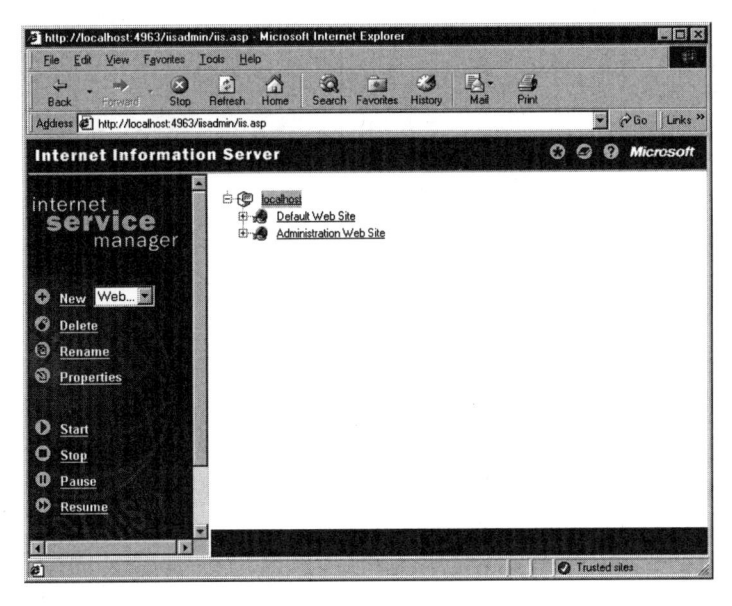

Figure 6-5
Manage SBS Web sites through a Web-based interface.

Microsoft Transaction Server

Microsoft Transaction Server provides an environment for creating and running Web-based applications. With Transaction Server and the appropriate development tools, you can create complete applications for doing business on the Internet.

For example, suppose you are processing an order that requires updating information in two databases—Client and Inventory. You wouldn't want to update one database without updating the other. If something occurs that prevents the Client database from being updated, for example, you want the transaction to fail so changes aren't made to the Inventory database.

Transaction Server offers a platform for processing transactions in a client/server environment. Because of the nature of programming, however, Transaction Server is for advanced users and programmers only.

Microsoft Index Server

Microsoft Index Server creates an index of the contents of your Web sites and provides a full-text search engine to help users find information on your intranet or Internet site. In addition to indexing Web pages on your site, Index Server also indexes the contents of plain text documents, as well as documents created by Microsoft Word, Microsoft Excel, and Microsoft PowerPoint. Once you install Index Server, it works in conjunction with IIS to index your Web site files.

Index Server comes with several sample forms that you can publish to your own Web site to provide search capabilities. A sample form is shown in Figure 6-6, which also illustrates how search results can be displayed.

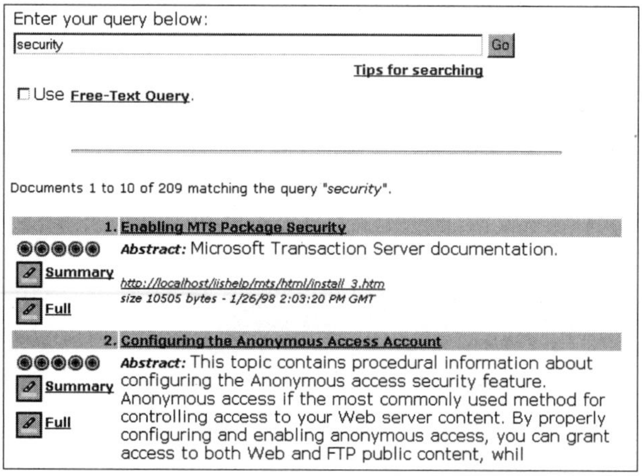

Figure 6-6

Search for documents on a Web site using Index Server.

Index Server can also report statistics so that you can keep track of Web site usage, as shown in Figure 6-7.

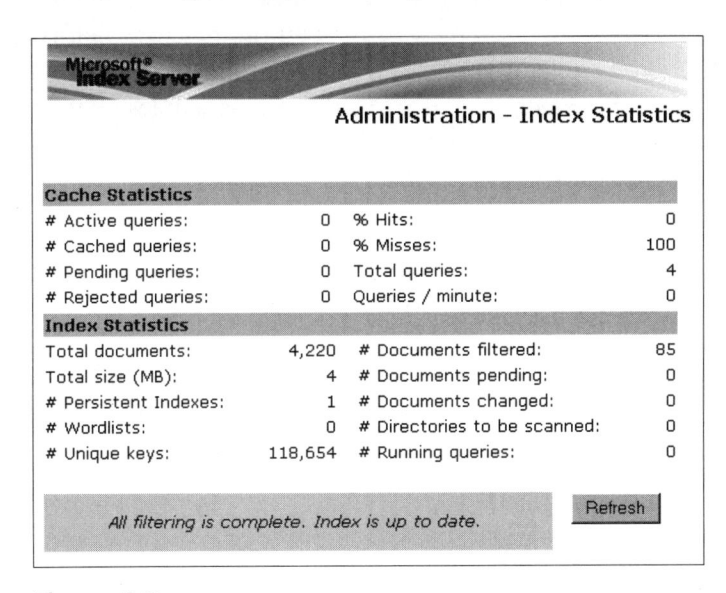

Figure 6-7
Use Index Server statistics to keep abreast of traffic on your Web site.

Microsoft Exchange Server

Microsoft Exchange Server is a full-featured messaging system for network communications and Internet e-mail. With Exchange Server, users in your office can send and receive e-mail via your company network and the Internet through an ISP. You can also arrange with your ISP to host your own *post office,* a centralized location for collection, distribution, and storage of e-mail. With a post office, you can create an unlimited number of mailboxes on your server with subnames, such as info@neibauer.net, sales@neibauer.net, and so on.

Exchange supports both the Internet Messaging Access Protocol (IMAP) and Post Office Protocol 3 (POP3). IMAP lets you maintain your mail on the server. You can choose which mail to read and which mail and attachments you want to download to your own computer. With POP3 mail, you connect to the mail server and download mail to your computer. Once you download mail, it's removed from the server.

Exchange Server also supports the Network News Transport Protocol (NNTP), which allows users in your company to access Internet newsgroups.

Microsoft Outlook

Microsoft Outlook serves as a mail client with Exchange Server to compose, send, retrieve, and read e-mail. Outlook is also a comprehensive calendar program with which you can schedule appointments and meetings and organize and track tasks. For example, you can check the schedules of other Outlook users and schedule a meeting with them.

Microsoft FrontPage

Use Microsoft FrontPage to create and manage intranet or Internet Web sites. You can design a site graphically with no programming experience and maintain it with FrontPage.

When you have a site that features FrontPage Server Extensions, you can use FrontPage to upload your Web site to the server on which it's hosted and to manage your site. This makes updating your site easy whenever you change your Web page in the IIS Web staging folder.

Microsoft SQL Server

Microsoft SQL Server is a relational database management system that can organize information of all types. SQL Server serves as the back end of a database system, providing data storage and management facilities. You access the data with a front-end database program that allows you to design queries and display data retrieved from the SQL Server database. See Figure 6-8. SQL Server databases can be up to 10 gigabytes large.

Microsoft Modem Sharing Service

This service lets everyone on the network share modems that are connected to the server. You designate the modem on the server that is to be shared and then configure the client workstations to access that modem when they connect to the Internet or send and receive e-mail. Two or more users can access the Internet through the shared modem and phone line at the same time.

If you have more than one modem on your network, you can create a modem pool. The modem sharing service finds the next available modem when a network user requests Internet connection.

Chapter 6: Client/Server Networking with Microsoft BackOffice Small Business Server

1. Front-end program on the client requests information from the server.

3. The client computer formats and displays the information.

SQL Server maintains the data and handles all client requests for database information.

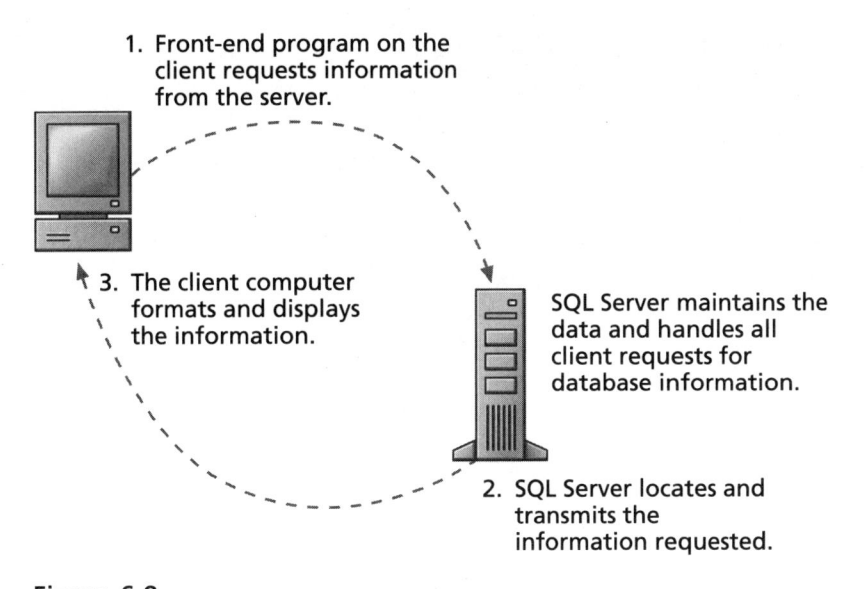

2. SQL Server locates and transmits the information requested.

Figure 6-8
Use SQL Server as a backend to your database system.

Microsoft Proxy Server

When you are connecting to the Internet through the network, Microsoft Proxy Server prevents unauthorized persons from accessing your network through the Internet. This is done by creating a firewall. You can also use Proxy Server to control which workstations on the network have access to the shared modem. You can create groups, for example, and allow only certain groups Internet access.

Proxy Server also performs caching—storing Web pages on the server's hard disk to increase overall performance. When a user tries to access a Web page, the Proxy Server cache is checked for an up-to-date version of the page. If an up-to-date version of the page is found in the cache, the page is quickly displayed in the user's browser from the hard disk rather than the browser accessing the page through a slower Internet connection on a Web site.

Microsoft Fax Service

Microsoft Fax Service allows everyone on the network to send and receive faxes and to share a common address database. It also provides complete status reports for tracking fax usage.

Because users share a common fax modem through which all faxes are sent and received, you can keep track of your fax and phone usage and provide standard cover pages. You can keep an archive file of faxes that you don't want to clutter up your hard disk but might need in the future.

Microsoft Office

Included with some versions of SBS are Microsoft Office 2000 Professional and enough licenses to use Office 2000 on all of the authorized workstations. In addition to Outlook, Office 2000 Professional includes:

- **Microsoft Word 2000** for word processing
- **Microsoft Excel 2000** for preparing spreadsheets, graphs, and maps; and analyzing numeric data
- **Microsoft Access 2000** for database management
- **Microsoft PowerPoint 2000** for creating graphical presentations
- **Microsoft Publisher 2000** for creating newsletters, reports, and other professional-looking documents
- **Microsoft Small Business Tools**, which include Small Business Customer Manager, Business Planner, Direct Mail Manager, and Small Business Financial Manager

SBS Console

To reduce the amount of technical expertise and time required to maintain the network, you also get the SBS Console. The Console, shown in Figure 6-9, is a system of menus and wizards that take you through all of the steps and tasks of network management.

Using the Console, you can easily:

- Add user accounts
- Create and manage user groups
- Share disk drives and folders
- Share printers and modems
- Install network software and track licenses
- Set up client workstations

Chapter 6: Client/Server Networking with Microsoft BackOffice Small Business Server

Figure 6-9
Use the SBS Console to manage an SBS-based network.

The Set Up Computer Wizard, for example, lets you use your SBS CD to set up and configure client workstations. After installing your NOS and components on the server, you can prepare the client computers for networking as well. The wizard installs these items on the client:

- **TCP/IP** to enable workstations to communicate with the server and the Internet
- **Internet Explorer** 5 Web browser
- **Modem Sharing Client** files to allow the workstation to access the server's modems
- **Fax Sharing Client** files to allow the workstation to access the server's fax modem
- **Proxy Client** to provide access to the Internet through the server firewall
- **Microsoft Outlook** for e-mail and calendaring
- **Microsoft Office** applications (if you have the version of SBS that includes Office)

> **Note**
>
> In a client/server network, the clients are the computers that use the resources of the server computer. Installing server software, such as Proxy Server, sets up the server to provide resources to the network. Client software, such as the Proxy Client, configures the workstation to access and use those resources.

Through the SBS Console you can also access folders for the staging areas of your intranet and Internet and manage users, shared folders, disks, printers, faxes, and modems.

SBS also includes a number of administrator tools and reports to help maintain the network. An Internet access report, for example, tracks Internet usage, peak access times, and frequently accessed Web sites. The fax report shows the date and time when faxes are sent and received, the sender and the recipient, and the number of pages. Logs of most server activities are kept so that you can track the usages of each server component.

There are numerous maintenance and configuration tools, as well. From within Windows, for example, you can manage disk partitions and check system hardware performance levels.

SBS Varieties

When you're investigating the best place to purchase SBS, you'll discover that the full name of the product is Microsoft BackOffice Small Business Server 4.5. This is the most recent version of the suite, as of this writing, and it includes the most recent versions of most of the programs it contains.

Another version of SBS will be released that will include the Windows 2000 Server operating system. Windows 2000, as you'll learn in Chapter 8, offers many improvements over Windows NT, including easier installation and configuration of hardware, but generally it has the same functionality as far as small business networks are concerned.

Another suite of networking programs, Microsoft BackOffice Server 4.5, is designed for larger corporate settings. In addition to Windows NT, Exchange Server, Proxy Server, and SQL Server, the BackOffice package includes these items:

- **Microsoft SNA Server 4.0** for integrating your local area network with mainframe and mid-range computer systems

Chapter 6: Client/Server Networking with Microsoft BackOffice Small Business Server

- **Microsoft Systems Management Server 2.0** for managing multiple site networks
- **Microsoft Site Server 3.0** for building more comprehensive intranet sites in conjunction with IIS
- **Seagate Crystal Info 6.0** for analyzing and reporting data from SQL Server and other sources

If you have a small business, SBS is the recommended package. BackOffice is more expensive, and most small businesses don't require the advanced technologies in that suite.

The next chapter shows you the advantages of using Exchange Server in your client/server network.

Chapter 7

When Does Your Business Need Microsoft Exchange Server?

If you have a peer-to-peer network, you can create an e-mail system to send and receive mail between network users and the Internet. A peer-to-peer network post office is ideal if your e-mail system consists of a limited number of network users, each with their own access to an Internet service provider (ISP) for Internet mail. As your company grows and as e-mail becomes an important way to communicate with staff and clients, however, you'll need the security and performance of a client/server messaging system.

Microsoft Exchange Server is a client/server network post office program that can handle all of your enterprise messaging needs. The program can manage e-mail from thousands of users—over the network, from the Internet, by remote dial-in access, and from other mail servers. If you have

Part 1: Choosing Among Network Options

a large organization, you can create more than one Exchange Server site and exchange messages between them.

Exchange Server provides the following services:

- A layer of security for network e-mail
- Communication with other mail systems, such as those used by your clients
- Mail services for networks in branch offices
- Public folders for sharing general company news
- Chat service for real-time conferencing
- Access to their mail for staff members who are on the road, either by dialing directly into the office or connecting to the office through the Internet

You can even arrange with your ISP to host your own mail server. You'll be able to set up an unlimited number of individual mailboxes at your Web site, including one for each staff member. If your site is *www.neibauer.net*, for example, you can have e-mail accounts such as info@neibauer.net, president@neibauer.net, sales@neibauer.net, and so on. See Figure 7-1.

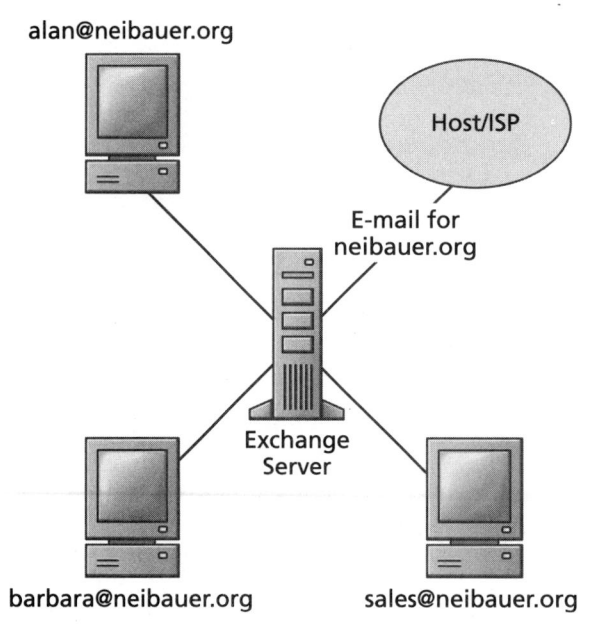

Figure 7-1

Host a mail server with your ISP, and you can set up an unlimited number of individual mailboxes.

Chapter 7: When Does Your Business Need Microsoft Exchange Server?

Exchange Server, which is tightly integrated with Microsoft Windows NT Server, can create a mail account and mailbox for each registered network user. In fact, if you use Microsoft Small Business Server (SBS), you create an Exchange mailbox at the same time you create a network user account. Exchange also relies on the security of Windows NT. Once users log on and are authenticated to use Windows NT resources, they can access their Exchange mailboxes.

How Exchange Server Works

Exchange Server maintains a *directory* of users who have mailboxes, as shown in Figure 7-2.

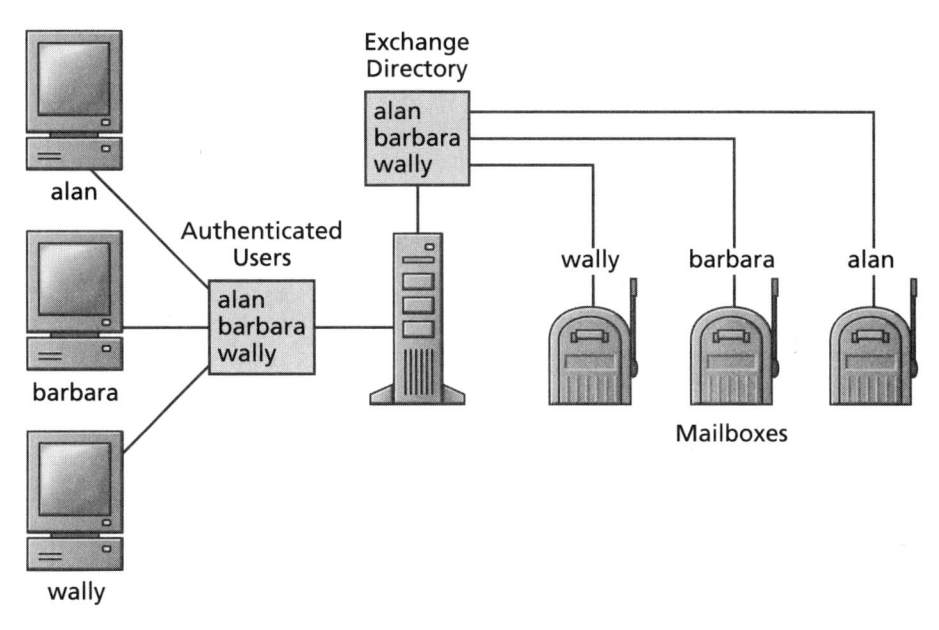

Figure 7-2
Users with mailboxes are listed in the Exchange Server directory.

When the server receives mail, the mail is placed in a central location called the *information store*. The address on the message is checked against the directory, and then the *message transfer agent* (MTA) sends the message to the recipient's mailbox, as shown in Figure 7-3.

Part 1: Choosing Among Network Options

```
          Incoming mail
               ↓
      ┌─────────────────┐
      │ Information store│
      └─────────────────┘
               ↓
      ┌─────────────────────┐
      │ Message transfer agent│
      └─────────────────────┘
           ↙    ↓    ↘
         alan barbara wally
         [📫]  [📫]   [📫]
             Mailboxes
```

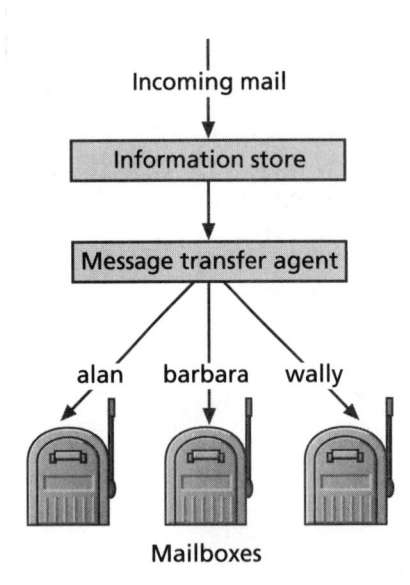

Figure 7-3

Incoming mail goes into the information store in Exchange Server and then is transferred by the message transfer agent to individual mailboxes.

When Exchange Server receives mail through the Internet from systems based on Simple Mail Transfer Protocol (SMTP) that use Post Office Protocol version 3 (POP3) and Internet Message Access Protocol (IMAP4), the *Internet Mail Service* handles the mail. The *System Attendant* keeps track of all e-mail messages regardless of where they're received.

Exchange Server has four optional features:

- **Security.** Key Management Server digitally signs and encrypts messages sent between users.

- **Microsoft Outlook Web Access.** Users can access their Exchange mailboxes and public folders through a Web browser window.

- **Connectors.** Exchange Server can accommodate mail from other systems, such as X.400, Internet Mail Service, Dynamic RAS, Microsoft Mail, and Lotus cc:Mail. You can use the Lotus cc:Mail connector, for example, to transfer messages to and from users who have Lotus cc:Mail rather than Exchange Server as their messaging system.

- **Microsoft Exchange Chat Service.** Users can participate in live conferencing over the Internet and intranet, for up to 10,000 users per server and 48,000 users per chat network.

Chapter 7: When Does Your Business Need Microsoft Exchange Server?

Public Folders

In addition to private mailboxes, Exchange Server lets you create and manage public folders. A *public folder* is a mailbox that network or Outlook Web Access users can access, so it's perfect for general discussions or project management.

When a user sends a message to a public folder, the message is posted to the folder rather than sent to a specific user mailbox. Network users with access to the folder can read and reply to messages, which are organized by subject. The initial message posted on a subject and all associated replies are grouped together in a *thread*, as shown in Figure 7-4.

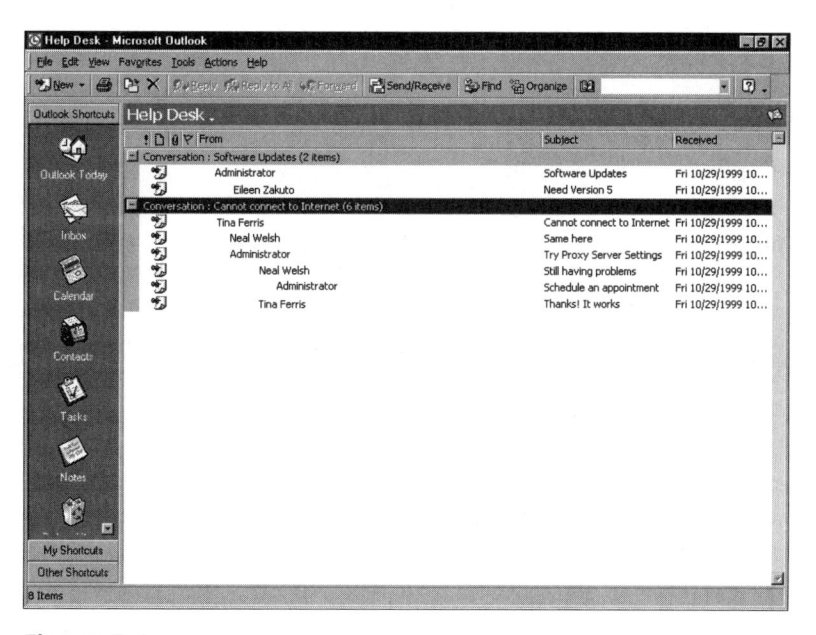

Figure 7-4
Related messages posted in a public folder are grouped in threads.

You can use a public folder to provide help desk support. A user can post a message asking for help. The messages are monitored by a technical support person who responds to the question by posting a public message in return or contacts the sender by private e-mail. Other network users can also respond with their own suggestions or with follow-up questions.

Because Exchange Server offers security features, you can limit access to a specific public folder to specific users. You can create a public folder, for instance, to share information with only the members of a project team.

Exchange also lets you create a *moderated* public folder. When someone posts a message to a moderated folder, it's first forwarded to a designated moderator who can determine the appropriateness of the message before posting it for public access.

Because Exchange Server supports the Network News Transport Protocol (NNTP), a public folder can be published as a newsgroup and accessed from any newsreader program. A Newsfeed Wizard will help you set up and configure NNTP, and you can arrange with your ISP to receive a USENET newsfeed so that users can post and read messages over the Internet.

If you have a large company with more than one Exchange Server site, you can *replicate* your public folders, copying them to other servers to equalize the workload.

Directory Access

You can also provide copies of your Exchange Server directory for offline use by users. This feature is useful because a staff member traveling with a laptop computer won't be able to access the directory to address e-mail messages. The directory, however, can be downloaded to a user's laptop when he or she is connected to the server. The user can then disconnect from the server and use the offline directory to address e-mail messages.

Exchange Server also conforms to the *Lightweight Directory Access Protocol* (LDAP). LDAP allows Internet users to search the directory as they would an address book. You determine what portions of the directory are published for access by nonauthenticated users. The public could access employee name, title, and office phone number, for example, while only authenticated users could also access mailing address and other employee information.

Client and Server

Exchange Server is the server end of the communication network. It maintains the messages on the server computer and handles requests for sending and receiving messages. It's similar to the e-mail server that your ISP offers, except the messages are stored on your own server.

In order to access the information on the server, users need a client program. The client lets them compose mail and send it to the server for transfer to the recipient and retrieve mail from the server so they can read

Chapter 7: When Does Your Business Need Microsoft Exchange Server?

and respond to it. Depending on how you set up the client software, messages can be stored in user mailboxes on the server even after they're read, or they can be downloaded to a mailbox on the user's own computer.

Users can access their Exchange Server mailboxes using virtually any messaging client because Exchange supports all of the popular messaging protocols. For example, they can use Microsoft Outlook Express and other e-mail programs or even a Web browser.

With the optional Outlook Web Access feature, users can also enter their mailbox and public folders over the Internet, just as if they were in the office. They can check their schedules, plan appointments or meetings, and search the Exchange directory for e-mail addresses.

Exchange Server includes two client programs—Microsoft Exchange client and Microsoft Outlook.

Microsoft Exchange Client

The Exchange client lets users send and receive mail through the network and over the Internet using both Exchange Server and a peer-to-peer post office. Users can also post messages to public folders and send and receive faxes if their computers are equipped with fax modems.

Installing the Exchange client places the Inbox icon on the Windows desktop, which users click to open their mailbox folders (shown in Figure 7-5). Installing the Exchange client also installs Microsoft Schedule+, a calendar program with which users can keep track of appointments and schedule meetings, as shown in Figure 7-6.

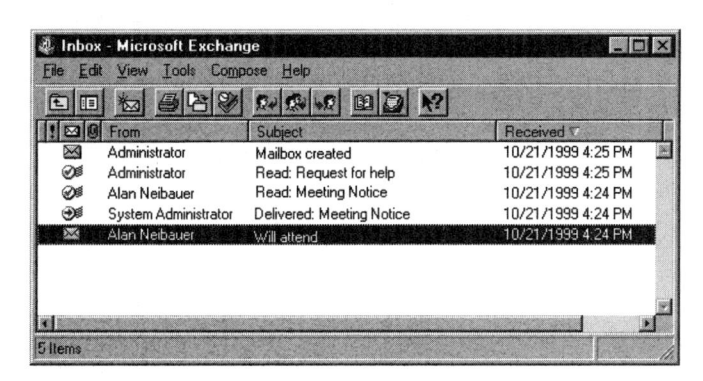

Figure 7-5
Double-click the Inbox icon on the desktop to open the Exchange client and access your mailbox.

Part 1: Choosing Among Network Options

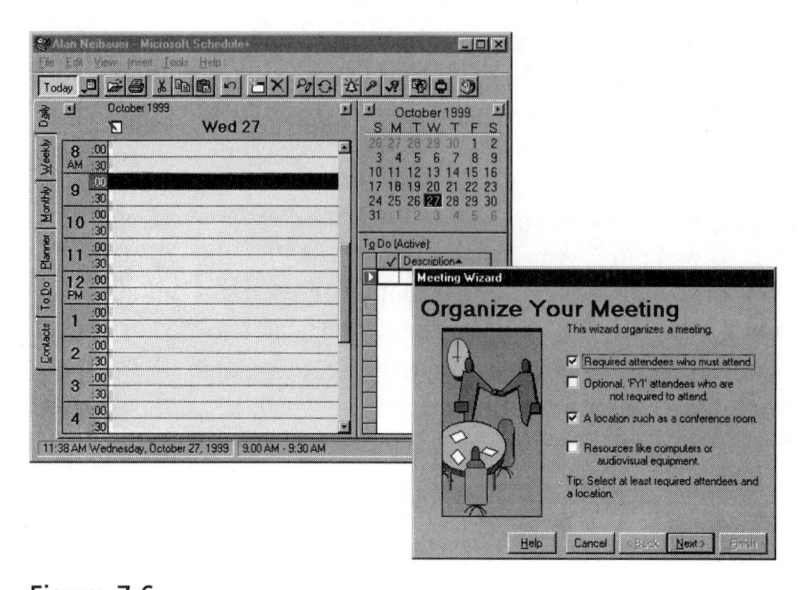

Figure 7-6
Schedule meetings with Microsoft Schedule+.

Using Microsoft Schedule+, users can even share information with other Exchange users by publishing their schedules to the server. Users can check other users' schedules to determine whether they're available for a meeting.

Microsoft Outlook

Outlook can be used in conjunction with Exchange Server as an alternative to the Exchange client. Outlook offers all the basic e-mail capabilities that the Exchange client does, such as the abilities to send and receive e-mail over the network and the Internet, send and receive faxes, and join in discussions in public folders. Figure 7-7 shows Microsoft Outlook in action.

Outlook also offers a lot of features that the Exchange client alone doesn't. With Outlook, users can manage their contact lists, schedule appointments and meetings, keep track of the tasks they have to perform, and record journals of Outlook and Microsoft Office activities.

Users can maintain e-mail messages and other Outlook information either on the server or on their computers. If they're using laptop computers, for example, they can keep Outlook files and the Exchange directory on the laptops' hard disks so that they can compose and address messages

Chapter 7: When Does Your Business Need Microsoft Exchange Server?

when they're away from the office. Users can also store copies of information from the server in *offline folders*. The information in offline folders is synchronized with the information on the server when users connect to the network.

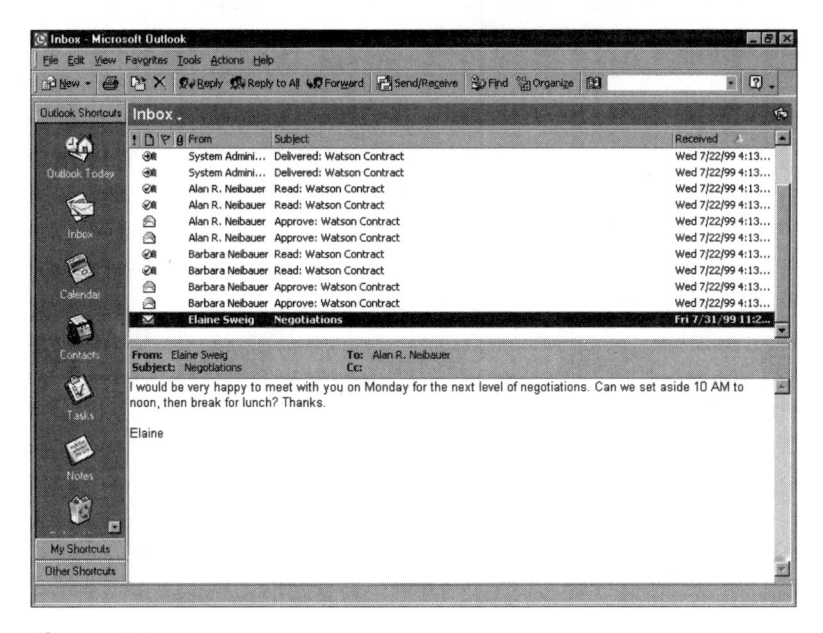

Figure 7-7
Use Outlook to send and receive e-mail, among other tasks.

> **Tip**
>
> Outlook has many features that can make work easier for staff members. The Journal is a perfect tool for generating invoices and reports. With it, you can create custom and automated forms to streamline office operations, such as a form for requesting office supplies.

With Outlook, messaging and scheduling functions are in one program. When you schedule a meeting, Outlook checks the server for the schedules of invitees. If any participant can't attend, Outlook can look for a time when all invitees are available. Outlook sends messages to each invitee about the meeting. If an invitee accepts the invitation, the meeting is placed on his or her schedule. As the meeting organizer, you can keep track of all of the responses to your invitation, as shown in Figure 7-8.

Part 1: Choosing Among Network Options

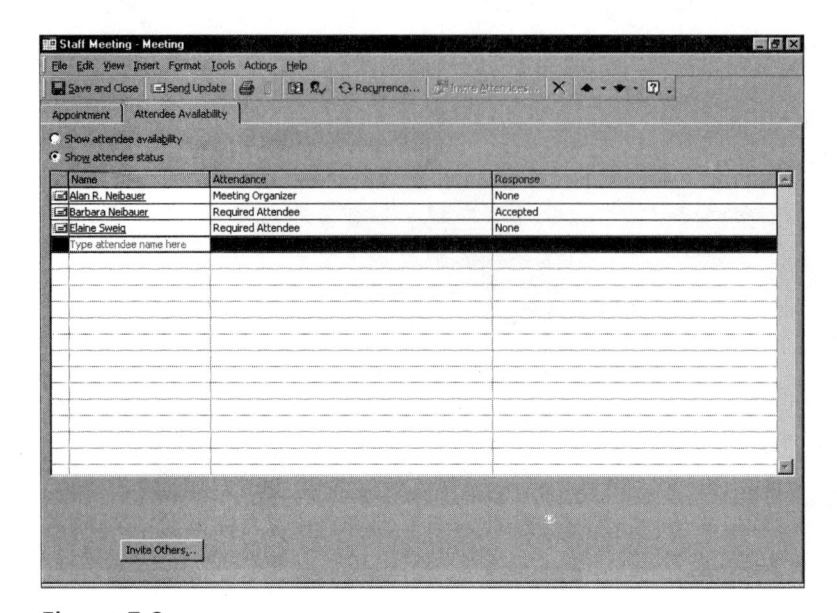

Figure 7-8
Track responses to a meeting invitation in Outlook.

Outlook also lets you keep track of responses to questions and votes. A feature called voting buttons lets you place buttons directly on an e-mail message, as shown in Figure 7-9. The recipient simply clicks on the appropriate button to indicate his or her response, which is also maintained in your record of the original sent message.

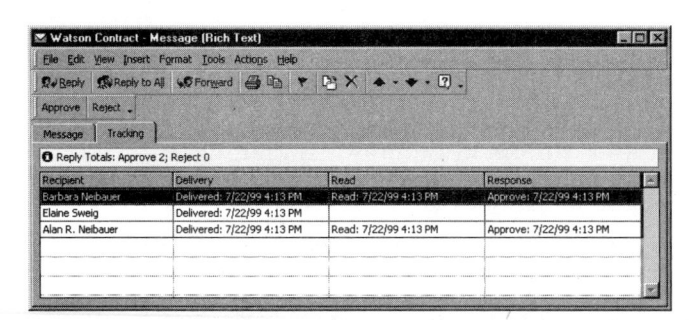

Figure 7-9
Use the voting buttons feature in Outlook to solicit answers to questions posed in e-mail and to track responses.

In Chapter 20 I'll look at installing and configuring Exchange Server. The next chapter covers the benefits to your small business of using Microsoft Windows 2000 Professional and Server.

Chapter 8

Does Your Office Need Microsoft Windows 2000?

If you're using Microsoft Windows 95 or Microsoft Windows 98 in an office setting, you might think about upgrading to Microsoft Windows 2000. In general, Windows 2000 blends the security and stability of Microsoft Windows NT with the ease of installation and use of Windows 98.

Windows 2000 comes in several versions, including Microsoft Windows 2000 Professional and Microsoft Windows 2000 Server. Windows 2000 Professional is designed for peer-to-peer networks, network clients, and non-networked computers. Windows 2000 Server is the network operating system for a client/server network. (Microsoft Windows 2000 Advanced Server contains enhanced memory support and features for large-scale networks.)

All versions offer file security and ease of installation. The server versions of Windows 2000, however, provide the greatest amount of scalability—the ability to handle any size network as your company grows. So if security and scalability are important to your business, you should definitely consider moving to Windows 2000.

In this chapter, I'll take a look at some of the benefits of Windows 2000 as compared to Windows NT and Windows 98.

Ease of Installation

Windows 95 and Windows 98 have been easy to install because they have plug-and-play support for most PC hardware and peripherals. When you install Windows 95 or Windows 98, it detects your computer's hardware and installs the necessary hardware drivers. If you later install a new peripheral, Windows detects the new hardware when it starts, and it takes you through the process of installing any necessary supporting software.

Windows NT doesn't have that level of plug-and-play support. While it might recognize some hardware when you install the operating system, it doesn't recognize the same scope of hardware as Windows 95/98, and it won't detect hardware that you add later. This means that you have to add and configure peripherals manually, using special Windows NT drivers that you find on the hardware's installation disk or that you download from the Internet.

Windows 2000 offers the same degree of plug-and-play support as Windows 95/98. It supports more than 7,000 device drivers and detects most Windows-compatible hardware, both plug-and-play and many older legacy devices. Like Windows 98, Windows 2000 also includes the Windows Update option on the Start menu, which connects to the Internet and downloads current versions of the drivers you need.

In addition, Windows 2000–supported drivers are *digitally signed*. This means that the drivers have been tested and verified to work with Windows 2000, and they contain a special identification, called a *digital signature*. If you try to install a driver that doesn't contain the digital signature, Windows will either warn you or prevent you from installing the driver, depending on how you configured your system.

The digital signature also ensures that the driver hasn't been modified or tampered with since verification. Sometimes hardware or software

Chapter 8: Does Your Office Need Microsoft Windows 2000?

manufacturers modify a driver in a way that makes it no longer compatible with the operating system. Because of digital signatures, a company must resubmit new versions of drivers for testing and verification.

Windows 2000 Server makes setting up a server easier with the Configure Your Server dialog box shown in Figure 8-1. You can use the options on the left of the dialog box to set up individual components, or you can use the options on the right to start a configuration wizard.

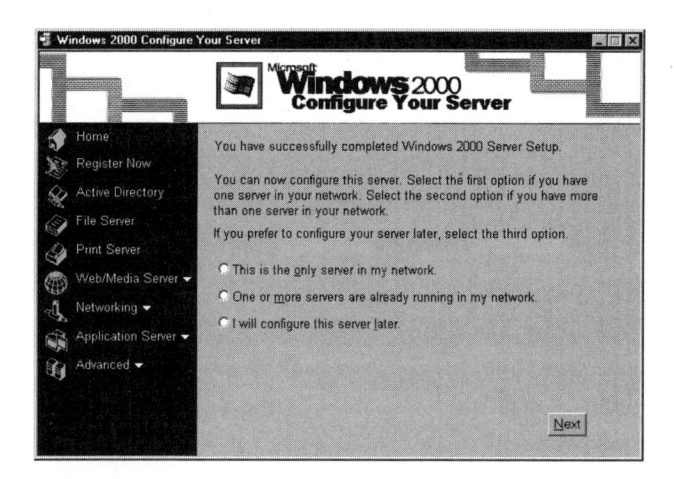

Figure 8-1
Set up your server using Windows 2000 Server configuration options.

Shared Files

A *dynamic-link library (DLL)* is a file that contains executable routines needed by a program. When you run a program or a Windows service, the program or service accesses the DLL it needs. In many cases, the same DLL is shared by a number of programs, including Windows itself. Some DLLs are provided with Windows and are in the System folder in the Windows directory. Other DLLs are supplied with specific software and might be stored in the System folder or elsewhere.

Sometimes, a software manufacturer modifies a common DLL slightly so that the DLL works better with its software. When you install the program, the new DLL will replace an existing one. In other cases, a software manufacturer might include an older version of a DLL with its program. When you install the software, the older version replaces a newer DLL, so programs that need the new version might no longer run on your computer.

Windows 2000 attempts to correct this problem by ensuring that critical system DLL files aren't overwritten. If installing a program replaces a system DLL, Windows 2000 copies the original system file over the new one. Using the Windows Update feature, you can periodically update system DLL files with the newest verified versions.

Errors also occur when you delete certain programs from your system. Deleting a program could possibly remove a DLL that's shared with other programs. Windows 2000 keeps track of shared files and prevents them from being deleted as long as an installed application needs them.

New Hardware Support

Windows 2000 supports new hardware and hardware standards that have been released since Windows NT came on the market, including the following:

- Accelerated Graphics Port (AGP)
- DVD players
- FireWire (IEEE 1394)
- Universal Serial Bus (USB)
- Advanced Configuration and Power Interface (ACPI)
- Infrared communication (IrDA)
- Multiple monitors

AGP is a high-speed video interface especially designed for 3-D graphics and multimedia programs. AGP video hardware is twice as fast as PCI video but requires a special AGP slot or integrated AGP on the computer's motherboard. Most new computers provide an AGP interface.

DVD players use a high-capacity type of CD—a DVD—that can store a full-length movie and are capable of holding from 4.7 gigabytes to 17 gigabytes of information. DVD players can also play standard CDs, so you can use the device to watch movies on your computer as well as install and access programs on a traditional CD.

FireWire, which was developed by Apple Corporation as an implementation of the IEEE 1394 standard, is a fast external interface that supports hot swappable devices such as video cameras at speeds up to 400 Mbps. *Hot swappable* means that you can plug in a FireWire device and load its

Chapter 8: Does Your Office Need Microsoft Windows 2000?

drivers without turning off and restarting your computer. The IEEE 1394 standard is supported by other companies under names such as I-Link and Lynx.

USB is another and currently more common external interface that supports hot swappable devices. Slower than FireWire, it's ideal for peripherals such as scanners, printers, and modems that don't need the real-time speed of video cameras.

ACPI lets your computer get the most from its power source, which is critical when you're using a laptop. Your computer can divert power to where it's needed rather than wasting power on unused resources. If you don't access your hard disk drive for a specific amount of time, for example, your system can shut off the power to the drive to conserve energy.

IrDA refers to the standards for infrared communications developed by the Infrared Data Association. With infrared communication, your computer can transfer data wirelessly to a peripheral or another computer. For example, you can use a laptop's built-in infrared port or an infrared device that you connect to a desktop's serial port to transfer information between two computers.

Multiple monitors let you create a wide virtual desktop that spans both displays. The use of multiple monitors, which was introduced with Windows 98, is also supported by Windows 2000. While Windows NT allows multiple monitors if you have two identical graphics adapters, Windows 2000 allows adapters from different manufacturers to be used and lets you specify which adapter to use as the primary display.

Accessibility Features

Windows 2000 offers a variety of features to enable hearing-impaired or sight-impaired persons to take full advantage of their computers. In Windows 2000, click Start and point to Program, Accessories, and then Accessibility to find the following utilities:

- **Accessibility Wizard**—The Accessibility Wizard takes you step-by-step through the process of choosing and configuring the most appropriate accessibility options. Dialog boxes, such as the one shown in Figure 8-2, let you choose options.

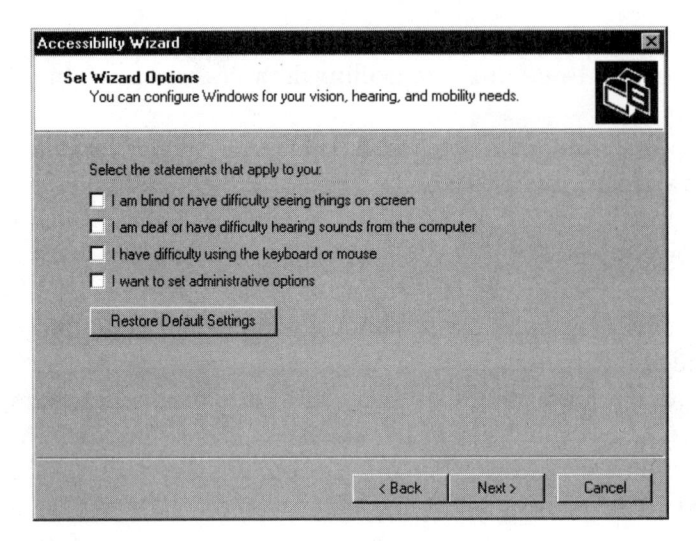

Part 1: Choosing Among Network Options

Figure 8-2
Use the Accessibility Wizard to configure Windows 2000 for hearing-impaired or sight-impaired users.

- **Magnifier**—The Magnifier inserts a pane on the screen that greatly enlarges the area under the pointer.

- **Narrator**—The Narrator "reads" the text in dialog boxes and menus under the pointer, as well as text that you type. The setup options for the Narrator are shown in Figure 8-3.

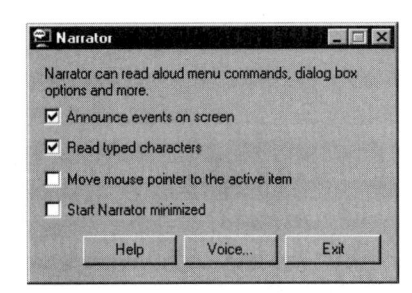

Figure 8-3
Set up the Narrator for visually impaired users.

- **On-Screen Keyboard**—This option shows a virtual keyboard that lets you type by using a mouse, joystick, or other pointing device.

Chapter 8: Does Your Office Need Microsoft Windows 2000?

- **Utility Manager**—Shown in Figure 8-4, the Utility Manager provides a central facility for controlling the accessibility features.

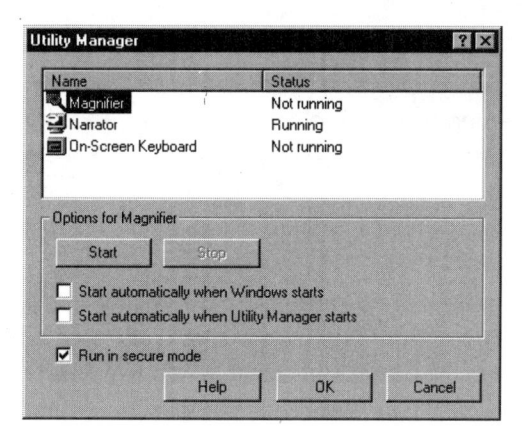

Figure 8-4
Control accessibility features with the Utility Manager.

Security

Windows 2000 offers two types of enhanced security for your files and folders:

- User-level permissions
- Encryption

User-Level Permissions

With user-level permissions, you can specify which network users, or groups of users, have access to your files. You can specify, for example, that Jane can only read files in a certain folder, that John can read and modify the files, and that Judy has no access to the folder at all.

In a peer-to-peer network with Windows 95/98, you have only share-level control. Share-level control means assigning a password to the folder. Anyone who has the password can access the folder. So if Joe surreptitiously learns the password, he can access your folder from any network client.

If you employ user-level access, however, Joe won't be able to access the folder unless he also learns the network logon password of an authorized user and logs on using that person's name.

Note

You'll learn more about sharing files and folders in Chapter 17.

File Encryption

You can use the NT File System (NTFS) and the Encrypting File System (EFS) in Windows 2000 to safeguard your files if your computer is lost or stolen. By encrypting files, your information can be read only after you log on and your password has been authenticated. EFS works on any file or folder stored on an NTFS disk.

To *encrypt* a file means to store the file in a coded format that can't be read or understood if an unauthorized user opens the file. As long as you're the authenticated user, you can work with the file as you would normally. When you open the file, it's decrypted so you can read it. You don't have to decrypt the file manually or take any special action to access it. When you save the file, it's encrypted to safeguard it. Anyone who accesses the file over the network by logging on to your computer without your password, or by stealing a Zip disk or other media with your encrypted files, is prevented from reading the file.

Encrypting a file or folder is easy:

1. Locate the file or folder using Windows Explorer.
2. Right-click the file or folder and choose Properties from the shortcut menu.
3. Click the Advanced button on the General tab to see the options in Figure 8-5.
4. Select the check box labeled Encrypt Contents To Secure Data.
5. Click OK in the Advanced Attributes dialog box and then in the Properties dialog box.

Chapter 8: Does Your Office Need Microsoft Windows 2000?

Figure 8-5
You can set attributes for a folder, such as indexing and encryption, in the Advanced Attributes dialog box.

6. If you're encrypting a folder, you'll be asked if you want to encrypt all files and subfolders within the folder, including all new files and subfolders you add to the folder. If you're encrypting a file, you'll be asked if you also want to encrypt the entire folder.

Tip

Clear the check box labeled Encrypt Contents To Secure Data in the Advanced Attributes dialog box if you want to decrypt the file or folder.

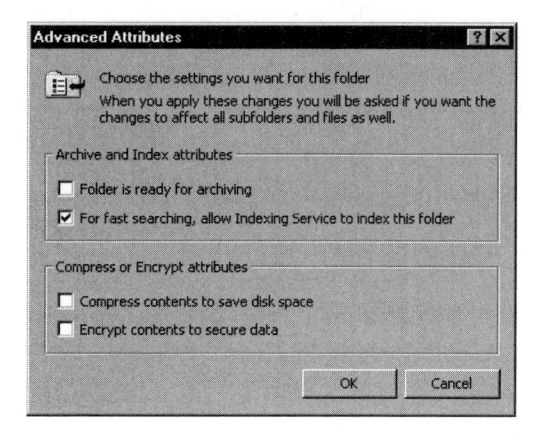

Working Remotely

The use of laptop computers has caused some significant changes in the way we work. You can connect your laptop to the network when you are in the office and then take the computer with you on the road. If you work with documents that are stored on your network, however, the documents won't be available to you when you're disconnected. You could copy the documents to your laptop, but you'd have to remember to copy them back to the network to record your changes when you connect again.

Part 1: Choosing Among Network Options

Windows 2000 makes working remotely with offline files easier. Using offline files, Windows 2000 copies documents from the location that you specify to your laptop so you can access them when you're away from the office. A Windows 2000 feature called Synchronization Manager synchronizes the files when you log on to the network, when you log off, or when your computer is idle. Synchronization ensures that the most recent versions of files are on both the network and your laptop.

Tip

You can also use offline files to work with network documents on your desktop computer so you can access the files if the network goes down.

By designating a file or folder as an offline file or folder, for example, you'll still be able to browse network drives and shared folders if you lose your connection. However, you'll be able to work with only the individual files that you've designated as offline.

To mark a file or folder for offline use, follow these steps:

1. Locate the file or folder on the network.
2. Right-click the file or folder and choose Make Available Offline. You can later clear this option if you no longer want to work with the file offline.
3. If this is the first time you've used this feature, the Offline Files Wizard lets you select several options. You'll be asked whether you want to synchronize your offline files when you log on and off the network and whether you want to see a reminder when you're working offline.

The file's icon will now have a special indicator—the two arrows in the lower left corner—showing it's ready for offline use:

letter to jim

Chapter 8: Does Your Office Need Microsoft Windows 2000?

If you disconnect from the network, the reminder appears in the Windows taskbar as shown here:

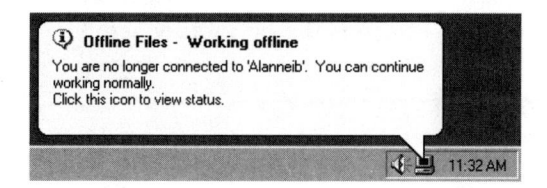

Offline Files - Working offline
You are no longer connected to 'Alanneib'. You can continue working normally.
Click this icon to view status.

Even though you're offline, you'll be able to access the file. Just right-click the Offline Files icon in the system tray of the Windows Taskbar (shown above) and choose View Files to display a list of offline files, as shown in Figure 8-6. Opening the offline file lets you work with it and save any changes you make to the offline file to your own hard disk.

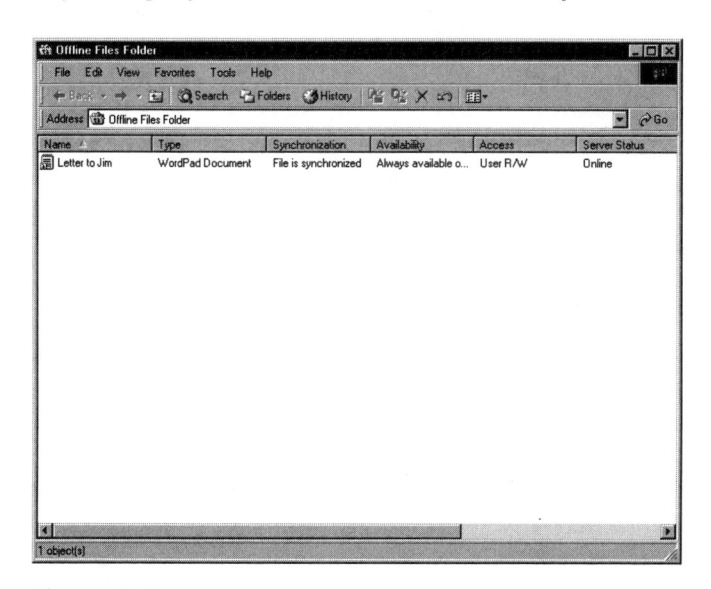

Figure 8-6
You can access offline files to read or edit them.

When you later reconnect to the network, the two versions of the files are synchronized. To control when your offline files are synchronized, click Start, point to Programs and then Accessories, and click Synchronize to open Synchronization Manager. Click the Setup button. By using the Setup feature in Synchronization Manager, you can specify whether offline files are synchronized when you log on and off the network (as shown in Figure 8-7), when your computer is online and idle, or on a periodic schedule.

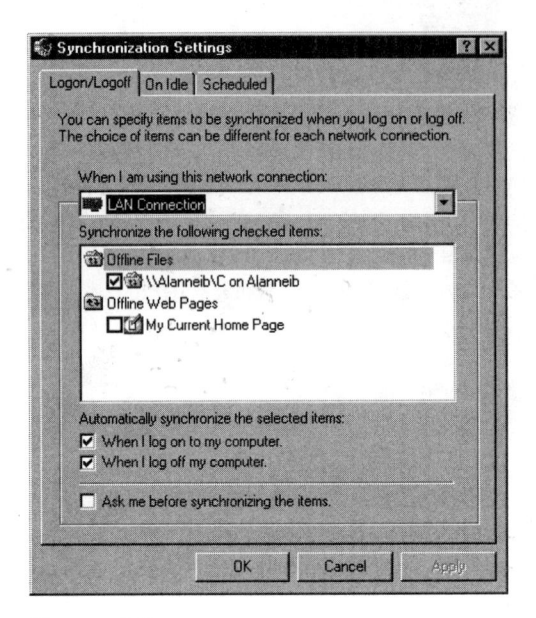

Figure 8-7
Use Synchronization Manager to specify whether offline files are synchronized when you log on or off the network.

IntelliMirror

Offline files are really part of a larger feature called IntelliMirror. On a client/server network, a feature called a *user profile* maintains information about each user's personal computer settings, files, software and data. This includes information such as your use of custom dictionaries, language settings, desktop layout and color schemes, as well as the network applications that you use.

IntelliMirror uses a variety of Windows 2000 features to maintain a user's overall environment regardless of the workstation he or she is using. IntelliMirror, for example, can restore missing device drivers, DLLs, and user settings if the user gets a new computer.

Chapter 8: Does Your Office Need Microsoft Windows 2000?

In addition to offline files, IntelliMirror takes advantage of group policies and Active Directory. *Group policies* assign user permissions and rights based on the user's membership in various groups or organizational units. Group policies make the job of managing a network easier by saving the administrator the task of assigning permissions to each user individually. You'll learn more about using groups in Chapter 14.

All of the information about users, groups, and network resources is stored in a database called *Active Directory*, shown in Figure 8-8. The Active Directory directory service presents a consistent interface and user database that's replicated on all servers in a large network. You work with Active Directory to manage users, computers, and services. You'll learn more about Active Directory in Chapter 13.

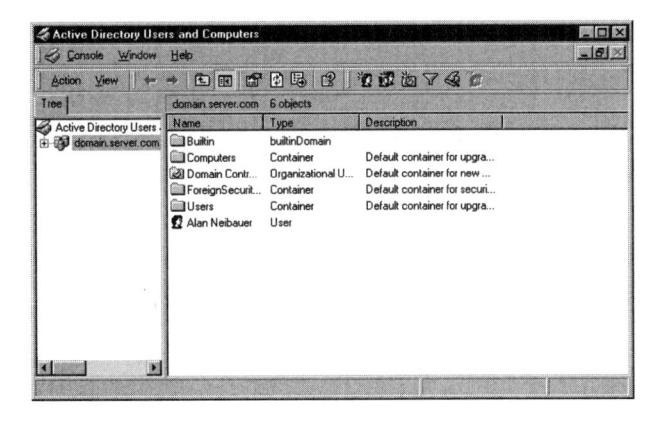

Figure 8-8
Manage your network through Active Directory in Windows 2000 Server.

By replicating the Active Directory database on all of your servers, Windows 2000 provides greater performance, fault tolerance, and load balancing.

Fault tolerance is the ability of the system to recover from hardware and software failures. If one server fails, for example, the replicated Active Directory database on another server can be used to authenticate users without any appreciable downtime. *Load balancing* distributes the processing, communications, and administrative overhead of a network across several computers, so no one server is overburdened.

Part 1: Choosing Among Network Options

By using features such as group policies and Active Directory, Windows 2000 Server makes managing large-scale networks easier and more secure. Windows 2000 Professional offers an upgrade path from Windows 95/98, when security and scalability for network workstations are issues.

Part 2, "Installing Hardware, Cards, and Cables," covers the hardware issues you'll need to consider when setting up your network. Chapter 9, the next chapter, looks at installing and using network interface cards.

Part 2

Installing Hardware, Cards, and Cables

9   Installing Network Interface Cards
10   Cabling Your Network
11   Hardware for Thin Servers
12   Hardware for Client/Server Networks

Chapter 9

Installing Network Interface Cards

The next step to setting up your office network is to purchase and install the network hardware: the network interface card (NIC), the hub, and the cables. If you're lucky enough to have computers that have NICs built-in, you can skip this chapter. While some office computers come equipped with NICs, many don't, so you'll likely have to install one yourself.

Are You Network-Ready?

Before going any further, you might want to check to determine whether your computers are already equipped with NICs. Your machines have NICs if you purchased computers that are ready to be connected to a network or if you inherited used computers that had NICs installed when you received them. If a computer is new, check its documentation or the specifications on the box in which the computer came. Chances are, if your computer is network-ready, the box will say so prominently.

If you aren't sure whether your computer is network-ready, check the back of the case. You should see one or two types of connectors: a small,

Part 2: Installing Hardware, Cards, and Cables

metal barrel that sticks out (this connects to 10Base2 coaxial cable) or an RJ-45 connector, which looks like a large telephone jack (this connects to twisted-pair cable). The two types of connectors are shown here.

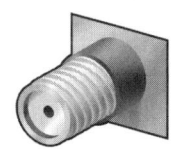

Connector for coaxial cable

Connector for twisted-pair cable

If you see neither type of connection, your computer isn't network-ready. If you see both, you're in good shape. If you see only one type of connection, it must be the correct type for the cable you'll use. Let's say you have inherited an older computer that has an NIC with just a coaxial-cable connection. You can't connect your computer to other computers that have twisted pair connections without replacing the NIC.

Note

If your computer is network ready, you can skip the rest of this chapter, unless you have to install an NIC in another office computer.

Working Without Cards

Perhaps installing the NIC makes you uncomfortable. As you'll learn later in this chapter, installing an NIC inside your computer is easy, but if you'd rather not open your computer case, you can either pay someone to do it for you or consider one of the alternatives discussed here.

You can find NICs that don't have to be installed in your computer. They plug easily into your computer's USB or printer port. Many of the USB devices are Ethernet and connect to twisted-pair cable just like an internal NIC. They have a USB connection at one end and a twisted-pair connection at the other. You plug the adapter into the USB port on your computer and connect a cable from the adapter to the network hub, to which all the cables from all the NICs are connected. To use a USB network device, you must be running Microsoft Windows 98 or Microsoft Windows 2000 and have at least one USB port on your computer, as shown here.

Chapter 9: Installing Network Interface Cards

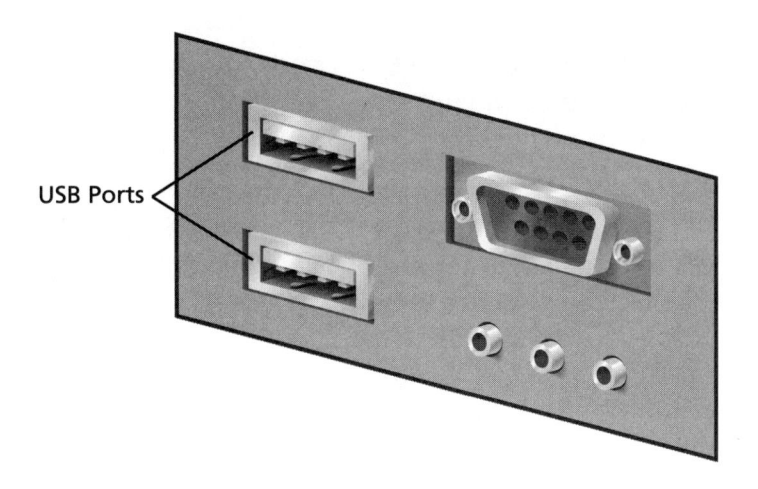

USB Ports

Most of the printer port-NICs, however, aren't Ethernet. They use neither twisted-pair nor coaxial cable. Instead, they transmit information through the telephone line, your office's power lines, or over a radio frequency without wires. Printer port devices are usually slower than Ethernet networks, but they're easier to install.

> **Note**
>
> You can also find network interfaces that are serial port devices, but they're more expensive and can be complicated to set up. Serial port devices are recommended for businesses with older computers.

Can You Do It Yourself?

If you decide that the speed advantages in using networking hardware that includes an internal NIC are for you, consider installing the card yourself or finding someone in your organization who can. Nothing is difficult or mysterious about the inside of a computer—it's just a collection of wires, circuit boards, and other paraphernalia. Lots of folks insert NICs, sound cards, and other kinds of cards themselves. They save a little money, and they get the satisfaction of having faced the computer monster and triumphed.

Other folks wouldn't operate on their computer even if you paid them. They'd rather have a professional do it. They save themselves frustration if something goes wrong, and they have the comforting feeling that they can just take the computer back to the professional who installed the hardware for them if anything else needs to be done in the future.

Installing an NIC Yourself

You don't have to be an electronics expert to install an NIC in your computer. You just need some patience, common sense, and the ability to use a screwdriver, which is likely the only tool that you'll need.

Of course, whenever you open a computer, you're exposing a lot of sensitive and expensive equipment. Certainly, pulling or poking the wrong part can damage your computer, but if you're careful, nothing will go wrong. A lot of wires are inside your computer. You can safely move them out of the way as long as you're careful not to disconnect them.

Just keep in mind that you shouldn't open your computer with wet hands, when the computer is plugged in, or while the kids, the spouse, the television, or the telephone are distracting you.

If you have more than two computers to connect to a network, start by buying enough hardware for two and no more. Setting up a network isn't difficult, but it takes time, and it's best to get two computers communicating before you invest your whole bankroll in connecting the rest of your computers to the network. Starting with just two gives you time to concentrate on the basics.

Tip

Purchasing hardware by mail order can be a money-saving alternative if you want to install it yourself.

Finding Someone Else to Do It

If you decide to have someone else install the hardware for you, that person can also set up the network drivers for your NIC and configure Microsoft Windows for the network. If you install the NIC yourself, you can learn about network drivers in Chapter 13.

The main drawbacks of having someone else install the hardware include:

- You'll have to carry the computer to the store or pay more to have a consultant come to your office to do it.
- You'll have to do without your computer for a while.

- You'll need to consider deleting any sensitive material you have on your hard disk.

If you take your computer to the store, you'll have to unplug all of the cables connected to the computer. You won't need to take the keyboard, mouse, or monitor—just the computer case itself. The shop will connect a keyboard and monitor for the installation process.

Some stores might be able to install the NIC while you wait, but others will make you drop off the computer and come back another day. It doesn't take long to install the card, but some shops are very busy, especially during holiday seasons. If you can't do without the computer for long, ask the store when they are least busy and try to schedule your visit for that time.

> **Tip**
>
> I suggest that you take your computer to the same store from which you originally bought it; you might get a price break on installation of an NIC. When you purchase a computer at a computer superstore, for example, you can usually have an NIC installed for a small, flat rate that will be worth the money for the peace of mind.

Buying and Installing an NIC

You'll need to decide what to buy, where to buy it, and whether you should buy separate components or obtain everything in a kit.

Selecting the Card

When you select hardware that includes an internal NIC, whether it works through Ethernet or the telephone line, you'll have to make sure you get the correct NIC for your computer. If you decide on an Ethernet network, the NIC you buy must use either twisted-pair or coaxial cable.

When you buy an NIC, make sure it's designed for the type of cable you select. You can play it safe by purchasing *combo cards*, which are NICs that have connectors for both coaxial and twisted-pair cables.

Next, consider whether you'll be satisfied with the 10 Mbps network speed of regular Ethernet or whether you want a 100 Mbps network (also called Fast Ethernet). For small office networks, 10 Mbps is fast enough,

Part 2: Installing Hardware, Cards, and Cables

but the price difference between 10 Mbps and 100 Mbps is so small that it almost doesn't pay to stay with the slower speed. Fortunately, you can mix 10 Mbps and 100 Mbps cards on the same network so you can always upgrade parts of the network to become faster.

For larger office networks, invest in 100 Mbps hardware, or if cost is no object, consider gigabit Ethernet and fiberoptic cable.

Fitting Your Computer's Bus

The *bus* is the part of the computer that moves information between all the components. The signals flowing in and out of the NIC and other parts of the computer flow through the bus, like traffic on city streets.

The NIC plugs into an expansion slot on the bus that's not already occupied by a video card, modem, or other device. An *expansion slot* is a socket inside your computer into which you slide a card that adds functionality to your computer, such as an NIC. Metal contacts in the slot mesh with the contacts on the card so that electronic information can pass between them.

Most computers today can have three types of slots, as shown in Figure 9-1.

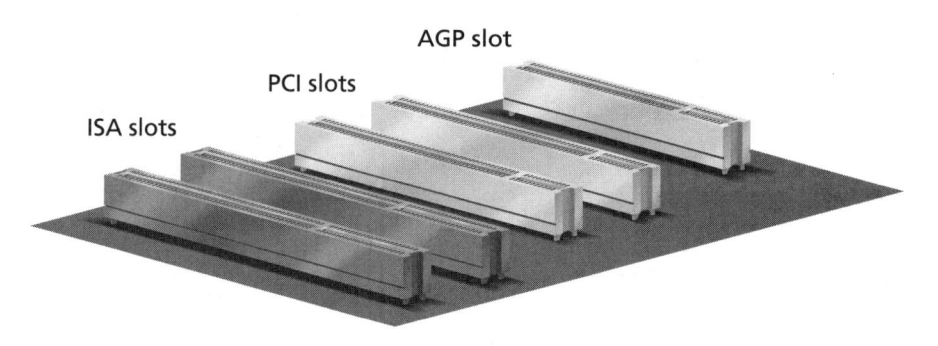

Figure 9-1

A typical bus can have three types of expansion slots.

- **Industry Standard Architecture** (ISA) slots are the type used in older machines, but they're still around today. They're usually black and have a plastic divider across the slot about two-thirds of the way from one end. The NIC fits into an ISA slot and has a space to accommodate the divider.

Chapter 9: Installing Network Interface Cards

- **Peripheral Component Interconnect** (PCI) slots are usually white. They are shorter than ISA slots and have a divider about three-quarters of the way from one end, which is accommodated by the space on the NIC.
- **Accelerated Graphics Port** (AGP) slots are shorter than the PCI slots. They also have a divider, and one end of the slot is set back further from the edge of the bus than the other slots. Most buses have only one AGP slot. The slot is used for a high-speed graphics card, so you can't use it for an NIC.

Note

Some older computers might have Extended ISA (EISA) slots, which look like ISA slots except that they're deeper and usually brown.

You must purchase the correct type of NIC for the type of slot that is open and available in your computer. You can often determine which slots are free by looking at a photograph or illustration in your computer's manual that shows the inside of the computer. The photograph or illustration should show you which slots are occupied and by what.

If the manual doesn't help, you might be able to tell by looking at the back of the computer for unused slots. If a slot is unused, you'll see a solid metal plate covering an opening.

If you still can't tell, open the computer and look for an empty slot on the main circuit board. If your computer doesn't have any empty slots, you'll need the type of NIC that connects to a port on the back of the computer, such as the USB port.

Note

If you need help opening your computer, read "Installing NICs" on page 130.

NICs that fit in PCI slots are the easiest NICs to install inside a computer because they require the least software configuration. In most cases, Windows will configure them when you plug them in and turn on the computer because they're *Plug and Play* compatible. This means that Windows senses that the card is installed and either installs the correct software by itself or prompts you to insert the disk that came with the NIC.

NICs that fit in ISA slots are usually more complicated to install, even those that are Plug and Play. You might have to change the settings on these NICs to avoid conflicts with other cards in your computer. *See "Installing NICs in ISA Slots" on page 133* to learn how to change the settings on the NIC.

Connecting Laptops

Although a few laptop computers have built-in NICs, laptops normally don't have internal slots into which you can plug an NIC. You can still connect a laptop to a network by using a network interface device on a PC Card or an external network interface device such as a USB card.

PC Cards are about the size of credit cards; they slide into a PC Card slot on your laptop. (A PC Card slot is also called a PCMCIA slot, which is named for the Personal Computer Memory Card International Association, the organization that developed the PC Card standard.)

PC Cards with a network interface device work just like other NICs. The network cable connects directly to the end of the PC Card sticking out of the computer or to a smaller cable that plugs into the card. Some cards use only twisted-pair cable, but others have adapters that can accept either twisted-pair or coaxial cable.

Installing a PC Card is a piece of cake. The label on the card is on top and the end of the card with the small holes fits into the PC Card slot, which is usually on the side of the computer.

Most laptops have two PC Card slots, an upper and a lower slot. If one slot already has something in it, like a modem, slide the PC Card into the other slot. Then push the card in firmly. This pushes out a small tab on the side of the slot, which you can press to remove the card.

Using Network Starter Kits

Because of the growing popularity of networking, many manufacturers package all the essentials for setting up a small network in one box: the *network starter kit*. Ethernet kits, for example, usually include two NICs, a hub, and a couple of network cables.

The kits are a good value because they often cost less than if you purchase the components separately. For $50 to $100, you can buy a complete kit that gives you everything you need to connect two computers. If you need to add computers, you can purchase additional cards and cables separately. With a kit, you can be relatively certain that all the parts have been designed to work together. Many network kits, including the Microsoft/3Com HomeConnect network kit, even come with a program that sets up Windows for networking, so you don't have to do any software configuration. In addition, most of the kits come with software that lets you share one Internet connection among all the people on the network. This means that everyone on the network can actually browse the Internet at the same time, using one phone line and one Internet account.

Note

You'll learn how to share Internet accounts in Chapter 21.

Kits have some disadvantages, however. While you might be able to find a kit that includes one internal NIC for a desktop and one PC Card for a laptop computer, almost all the kits offer two cards of the same type. That's fine if that's what you need, but otherwise, you might have to purchase a card of a different type separately. The other disadvantage is that if one of the cards is defective, you might have to return the entire kit to have the company replace the card, which means you'll have to remove both cards and the hub, even if only one component is bad.

As an alternative to a kit, you can purchase each component separately. You can then buy different cards for different machines and return individual pieces if need be. Because all Ethernet cards work together, you can even purchase NICs and hubs from different manufacturers.

Where to Shop?

Now that you've made some basic decisions about the type of components to buy, you're ready to get out the charge card and go shopping. But where?

You'll find the best prices at computer superstores—those large stores that carry only computer hardware and software—and through mail order. The superstore will have a good selection of kits and individual components. There you'll be able to purchase the kit and take it home the same day, and you'll have a local place to go if you must return anything. If you can't find items locally, you should opt for buying them through mail order.

Part 2: Installing Hardware, Cards, and Cables

Mail-order and online retailers such as PC Connection, CDW, Insight, Outpost.Com, Buy.Com, and others, also offer great prices and often a better selection than local stores. While you have to pay for shipping, most mail-order companies don't charge sales tax. They offer the same return policy as local stores and often provide overnight or two-day shipping for the same price as regular ground shipping. You'll have to install the hardware yourself, however, and it'll take longer if you have to return or exchange something.

As an alternative, you can purchase hardware at large chain appliance stores, electronic boutiques in malls, and independent computer stores. But while the prices at appliance stores might be good, you'll rarely get the sales help you need. Expect to pay slightly higher prices at electronic boutiques in malls that carry computer games, magazines, and some hardware. Again, the salespeople aren't usually computer experts, although they'll probably know a lot about the most awesome computer games. Also expect to pay slightly higher prices at local independent computer stores. However, it's at your local computer store that you'll probably find the most knowledgeable salespeople and most helpful technical support. Try to pick a shop that's been around for a while. Plenty of little computer stores pop up, only to go out of business by the time the stoplight on the corner changes. Nothing is wrong with these places, but it's nice to have a place to go down the road if something goes wrong.

One other place you should consider as a source for computer hardware is computer shows. If you live near a metropolitan area, look for computer shows periodically at convention centers, schools and colleges, or other meeting grounds. You might have to pay a small entrance fee, but you'll have access to a wide selection of vendors and products. While some vendors simply travel from show to show, look for those from local computer stores. You might have difficulty tracking down a traveling vendor or one who's based in another area if you need support later.

My recommendation? Purchase a kit from a computer superstore in your area. Check the return policy, and install and test the hardware before the return period ends. If you don't want to install the hardware yourself, have the techies at the superstore do it for you.

If no superstore is in your area, find a local computer shop that's been around for some time. Tell them what you want and that you want to spend as little money as possible.

Preparing for the Installation

If you've chosen to install the NICs yourself, a little preparation will make the job easier and faster.

Note

If you're installing an ISA NIC, refer to "Installing NICs in ISA Slots" on page 133 of this chapter before attempting the installation.

- Make sure you have a Phillips screwdriver; a small one will usually do. Don't use a magnetic screwdriver because the magnetism in the screwdriver might scramble information stored in computer chips.

- Find a small container, such as a paper cup. You'll be removing small screws and you'll want a place to put them so they don't get lost.

- While it's not necessary, you might find it handy to have needle-nose pliers available in case you drop a screw and need to fish it out of the computer. You might also need a flat-bladed screwdriver to pry off a cover plate. And you'll need a scalpel and forceps (only kidding, of course).

- Next, remove rings, necklaces, and any other metal jewelry that might hang down or make contact with the inner workings of the computer. Metal is a conductor of static electricity, and necklaces can get caught inside the computer.

- Find a place to work. You should have plenty of room on all sides of the computer, so pick the center of a room or a hallway where you won't be disturbed by foot traffic. It's best to find a spot near a phone line, because many manufacturers supply a telephone number that you can call for support. With the phone close to your workspace, you can describe to the support technician what you see and what you're doing.

- Make sure the work area is as free from static electricity as possible. Rub your hands on your pants or skirt and touch something metal. Did you get a shock? If so, static electricity is present, and it's a danger to the components in any computer. Try working in a room without a carpet and discharge any static

Part 2: Installing Hardware, Cards, and Cables

electricity by touching the computer case before working inside. You can also purchase an anti-static band that wraps around your wrist and connects to the computer case. Any static flows through the band to the case rather than through the delicate electronic equipment inside the case.

- Leave the NIC in its anti-static packet until you're ready to insert it in a slot. Never touch the surface of the card or the metal connectors on the bottom and handle the card by only its edges.

Installing NICs

When you're ready to start, work on just one computer at a time; don't take two or more computers apart at the same time because you might mix up their parts.

Follow these steps:

1. Unplug the computer.

   ### Caution

   Don't just turn off the computer or turn off the power strip to which it's attached. The computer must be unplugged.

2. Unplug the wires from the keyboard, mouse, printer, scanner, and any other device. Think of this as a good opportunity to dust behind the computer and straighten out all the cables.

3. Move the computer case to a work area. Don't try squeezing in beside the desk or balancing the computer on your lap.

4. Remove the computer's cover and put any screws that you remove into your small container.

   If you have a desktop computer, you might need to remove only the top panel. Some cases have tabs on the back that you press to release and lift off the cover. In other cases (pardon the pun), you must remove several screws at the back of the computer and slide the case forward or backward to remove it. If you have a tower computer that sits on the floor, you can remove one or both side panels. Look carefully at the case to determine whether the two side panels appear to be separate from the rest of the case. If they are, you need to remove only the screws on one side and slide the

Chapter 9: Installing Network Interface Cards

panel away. Which side? Sometimes you just can't tell. If you take one side off and you don't see the row of cards and slots, replace the panel and remove the other side.

The screws you need to remove are probably near the edge of the case. Don't remove any screws from the middle, especially ones near the power supply—where you plug in the power cord—because they might hold the power supply in place.

5. Remove the metal slot cover plate behind the empty slot in which you plan to place the network card, shown in Figure 9-2.

    You might need to either remove the screw that holds the cover in place or break off the small tab that holds the cover. Use a flat-bladed screwdriver to gently pry the cover away and then work the plate back and forth until it comes out.

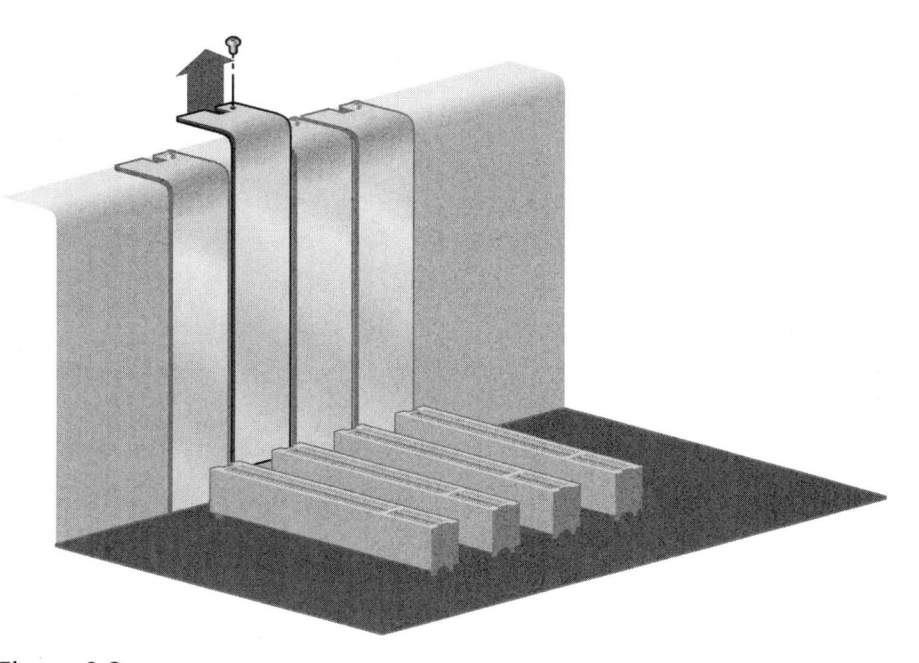

Figure 9-2
Remove the cover plate to expose the slot.

6. Position the card so the connectors are toward the back of the computer. The metal back of the card will replace the blank slot cover that you've removed.

Part 2: Installing Hardware, Cards, and Cables

7. Line up the bottom edge of the NIC with the slot and confirm that they match. (Some ISA cards won't fill the entire ISA slot, just the front section.) See Figure 9-3.

    If any wires or cables are in the way, gently move them aside without disconnecting them. Although most cables inside the computer are connected snugly, make sure you don't dislodge the smaller and more delicate cables, such as those that connect a CD drive to the sound card, while moving them aside to access the slot.

8. Push the card down into the slot, exerting steady, firm pressure. As the card goes into the slot, the metal back should slide down and fit where the cover plate was. The top of the back should rest on the screw hole. If it doesn't, the card isn't down all of the way.

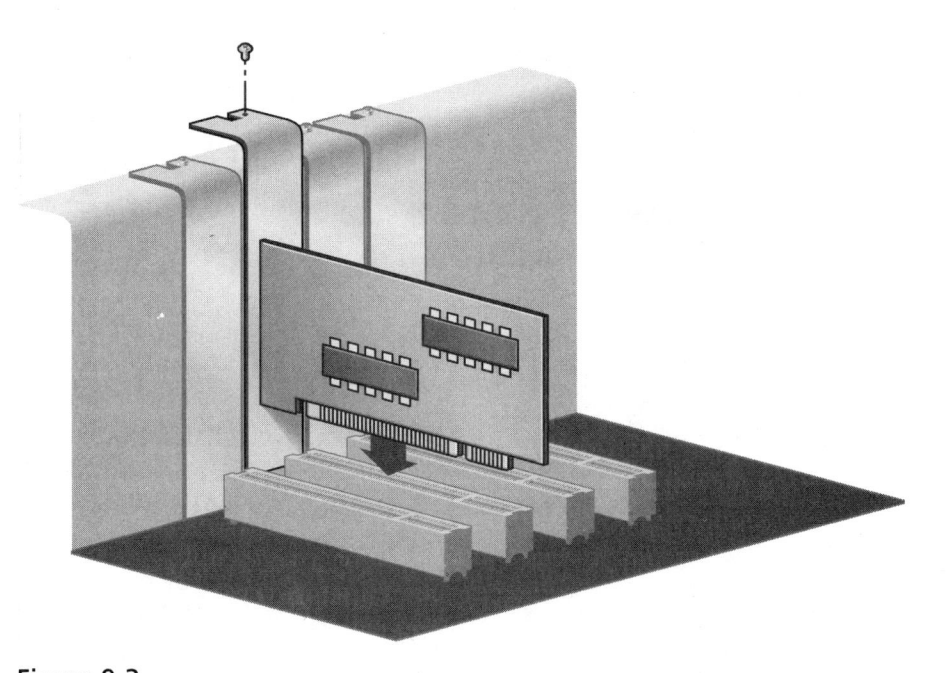

Figure 9-3
The edge of the NIC should fit within the slot.

Try not to bend the card to either side, rock it back and forth, or touch its surface. Just hold the card by its edges and apply firm, downward pressure.

Chapter 9: Installing Network Interface Cards

9. Being careful not to drop the screw into the computer, screw the metal back of the card into the frame of the computer. This screw is important because it keeps the card firmly seated in the slot.
10. Replace the computer cover and be careful not to trap any wires.
11. Before putting the computer case back in its place, clean around the area, straighten out the cables, and make sure you have no extra screws in the container.
12. Plug everything back in. Plug in the power cord last.

Installing NICs in ISA Slots

Installing NICs in ISA slots often requires you to change special settings on the card, such as the IRQ and I/O address. *IRQ* stands for interrupt request. Imagine the IRQ as a telephone number. Each device in your computer has a different IRQ number that it uses to communicate with the computer. Your computer scans each IRQ line to see which device is requesting service—that is, to send or receive information through the computer bus. Only one device is allowed on an IRQ line at one time. If more than one ISA device uses the same IRQ, their signals might conflict.

> **Note**
>
> Some devices, such as PCI cards, can share an IRQ.

The *I/O address* (I/O stands for input/output) is the location in your computer's memory where the signals from the device are stored. No two devices can have the same I/O address or their signals will conflict.

The IRQ and the I/O address of an ISA device are changed either by hardware or software. If your card's documentation tells you that the IRQ and I/O address are set up through software, you can skip this section for now.

On some older cards, you make these settings by changing a small switch or moving a *jumper*, which is a small device with metal prongs, as shown in Figure 9-4. A plastic cap fits over two of the prongs. The pair of prongs that the cap is on determines the IRQ that's assigned to the device. The card's documentation will show you which switch or jumper to change.

Part 2: Installing Hardware, Cards, and Cables

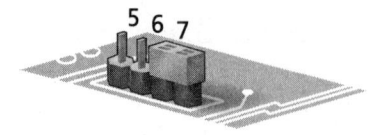

Figure 9-4.
Position a jumper to set the IRQ to 7.

> **Note**
>
> NICs that fit in PCI slots share IRQs automatically, so no special setup is required.

Before you can pick an IRQ setting for the card, you must check to see what's available on your system to avoid a conflict. To check which IRQs are already being used, follow these steps:

1. Look at the documentation on the card for possible IRQ and I/O settings.
2. Right-click My Computer on the Windows desktop.
3. Choose Properties from the shortcut menu.

If you're using Windows 95 or Windows 95, continue with these steps to see which IRQ and I/O settings are available:

4. In the System Properties dialog box, click the Device Manager tab.
5. Double-click Computer at the top of the list.
6. Click the Interrupt Request (IRQ) button. The IRQs, usually numbered from 0 to 15, are listed.
7. Look for an unused IRQ or one that's assigned to a device you don't plan to use, such as an unused COM port. Don't worry if some IRQs are used by more than one device in the list. Some devices can share IRQs.
8. Click the Input/Output (I/O) button.
9. Check to see which of the addresses that your card can use are available.
10. Click Cancel to return to the Device Manager tab.
11. Click Cancel again to close the System Properties dialog box.

If you're using Windows 2000, continue with these steps to check for available IRQ and I/O settings:

Chapter 9: Installing Network Interface Cards

1. In the System Properties dialog box, click the Hardware tab, and then the Device Manager button.
2. In the Device Manager window that appears, choose Resources by Type from the View menu.
3. Click the plus sign next to the Interrupt Request (IRQ) option. The IRQs, usually numbered from 0 to 15, are listed.
4. Look for an unused IRQ or one that's assigned to a device you don't plan to use, such as an unused COM port. Don't worry if some IRQs are used by more than one device in the list. Some devices can share IRQs.
5. Click the plus sign next to the Input/Output (I/O) option.
6. Check to see which of the addresses that your card can use are available.
7. Close the Device Manager window and then the System Properties box.

Set the switches or jumpers on the card to settings that won't conflict, and then install the card and restart your system.

Your NIC is now installed. If you installed the NIC yourself, you must still install the NIC drivers and configure Windows, and that's the subject of the next chapter. If you had it installed by someone, your network drivers and Windows software should also be set up and ready to go, although you might still want to go through the next chapter to make sure your network is ready.

The next chapter covers how to run cable for your network.

Chapter 10

Cabling Your Network

Now that you have network interface cards (NICs) installed in your computers, you're ready to connect the computers with cable. Just as a chain is only as strong as its weakest link, though, your network is only as sound as the connections between computers, so you'll want to consider the suggestions in this chapter carefully.

Before Proceeding

Proper cabling is a critical step in creating your network. Even cables that appear to run between rooms correctly can lead to problems. You might consider hiring a professional company to run and test your office cables if any of these factors apply to your situation:

- You don't have a suspended ceiling in which to easily run cables between rooms.
- You have concrete or block walks that are difficult to drill through.
- Your office is very large and spread out.

If you're building or remodeling an office, you might have the opportunity to run and test your cables before insulation is added and the walls are completed. In this case, if you find a problem connection, you can replace the cable while it's still exposed.

You can test a cable by actually connecting it to a hub and a computer. As an alternative, you can purchase testing equipment through companies such as Data Comm Warehouse (*www.warehouse.com/datacomm*) that will tell you if the cable is capable of carrying an Ethernet signal.

If you decide to wire the office yourself, you must choose whether you want to use patch cables or premises wiring.

Patch Cables

Lengths of cables with connectors already installed at both ends are called *patch cables*. You can purchase patch cables of various length, or you can make your own, as explained in *"Making Your Own Network Cables" on page 150*. Simply plug one end of the cable into the NIC that's in the computer you wish to connect and the other end into the hub. Running patch cable doesn't require any special tools.

If you have to run cable outside of the walls to reach a computer on the far wall, you can purchase raceways and floor cable covers to provide a professional-looking appearance and to avoid tripping over exposed cables. *Raceways* are usually made of a non-conductive material such as vinyl; they attach to walls, ceilings, or floors to hide cable and keep it safe. Most raceways have curves, as shown here, for use in the corners of rooms to keep the cable from bending too sharply:

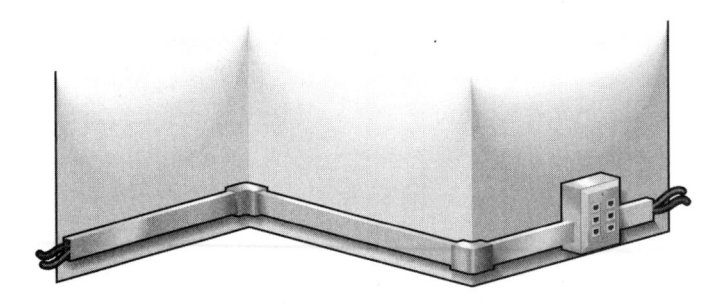

Floor cable covers are plastic or rubber, and they cover a cable that might be stepped on. Depending on their design, you run the cable under the floor cable covers or through them, as shown above.

Premises Wiring

With *premises wiring,* cables run through the walls and connect to Ethernet sockets on the wall. Ethernet sockets look like phone sockets or cable video sockets, but they're for network cables instead. The sockets help to create a more attractive look and avoid clutter. Premises wiring requires either special tools or special costly connectors that can be installed without tools.

I recommend premises wiring for all but the smallest networks, especially when network computers are spread throughout an office. With premises wiring, there is less chance that someone will trip over cables or damage cables by rolling over them with chairs or other office equipment. It's a more professional installation and encourages a more organized and planned network.

Planning for Network Hubs

An Ethernet network using twisted-pair cable requires some device that serves as a central location through which all network signals flow. The least expensive device is a hub, at which all of the cables from the NICs converge.

> **Note**
>
> Hubs are also called *concentrators*.

Selecting the proper hub and planning its location is critical to the performance of your network. Its location will also determine where you have to run your cables. Before discussing hubs and their alternatives, however, I'll look at a way to create a very small network of just two computers without a hub.

Hubless Networks

If you want to create a small peer-to-peer network of only two computers, you can avoid using a hub by connecting the computers' NICs with a special cable called a *crossover* or *cross-pinned* cable. As shown in Figure 10-1, straight wires connect each of the pins or connections in one end of a standard Ethernet cable to the corresponding pins at the other end. In a crossover cable, several of the wires aren't straight but cross over one another as they connect pins in one end to non-corresponding pins at the other end.

Part 2: Installing Hardware, Cards, and Cables

standard Ethernet cable

crossover Ethernet cable

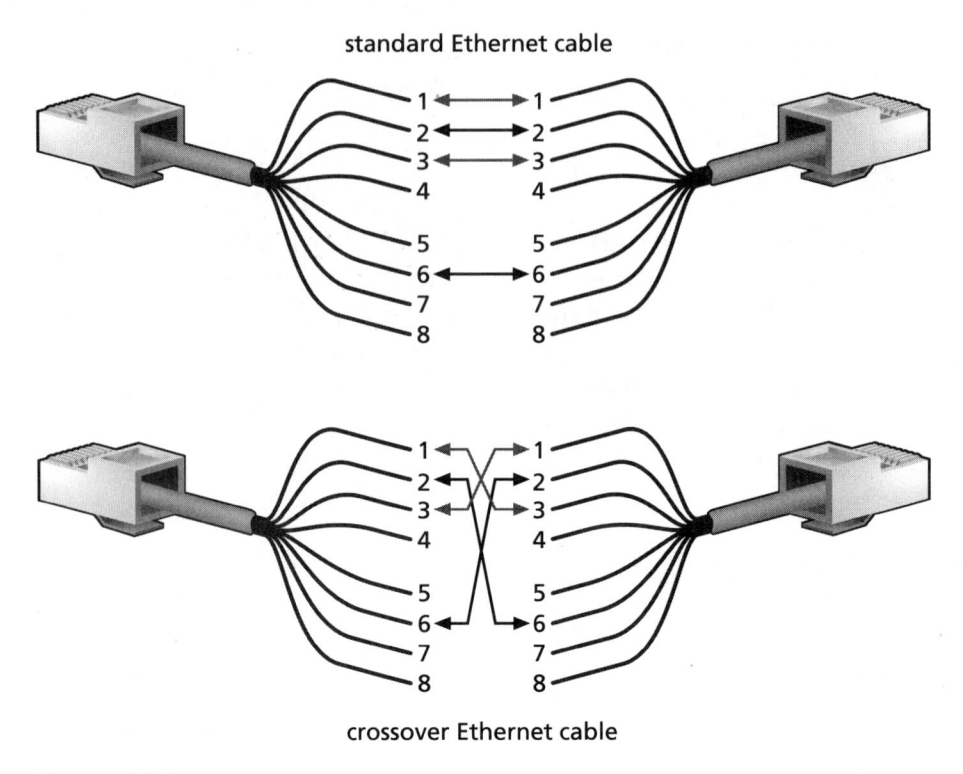

Figure 10-1
In a standard Ethernet cable, interior wires are straight, while in a crossover cable the wires cross over one another.

The wires have to be crossed over because you're making a direct connection between computers. Certain pins in the Ethernet plug of an NIC are designed to send information out, while others bring information in. When you connect cables through a hub, the hub accepts information on the computer's outgoing pins and sends it to other computers on their incoming pins.

If you connect a regular Ethernet cable directly between two computers, the outgoing pins of both interfaces will be connected. When one computer sends information to the other, the information will be transmitted to the outgoing pin of the other computer and won't be accepted. To connect two computers directly together, the outgoing pins of one must be connected to the incoming pins of the other, which is the function of a crossover cable.

Plug one end of the crossover cable into the NIC of one computer, and plug the other end into the NIC of the other computer. No other hardware is required, and the cable can even be 100 feet long or more. A crossover cable is inexpensive; a 10-foot cable might cost $20 or less. Unfortunately, crossover cables aren't that easy to buy because few computer stores carry them.

If you go to a computer store to purchase a crossover cable, make sure you don't get a regular patch cable, the standard cable for networking. If you can't find a crossover cable at the local computer superstore, try ordering one from a mail order company, such as Data Comm Warehouse. You can also go to a small, local computer store where the staff might know about such things and can make one for you. In fact, take a copy of Figure 10-1 with you so you or the staff don't make any mistakes.

Tip

Because crossover and regular patch cable look the same, you might want to wrap a small piece of duct tape or adhesive tape on one end of the crossover cable and write *crossover* on it. This will help you distinguish the crossover cable from your regular patch cables.

Getting to the Hub of the Matter

When you want to connect three or more computers or connect a printer directly to the network, you'll need a hub. Consider a hub even when you need to connect only two computers. Hubs are so inexpensive that buying one might cost less than having a crossover cable custom made.

Note

You'll need a hub for any Ethernet network of three or more computers that uses twisted-pair cable. This includes networks with computers using external universal serial bus (USB) NICs.

The hub you need depends on how many computers you want to connect to the network. You can get 10-Mbps hubs, 100-Mbps (Fast Ethernet) hubs, dual-speed 10/100-Mbps hubs, and even gigabyte hubs. The dual-speed hubs are perfect for networks that use both 10-Mbps and 100-Mbps NICs because you'll get the maximum speed from each NIC.

The least expensive hubs have ports for up to five computers. You can also get hubs that handle more than five computers, and you can connect hubs together to increase the number of connected computers.

Connecting Hubs

Most of the ports on the hub are designed to be connected to an NIC using a standard unshielded twisted-pair (UTP) cable. You can't use a standard cable to connect two hubs via standard ports. As a solution, many hubs have an extra connector called an *uplink port* that lets you connect hubs and link them in a chain. This port is designed so you can connect it to a standard port of another hub. In some cases, a switch on the hub changes a port from standard to uplink.

Tip

If a hub has a switch that changes a standard port to an uplink port, the uplink position is often labeled Xon. If the switch is in the standard port position (Xoff), treat the port as a standard port.

Here are four different ways to connect two hubs:

- Both hubs have an uplink port. A UTP cable connects the uplink port of one hub to *any* standard port on the second hub but not to its uplink port. This system allows up to nine computers to be on the network.
- The uplink ports of both hubs are connected using crossover cable. You can have 10 computers on your network with this system.
- Only one of the hubs has an uplink port. Again, a UTP cable connects the uplink port of one hub to *any* standard port on the second. With this system, you can connect up to 10 computers to the network.
- Neither of the hubs has an uplink port. The two hubs are connected, however, by a crossover cable from any port on one hub to any port on the second hub. This configuration leaves 10 free ports for connecting computers.

Chapter 10: Cabling Your Network

> **Tip**
>
> If your hub has an uplink port, check the hub's documentation. In some hubs, the uplink ports share the same resources as a standard port—usually the one next to it. This means that if you plug a cable into the uplink port to connect the hub, you can't use the standard port beside it. So, if you have a 5-port hub with an uplink port that shares resources, using the uplink port means that only four computers can be connected to the hub.

When you need more than two hubs for your network, you can link additional hubs together. In Figure 10-2, for example, three hubs are connected in a series, with workstations connected to each of the hubs. If the connection between any two of the hubs happens to break, the computers that are still connected remain in the network. This is often called the *star bus topology* because the hubs are linked together like a bus network—the hubs are connected directly together rather than through a central point—while the workstations are connected to hubs in a star configuration.

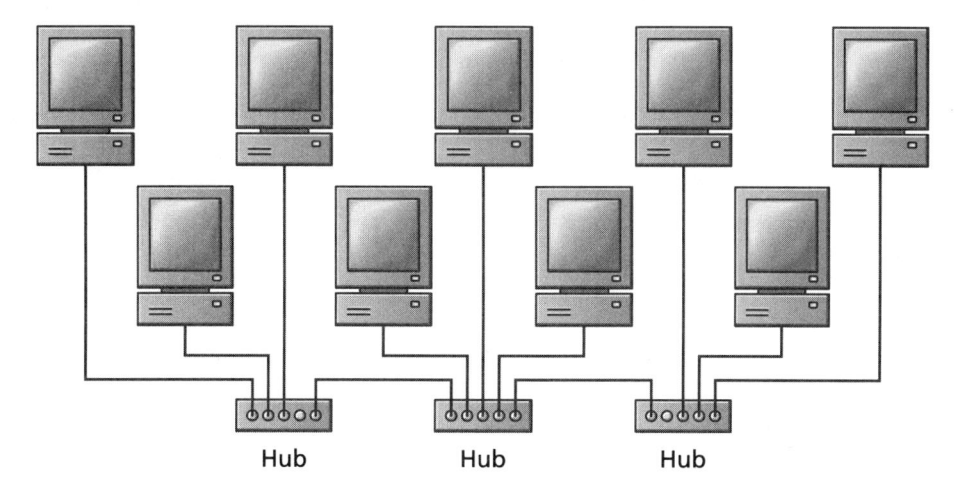

Figure 10-2
Connect hubs together in series to form a star bus topology.

> **Note**
>
> In any of the examples given here, the computers connected to the hubs can be workstations or a server computer. The server can be connected to any hub.

Another way to join hubs is to connect them to one main hub. All of the hubs aside from the main hub service workstations connected to the network.

On some networks that use twisted-pair cable to connect workstations to the hubs, you can connect the hubs together with ThinNet coaxial cable. These hubs have one or more coaxial ports in addition to the standard ports. That way, you can use all of the standard ports to connect workstations to the network. You don't have to worry which port to use to connect the hubs to each other because all of the hub-to-hub traffic is carried over the coaxial cable. You can also use these types of hubs to combine twisted-pair and coaxial cable in one network. Just connect the free end of the coaxial cable from a computer to the coaxial port of the hub.

Placing Hubs

Placing a hub requires some thought. The hub must be plugged into an electrical source for power, so make sure it's near an outlet. You might be leaving the hub turned on at all times, so connect it to an outlet that isn't controlled by a wall switch. The hub needs some air circulating around it, so don't put it in a cabinet or drawer. And be sure to keep it away from direct sunlight, heat, radios, fluorescent lights, or transmitters of any kind that can cause interference.

The main trick in placing a hub is to make it convenient to all your computers, so you can easily connect cables from the computers to the hub, passing through the least number of walls, floors, and rooms. If you're connecting two computers in the same room, just place the hub near an electrical outlet and run the cables along the baseboard from each computer to the hub. If you're connecting computers in adjacent rooms, place the hub near the hole you've made in the wall or in the floor between the rooms.

Because you have to run separate wires from every computer to the hub, sometimes the central location where you'd like to place the hub isn't ideal, especially when you have to run the cable through walls and along baseboards. Select a location that requires the least amount of cable and the least amount of fishing the cable through walls, floors, and ceilings.

If you need more than one hub for your network, they don't necessarily have to be in the same room. You can separate the hubs if it helps to reduce the amount of cable you have to run through walls. You can also use multiple hubs only where running cables is difficult or where running multiple cables along the same path isn't desirable.

Alternatives to Hubs

Most of the inexpensive hubs on the market are called *passive hubs*. They simply provide a means of linking all of the computers together through UTP cable. No matter how many passive hubs you have linked together, they're all one network segment to the server. This network segment is comparable to a group of networked computers that are all connected by the same length of cable.

To understand the problems that you can encounter with hubs, you have to understand a little about the way Ethernet works. Information is carried across the network in groups of data called *packets*. When the hub receives a packet from a computer, it sends the packet to every other computer connected to it, regardless of the computer to which the packet is being sent. All of the computers on the network can see the packet but only the one to which the packet is being sent does anything with it.

As an example, suppose you connect to the network and ask to see a directory of the files on another workstation. The list of files is transmitted in one or more packets to every networked computer. Because you asked for the list, only your computer displays it. This repetition of packets being sent to workstations not interested in them is a waste of resources.

Because information is transmitted to every computer on the network, it's as if all of the workstations are competing for the same space on the cable. As your network traffic increases, more than one packet might be on the cable at the same time. If they collide in what is called a *network collision*, neither packet might reach its destination.

A limited number of computers can be connected to one segment, with a limit of 90 meters of cable between each computer and the hub.

To get around some of these problems, other types of hubs are available, such as the following:

- An *active hub* can amplify the network packet to allow greater distances.

- A *managed* or *intelligent hub* contains built-in software to manage network transmissions to avoid packet collisions and increase performance, as well as configure the ports on the hub and provide network statistics.

- A *stackable hub* uses a special high-speed bus to carry network packets from one hub to another and acts as a repeater to maintain signal strength.

Part 2: Installing Hardware, Cards, and Cables

> ### *Token Ring Networks*
>
> An alternative to Ethernet networks is the token ring network. In a *token ring network,* the computers are logically connected in a complete circle.
>
> To avoid collisions, a special packet called a *token* is continuously passed from one computer to another. A computer must have possession of the token to transmit a packet on the network. So when a computer needs to send a packet, it waits until it receives the token to send its packet. The packet travels with the token around the network in one direction. When the packet returns to the sending computer, the computer removes the token from the packet and sends the token along the network for the next workstation that needs it.
>
> Physically, the computers in a token ring network are connected by twisted-pair cable to a central hub-like device called a *multi-station access unit (MAU).*

In place of a hub, you can also use a device called a *switch* or *switching hub.* Switches work by filtering packets. The software within the switch looks at the destination address of the packet—the address of the computer to which the packet is being sent—and transmits the packet directly to that computer's port on the switch.

With a switch, the network appears to have a separate connection to each of the computers. Each computer is seen as its own network segment, so they don't compete for the same bandwidth or have network collisions. You can use a switch to replace a hub in a peer-to-peer network.

You can also use a switch to connect multiple network segments together, where segments have their own bandwidth and speed requirements. A client/server network, for example, can use a switch to connect two 10Base-T network segments with a 100Base-T segment. Using a switch in place of a main connecting hub increases network performance.

In addition to hubs and switches, consider other network devices, such as the following:

- A *repeater* allows the distance between devices to be extended by amplifying the network signal but doesn't avoid collisions or increase network speed.
- A *bridge* connects two network segments together so each appears as its own network. Each segment can have its own hub, and each segment has its own limitations in terms of distance

between each computer in the segment and bandwidth. The bridge filters packets so only packets sent to computers on the other side of the bridge are transmitted through the bridge.

- A *router* also divides a network into segments and acts as a bridge. While a bridge separates transmissions at the message level, a router can separate a network logically at the protocol level. The *protocol* is the system used by a network to send and receive information. By working at this level, a router can act as a firewall and prevent information from leaving or entering areas of the network. Routers can determine the optimal route for sending network information based on network load, speed, and other factors that affect network performance. Some routers are designed for specific purposes, such as remote connections or Internet access.
- A *gateway* connects different types of networks together, such as those using different protocols.

The Network Backbone

When you connect two or more networks together using a bridge, router, or other device, you're creating a network *backbone*. The backbone is usually a higher speed connection that can run longer distances than the standard cable between computers within a network.

In some cases, you can use coaxial or fiberoptic cables as a backbone to which any number of twisted-pair Ethernet networks are connected. The higher speed backbone handles the traffic between networks.

Running the Cables

Connecting together two or more computers in the same room is relatively easy, but when the computers are in different parts of the office, running cables between them can be more of a challenge.

Note

If you need custom cable lengths, see "Making Your Own Network Cables," on page 150.

Running Cables Within a Room

You can often run the cable between devices in the same room along or even under the baseboard molding. In some rooms, you might be able to hide the cable by pushing it between the carpet and the bottom of the molding. If not, run the cable on the top of the baseboard molding. Of course, using a cable that's the same color as the molding looks best. When you get to the corner of a room, don't bend the cable sharply, even if this means that the cable has to stick out slightly from the corner.

Running Cables Between Rooms

If you need to connect two computers that are in adjacent rooms, you can drill a hole in the wall between the rooms and feed the cable through. Of course, if the computers are on opposite sides of the wall, you won't even have to run the cable along a baseboard. Alternatively, you can run the cable through the ceiling, either within a suspended ceiling or between the ceiling joists. You'll then have to make two holes, one where the cable enters the ceiling in one room and another where the cable exits the ceiling in another room. If there's a heating duct or a return that runs between rooms, you can also run the cable through it, but if you make holes in the metal to get the cable into the duct, stuff some insulation around the cable to prevent air loss around the holes.

If you want to connect a computer that's directly upstairs, look for a closet. If you drill a hole in the closet ceiling and run the cable through it, you can avoid unsightly hanging wires in your office. Because floors can be 8 inches thick or more, you might have to use a coat hanger to fish the cable through the hole. After the cable reaches the other floor, you can run it along the baseboard.

If you'd rather not drill holes in a closet, look for other wires, pipes, or ducts that go between floors. You might find some space that you can use for your network cables next to pipes or other wires. If the space you must go through is insulated, be sure to replace any insulation that you remove. In some localities, the fire code requires that all spaces between floors be insulated as a fire stop.

If the computers you want to connect aren't in adjacent rooms, you might need to run cable through a suspended ceiling, in an attic or basement, or even along the outside of the building.

Using Twisted-Pair Cable

When you're using twisted-pair cable for the network, you must run a cable from the NIC in each computer to the hub. If you purchased an Ethernet kit, you probably have a hub and two lengths of cable. You plug in the cable just as you would a telephone cable.

If a cable you have is too short, you can join cables end to end with a *coupler,* which has two female RJ-45 sockets. A coupler for network cable looks just like a coupler for telephone cable, only it's bigger, as shown here:

Avoid getting cables that are too long. You'll have to coil up their extra length, and coils actually slow down network connections and make them unreliable.

Making the Grade

You can purchase several *categories,* or grades, of twisted-pair cable. The higher the category, the better the cable and the more stable the connection. The standard grade for small networks is called Category 5, or Cat 5. In fact, most stores sell only Cat 5 cable because the price difference between categories is negligible for short patch cables. Another category of cable, called Cat 5e, falls between Cat 5 and Cat 6 in price and quality. Cat 6 and Cat 7 are designed for high-speed networks that must span long distances.

Note

Cat 2 cable is used to wire alarm systems and telephone lines, and Cat 3 and Cat 4 cables are used for networks running at speeds slower than that of Ethernet networks.

You can purchase twisted-pair cable in various lengths and colors. Most local stores carry only one or two colors, such as gray and white, but additional colors are available through mail order. You can also get cables that have *molded* or *booted ends,* which have plastic or rubberized material that covers the connection between the wire and the plug. This strengthens the connections and makes them more suitable for installations where you'll be frequently removing and reinserting cables.

Making Your Own Network Cables

If you have a lot of wiring to do, you might want to consider making your own patch cables. That way, you can get cables that are just the right length and you can save some money too. Rather than purchase patch cable that already has connectors on both ends, you can purchase bulk cable, long lengths of twisted-pair cable without any connectors. Although you must usually buy lengths of 250 feet or more to get bulk cable, cable at that length is relatively inexpensive. A 250-foot roll of bulk cable can cost about the same as two 50-foot patch cables. Buying bulk cable in even longer lengths, such as 500 or 1000 feet, is even cheaper per foot.

> **Note**
>
> You can also purchase a patch cable, cut one end off to make it the proper length, and install a connector on the end yourself.

In addition to bulk cable, you'll need a supply of connectors and two special tools—a *stripper* and a *crimper*. The stripper cuts away the coating around the cable so you can place the wires that are inside in a connector in a specific order. The crimper tightens the connector onto the wires. Complete kits of connectors and tools aren't expensive, but some dexterity is required in stripping and crimping the cable and in arranging the wires in the correct order.

When you purchase bulk cable, you might have a choice between *polyvinyl chloride (PVC) plastic* or *plenum-grade*. Both terms refer to the outer jacket on network cable. PVC plastic is less expensive than plenum-grade but shouldn't be used when running cable through suspended ceilings, air ducts, or ventilation returns. These areas are called *plenums*. In the event of a fire, burning PVC emits a poisonous gas that would spread throughout the building through the ventilation system. Plenum-grade

Chapter 10: Cabling Your Network

cable is covered in a fire-resistant material that emits minimal smoke and gas when burning.

If you install Ethernet sockets for premises wiring, you can purchase cable that doesn't require a crimping tool. You'll need only a stripper to expose the wires in the cable and a faceplate to hold the socket on the wall, as shown in Figure 10-3. Some faceplates can hold two, four, or more sockets. You'll need one of these faceplates for the location where all the cables connect to the hub.

Figure 10-3
A faceplate holds sockets in the wall so cables can connect to them.

Tip

If you're running patch cable along baseboards, you can purchase surface-mounted jacks that attach directly to the baseboard. You then plug the patch cable into the jack.

Using ThinNet Coaxial Cable

When you use coaxial cable, you don't need to connect the network cables to a hub. Instead, you simply connect cables from one NIC to another to form a continuous chain. Of course, to use coaxial cable on your network, the NICs must have BNC connectors instead of, or in addition to, RJ-45 connectors.

At the end of each length of coaxial cable is a male *BNC connector* (BNC is short for bayonet-Neill-Concelman—Neill and Concelman developed the BNC connector, and bayonet refers to the way that BNC connectors fit together, which is similar to the way a bayonet fits on a rifle). The connector has a pin in the center and an outer ring that rotates. If you look into the end of the connector, you'll see that this ring has two grooves, as shown here:

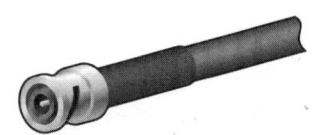

The BNC male connector attaches to a BNC female connector, which has two small stubs and no outer ring, as shown here:

You join the male and female connectors by inserting the male connector into the female connector, so the stubs fit into the grooves, and then rotating the ring on the male connector clockwise to lock the connectors together.

To connect a cable to an NIC, you need a T-connector. The *T-connecter* has a BNC male connector at the base and a female connector at the end of each arm, as shown here:

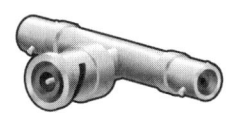

A T-connector allows you to connect the cable to the computer as well as continue it to the next computer in the chain. Attach the BNC connector on the cable to a T-connector, and then attach the T-connector to the NIC. Slide the male BNC connector on the cable onto one arm of the T-connector and then rotate the connector clockwise so it locks into place.

After you've connected the cable to the T-connector, slide the T-connector onto the connector on the NIC and rotate the T-connector clockwise until it locks into place. This leaves an unused connector on the other side of the T that'll be connected to another computer.

If you're connecting only two computers, connect the other end of the cable to the unused end of the T-connector that's attached to the second machine. If the machines are in adjacent rooms, attach one end of the cable to the computer in one room, bring the cable through the wall, and connect it to the T-connector on the other computer.

One arm of the T-connector on the last computer on both ends of the cable won't be connected to a cable, but you can't leave it empty. If you did, the signal traveling through the cable would reach the end and then bounce back in the other direction. The rebounded signal would interfere with the normal network traffic, preventing any communications between computers. This is called *signal bounce*.

To avoid signal bounce, install a terminator on each unused arm of the T-connector. A *terminator* is a cap that is grounded so the signal flows off the network rather than bouncing back along the cable.

By the time the packet reaches the terminator, either it has already been received by its designated workstation or the workstation isn't on that end of the cable, so the packet can safely be discarded through the terminator.

Just picture the network as a chain of computers with coaxial cable running from the computer at the start of the chain to the computer at the end of the chain. Add additional computers to the chain by connecting them to the unused connections at the ends of the chain or by inserting them in the middle of the chain. To insert a computer in the middle of the chain, just take the coaxial cables from the computers on both sides and connect them to the T-connector on the new computer.

If at all possible, use continuous lengths of cable between computers. Connections are the most common places for problems to occur, so eliminate as many connections as possible to make sure your network runs well. If you don't have a length of coaxial cable that's long enough, you can join two cables end to end in the same way that you'd use an extension cord. To join the cables, use the two arms of a T-connector without attaching the base of the T-connector to anything. You can also use a barrel connector, which is the top part of a T-connector with two BNC female connectors, as shown here:

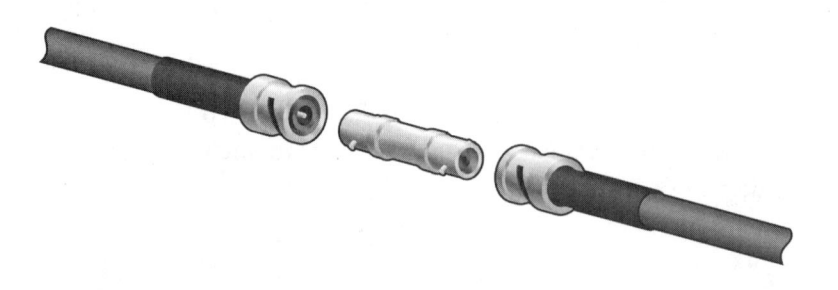

Making Your Own Coaxial Cable

You can create your own custom lengths of coaxial cable by using bulk cable and connectors. You can even attach "twist-on" connectors to the end of bulk coaxial cable without crimping. These connectors work like the twist-on connectors you can use on cable TV wire. Bulk ThinNet coaxial cable is about $80 for 500 feet, and twist-on connectors are only about $2 each.

If you want to run coaxial cable through walls, you can purchase male connectors, BNC sockets, and faceplates, which resemble cable TV outlets.

Making your own coaxial cables can save you money, but be sure you create tight connections. If ThinNet coaxial cables become disconnected, the entire network will go down. Not only is the path between computers broken, but the resulting non-terminated ends will create signal bounce on the network segments that are still connected.

Using Fiberoptic Cable

Fiberoptic cable is ideal for large networks because of its speed and bandwidth. It's difficult to run through an office, however, because fiberoptic cable is less flexible than other types of cable and must never be bent sharply around corners. A sharp bend can break the cable's inner core, preventing the light pulses from being transmitted.

You need special NICs, hubs, and other hardware for fiberoptic cable. These components cost more than their twisted-pair or coaxial counterparts and aren't as widely available. It is unlikely, for example, that you'll find fiberoptic patch cables and NICs at local computer stores.

A good use of fiberoptic cable, however, is to connect two network segments. You can use a repeater or bridge that has UTP or coaxial inputs and a fiberoptic output. That way you can use less expensive NICs in the computer workstations that connect to twisted-pair or coaxial cable. With twisted-pair to fiberoptic converters you can can extend the distance between network segments to more than 1 mile.

You can purchase fiberoptic patch cables in lengths up to 30 meters or bulk fiberoptic cable and connectors. Couplers are also available to connect two patch cables. A 1-meter fiberoptic patch cable, however, might cost around $30, compared to a twisted-pair patch cable the same length for around $10.

Because of the complexity of working with fiberoptics, consider hiring a professional installation company if you want to install fiberoptic cable in your office.

Good Cables Equal Good Networking

Now that you're familiar with the basics of cabling your network, here are some overall rules that you should consider.

Use Continuous Lengths

Twisted-pair cables running from computers to the hub or coaxial cables running from computer to computer should be continuous lengths. Although you can join two cables end to end with a coupler, the connections at the coupler can come loose, and moisture or dust can disturb the metal contacts inside the coupler. Therefore, the coupler is the first place to look if something goes wrong with the network and the problem seems to be in the cable. Don't place the coupler in a wall, in case it needs to be reached or replaced.

Prevent Bends at Sharp Angles

As you run the cable, don't bend it at sharp angles. If you have to go around a corner, for example, don't bend the cable so it folds or creases, and don't pull the cable very tight. The wires inside cables are strong and flexible, but they can break if you bend a cable back and forth during installation or sharply fold it in the corner of a room. Although these wires might not break immediately, they might deteriorate over time.

Keep a Tidy Appearance

To preserve the appearance of your rooms, try to run cable in a wall or above the ceiling whenever possible. Try to avoid running it on the outside of a wall, along the baseboard. Many businesses have ceilings that are dropped just so network and other cables can easily be run from room to room, but you might not have that luxury. If you must run cable along a baseboard or up a wall, secure it to the surface. Rather than nail or staple directly into the cable, use U-shaped nails, which you can purchase at a hardware store or home center. Never put a cable where it can be tripped over or kicked, and never put it under the carpet where it can be stepped on. Although you might find it tempting to run the cable under an area rug rather than around the perimeter of a room, continuously walking over it, rolling over it with a chair, or vacuuming over it can wear the cable down and eventually ruin it. And no matter how thick your carpet is, you'll soon see the telltale sign of a cable bulging through.

Don't Force Cables

If you have to drill a hole in a wall to run the cable through, make the hole larger than the connector at the end of the cable. Never force a cable through a smaller hole because you could damage the connector. In fact, always be particularly careful with connectors at the end of the cable. The plug at the end of a twisted-pair cable has small metal contacts and a plastic tab that helps hold the plug in place. Don't step on the end or break off that tab. Also, take care to avoid cutting or bending the small wire at the end of a coaxial cable.

Use a Fish

The worst part of running wire is fishing it through walls: getting it to go from one location to another when you can't see where it's going. Sometimes fishing cables is easy, such as when you have to run them between two adjacent rooms, but sometimes fishing is so frustrating that you'll want to give up and send all your mail by carrier pigeon.

If you have trouble feeding the cable through a wall, you can open a metal coat hanger and push one end through. Alternately, you can purchase a *fish* at a hardware store. A fish contains a coil of metal that you can unwind as needed. Once you get the coat hanger or fish through the wall, tie the end of the cable to the end of the hanger or fish, and then pull the cable through the other end.

Chapter 10: Cabling Your Network

Expanding Your Network

As your needs and your business grow, you might want to add more computers to the network. As you've seen, adding computers to a network that uses ThinNet coaxial cable is easy. You just remove the terminator at one end of the chain and connect the cable from the additional computer.

If you use twisted-pair cable, you must have enough ports on the hub for all the computers that you want to connect or have additional hubs. As your network grows, you might upgrade from a passive hub to a stackable hub or a switch to increase performance and then upgrade to bridges to divide larger networks into two or more individual segments. You might need a remote access router if you're providing remote access to your office network or a Web router to share your Internet connection with multiple users.

In this chapter, you learned how to connect computers using twisted-pair wire, with and without a hub, and how to use coaxial cable. The next chapter covers hardware issues involved with using thin servers.

Chapter 11

Hardware for Thin Servers

In Chapter 5, you learned how thin servers could add efficiency and functionality to peer-to-peer and client/server networks. This chapter looks at some of the hardware options for thin servers and how to connect them to your network.

Choosing a Thin Server

You can purchase one thin server that offers file, modem, and printer sharing, or you can get individual pieces of hardware for each function. Both solutions have their advantages.

Multipurpose thin servers might cost less than the combined cost of the individual components. The server, and thus all of its shared resources, can be controlled and configured from one location using a single interface. You need to assign only one network address to the device, and you need only one port on your network hub. However, if the thin server's disk crashes or you need to take the unit offline for repair, file, printer, and modem sharing are no longer available.

Purchasing separate thin servers might cost more than a multipurpose server, but each device is a separate piece of hardware. You can take the modem server or print server offline, for example, and still provide access to network storage. However, each thin server must be connected to the network, configured, and controlled separately. Each thin server requires its own network address and port on the hub. In addition, you'll need to learn how the interface for each thin server works.

Look for a thin server that meets industry standards. You should be able to set up plug-and-play thin servers, even multipurpose ones, in five to ten minutes. They should require no special cables or complicated configuration and cause minimal disruption to the network. Many thin servers need little or no special setup on each client computer. When connecting a network-attached storage (NAS) server, for example, look for one that plugs into the network and requires only simple configuration to make it available to every network user. You want to avoid having to reconfigure individual workstations to access the server.

Some types of thin servers are easier to install than others. NAS servers, such as hard disk and CD drives, are usually the easiest. Once you assign a network address to an NAS server, usually through a program on one of the workstations, the NAS server is accessible from all of the workstations.

Print and modem servers that are part of a multipurpose thin server are also easy to install. The workstations treat the shared modem or printer as if it were connected to another workstation. Sharing a printer on the multipurpose device, for example, is as easy as sharing a printer on a workstation. Setting up individual print and modem servers, however, isn't always that easy, although it varies with the model of server used. Dealing with network protocols and addresses and loading special software or drivers into the workstations can take some time.

Connecting Thin Servers

Connecting a thin server to a network is comparable to connecting a workstation to the network. The thin server will have a connector for twisted-pair or coaxial cable or both. If you're using twisted-pair wiring, simply plug one end of a cable into the thin server and the other end into the hub. With coaxial cable, you plug in the device as you would a workstation and attach a terminator if the server is at the end of the cable.

In some cases, the thin server might include a hub. You can connect your workstations to the thin server's hub or connect the thin server to another hub to connect a greater number of workstations to the network.

Depending on your network, however, you might have to configure the thin server to communicate using your network's protocol. For example, most thin servers use the TCP/IP protocol. As a result, you have to set the thin server for a specific *IP address*, a 4-byte number that uniquely identifies a computer on the network, or allow it to get its IP address from the network. You should check the documentation before purchasing the device to make sure it's compatible with your network setup. You'll learn about IP addresses and network configuration in Chapter 13.

Note

Some thin servers are able to assign IP addresses to each computer connected to the network. See "Using Server-Assigned IP Addresses" on page 208.

The Microsoft Windows–Based Server Appliance

One of the most powerful thin servers you can add to a peer-to-peer network is a Microsoft Windows–based server appliance. Available from a variety of manufacturers, the appliance offers a network hub, file server, modem server, and print server in one easy-to-use package.

The file server lets network users access public or private folders stored on the server. Every network user can access public folders. Only the user who creates a private folder can access it. By using both public and private folders, you offer network users easy access to company-wide files along with personal security for their own documents.

The modem server allows more than one user to access the Internet through a single Internet account and connection using a 56K modem or broadband connections such as DSL and cable modems. If the appliance has a built-in 56K analog modem, for example, multiple users can share the modem to browse the Web and send and receive e-mail at the same time.

The print server allows users to access a printer connected to the server's printer port. The embedded operating system, Microsoft Windows for Express Networks, has drivers for most printers. If your printer isn't in its driver database, you can load the drivers from the workstation you use to set up and maintain the server.

Part 2: Installing Hardware, Cards, and Cables

The appliance doesn't have a keyboard, mouse, or monitor. Instead, it has a small LCD panel and a series of lights indicating the status of the machine.

Icons on the LCD panel indicate such items as

- The disk drive is available, busy, or has an error that requires attention.
- The server is connected to the network, information is being transmitted across the network, or the server can't connect.
- The server's modem is connected to the Internet, transmitting information, or has an error.

The lights indicate the status of the *CMOS* (the memory where the server's startup parameters are stored), RAM, and hard disk drive. The lights also show whether the computer started or booted successfully and whether operating system errors occurred. By watching the LCD panel and status lights, you can determine whether any problems are affecting the server's performance.

If you haven't already created a network, simply plug the Ethernet cables from your workstations into the built-in hub. You can also attach the appliance to another hub to add additional capabilities. A switch or button near the built-in hub determines whether one port on the appliance functions as a standard network port or as an uplink port for connecting to an external hub.

The Windows-based server appliance comes in a variety of configurations, but the most common includes a primary hard disk drive and a secondary hard disk drive that serves as a mirror drive. Everything recorded on the primary disk is also copied to the mirror drive.

When the appliance boots, it checks to make sure that the primary and secondary drives contain the same information. If your primary drive fails and you have to replace it, for example, your data can be restored from the mirror drive so nothing is lost.

You control and manage the appliance through a Web-based interface from one of the workstations connected to the appliance. From the workstation, for example, you set up the modem to connect to the Internet, install printers, and even see reports about the service's status, such as its operating temperature and voltage.

The person who initially sets up the appliance is the administrator. The administrator can choose to let every network user access the server's resources or to create permissions for using the Internet and printers and accessing files. With security features enabled, for instance, the administrator can create a user account for each workstation and a private folder for the user's files. The user account includes a user name and password. A person's name and password must match those in the user account for the person to access the server.

> **Note**
>
> You'll learn more about setting up Windows-based server appliances in Chapter 15.

Other types of thin servers are available in addition to the Windows-based server appliance. The Boffin Limited KwikSTOR network device (*www.boffin.com*), for instance, includes a file and print server, but no modem. A series of LEDs on the front panel indicate the device's status, when the internal disk is being accessed or when an error condition occurs. The LEDs—whether they're on, off, or blinking—indicate items such as

- The hard disk is full.
- The server is shutting down.
- The server is unable to connect to the network.
- A printer error has occurred.

When you as the administrator set up the device, you assign it an IP address and workgroup name. The workstations on your network will be able to access its drive and printer just as if it were another workstation. You don't need to install any special software on the workstations or change their configuration. For instance, the entire configuration for the KwikSTOR network device is handled in one menu.

Network-Attached Storage

An alternative to a Windows-based server appliance is a network-attached storage (NAS) server. These devices offer hard disk space but not printer or modem sharing. Use an NAS server when you want to create a data-centric network model.

Part 2: Installing Hardware, Cards, and Cables

Most traditional networks are server-centric. As shown in Figure 11-1, a server-centric network routes all requests for data through the server, so all workstations connected to the server compete for server time and resources.

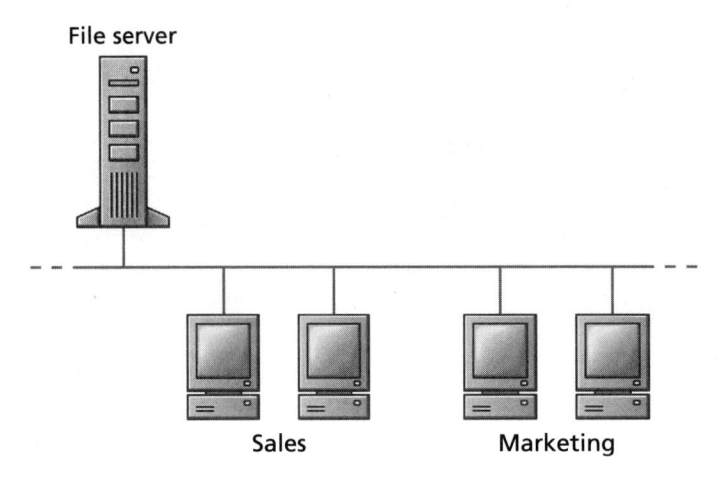

Figure 11-1

All requests for data from client workstations are routed through the server in a server-centric network.

In a data-centric network model, shown in Figure 11-2, stand-alone NAS servers provide data access to workstations, relieving the server of the burden. In a peer-to-peer network, the NAS servers offer central storage and access without the overhead of a server. You can even use several NAS servers organized around departments or workgroups.

Many NAS solutions are on the market. The Netgear Network Disk Drive (*www.netgearinc.com*), for example, comes in 8-gigabyte and 20-gigabyte models. About the size of the average hardbound book, the device fits easily on a desktop or even under a network hub or external modem. It's basically an external hard disk drive that connects to your network hub using a variety of protocols, including TCP/IP, and at either 10Base-T or 100Base-T speeds.

The NetFORCE line from Procom Technology (*www.procom.com*), on the other hand, offers a number of NAS servers in models from 20 to 900 gigabytes. An LCD panel on a NetFORCE NAS server indicates system status, and buttons on the front panel set the device's network address without the need for software. The drives are mounted from the front for

Chapter 11: Hardware for Thin Servers

easy removal and replacement. An optional connector at the rear of the device connects to a high-speed tape backup, and a backup utility program can save data at a rate of 14 gigabytes per hour. Other built-in software sends an e-mail notification of a device failure. Procom Technology also offers a series of DataFORCE CD/DVD servers.

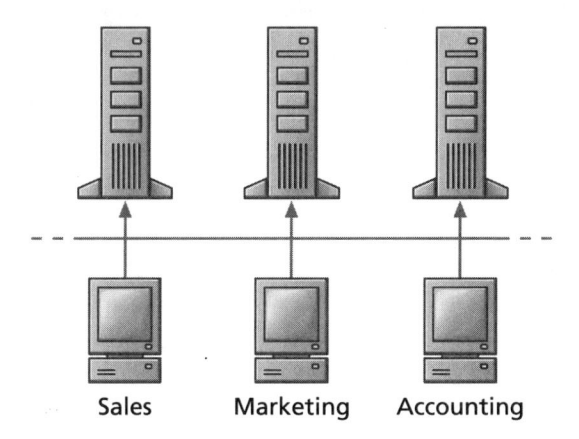

Figure 11-2
In a data-centric network, NAS servers handle requests for data from client workstations.

Axonix (*www.axonix.com*) markets the ProLinQ series of NAS servers. The series includes

- SuperCD—an NAS server with a single CD drive and multiple hard disk drives on which you can store CD data
- CD Sharer—an NAS server with multiple CD drives
- Jazsharer—an NAS server with one to seven Jaz drives
- HD Sharer—an NAS server with multiple hard disk drives
- Super Sharer—a customized NAS server with multiple CD, hard disk, and Jaz drives

Creative Design Solutions (*www.creativedesign.com*) manufactures the Plug & Stor brand of NAS servers. The NAS servers include an extra port to which external hard disk, CD, Zip, or Jaz drives can be connected to expand the storage capability. Built-in software provides e-mail failure

Part 2: Installing Hardware, Cards, and Cables

notifications and system monitoring; a front panel LCD and buttons provide for system control and status.

Hewlett-Packard offers NAS CD servers from the single-disk SureStore 32X to a tower with room for seven or more CD drives. Other manufacturers include Axis Communications (*www.axis.com*), REALM Information Technologies (*www.realminfo.com*), Quantum (*www.quantum.com*), and dozens of other companies.

NAS servers are just one type of thin server. Thin servers also include stand-alone print and modem servers, remote access and Internet servers, and time servers. Each type of device performs a single server function to the network workgroup. You'll learn about print and modem servers in later chapters.

In the next chapter, you'll learn about hardware you need to set up a client/server network.

Chapter 12

Hardware for Client/Server Networks

The hardware required by a client/server network depends largely on the number of computers you want to network, how you want to administer the network, and the nature of the tasks the network will perform.

If you're using a client/server network for basic file, printer, and modem sharing among a few workstations, your hardware will be similar to that used in a peer-to-peer network. Each computer, including the server, can be connected to a network hub, but all computers will share the resources of the server.

The configuration of a basic client/server network is not unlike a network that uses a multipurpose thin server for file, printer, and modem sharing. One of the primary differences between a client/server network and a peer-to-peer network using thin servers is that the server on a client/server network authenticates users as they connect to the network to ensure they have permission to use the shared resources.

A basic client/server network would easily serve a network of 25 workstations that are connected to a server using hubs or switches, as explained in Chapter 10. If your network has a larger number of workstations or performs mission-critical work, the hardware requirements and complexity of organizing the network increases. I'll take a look at some of these issues in this chapter.

Using Domain Controllers

Before looking at specific hardware issues, you should understand a little about the way larger client/server networks operate in Microsoft Windows NT and Microsoft Windows 2000.

Among other functions, a server authorizes workstations to connect to the network and use network resources. The server and all of the workstations that are authorized by it are called a *domain,* and the server is called the *domain controller.* If you have a very large network, you may group the workstations into more than one domain and have a domain controller for each group of workstations.

Windows NT and Windows 2000 handle the task of controlling the domain differently, as you will soon learn. But understanding the process of controlling a domain is important in understanding the hardware requirements of a client/server network.

Domain Controllers in Windows NT

Each server on a Windows NT network can access a database of authenticated users, called the *Security Accounts Manager (SAM)* database, to verify that users have permission to access network resources when they log on. The server that stores the database is called the *Primary Domain Controller (PDC).* If the SAM database becomes corrupted by some hardware or software glitch or the hard disk drive on the PDC crashes, no one will be able to log on to the network. The network administrator has to recreate the SAM database either by using a backup file or by reentering user account information.

As a safeguard, you can maintain one or more other servers on the network that store a copy of the database in case the PDC fails. A server that has a copy of the database is called a *Backup Domain Controller (BDC).* The BDC contains a read-only replica of the PDC database. The BDC is synchronized with the PDC, so any changes you make to the SAM on the PDC are recorded on the BDC as well. If the PDC crashes, the BDC can be promoted to the PDC with little interruption of service.

Chapter 12: Hardware for Client/Server Networks

> **Note**
> With a peer-to-peer network or workgroup running Windows NT or Windows 2000, authentication is performed when a workstation tries to access files on another workstation.

Purchasing and maintaining a BDC, however, can be costly. Instead, you can make a backup copy of the SAM on a tape, on some other removable media, or even on a user's workstation.

Restoring the SAM database from a tape or other device, however, takes longer and results in greater disruption to the network than promoting a BDC to a PDC. You have to weigh the downtime that users would experience while you're restoring the database against the cost of a BDC. If you have less than 100 users, you might find it economically feasible to recover your SAM from a backup tape or disk if the PDC fails. If you have more than 100 users, a BDC is recommended.

If you maintain a BDC, it should be connected to the PDC so information doesn't have to travel through many links, such as from hub to hub. The BDC should have the same general specifications as the PDC in terms of memory and hard disk space, since it might have to perform as your server until the PDC is restored.

Multiple Domains

Maintaining the SAM database and authenticating users takes up quite a bit of the server's resources. While a PDC can accommodate 25,000 or more users, for best performance you should limit a PDC to about 2000 users.

When you have more than 2000 users, you can divide them into more than one domain and have a server for each domain. If you want the users of one domain to access the resources of the other, you create a trust relationship between the domains. A *trust relationship* exposes the resources in one domain to user accounts in another. Trust relationships between two PDCs can be one-way or two-way.

In a *one-way trust,* every authenticated user of the Main Office domain can access the resources of the Field Office. The Field Office domain is called the *trusting domain,* while the Main Office domain is called the *trusted domain.* This means that the Field Office domain trusts users who have been authenticated by the Main Office domain. However, since the relationship is one-way, authenticated users in the Field Office domain don't have access to the Main Office domain.

This one-way relationship might be used, for example, when you want administrative personnel to access the records in the field office for invoicing or other purposes, but you don't want field office personnel to access records or other resources in the main office.

In a two-way trust relationship, the authenticated users of either domain can access the resources of the other. Both domains are *trusted* and *trusting*. Use this relationship if you're dividing your network into multiple domains to share the PDC function across a great number of users or to span a wide geographic area. Keep the PDC near the users that it's serving so the network performs more efficiently and is easier to administer. Multiple servers help balance the workload, spreading out the burden of client authentication and resource sharing across the network.

Providing a two-way relationship doesn't mean that you give up security or privacy for folders or other resources. The relationship means only that an authenticated user on one domain is seen as an authenticated user on the other. You can still assign permissions to folders, printers, modems, and other resources to restrict access as needed.

Tip

In Windows NT, you create a trust relationship using a utility called User Manager For Domains.

Domain Controllers in Windows 2000

Microsoft Windows 2000 has a different method of authenticating users on a network than Windows NT does. Rather than using a PDC and a subordinate BDC, a Windows 2000 network uses the Active Directory to maintain peer domain controllers, each of which has a copy of the user database. Using a feature called *master replication*, Windows 2000 copies the Active Directory domain information to all domain controllers on the network whenever the user database is updated. Any domain controller can modify the user database since the information is updated in all domains. Individual domain information is maintained within the Active Directory so that trust relationships can be maintained.

Domain Administration

The organization of your network should be based on administrative priorities as well as the technical aspects of server performance. Rather than organize domains by geography, for example, you can assign domains by function.

As an example, suppose your organization is divided into groups such as research, marketing, and accounting. Assuming that all of the members of a group use the same basic applications and must access the same data and resources, you can create a separate domain and PDC for each group.

Each domain will be assigned its own administrator who controls user accounts and resources for that domain. The administrators will know the members of their groups and will be able to communicate with them more effectively than would a single administrator for the entire network. Each administrator will be able to control trust relationships with his or her domain, deciding which other domains will be trusted.

Selecting Client/Server Hardware

Selecting the proper hardware for your server is critical because of the load the network places on a server. Before making any hardware decisions, check the Hardware Compatibility List (HCL) provided by Microsoft. The HCL shows specific models of computers and peripherals that have been tested for use with Microsoft Windows 98, Windows NT, and Windows 2000. You can find the list on the Windows NT, Windows 2000, or Microsoft BackOffice Small Business Server (SBS) CD or at the HCL Web site: *www.microsoft.com/hcl*.

On the HCL Web site, you can check hardware either by type or category, such as an entire desktop system or a specific component (such as a sound or video card), or by manufacturer. See Figure 12-1.

If you already have a desktop computer that you're considering for use as your server, for instance, you can type the manufacturer's name in the Search For The Following box on the HCL Web site and then click Go. In the list that appears, look for the model number of your desktop computer.

Part 2: Installing Hardware, Cards, and Cables

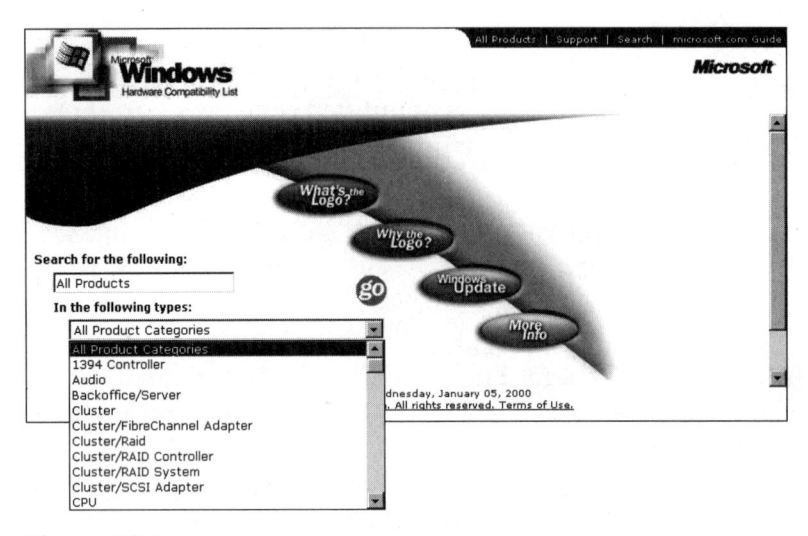

Figure 12-1
You can check the HCL Web site to see if your hardware is compatible with Windows.

If you're shopping for a new computer, choose System/Desktop Uniprocessor from the In The Following Types list on the HCL Web site and click Go for a comprehensive list of tested models that are compatible with Windows, shown in Figure 12-2.

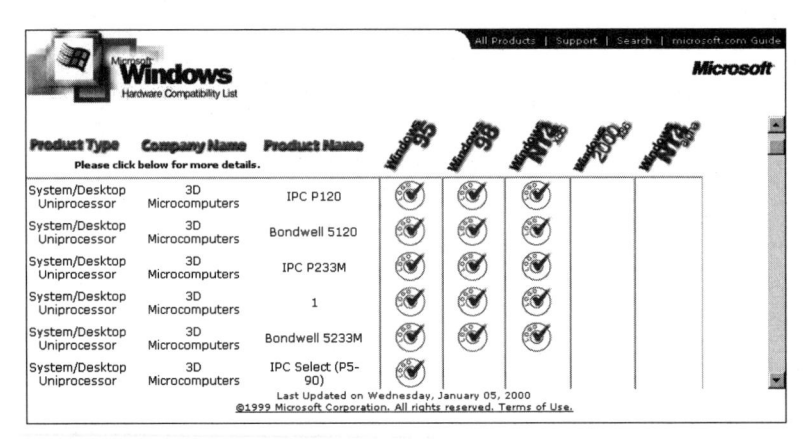

Figure 12-2
The HCL Web site can provide you with a list of new computer models that are compatible with Windows.

Just because your hardware might not be on the list doesn't mean you can't use it on your server. Many unlisted components work fine with

Chapter 12: Hardware for Client/Server Networks

Windows NT and Windows 2000. Your computer might contain unlisted components that are comparable to similar components that have been tested. In addition, the manufacturers of unlisted components might not have submitted their hardware to Microsoft for evaluation of compatibility with Windows.

Generally, a computer should have at least a 200-MHz Pentium or compatible processor, 32 MB of RAM, 2 GB of available hard disk space, and a CD-ROM drive to install and run Windows NT or Windows 2000. If you want to add Microsoft Exchange Server to your network or install SBS, then you'll need at least 64 MB of RAM and 4 GB of hard disk space. You'll also need a network interface card (NIC), video display adaptor, and monitor that are supported by Windows NT or Windows 2000.

Before installing Windows NT, Windows 2000, or SBS, you should make sure you have the appropriate drivers for your peripherals, such as modems or tape drives. Some peripherals are de facto standards, so the appropriate drivers are provided on the Windows NT, Windows 2000, or SBS CD. However, many peripherals are designed primarily for Windows 95/98 and aren't automatically recognized by Windows NT, Windows 2000, or SBS. The disk that came with the peripheral should contain the drivers needed, and the printed or online documentation for the peripheral should explain how to install the drivers.

If the appropriate drivers aren't on the CD, check the manufacturer's Web site. Many hardware manufacturers allow you to download the most recent drivers from their Web sites.

Note

See Chapter 10 for a discussion of hubs, switches, and other hardware needed for your network.

In addition to computers, you'll need modems and printers suitable for a client/server environment. If you're sharing a modem across a network, get a modem with the highest speed and bandwidth available. A standard 56K analog modem might be suitable for one or two simultaneous users but no more. Consider an ISDN, DSL, or cable modem for faster Internet connections and communications.

The same consideration should be given to printers. You'll need a printer capable of handling the projected workload, in terms of speed and duty cycle. The *speed* is the time a printer takes to print an average page.

The slower the printer, the longer each document takes to be printed, and the greater the waiting time for print jobs to be done. *Duty cycle* refers to the average number of pages that can be printed each month without causing a problem with the printer. In selecting a network printer, estimate the number of pages that will be printed per day and month, and look for a printer with the appropriate speed and duty cycle.

Servers and Thin Servers

Chapter 11 looked at using thin servers to supplement a peer-to-peer network. You can also use thin servers with a client/server network to balance the workload placed on the network.

Your network can be used for these types of functions:

- User authentication
- Application sharing
- File storage
- E-mail
- Printer sharing
- Modem sharing
- Fax sharing
- Intranet

While a single domain server can be used for all of these functions, fielding requests for service from a number of workstations can severely degrade performance of the server. One server might be appropriate if you have just a few workstations. But on larger networks, one server won't be able to handle all of these tasks efficiently.

One alternative is to use multiple servers on the network. One or more servers perform user authentication, while other servers handle other network tasks, such as modem and printer sharing. The servers share resources with other computers, but no one server handles every network task.

Another alternative is to use thin servers to perform specific network tasks in a data-centric or function-centric organization, as shown in Figure 12-3. In this example, file sharing, modem sharing, and printer sharing are performed by thin servers. You can keep the thin servers close to users to make it convenient for them to change CDs in a CD server or retrieve documents from a workgroup printer.

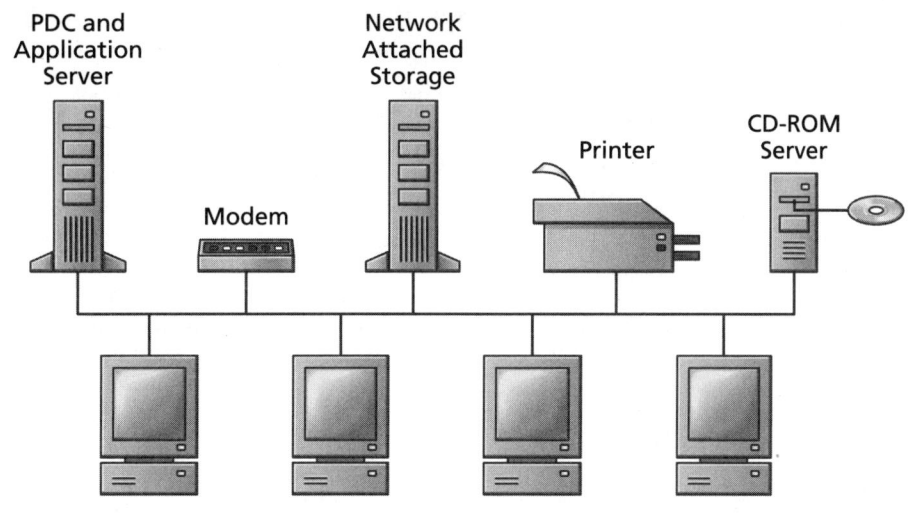

Figure 12-3

Using thin servers on a client/server network can reduce the burden on the server and improve network performance.

Setting Up Client/Server Hardware

Setting up a client/server network with just a few workstations is as easy as setting up a peer-to-peer network. Put the hub in a convenient location, and run twisted-pair cable from the hub to the server and to each workstation.

As your network grows, however, running cable and setting up hardware becomes more complex. Just imagine the number of cables in your office if you have 25 or 50 workstations or multiple servers.

Special hardware is available for larger networks to tame the jungle of cables and to make checking or changing connections easier.

The Computer Room

You might want to start by isolating servers in a separate computer room. The room should have environmental and security controls to ensure safe and continued operation of the servers. Access to the room would be limited to system administrators and perhaps maintenance personnel who would need to adjust air-conditioning and heating controls.

The computer room also serves as the central location where the various cables emerge; the room can be built with a drop ceiling or even on a raised floor to accommodate the cables. The room should also have the following characteristics:

- A location that's near the network administrator or other support staff and that can be easily observed
- A lock or other method to secure the room
- A climate-controlled environment to protect the servers, which is accomplished most easily when the room is located within an interior of the building so it has no exterior windows or doors
- Adequate ventilation and lighting
- A separate electrical circuit to avoid power brownouts and surges
- An uninterruptible power supply (UPS) that can provide power to all of the equipment long enough for a proper shutdown in the event of a power failure

Racks, Panels, and Blocks

If you picture the computer room as a place where hundreds of cables converge, then you might realize how difficult the room can be to organize. Just look at the unruly mess made by the cables on the back of a typical computer desk: cables for a computer, a monitor, a mouse, a printer, and speakers. Now imagine the number of cables needed for servers, hubs, routers, and other hardware on the network and all the cable connections these pieces of equipment have to workstations, modems, printers, and other devices spread throughout your company.

Fortunately, special equipment designed to handle the cables of a busy computer room is available.

Racks and Cabinets

You'd need a rather large room if you had to spread out your network equipment horizontally on tables or desks. To reduce the size of the computer room, you can place your hardware vertically on racks or in cabinets.

A *rack* is a freestanding, floor-mounted frame in which you can slide a number of computers, hubs, routers, modes, power supplies, and other hardware, as shown in Figure 12-4. Most racks also have space for a

Chapter 12: Hardware for Client/Server Networks

monitor, keyboard, and mouse, which the system administrator uses to control the server. A *cabinet* is a rack that's enclosed on three or four sides with movable doors or panels for easy access.

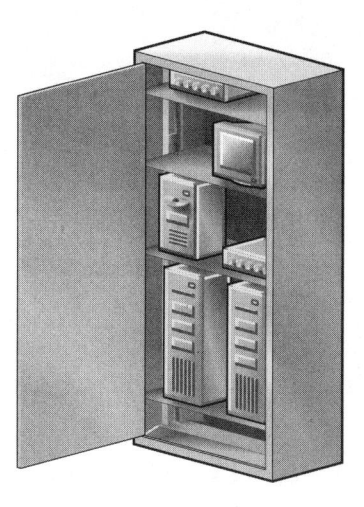

Figure 12-4
Store hardware vertically on computer racks or cabinets.

Some racks are very plain; they're little more than metal frames with shelves on which to place equipment. Other racks resemble desks but with several levels of shelves to accommodate multiple computers, monitors, keyboards, and other equipment.

One rack or cabinet might accommodate a PDC, BDC, monitor, keyboard, network hub or switch, routers, and modems. An entire wall of racks would use little floor space but could accommodate a rather large network.

Tip

If you have several servers in the computer room, you can control them all with one monitor, mouse, and keyboard by using switch boxes.

Patch Panels

When you have multiple cables running to one location, you might have difficulty keeping them orderly. A patch panel can help. A *patch panel* contains a number of RJ-45 Ethernet ports, as shown on the following page.

Part 2: Installing Hardware, Cards, and Cables

You might have a small patch panel to which the cables from all of the workstations in the office connect. From the patch panel, cables travel through the wall, floor, or ceiling to the computer room. The computer room has a larger patch panel, to which all of the cables from workstations, servers, and thin servers connect.

Each port on the patch panel is labeled to help you keep track of which cable belongs to which piece of equipment. The patch panel makes it easy to connect and disconnect cables from network equipment and to troubleshoot network problems. If you're having problems logging on to a network, for example, the system administrator should be able to confirm quickly whether the cable from your computer is connected properly to the network in the computer room.

Connect Blocks

A *connect block* is similar to a patch panel. Instead of having RJ-45 Ethernet ports, however, the block has a series of connectors to which bare wire is attached.

The cables going to the block don't have RJ-45 connectors on the end. Instead, the ends of the wires are *stripped*—the insulation material on the wire is removed so that the metal conductor is exposed. The wires are twisted and screwed around connectors on the block. This type of connection provides a stronger and more permanent connection than a plug-in RJ-45 connector, and it allows technicians to test the continuity between cables.

Using a connect block is more difficult and time-consuming than using a patch block, however, because all of the cable ends must be exposed and connected individually. If a single Ethernet cable has eight wires, hooking up 20 workstations to a connect block means stripping and attaching

160 separate wires. In addition, the eight color-coded wires within each cable must be attached to the correct connector in the block. So connect blocks are recommended only when a semi-permanent connection is needed and the installer knows to which connector a color-coded wire should be attached. Semi-permanent connections, which are often more dependable than using patch cables and panels, are used in instances where the arrangement of computers and cabling isn't likely to be changed.

Using Thin Clients

In the early days of computers, organizations used large, central computers called *mainframes,* which typically processed and stored all the data used by the organization. Individual users at an organization connected to the mainframe using terminals rather than individual PCs. A *terminal* is basically a keyboard and monitor that's used to access a central computer. A terminal has no ability to process or store data; all of the programs and data needed by the organization are maintained on the central computer or mainframe. This method of computing is known as a *central processing system*.

Mainframes, however, were expensive. As PCs became cheaper and more popular, organizations started using them to process and store business information instead of using terminals connected to a mainframe, and a distributed processing system was created. In a *distributed processing system,* the burden of running programs and processing and storing information is distributed among several computers. Some disadvantages of such a system are that PCs cost more than terminals and are more difficult to maintain because they are more complex. Distributed processing also makes controlling and coordinating the various uses of company information more difficult because the information is processed and stored on individual PCs rather than in one central location.

However, now that PCs have become more powerful and can function as servers or central computers, some organizations are beginning to implement central processing systems using PC servers and thin clients. See Figure 10-9. A *thin client* is a device that is used to connect to a server and that has little or no ability to process or store data. In an office, thin clients can be terminals or they can be PCs with a minimum amount of memory and storage. Often called *network PCs*, thin clients don't even need a hard disk drive because the operating system needed for them to start and to connect to the network is embedded in their electronics. All of the programs to be used by the thin client are stored in the server. They don't need a CD drive, a modem, or even a printer port if those resources are being provided by the server or by a thin server.

You can use thin clients with a client/server network to provide a single point of control. When a program update is received, for example, it needs to be installed only on the server. Because no programs are maintained on the thin clients, you are assured that users are all using the same version of each program, so all document formats are compatible.

One example of a thin client system is used by bank tellers. When you make a bank deposit, the teller enters your account number and deposit amount into a terminal at the branch. The actual record of your account, however, is maintained in the bank's central computer system. The teller doesn't need a hard disk drive or any other hardware at the branch; she simply needs a way to input the information and see a report of your account status.

Universal product code (UPC) scanners are also thin clients. When workers in a warehouse that uses UPC scanners take inventory, for instance, unit counts are maintained temporarily in each scanner's memory. The totals are later transferred to a computer for processing.

Windows-Based Terminals

Windows-based terminals (WBTs) are a special type of thin client. Terminals of old were simply text-based—they could display only text, not graphics. Windows-based terminals, on the other hand, support the graphic interface of the Windows environment. The terminal has the same look and feel as a PC running Windows.

Windows NT Server 4.0, Terminal Server Edition, and Windows 2000 Server Terminal Services support the use of WBTs. The server runs Windows-based applications, sending just the application's display across the network to terminal screens. It can run multiple instances of an application so multiple terminals can access the application simultaneously. As with other thin-client systems, data is stored on the server rather than on the terminals.

Chapter 12: Hardware for Client/Server Networks

WBTs run Windows-based Terminal Professional, based on Windows NT Embedded 4.0, or Windows-based Terminal Standard, based on Microsoft Windows CE, and are manufactured by a variety of companies. You can find more information on WBTs at *www.microsoft.com/ntserver/ terminalserver/vendors/default.asp*.

In Part 3, "Setting Up Computers on a Network," I show you how to install and configure workstations and thin servers on the network. In the next chapter, I'll cover the software you'll need for a client/server network.

Part 3

Setting Up Computers on a Network

13 Installing Software on Network Workstations

14 Configuring Personal Profiles

15 Setting Up a Windows-Based Server Appliance

16 Setting Up Clients on Microsoft BackOffice Small Business Server

Chapter 13

Installing Software on Network Workstations

Now that you've installed the network hardware, you're ready to deal with the software. Your network interface card (NIC) won't do you any good unless you configure Microsoft Windows to use it and to communicate with other computers on the network. In this chapter, you'll learn how to install the software that controls your NIC and allows your computer to communicate with the rest of the network.

Before you do anything else, however, check the manual that came with your hardware. Some types of network hardware require a number of steps to set up. Others come with a completely automatic setup program. Networking kits from Microsoft, for example, install all the necessary software and configure Microsoft Windows. Once you've run the setup program, you're ready to connect to your network without any further configuration.

Part 3: Setting Up Computers on a Network

> **Note**
>
> If you're using a Windows-based server appliance as your server, the software that came with it will set up and configure your network for you.

While not every networking kit is as automatic as Microsoft's, many have their own special ways of installing drivers and configuring Windows. So it pays to look at the hardware manual first and run any installation program the manufacturer provides.

Installing Network Drivers

Network drivers for your NIC are the first software you have to install. If a disk or CD came with your hardware, it probably contains the network drivers for the hardware.

Drivers are installed in one of three basic ways, depending on the type of hardware.

- The Good: Windows installs drivers automatically for plug-and-play devices.
- The Bad: You must install drivers manually using Windows or special software that comes with the hardware.
- The Ugly: You must install drivers for non–plug-and-play NICs and configure the NICs manually to avoid hardware conflicts.

Loading Drivers Automatically

If you install a plug-and-play NIC, Windows will sense that the card is installed and load the drivers for it. The drivers for some NICs are already on your hard disk. Drivers for other NICs are on the Windows CD. (Have the CD handy, just in case Windows needs to copy the drivers from the disc.) In other cases, the drivers will be on the disk that came with the NIC.

To install the drivers for your NIC on a Windows system, follow these steps:

> **Note**
>
> Different wizard dialog boxes might appear depending on your version of Windows, but the general process is the same as that described here.

Chapter 13: Installing Software on Network Workstations

1. Turn on your computer and watch the screen.

    Windows, sensing that a new card has been installed, briefly displays the New Hardware Found message on the screen and then starts the Add New Hardware Wizard. This wizard takes you step-by-step through the process of installing the drivers.

    The first dialog box of the Add New Hardware Wizard identifies the new hardware that has been detected.

Note

If Windows doesn't detect your NIC, go to Control Panel and double-click Add New Hardware (for Microsoft Windows NT) or Add/Remove Hardware (for Microsoft Windows 2000). Follow the directions that appear until the wizard identifies your NIC.

2. Click Next.
3. The next dialog box asks whether you want Windows to search for new devices or whether you want to select the device from a list. Choose the first option, Yes (Recommended), and then click Next.
4. Select the check boxes next to one or more of the options to look for the drivers: Floppy Drive, CD-ROM, Microsoft Windows Update, and Specific Location.

    Select Floppy Disk if your NIC came with a disk. Insert the disk in the floppy disk drive. If you chose CD-ROM, insert the Windows CD or other CD in your CD drive. If you selected Microsoft Windows Update, you'll need to have an active Internet connection because this option will open the Windows Update Web site. If you selected Specific Location, you'll need to type the path to the drivers, such as D:\WIN98.

5. Click Next to have the wizard look for the appropriate drivers.

    The next wizard dialog box shows where the drivers are located.

6. Click Next, and then click Finish.

After the drivers are installed, the wizard will ask whether you want to restart your computer. Windows won't recognize the drivers properly until you restart, so click Yes.

Part 3: Setting Up Computers on a Network

Installing Drivers Manually

If the Add New Hardware Wizard doesn't detect your NIC, you can load the drivers manually.

Microsoft Windows 95/98

To install NIC drivers manually in Windows 95 or Windows 98, follow these steps:

1. Double-click My Computer on the Windows desktop.
2. In the My Computer window, double-click the Control Panel icon.
3. In the Control Panel window, double-click the Network icon.
4. Click Add to see the Select Network Component Type dialog box, shown here:

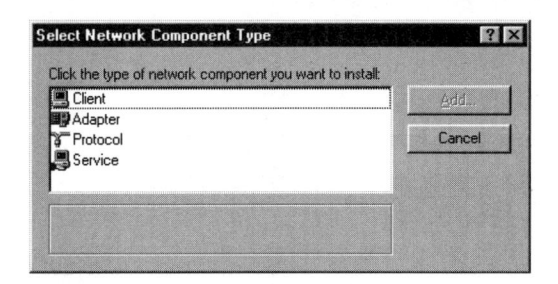

5. Click Adapter in the list, and then click Add to open the Select Network Adapters dialog box shown in Figure 13-1.
   On the left side of the dialog box is a list of manufacturers whose drivers are provided with Windows.
6. From the list of manufacturers, select your NIC manufacturer.
   On the right side of the dialog box is a list of network adapters made by the selected manufacturer.

Note

If your manufacturer or NIC isn't listed, but the NIC came with a disk of drivers, click Have Disk in the Select Network Adapters dialog box, and navigate to the disk that contains the drivers.

7. From the Network Adapters list, select the model of your NIC.

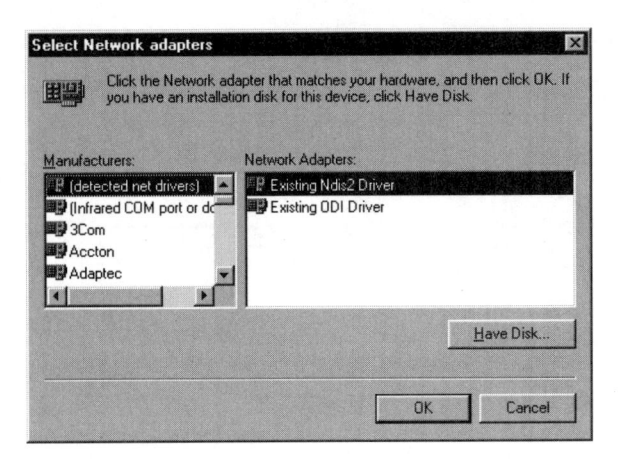

Chapter 13: Installing Software on Network Workstations

Figure 13-1
The Select Network Adapters dialog box allows you to select the make and model of your NIC.

8. Click OK.

9. Click Yes when you're asked whether you want to restart your computer.

Microsoft Windows 2000

If you're using Windows 2000, follow these steps to install NIC drivers manually:

1. In the Control Panel window, double-click Add/Remove Hardware.

2. Click Next twice. Windows displays a list of devices. Select Add A New Device, and then click Next.

3. Select No, I Want To Select The Hardware From A List, and then click Next to display the Hardware Types list, which is shown in Figure 13-2.

4. Choose Network Adapters, and then click Next. On the left side of the dialog box is a list of manufacturers whose drivers are provided with Windows.

5. From the list of manufacturers, select your card manufacturer.
    On the right side of the dialog box is a list of network adapters made by the manufacturer.

Part 3: Setting Up Computers on a Network

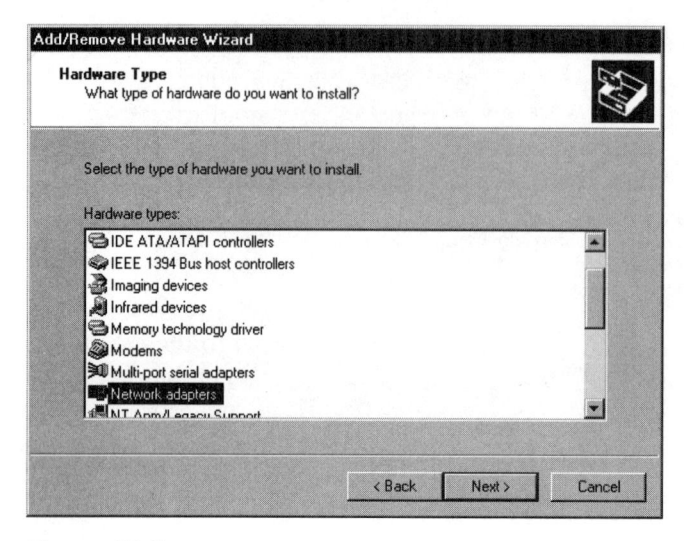

Figure 13-2
Select your adapter from the Hardware Types list.

Note

If your manufacturer or NIC isn't listed, but the NIC came with a disk of drivers, click Have Disk in the Select Network Adapters dialog box and navigate to the disk that contains the drivers.

6. From the Network Adapters list, select your NIC model.
7. Click OK.
8. Click Yes when you're asked whether you want to restart your computer.

Installing Drivers for Non–Plug-and-Play NICs

In Chapter 9, you learned how to install an ISA card and how to set switches and jumpers if the IRQ and I/O addresses need to be set on the card itself. Some ISA cards, however, let you change these settings using software. Such cards come with a setup or installation program on disk that either makes the settings for you or guides you through the process.

Chapter 13: Installing Software on Network Workstations

> **Tip**
>
> If other devices are already using all your IRQ addresses, you might encounter difficulties when setting up an ISA card. Exchanging the card for another ISA NIC might not solve the problem—you might need a PCI card or an external network device that connects to your universal serial bus (USB) or printer port.

Run the installation program that came with the NIC. The program might check your PC and assign the best settings to the card. If the program asks you to select the settings, however, cancel the program so you can check which IRQs and I/O addresses are free. The NIC manual should include a list of the possible addresses to which you can set your card. Here's a quick reminder about how to find out which of these addresses are actually available.

Microsoft Windows 95/98

If you're using Windows 95 or Windows 98, check the IRQ and I/O addresses by following these steps:

1. Right-click My Computer on the Windows desktop, and choose Properties from the shortcut menu.
2. Click the Device Manager tab in the System Properties dialog box.
3. Double-click Computer at the top of the list.
4. In the dialog box that appears, make sure the Interrupt Request (IRQ) option is selected.
5. Look for an unused IRQ. You might also be able to use the IRQ assigned to an unused serial port.
6. Select the Input/Output (I/O) option.
7. Check to see which of the unused addresses your card can use.
8. Click Cancel to return to the desktop.

Now run the installation program that came with the NIC and select an IRQ and I/O address not in use by another device.

Part 3: Setting Up Computers on a Network

Microsoft Windows 2000

If you're using Windows 2000, check the IRQ and I/O addresses by following these steps:

1. Right-click My Computer on the Windows desktop, and choose Properties from the shortcut menu.
2. On the Hardware tab, click Device Manager.
3. Select Resources By Type from the View menu.
4. Click the plus sign next to Interrupt Request (IRQ).
5. Look for an unused IRQ. You might also be able to use the IRQ assigned to an unused serial port.
6. Click the plus sign next to Input/Output (IO).
7. Check to see which of the unused addresses your card can use.
8. Close the window.

Now run the installation program that came with the NIC and select an IRQ and I/O address not in use by another device.

Checking Hardware Conflicts

After you install the drivers, you should confirm that no hardware conflicts exist. Here's how to do it:

1. Right-click My Computer on the Windows desktop, and choose Properties from the shortcut menu.
2. In Windows 95/98, click the Device Manager tab in the System Properties dialog box. In Windows 2000, click the Device Manager button on the Hardware tab.

    If your network device isn't working properly, you'll see an exclamation point or X next to its name.

If your network device has a problem, follow these steps to troubleshoot it:

1. In the list of devices on the Device Manager tab, click the name of your NIC in the Network Adapters list, and then click Properties. In Windows 2000, click the Properties button on the toolbar.

Chapter 13: Installing Software on Network Workstations

2. In the Properties dialog box for your network device, look in the Device Status area of the General tab.

    If you see a message that says, "This device is either not present, not working properly, or does not have all the drivers installed," you have either a bad NIC or a conflict.

3. Click the Resources tab.

    The Conflicting Device List section shows where the conflict is occurring.

Try rerunning the NIC's installation program and selecting other settings; if that doesn't work, change the settings manually in the device's Properties dialog box.

Changing the settings yourself is a last-ditch option. You have no guarantee that the NIC will work, and you could create a new conflict with another device, such as a modem or printer, causing that device to fail as well. If you do want to try changing the settings manually, follow these steps:

1. On the Resources tab of the Properties dialog box, make a note of which settings are being used.

    This information will allow you to restore the original settings, if necessary. Restoring the original settings won't do anything for the NIC, but it might restore some other device that you disabled by changing the settings manually.

2. Click the Use Automatic Settings check box to clear it.
3. In the Resource Type list, click the setting you want to change.
4. Click Change Settings.
5. In the dialog box that opens, change the setting, and then click OK.

Restart your computer and test all your devices. If the new device doesn't work, repeat the process but restore the original settings. Perhaps it's time to take your computer to a shop for the installation or to remove the card and exchange it for a plug-and-play PC model.

Configuring Windows for Networking

The next step in creating your network is to configure Windows for networking. This involves four procedures:

Part 3: Setting Up Computers on a Network

- Adding the network client
- Installing the network protocol
- Selecting network services
- Identifying your computer on the network

Choosing a network client determines how users gain access to the network. You can choose whether everyone who uses a networked computer must log on by typing a user name or by selecting the name from a list. In either case, a user must type a password for access to the network.

A *protocol* allows computers on a network to send information back and forth and understand what other computers are saying. A protocol is a sort of language, with its own vocabulary and rules of grammar, that all computers on a network have to speak in order to understand each other. If two computers are using different protocols, they can't communicate.

Network services are the resources you want to share. For example, you can choose to share your files and to let other network users access your printer.

A *workgroup* is simply a collection of computers that can interact and communicate with each other on a network. Everyone on the network who wants to share resources with others in a particular workgroup must belong to that group and must be identified by a computer name. You must type the workgroup name for each computer when you set up the network.

Adding the Network Client

The first step in configuring Windows for networking is to determine how members of your staff log on to the network when they start the computer or restart Windows. Do this by installing one of two network clients:

- **Client for Microsoft Networks** lets you start your computer and log on to the network by typing your name and password in a dialog box when Windows starts.
- **Microsoft Family Logon** lets you start your computer and log on to a network by selecting your user name from a list. You can use this option if a computer is used by more than one person. This option isn't available in Windows 2000.

Microsoft Windows 95/98

Follow these steps to select your network client if you are using Windows 95 or Windows 98:

Chapter 13: Installing Software on Network Workstations

1. On the Start menu, point to Settings, and then click Control Panel.
2. Double-click the Network Icon to open the Network dialog box.
3. Look for either Client For Microsoft Networks or Microsoft Family Logon in the Primary Network Logon box. If one of these is already installed and you don't want to change to the other, you can skip the rest of this procedure. If neither is installed or you want to select the other client, continue to the next step.
4. Click Add.
5. In the Select Network Component Type dialog box, click Client.
6. Click Add.
7. In the Select Network Client dialog box, click Microsoft in the Manufacturers list.
8. From the list of Network Clients in the Select Network Client dialog box, select Client For Microsoft Networks or Microsoft Family Logon.
9. Click OK to close the Select Network Client dialog box.
10. Click OK to close the Network dialog box.
11. Click Yes when you are asked whether you want to restart your computer.

You can have both Client for Microsoft Networks and Microsoft Family Logon installed at the same time. After adding one client, repeat the steps above but choose the other option. To choose which client to use as the default, follow these steps:

1. On the Start menu, point to Settings, and click Control Panel.
2. Double-click the Network icon to display the Network dialog box.
3. From the Primary Network Logon drop-down list, choose either Client For Microsoft Networks or Microsoft Family Logon.
4. Click OK.

If you have a client/server network using Windows NT or Windows 2000, you can set your workstation so it connects to the server whenever you start your computer. To do this, open the Network dialog box in Control Panel. Select Client For Microsoft Networks on the Configuration tab, and click Properties. In the Logon Validation area of the dialog box that appears, select the check box and type the name of your Windows NT domain.

Microsoft Windows 2000

For Windows 2000, follow these steps to configure the network client:

1. On the Start menu, point to Settings, and then click Network And Dial-Up Connections.
2. In the window that appears, right-click Local Area Connection and choose Properties from the shortcut menu to display the Local Area Connection Properties dialog box.
3. If Client For Microsoft Networks is listed, you can skip the rest of this procedure. If it isn't installed, continue as follows.
4. Click Install to open the Select Network Component Type dialog box.
5. Select Client, and then click Add to display the Select Network Client dialog box.
6. Select Client For Microsoft Networks, and click OK.
7. Click Close to close the Local Area Connection Properties dialog box.

Installing Protocols

Your next step is to install one or more protocols that will allow your computer to communicate with other computers. Three basic protocols are used in small business networks:

- **Transmission Control Protocol/Internet Protocol** (TCP/IP) is the protocol used to dial in to an Internet service, so odds are you already have it installed. However, it's not often used in smaller networks, because it requires a few more steps to set up than the other protocols do.
- **Internet Packet Exchange** (IPX/SPX) was originally developed for an office networking system called Novell NetWare, although it can be used for any type of network.
- **NetBIOS Extended User Interface** (NetBEUI) is an easy-to-set-up network protocol for smaller networks.

You can actually have all three protocols installed on one PC at the same time for compatibility with any type of network to which you connect. In fact, they might already have been installed on your computer by the manufacturer. Some NIC installation programs, such as the one from

Chapter 13: Installing Software on Network Workstations

Microsoft, set up and configure all three protocols when they install the network drivers.

Note

If you plan to add shared modems and printers to your network, consider using TCP/IP because it's often required for connecting devices directly to the network. See "Configuring TCP/IP" on page 204.

With all three protocols installed, your network will probably work perfectly well by choosing the best protocol when the computers begin communicating. The IPX/SPX and NetBEUI protocols require virtually no special configuration, so once you install them and start the network, your computer should be ready to communicate with other computers on the network.

Microsoft Windows 95/98

To see which protocols are already installed and to add new ones, follow these steps for Windows 95 or Windows 98:

1. On the Start menu, point to Settings, and then click Control Panel.
2. In the Control Panel window, double-click the Network icon to display the Network dialog box shown in Figure 13-3. Any network protocols and services that are already installed are listed.

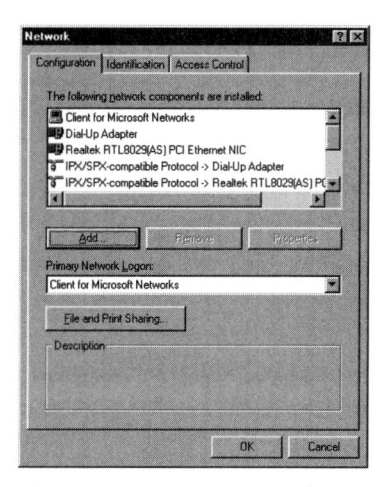

Figure 13-3

The Network dialog box lists the protocols installed in your system.

Part 3: Setting Up Computers on a Network

3. Click Add.
4. In the Select Network Component Type dialog box, select Protocol and click Add to open the Select Network Protocol dialog box.
5. Choose Microsoft from the list of manufacturers.
6. Click a protocol in the Network Protocols list—IPX/SPX, NetBEUI, or TCP/IP.
7. Click OK to close the Select Network Protocol dialog box.
8. Click OK to close the Network dialog box.
9. Click Yes when you're asked whether you want to restart your computer.

Now reopen the Network dialog box. You should see a listing for each of the protocols followed by the name of your network card in this form: TCP/IP -> NETGEAR PCI Fast Ethernet, for example. This is called a *binding entry* showing that the protocol is associated with your NIC.

Microsoft Windows 2000

To see which protocols are already installed and to add new ones in Microsoft Windows 2000, follow these steps:

1. On the Start menu, point to Settings, and then click Network And Dial-Up Connections.
2. Right-click Local Area Connection, and choose Properties from the shortcut menu to display the Local Area Connection Properties dialog box. Any network protocols and services already installed are listed.
3. Click Install.
4. In the Select Network Component Type dialog box, select Protocol and click Add to open the Select Network Protocol dialog box.
5. Click a protocol in the Network Protocols list—IPX/SPX, NetBEUI, or TCP/IP.
6. Click OK to close the Select Network Protocol dialog box.
7. Click OK to close the Select Network Component Type dialog box.

Chapter 13: Installing Software on Network Workstations

8. Click Yes when you're asked whether you want to restart your computer.

Now reopen the Network dialog box. You should see a listing for each of the protocols. At the top of the box is the name of your network card. The check mark next to the protocol indicates that the protocol is associated (bound) with your network card.

Check Your Bindings

Setting up a network is really a combination of hardware and software. You have installed your NIC and the necessary protocols and services. You should now check to make sure that the hardware and network services are linked together, so the NIC can use the services in each of the protocols. These links are called *bindings*.

1. Click Start on the Windows taskbar, point to Settings, and click Control Panel.
2. Double-click the Network icon to open the dialog box.
3. Select one of the protocols for your network card, and click Properties.
4. Click the Bindings tab. You should see that each of the installed network services is enabled for that protocol. If you want, you can disable one of the boxes to turn off the service for just that protocol.
5. Click OK.
6. Now in the same way, check the bindings for the other protocols you have installed.

You can use the binding feature on smaller networks to create a firewall that prevents access to the network from unauthorized Internet hackers. Use NetBEUI as your network protocol and turn off the Client For Microsoft Networks and File And Printer Sharing For Microsoft bindings under TCP/IP for your network card. This prevents access to your network using the TCP/IP protocol that's used on the Internet.

Part 3: Setting Up Computers on a Network

Selecting Network Services

Network services allow you to share resources—primarily files and printers—on the network.

File sharing lets other network users access your files. If you don't allow file sharing, other users can tell that you are on the network, but they won't be able to use any of your folders or files. Because sharing files is one of the main reasons to create a network, it makes sense to turn on this feature. You always have the option to specify which folders might be shared and how the files they contain can be used.

Because sharing a printer is another big advantage of networking, you'll want to turn on printer sharing as well.

Before you can activate file sharing and printer sharing, however, you have to install the Windows service that allows sharing in the first place.

Microsoft Windows 95/98

Here's how to add network services in Windows 95 and Windows 98:

1. On the Start menu, point to Settings, and click Control Panel.
2. In the Control Panel window, double-click the Network icon to open the Network dialog box.
3. In the list of network components that are installed, look for File And Printer Sharing For Microsoft Networks. If it's installed, you can skip the rest of these steps. If not, continue as follows.
4. Click Add.
5. In the Select Network Component Type dialog box, click Service.
6. Click Add.
7. In the Select Network Service dialog box, click File And Printer Sharing For Microsoft Networks.
8. Click OK.
9. Click OK to close the Network dialog box.
10. Click Yes when you're asked whether you want to restart your computer.

After your computer restarts, you're ready to turn on file and printer sharing.

1. On the Start menu, point to Settings, and then click Control Panel.

Chapter 13: Installing Software on Network Workstations

2. In the Control Panel window, double-click the Network icon to display the Network dialog box.
3. Click the File And Print Sharing button.
4. Select both check boxes in the File And Print Sharing dialog box.
5. Click OK.
6. Click OK to close the Network dialog box.

This doesn't mean that your files and printer are now shared. It only means that you've turned on the service that allows sharing.

Microsoft Windows 2000

Follow these steps to add network services in Windows 2000.

1. On the Start menu, point to Settings, and then click Network And Dial-Up Connections.
2. Right-click Local Area Connection and choose Properties from the shortcut menu.
3. In the list of network components that are installed, look for File And Printer Sharing For Microsoft Networks. If it's installed, you can skip the rest of these steps. If not, continue as follows.
4. Click Install to open the Select Network Component Type dialog box.
5. Select Service, and then click Add to open the Select Network Service dialog box.
6. Select File And Printer Sharing For Microsoft Networks, and click OK.
7. Click OK again to close the Select Network Component Type dialog box.
8. Click Yes when you're asked whether you want to restart your computer.

Identifying Your Computer on the Network

The final step in configuring Windows for networking is to make sure that your computer has a name and that you're a member of the same workgroup as the other computers on the network.

Part 3: Setting Up Computers on a Network

Microsoft Windows 95/98

If you're using Windows 95 or Windows 98, identify your workstation by following these steps:

1. On the Start menu, point to Settings, and click Control Panel.
2. In the Control Panel window, double-click the Network icon to open the Network dialog box.
3. In the Network dialog box, click the Identification tab to see the options shown in Figure 13-4.

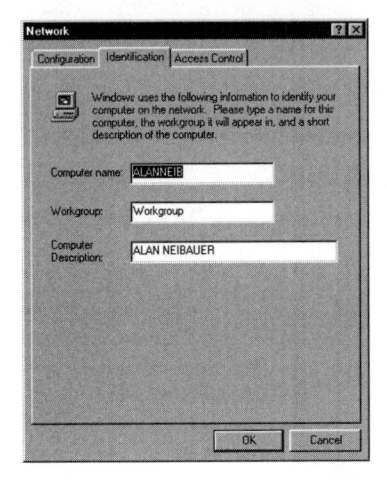

Figure 13-4
Identify yourself and your workgroup on the Identification tab.

4. If you want, change the name for your computer.
5. Make sure the workgroup name is the same one you use for other computers on your network. Windows uses the name Workgroup by default.
6. Type an optional description that others who browse the network will see.
7. Click OK to close the Network dialog box.
8. Click Yes when you're asked whether you want to restart your computer.

Chapter 13: Installing Software on Network Workstations

Microsoft Windows 2000

To identify your workstation using Windows 2000, follow these steps:

1. On the Start menu, point to Settings, and click Network And Dial-Up Connections.
2. In the Network And Dial-Up Connections window, choose Network Identification from the Advanced menu to display the Network Identification tab of the System Properties dialog box.
3. If you want to change the name of your computer or the workgroup, click Properties to display the Identification Changes dialog box.

Tip

The Network ID button in System Properties allows you to use a wizard to connect your computer to a network domain.

4. In the Identification Changes dialog box, shown in Figure 13-5, you can change the computer name and the workgroup name. If you log on to a server domain, click Domain and type the domain name.

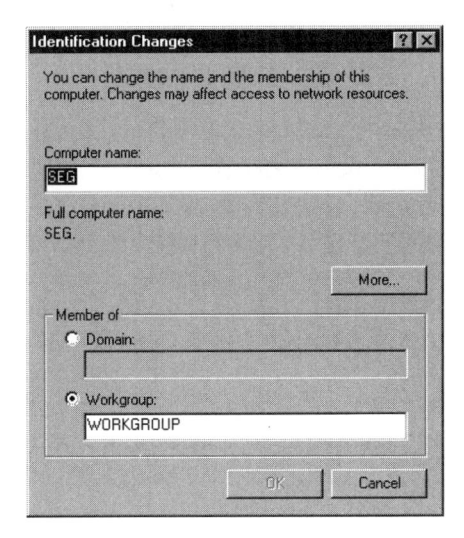

Figure 13-5

Change your identification settings.

Configuring TCP/IP

Once installed, the NetBEUI network protocol usually doesn't require any further configuration to get it working. With TCP/IP, however, you must check some settings to make sure that the computers on the network can communicate.

If you have a dial-up Internet account, your computer is probably already using TCP/IP to connect to the Internet. In the Network dialog box, you see a listing for TCP/IP -> Dial-Up Adapter showing that the protocol is installed.

Tip

If you get a message stating that file sharing is turned on when you first connect to the Internet, turn it off and restart your computer. This will protect your files from unauthorized use by Internet hackers.

TCP/IP requires that each computer on the network have its own *IP address*—a string of numbers that identifies every computer linked to the Internet and every computer linked to a TCP/IP network. No two computers on the Internet or on your network can have the same IP address. If you have a dial-up Internet account, most Internet service providers assign an IP address to your system each time you connect to the Internet.

For a small network using TCP/IP, you can have Windows assign an IP address to your computer every time your computer is started, or you can assign an IP address to your computer that will be unique on your network. I'll show you how to assign IP addresses later in this section. For most small networks, letting Windows assign the IP address is your best bet, because it's faster and easier. The address is dynamic, meaning that it might change each time you connect to the network depending on what other computers have connected before you.

You'll need to type a specific IP address only if you plan to use your computer with peripherals, such as a network modem or printer, that require a certain address. This is called a *static address* because it's the same each time you start your computer.

When you type an IP address, you do so as four sets of numbers, with up to three digits in each set. On the Internet, no two computers can have the same IP address. Your ISP will assign you an Internet IP address when you connect, so you have to select a network IP address that's guaranteed not to conflict with that address. To make this easy to do, three ranges of

Chapter 13: Installing Software on Network Workstations

numbers have been set aside that can't be used as Internet addresses, and you can safely choose any IP address in these ranges:

- 10.0.0.0 through 10.255.255.255
- 172.16.0.0 through 172.31.255.255
- 192.168.0.0 through 192.168.255.255

For a small office network, for example, you can use IP addresses starting with 192.168.0.1 and just increment the last number for each computer. (To set up the second computer in your network, for example, type *192.168.0.2* as the IP address.) Press the period key between each number to separate the numbers into four sets.

You also have to designate a subnet address. Because the number of IP addresses available to computer users is limited, another set of numbers, called the *subnet mask*, is used to define the specific IP address of a computer further. All the computers on your network must be in the same group of IP addresses, so each must have the same numbers in the Subnet Mask field.

You should be aware that using TCP/IP might cause conflicts. Some computers with older versions of Windows 95 have difficulties when TCP/IP is used for two devices at the same time, such as your NIC and your modem—one device or the other might not work properly. When you connect to a computer on the network, your Web browser might try to connect to your ISP through Dial-Up Networking. Communications programs, such as some versions of CompuServe software, might not be able to connect to the ISP when TCP/IP is being used as a network protocol. The easiest way to resolve these conflicts is to use NetBEUI as your network protocol instead.

For larger networks, however, TCP/IP provides fast connections and communications, and it's compatible with a wider variety of other network devices.

Microsoft Windows 95/98

To set the IP address of a Windows 95 or Windows 98 workstation on the network, follow these steps:

1. On the Start menu, point to Settings, and then click Control Panel.
2. In the Control Panel window, double-click the Network icon to open the Network dialog box.

Part 3: Setting Up Computers on a Network

3. In the list of network components, click the TCP/IP setting for your NIC, and click Properties to see the options shown in Figure 13-6.

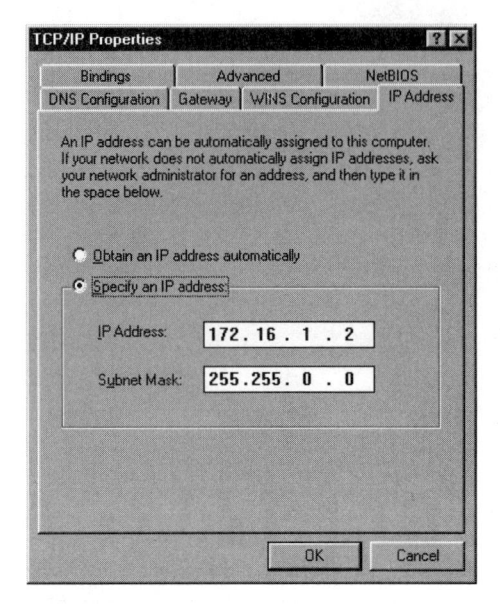

Figure 13-6
The TCP/IP Properties dialog box displays two TCP/IP addresses: IP Address and Subnet Mask.

4. Make sure Obtain An IP Address Automatically is selected if you want Windows to assign an IP address to your computer whenever it's started, and then click OK.

5. If you want to assign your own IP address, continue with the following steps.

6. Select Specify An IP Address.

7. Type an IP address in the text box.

8. Type 255.255.0.0 as the subnet mask in this and every other computer on the network.

9. Click OK to close the Network dialog box.

10. Click Yes when you're asked whether you want to restart your computer.

Chapter 13: Installing Software on Network Workstations

Tip

When you type an IP address or subnet mask, Windows will move from one set of numbers to the next when you type the third digit. If you want to enter only one or two digits in a set, either press the period to move to the next set, or click in the spot for it.

Ethernet Addresses and IP

Every Ethernet network device contains a special number hardwired into its electronics called the *Ethernet Address*. Although you don't normally need to know a device's Ethernet Address, you'll usually find the Ethernet Address of a device on a label somewhere on the device itself.

The number is written in hexadecimal form, such as 00:53:78:31:1B:3D. The first three sets of numbers identify the manufacturer; the second three sets identify the specific device. No two devices have the same combinations of numbers.

Communication between devices is done at the Ethernet Address level. For two computers to exchange information using the TCP/IP protocol, each device is assigned an IP number. When the two devices need to communicate, Windows uses the IP number to locate the device's actual Ethernet Address.

Microsoft Windows 2000

To configure TCP/IP on a Windows 2000 workstation, follow these steps:

1. On the Start menu, point to Settings, and then click Network And Dial-Up Connections.
2. Right-click Local Area Connection and choose Properties from the shortcut menu to display the Local Area Connection Properties dialog box.
3. In the list of network components, click Internet Protocol (TCP/IP), and click Properties to see the options shown in Figure 13-7.

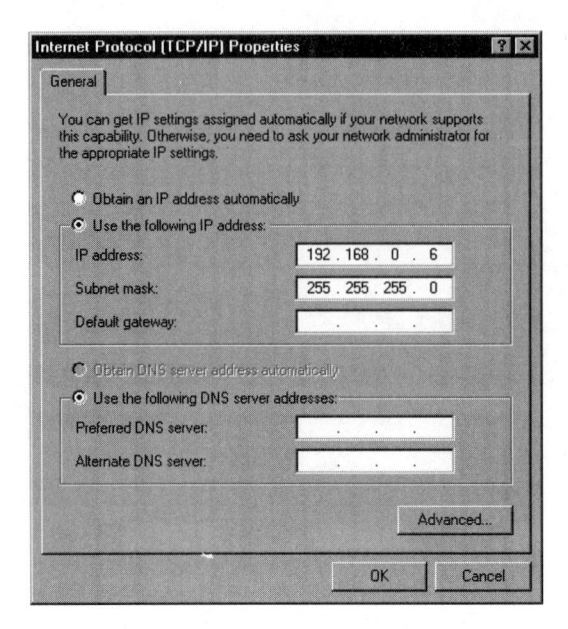

Part 3: Setting Up Computers on a Network

Figure 13-7
The TCP/IP Properties dialog box displays two TCP/IP addresses: IP Address and Subnet Mask.

4. Make sure Obtain An IP Address Automatically is selected if you want Windows to assign an IP address to your computer whenever it's started, and then click OK.

5. If you want to assign your own IP address, continue with the following steps.

6. Click Use The Following IP Address.

7. Type an IP address in the text box.

8. Type *255.255.255.0* as the Subnet Mask in this and every other computer on the network.

9. Click OK to close the TCP/IP Properties dialog box.

10. Click OK to close the Local Area Connection Properties dialog box.

11. Click Yes when you're asked whether you want to restart your computer.

Using Server-Assigned IP Addresses

If you're on a client/server network with Windows NT or Windows 2000, you can have the server assign IP addresses to all of the workstations. This

Chapter 13: Installing Software on Network Workstations

saves you the trouble of figuring out which IP addresses to use and typing them for each of the workstations.

Microsoft BackOffice Small Business Server (SBS) can act as a Dynamic Host Configuration Protocol (DHCP) server. When a workstation connects to the network, the DHCP Server assigns an unused IP address to the workstation. DHCP service might actually be turned on by default after you install SBS. To take advantage of DHCP, make sure each workstation is set to Obtain An IP Address Automatically when you configure its TCP/IP settings.

While DHCP seems to be beneficial, it isn't always recommended. Some network devices, such as printer servers, aren't compatible with DHCP. The device must have a specific IP address assigned to it in order to communicate with the network. Other devices, such as LAN modems, have their own DHCP servers built into them and you can have only one DHCP server on a network.

In addition to DHCP, Windows NT provides another feature that makes it easier to manage a large number of workstations in a TCP/IP network—the Windows Internet Naming Service (WINS). WINS maintains a database associating each computer's name that you see in Network Neighborhood with its IP address. When DHCP assigns a computer an IP address, the WINS database is updated. When a computer tries to contact another computer on the network by its name, the IP address is quickly found in the WINS database.

Note

The Domain Name System (DNS) is similar to WINS but works over the Internet. The DNS server maintains a database of domain names and their IP addresses. When you type a domain name in your browser's Address box, your ISP consults the DNS server for its IP address.

Welcome to the Neighborhood!

With all your hardware and software properly installed, your network is now complete. All the computers on the network are ready to communicate, and they should be able to "see" each other.

Microsoft Windows 95/98

If you're using Windows 95 and Windows 98, double-click the Network Neighborhood icon on your Windows desktop to find other computers on the network. You should see icons for each of the computers on the network, as well as one labeled Entire Network.

> **Tip**
>
> Your computer might take a few minutes to "see" the other computers on the network. If no other computers appear in Network Neighborhood, close the Network Neighborhood window and try again in a few minutes.

To access one of the computers on the network, double-click its icon in Network Neighborhood. You should see all the resources on that computer that can be shared. Don't worry if nothing appears when you try this now—you'll learn how to share resources in Chapter 17.

If you double-click the Entire Network icon in Network Neighborhood, you'll see an icon representing the workgroup. Open that icon to display the computers in your workgroup.

Network Neighborhood will appear in Windows Explorer and the File Open and File Save dialog boxes of Windows applications. If you're using Microsoft Word, for example, you can open or save a file on a connected computer by choosing Network Neighborhood in the Look In list that appears in the Open or Save dialog box.

Another way to access a computer on the network is by using the Find command as follows:

On the Start menu, point to Find, and then click Computer.

Type the name of the computer in the Find Computer dialog box, and click Find Now.

Microsoft Windows 2000

To find other computers using Windows 2000, follow these steps:

1. Double-click the My Network Places icon on your Windows desktop to see these two options:
    - **Entire Network** includes your workgroup and a server domain.
    - **Computers Near Me** includes computers in your workgroup.

Chapter 13: Installing Software on Network Workstations

2. Click Computers Near Me to see icons for each of the computers on your workgroup. If you click Entire Network, double-click Microsoft Windows Network to see an icon labeled Workgroup and an icon for your server's domain. Double-click the icon for the computer you want to locate.

3. To access one of the computers on the network, double-click its icon. You should see all the resources on that computer that can be shared.

My Network Places will appear in Windows Explorer and the File Open and File Save boxes of Windows applications.

Troubleshooting

Theoretically, every part of your network should be humming along now. But sometimes, even with the best planning, things can go wrong. If you can't access the other computers on your network, you'll have to take some time to check out each aspect of the installation.

Accessing the Network

You can often access a computer before it shows up in Network Neighborhood. Try locating it using Find Computer on the Start menu if you know the name of another computer.

If that fails, check all the cable connections to the computers and to the hub. Make sure the hub is plugged in and turned on and that all of the cables are securely connected.

If you still can't access the network, the problem might be the configuration of the NICs.

Checking Network Settings

The next place to troubleshoot the network is in the Network dialog box.

Make sure you're using the same workgroup name for each computer, with the same spelling and the same combination of uppercase and lowercase characters. If any computer is using a different workgroup name, change it to match the others, restart the computer, and try Network Neighborhood again.

Next, make sure you have all three protocols installed and that the Network dialog box displays a listing for each protocol. The same protocols should be installed on every computer in the network.

If you're using TCP/IP, make sure either that your computer or network is assigning IP addresses automatically or that each machine has a different address. Check that the subnet mask is the same for every machine.

Tip

If all else fails, remove all the protocols except NetBEUI from all of the computers and try again. NetBEUI is the easiest protocol to use because it requires no special configuration.

Diagnosing Hardware Conflicts

Finally, if your network still doesn't work, check for conflicts between the NIC and other hardware on your computers. One way to check for conflicts is by using the Windows 98 System Information program:

1. On the Start menu, point to Programs, Accessories, and System Tools, and then click System Information.
2. In the Microsoft System Information window, click the plus sign next to Hardware Resources.
3. Under Hardware Resources, click Conflicts/Sharing and see whether any conflicts are listed in the right pane of the window or if your network card is using the same IRQ as another device.
4. Click Forced Hardware. This will show devices that you set up manually using settings other than those chosen by plug-and-play.
5. Click I/O, and look for addresses that are shared by two devices.
6. Click IRQs, and scan the list for any possible conflicts.
7. Click the plus sign next to Components.
8. Under Components, click Network.
9. Scroll through the list on the right to confirm that your network card, TCP/IP, and network clients are all listed. If they're not listed, go back to the beginning of this chapter and reinstall the network drivers, protocols, and clients.

Chapter 13: Installing Software on Network Workstations

Depending on your NIC, setting up your hardware can be either a breeze or a windstorm. Fortunately, almost all NICs you get these days are plug-and-play, or they include software that guides you through the process.

In the next chapter, I'll cover how to configure personal profiles for users.

Chapter 14

Configuring Personal Profiles

If you have a small office, more than one person will likely use the same computer. People often share computers when you hire temporary help or have several part-time employees assigned to the same desk, office, or computer. However, you might not want a temporary person or a particular employee accessing the network in the same way as someone else who shares the computer.

If you use Microsoft Windows, individual users can have their own personal settings that go into effect whenever they log on to the network. These settings personalize their screen displays, such as their screen savers and desktop themes, and they maintain other preferences, such as which folders and files to share with other users.

These personal settings are stored in a feature called a *profile*. Each user creates a profile, which is associated with a user name. When each person types a user name upon starting Windows, the correct profile is used. One set of default settings is reserved for users who don't have profiles of their own.

To use profiles, you have to turn them on and create a user name for each person who will be using your computer.

Part 3:   Setting Up Computers on a Network

What's in a Profile?

In addition to the user name and password, a personal profile might include the following items:

- Display settings, such as the screen saver, desktop theme, and Windows color scheme
- Icons and other items on the desktop
- Internet cookies and downloaded files
- Files contained in the My Documents folder
- Recently used files in the Documents list
- Programs on the Start menu
- Favorites in the Favorites folder
- E-mail shown in certain e-mail programs, such as Microsoft Outlook Express

You can probably see just from this list how useful the profiles feature can be.

For example, when you have your own user profile, your Web browser saves all of your Internet cookies in a file reserved just for you. A *cookie* is a small file that a site on the Internet saves on your hard disk. When you later revisit that site, it reads the information in the cookie file to identify you and any settings or options that you selected on your last visit. Your own personalized settings will show up when you return to many Web sites because your browser retrieves your cookies rather than the cookies stored for other users. Sites that sell books, such as Amazon.com, save your book-buying preferences in a cookie. When you log on to the site, you might see a list of books that match your interests. If every user of your computer used the same profile, you'd see books of interest to them, as well.

On the desktop, the My Documents folder and Documents list show only your files, so you can quickly open files that you've worked on, instead of seeing a multitude of files from other users.

If you share your computer with an avid game player, your profile lets you avoid seeing a long list of somebody else's games in the Start menu. Those games appear only when the other player logs on with a different user name and password.

A personal Favorites list means that only the Web sites you want to visit are listed in the Favorites menu—both on the Start menu and in

Microsoft Internet Explorer. You won't need to scroll through a long list of favorites chosen by other users.

The same applies to e-mail messages in programs such as Outlook Express. Each user sees only his or her messages in the Inbox and Sent Items folders; every other user's mail is kept private.

Turning On Profiles

In order to use the profile feature, you have to specify that you want other users to have their own settings. Otherwise, Windows displays the same desktop and uses the same settings for everyone who uses your computer.

> **Note**
>
> This section discusses profiles with Microsoft Windows 95 and Windows 98. For creating and using profiles with Windows 2000, see "Microsoft Windows 2000 Profiles" on page 226.

Here's how to turn on the profiles feature:

1. On the Start menu, point to Settings, and then click Control Panel.
2. In the Control Panel window, double-click the Passwords icon to open the Passwords Properties dialog box.
3. Click the User Profiles tab.
4. Click Users Can Customize Their Preferences And Desktop Settings.
5. Click to select the two check boxes in the User Profile Settings section.

    These settings allow individual users to add icons to the desktop and programs to the Start menu that appear only when they select their profile.
6. Click OK to close the Passwords Properties dialog box.
7. Click Yes when you're asked whether you want to restart your computer.
8. After Windows restarts, type your user name and password, and then click OK.
9. Click Yes when you're asked if you want to retain the current settings in your profile.

You now have your own profile, containing all the settings you created when you were the computer's only user.

Adding Users

The next step is to specify who the users of your computer will be, so that each can have a personal profile. You can add as many users as you like, whenever you like, or users can create their own profiles in order to keep their passwords confidential.

To add a new user, you can simply type a new name and password when you start Windows, or you can go to Control Panel and select user options.

> **Note**
>
> Adding a new user through Control Panel is possible only if you have Internet Explorer version 4 or later on your computer.

Adding Users When You Log On

It's easy to add a new user when you start Windows, but then you'll have to go to Control Panel to select options. Here's how to do it:

1. When you start Windows or use the Log Off option from the Start menu to log on as another user, type a new name and a new password in the Enter Network Password dialog box, and then click OK.

   > **Note**
   >
   > A password is optional. If you don't want to use one, just leave the Password text box blank.

   Because you've typed a new user name, the Set Windows Password dialog box appears, asking you to retype your password to confirm it.

2. Type a password, and then click OK.
3. When a message appears asking if you want to save your own Desktop settings, click Yes.

Adding Users Through Control Panel

If you have Internet Explorer version 4 or later, you can add users and select certain profile settings with Control Panel. The first time you add a user this way, Windows runs the Add User Wizard, which takes you through the process step-by-step:

1. On the Start menu, point to Settings, and then click Control Panel.
2. In the Control Panel window, double-click the Users icon to open the User Settings dialog box.
3. Click New User to start the Add User Wizard.
4. Read the explanation shown in the dialog box, and then click Next.
5. In the Add User dialog box, type a new user name, and then click Next.
6. In the Enter New Password dialog box, type the password in both the Password and Confirm Password text boxes, and then click Next.
7. In the Personalized Items Settings dialog box, shown in Figure 14-1, click to select the check boxes for the items that you want in your personal profile. If you leave a check box cleared, you won't have a custom copy of that item.

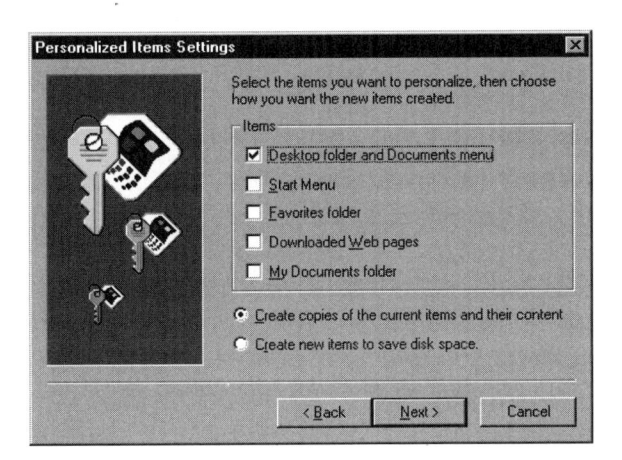

Figure 14-1
The Personalized Items Settings dialog box allows you to choose the contents of your profile.

8. Select one of the two option buttons near the bottom of the dialog box to determine how you want your personal profile set up.
   If you select the first option button, Windows will make a copy of all of the items in the profile currently being used as the basis for your personal profile. If you choose the second option button, you'll have to create all of the items yourself from scratch.
9. Click Next, and then click Finish.
   Windows creates your personal desktop and displays the User Settings dialog box.
10. Click Close in the User Settings dialog box.

If you prefer to use the desktop settings of another user, it's possible to copy those settings to a new personal profile that you can use. Follow these steps to start a new profile using someone else's settings:

1. Double-click the Users icon in Control Panel.
2. Click the name of the user whose settings you want to copy.
3. Click Make A Copy to start the Add User Wizard.
4. Follow the steps of the wizard, selecting just the items you want to copy in the Personalized Items Settings dialog box. For example, you can clear the My Documents Folder check box if you don't want to see the other user's documents displayed in your My Documents folder.
5. Click Finish in the last dialog box of the wizard.

Changing User Settings

Changing your password and profile settings is as easy as adding a new user.

1. Double-click the Users icon in Control Panel.
2. In the User Settings dialog box, click your user name.
3. Click Set Password to change your password. You'll have to type your current password, and then type and confirm the new one.
4. Click Change Settings to open the Personalized Items Settings dialog box, and then change your settings.

Note

If you're not using Internet Explorer version 4 or later, see "Changing Passwords," on page 223, to learn how to change your password.

You can also delete a user profile. This eliminates not only the user name and password, but also all folders associated with the user name, such as the My Documents and Favorites folders. If you don't want to delete the contents of these folders, copy the files or favorites you want to save to another location before deleting the user. Then click the user name in the User Settings dialog box and click Delete.

Tip

You can't delete a user who is currently logged on.

Logging On as a Different User

You can start Windows on any computer by logging on with your own user name. If you forget your password, you can bypass the logon process and use the default desktop—the desktop that existed when the profile feature was originally enabled.

To log on to any computer, start the computer and type your user name and password in the Enter Network Password dialog box. Leave the Password text box blank if you didn't type a password when you created your profile.

If you want to log on using the default desktop, just click Cancel in the Enter Network Password dialog box or press the Esc key. Windows will start using the settings of the default profile. Any files that were in the My Documents and Favorites folders of your personal profile won't be available on the default desktop.

If your computer is already started and you want to switch to another user profile, you have to log off and then log on again using the other profile. You might want to do this if you bypassed the logon when you first started and now want to access your personal profile files. To switch profiles in Windows 98, follow these steps:

1. On the Start menu, click Log Off.
2. Click Yes when you're asked if you are sure you want to log off.
   The Enter Network Password box appears.
3. Type the user name and password you want to log on with, and then click OK. You can also click Cancel or press Esc to log on using the default profile.

If you're using Windows 95, the procedure for switching profiles is a little different:

1. On the Start menu, click Shut Down.
2. In the Shut Down dialog box, click Close All Programs And Log On As A Different User. Windows will restart so that you can type another user name and password.

Using the Microsoft Family Logon

If a number of staff members are using one computer, you can save them the trouble of typing user names by choosing the Microsoft Family Logon feature. In Chapter 13, you learned how to install Microsoft Family Logon as a network client when setting up Windows for your network.

When a staff member starts a computer on the network, a dialog box lists the profile names of all users. The staff member can choose a user name from the list, type a password, and then click OK to log on using the correct profile.

If you installed Microsoft Family Logon and want to use it, follow these steps to select it as the default logon option:

1. On the Start menu, point to Settings, and then click Control Panel.
2. In the Control Panel window, double-click the Network icon to open the Network dialog box.
3. In the Primary Network Logon drop-down list, select Microsoft Family Logon, and then click OK.

Note

If you no longer want to use the Microsoft Family Logon feature, select Client For Microsoft Networks in the Primary Network Logon drop-down list instead.

Locating Your Folders

The profiles that are set up on a computer are stored in folders in the Profiles folder, which is in the Windows folder. To locate a profile folder, use either My Computer or Windows Explorer to navigate to the Profiles folder. In the Profiles folder, you'll see folders with the profile names.

Chapter 14: Configuring Personal Files

Double-click the profile name you're looking for to display all of the folders in that user's profile:

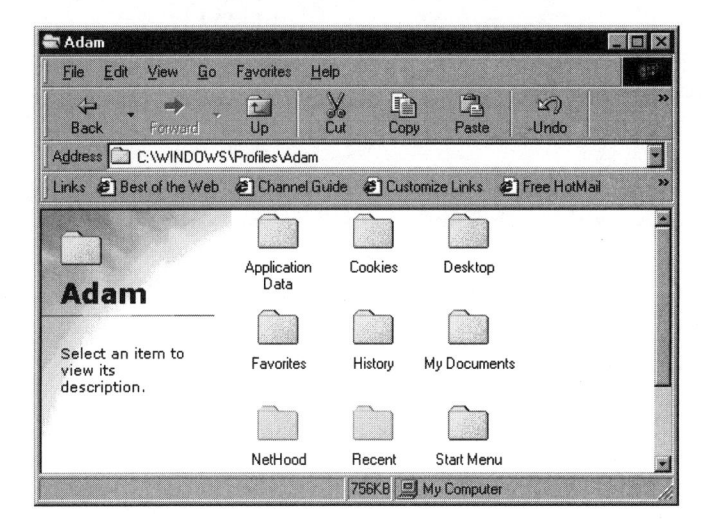

Changing Passwords

If you're using Internet Explorer version 4 or later, you can set and change your password in the Users dialog box. But no matter what version of Internet Explorer you're using, you can always change passwords with the Password program in Control Panel. Here's how:

1. In Control Panel, double-click the Passwords icon to display the Passwords Properties dialog box.
2. Click the Change Passwords tab.
3. Click Change Windows Password.
4. In the text boxes, type your current password, and type and confirm your new password.

Note

The Change Other Passwords option, which isn't available on all systems, lets you change the passwords you use to log on to a network server.

You'll learn how to password protect individual folders and files in Chapter 17.

Surviving Password Forgetfulness

What happens if you forget your password? What you *don't* want to do is log on as a different user and delete your entire profile. This will delete settings and files that you probably want to retain.

After the initial panic wears off, you can easily delete your password and start over. Passwords are stored in files with a .pwl extension. To locate your password file, follow these steps:

1. On the Start menu, point to Find, and then click Files Or Folders.
2. In the Find All Files dialog box, type *.pwl in the Named text box and click Find Now.
   You'll see a list of files with the .pwl extension.
3. Click the file that has your user name, press the Delete key, and click Yes to confirm the deletion.

Note

After you delete your password file, you'll have to retype your ISP password when you next log on to the Internet or check your e-mail.

You can now log on using your own user name and no password. You can also create a new password—one that you might not forget so easily. Either type a new password in the Enter Network Password dialog box or create the new password in the Users or Passwords dialog box from Control Panel.

Deleting All Profiles

If you ever decide that you no longer want to share your computer, you can delete all user profiles from Windows. To do so, however, you need to use the Windows Registry Editor, and this can be tricky. Because the registry is where Windows stores all of its settings, you must be extremely careful not to change a setting you don't want to change. If you do decide to delete all your profiles, follow these steps exactly:

1. Restart your computer and click Cancel when the Enter Network Password dialog box appears.
2. Double-click the Password icon in Control Panel.
3. On the User Profiles tab, click All Users Of This PC Use The Same Preferences And Desktop Settings.

Chapter 14: Configuring Personal Files

4. Click OK, and restart your computer.
   When the computer restarts, follow these steps:
5. On the Start menu, click Run.
6. In the Run dialog box, type *regedit*, and then click OK.
   The Registry Editor starts.
7. Click the plus sign in front of HKEY_LOCAL_MACHINE to expand this section, as shown in Figure 14-2.

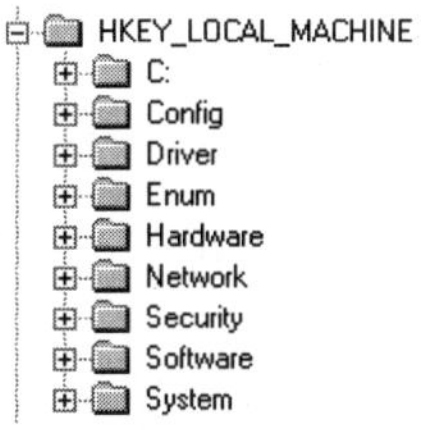

```
HKEY_LOCAL_MACHINE
    C:
    Config
    Driver
    Enum
    Hardware
    Network
    Security
    Software
    System
```

Figure 14-2
The Registry Editor lets you change settings in the Windows registry.

8. Click the plus sign in front of Software.
9. Click the plus sign in front of Microsoft.
10. Click the plus sign in front of Windows.
11. Click the plus sign in front of Current Version.
12. Click ProfileList. The status bar at the bottom of the Registry Editor should read My Computer\HKEY_LOCAL_MACHINE\Software\Microsoft\Windows\CurrentVersion\ProfileList.
13. Press the Delete key, and then press Enter if you are asked to confirm the deletion.
14. On the Registry menu, click Exit.
    Now that you've edited the registry, follow these steps:
15. Double-click My Computer on the desktop.
16. Double-click the icon for your hard disk drive.
17. Open the Windows folder and click Show Files to display the contents of the folder.
18. Click the Profiles folder.
19. Press the Delete key to delete the folder.
20. Click Yes to confirm that you want to move the folder to the Recycle Bin.

Microsoft Windows 2000 Profiles

In Windows 2000 Professional profiles work about the same way as in Windows 95 and Windows 98. The main difference is that Windows 2000 lets you assign users to groups. A group defines the rights of users who have been assigned to the group. This saves you the trouble of specifying permissions for each user individually.

Windows creates six default groups:

- **Administrators** have full access to the computer or network domain.
- **Guests** and **Users** can use the computer and save their documents, but they can't install programs or change system files and settings.
- **Backup Operators** can only back up files and folders from the computer.
- **Power Users** can install programs and change computer settings, but they can't read other users' files.
- **Replicator group** supports file replication.

To add a new user, you need to log on as an administrator. When you set up Windows 2000 Professional for the first time and log on, you'll be an administrator.

Open Users And Passwords in Control Panel to see a list of currently defined users, as shown in Figure 14-3. Windows 2000 creates a user called Administrator and a user account for the person who installed Windows. Windows 2000 also creates default users called Guest (for others with whom you want to share the computer), IUSR (for an Internet Guest Account), and IWAM (for someone to launch IIS Process Account programs).

To add a new user, follow these steps:

1. Click Add in the Users And Passwords dialog box.
2. In the Add New User dialog box, type the user name, full name, and description, and then click Next. In the box that appears, type and confirm the password, and then click Next.
3. Select the group to which you want to assign the users. If you want a group other than Power User or User, click Other and select the group from the list.
4. Click Finish.

Chapter 14: Configuring Personal Files

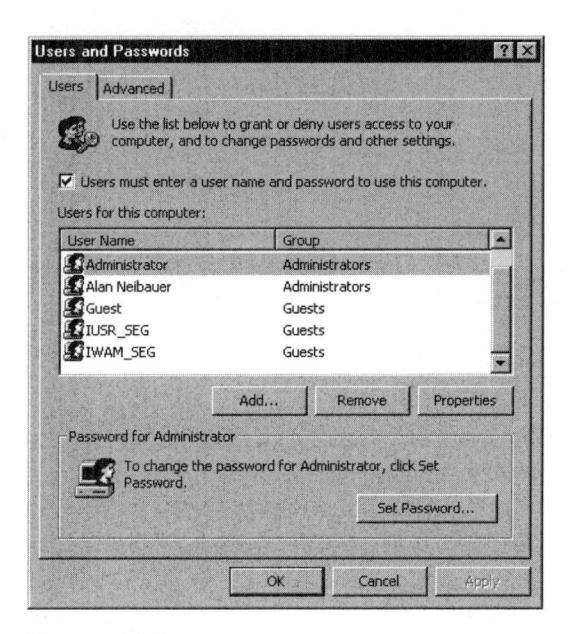

Figure 14-3
See currently defined users and groups in the Users And Passwords dialog box.

The new user will be listed in the Users And Passwords dialog box and can now log on to the system. If you need to change the user's name or group assignment, select the user's name and then click Properties.

You can create new groups and make changes to the user's profiles in the Computer Management dialog box, shown in Figure 14-4.

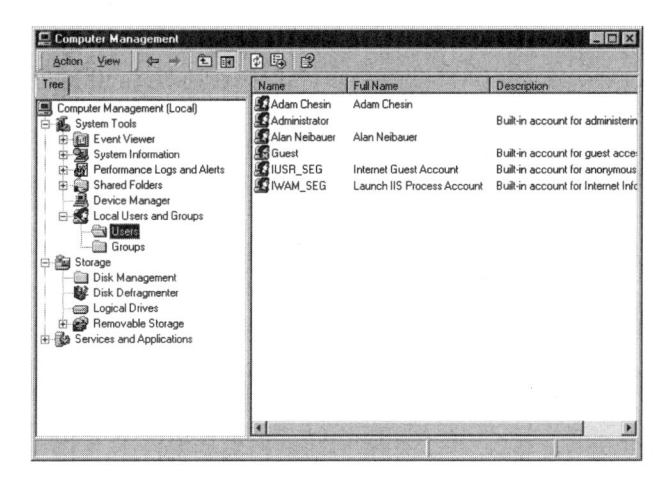

Figure 14-4
Create groups in the Computer Management dialog box.

Part 3: Setting Up Computers on a Network

To display the box, open Administrative Tools in Control Panel, and then open Computer Management. To change a profile, click the plus sign next to Local Users And Groups and then click Users to list the users on the right side of the window. Select the user whose profile you want to change, and then select Properties from the Action menu. The user's Properties dialog box appears, as shown in Figure 14-5.

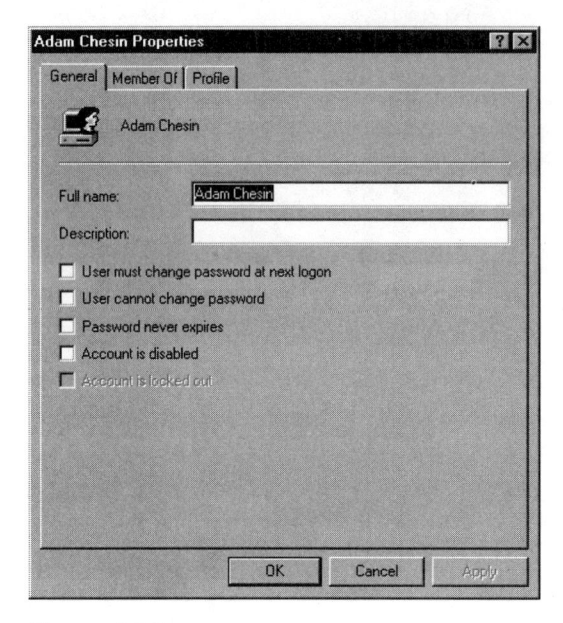

Figure 14-5
Change a profile in the User Properties dialog box.

On the General tab of the dialog box, you can designate whether the user must change his or her password the first time he or she logs on to the computer, whether the password never expires, or whether the account is disabled. Use the Member Of tab to change the groups to which the user belongs.

The Profile tab lets you create a roaming or a mandatory profile location. A *roaming profile* allows a user to log on to the computer remotely and have the profile information downloaded from the server to the remote computer. A *mandatory profile* is one created by the administrator that can't be changed by the user.

To create a new group from the Computer Management dialog box, click Groups in the Local Users And Groups area, and then choose New Group from the Action menu. In the dialog box that appears, type the group name and then click Create.

> **Note**
>
> Setting the permissions assigned to a group is a more complicated matter. It's performed from the Local Security Policy option in the Administrative Tools window and is beyond the scope of this book.

In the next chapter, you'll learn how to set up clients on a network when you're using thin servers.

Chapter 15

Setting Up a Microsoft Windows–Based Server Appliance

Many thin servers are plug-and-play and thus require very little configuration. This chapter will look at setting up and using a Microsoft Windows–based server appliance to add file, printer, and modem sharing to your network.

Assigning IP Addresses

Because thin servers connect directly to the network, they have to be set up for your network protocol so they can communicate with workstations. Most thin servers communicate with your network using the TCP/IP protocol, which you learned about in Chapter 13. So your first step in setting up a thin server is to assign it an IP address, just as you would do if you were setting up a workstation.

Some thin servers, however, can also be used as Dynamic Host Configuration Protocol (DHCP) servers. This means that the thin servers can assign IP addresses to each workstation as it connects to the network. With the thin server's DHCP feature enabled, the thin server uses a default IP address provided by the manufacturer and assigns other addresses in the same range to workstations.

If you want to assign workstations their own IP addresses yourself, you have to disable the thin server's DHCP feature and assign the thin server a fixed IP address. This is necessary if you're using another thin server that requires a fixed IP address and that won't accept an address from DHCP. Some print servers fall into this category.

You might be using a program that provides DHCP services to your network. Many Internet sharing programs, for example, use their own DHCP service as the mechanism for sharing the modem. While you might be able to use fixed IP addresses with these kinds of programs, it's difficult to do, if not impossible, when another DHCP server is on the network.

You can have only one DHCP server on a network. If you're using the Microsoft Windows NT DHCP Server or the Microsoft Windows 2000 DHCP Service, you must disable DHCP services provided by a thin server or an Internet sharing program.

In Chapter 18, you'll learn about using thin servers for sharing a printer on the network, and in Chapter 21, you'll learn about using thin servers for sharing a phone line and an Internet account. To set up and configure these thin servers, you have to perform two steps:

1. Set the device for your network protocol and addresses.
2. Configure your workstations to access the printer or the Internet through the thin server.

The documentation that comes with your thin server will show you how to configure it for the protocols your network uses and how to set up your workstations. Read the documentation carefully and check with the manufacturer's online or telephone support service if you have any questions.

Network-attached storage (NAS) servers also have to be configured for the protocols on your network. However, you normally don't need to set up special software or configure your workstations. Your workstations will be able to access the NAS server through Network Neighborhood just as they can any other computer on the network.

Chapter 15: Setting Up a Microsoft Windows–Based Server Appliance

Using a Microsoft Windows–Based Server Appliance

Windows-based server appliances are as easy to set up and use as an NAS server. Because they also provide modem and printer sharing and folder security, however, several steps are involved, including:

- Configuring the protocol
- Setting folder security and user accounts
- Configuring printer sharing
- Configuring modem sharing

Installing the Appliance

You set up a Windows-based server appliance from one of the network workstations. Choose the workstation that you will use as the appliance's administrator. As administrator, you determine who can access the appliance to share its hard disk drive and modem, and you set up and configure it for printer sharing.

> **Tip**
>
> If you're creating a new network and haven't set up any computers yet, you can use the appliance setup software to configure your workstations.

Start by connecting the appliance to the network. Either plug your workstations into the back of the appliance or plug the appliance into an existing hub. One of the ports can serve as an uplink to another hub through regular twisted-pair patch cable. Check the documentation that came with your appliance to determine which port can be used for an uplink and how to set it.

Next, insert into your computer the setup CD that came with your appliance to begin the setup process. You'll see a series of wizard dialog boxes. Several times during the process you might be asked to restart your computer. The program has to restart your computer and the appliance each time it changes an IP address so the devices will be able to communicate. After your computer restarts, the setup program will continue. Just respond to each dialog box as it appears, clicking Next to proceed.

One of the first options you'll get is to select either the user or the administrator setup. Choose Administrator if you're setting up the appliance for your network. The User option is for workstations that access the appliance.

You'll also be asked to assign a name to your computer. If you're on a network, your computer will already have a name. You can type the same name or a new one to rename your computer. The name can be up to 15 characters and can't contain periods.

The setup program then asks if you want to change the appliance's IP address or set your computer for dynamic addressing. By default, the appliance is set as a DHCP server and can assign IP addresses to workstations. If you want to use the appliance's DHCP features, select the dynamic addressing option. This will set the TCP/IP properties of your computer so that your computer will get its IP address automatically.

Caution

Just remember that if your network used static IP addresses, selecting this option might disable your computer from communicating with other computers on the network. You'll need to set all of the workstations for dynamic addressing either by using the appliance's User option or by configuring each workstation manually in Control Panel.

If you want to assign IP addresses manually on your workstations, don't use the appliance's DHCP feature. Choose the option to change the appliance's IP address. You'll see a dialog box in which you can type the IP address and subnet mask, as shown in Figure 15-1. Type the IP address that you want to assign to the Windows-based server appliance. It should be in sequence with the IP addresses you have assigned to your workstations. Enter the same subnet mask that you assigned to the workstations.

Tip

If you assign the appliance a static IP address and change your mind, restart the appliance by pressing its On/Off button twice in one second to return the appliance to the default DHCP settings. Then rerun the appliance's setup program from the CD.

Chapter 15: Setting Up a Microsoft Windows–Based Server Appliance

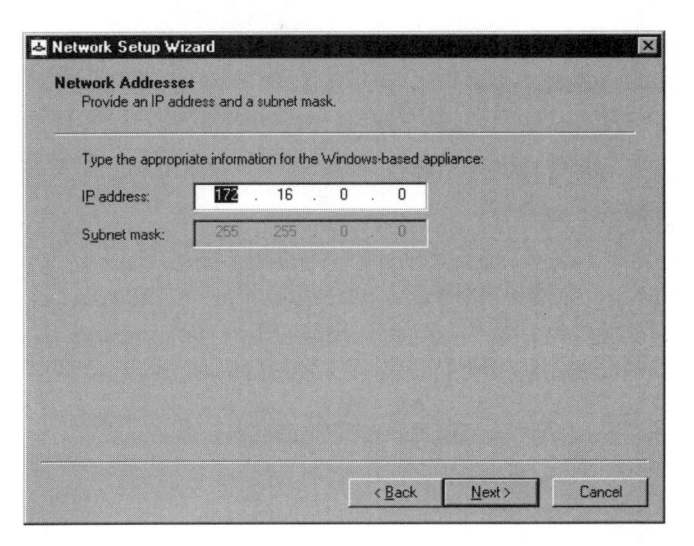

Figure 15-1
Type the IP address and subnet mask for your Windows-based server appliance.

After one or two restarts, the Microsoft Windows For Express Networks setup page opens in your Web browser, as shown in Figure 15-2.

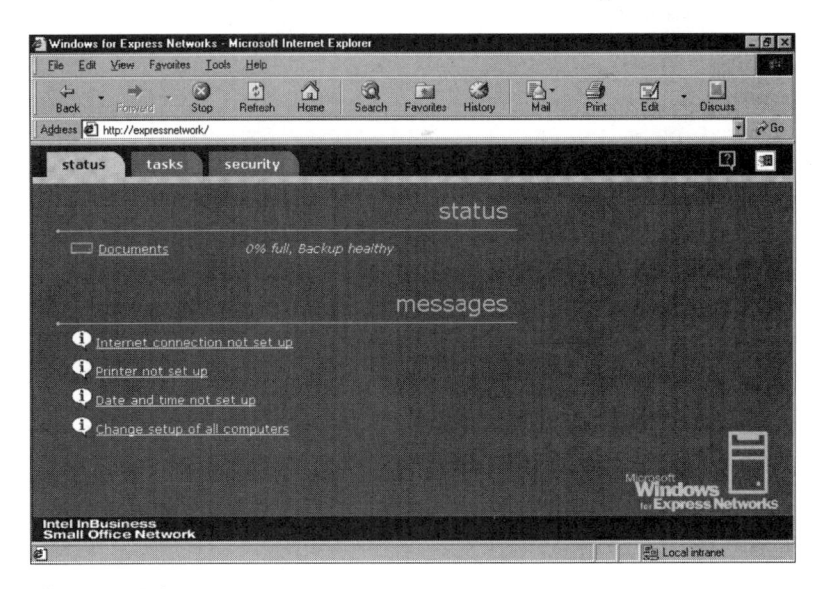

Figure 15-2
Use the Windows For Express Networks page to set up your computer.

Part 3: Setting Up Computers on a Network

The setup page has three tabs—Status, Tasks, and Security. The Status tab reports the state of the appliance's features. In Figure 15-2 for example, the Status section shows that the appliance hard disk is empty of user files and the mirror backup drive is working. The Messages section on the Status tab shows that the administrator has not set up Internet and printer sharing or set the appliance's date and time. To perform any of the tasks in the Messages section, such as setting up the Internet connection or the printer, just click the task. The Tasks tab, shown here, lets you perform common appliance functions, such as changing Internet sharing and printer sharing settings:

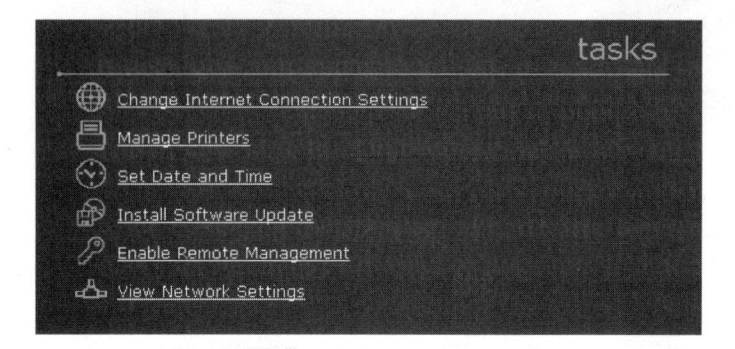

```
                                                        tasks
    Change Internet Connection Settings
    Manage Printers
    Set Date and Time
    Install Software Update
    Enable Remote Management
    View Network Settings
```

The Security tab lets you assign users to the appliance and create password-protected user folders. Until you assign users to the appliance, which is optional, every network user can access files and other shared resources. Once you assign users, however, only authenticated users can connect to the appliance.

While the window appears when you first set up the appliance, you can access it at any time to change settings. Click Start, point to Programs and then to Windows For Express Networks, and click Manage Express Network.

Setting Up an Internet Connection

If you want to share the appliance's modem with network users, you have to set up an Internet connection. This gives the appliance the information it needs to connect to the Internet.

Click Internet Connection Not Set Up on the Status tab to begin the Internet Connection Wizard. In the series of dialog boxes, you'll be asked to specify the connection information. In one of the first boxes, for example, you'll be asked to supply a primary and secondary phone number for your

Chapter 15: Setting Up a Microsoft Windows–Based Server Appliance

ISP. If you have only one number, enter it as both the primary and secondary numbers.

You'll then be asked for your user name and password. This is the user name and password you use to connect to your ISP. You probably already entered the name and password if you set up Dial-Up Networking in Microsoft Windows 95 or Microsoft Windows 98. You have to type the password twice to confirm it. Another dialog box asks for the location of a script file if your ISP requires one—most don't.

Yet another dialog box requests the IP address of your ISP's DNS server. Some ISPs assign the DNS address dynamically every time you log on. Others have fixed primary and alternate IP addresses that you must enter in this dialog box.

You will also be asked to set the number of minutes to allow your connection to be idle before hanging up, and you'll be asked whether you want to test your Internet connection.

Setting Up Printer Sharing

The appliance includes a parallel port to which you can connect a printer that will be shared with other users of the network. All of the printer drivers

---

Automatically Connecting to Your ISP

When you try to access the Web-based interface on the appliance, your computer might automatically try to connect to your ISP. To use the appliance's interface, you should turn off automatic dialing. Here's how:

1. Right-click the Microsoft Internet Explorer icon on your desktop, and choose Properties from the shortcut menu. You can also double-click the Internet Options icon in Control Panel.
2. Click the Connections tab.
3. Choose the option Never Dial A Connection.
4. Click OK.

You can now connect to the appliance's interface without dialing your ISP. When you want to connect to the Internet later, return to the Connections tab in the Internet Explorer Properties dialog box and select Always Dial My Default Connection.

Part 3: Setting Up Computers on a Network

that were available when your appliance was shipped are included on its hard disk, so setting up a printer is as easy as setting up a printer using Windows NT. If you have a newer printer whose drivers aren't on the appliance, you can set up the drivers from your workstation using the disks that came with the printer.

To set up a printer on the appliance, just follow these steps:

1. Click Start, point to Programs and then to Windows For Express Networks, and click Manage Express Network.
2. Click the Tasks tab, and then click Manage Printers.
3. In the dialog box that appears, click Add to start the Add Printer Wizard, and then click Next. The wizard asks you to select the port to which your printer is attached, which is usually LPT1.
4. Select the port, and click Next to display the options shown in Figure 15-3.

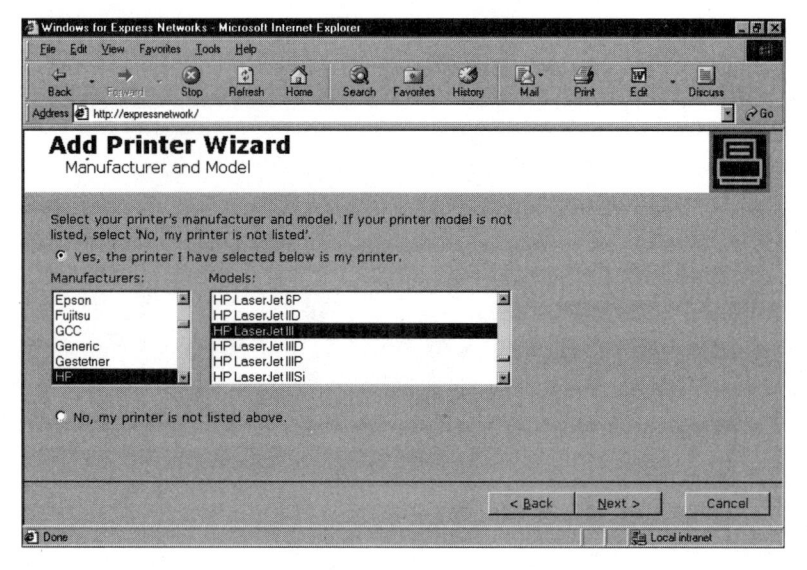

Figure 15-3
Use the Add Printer Wizard on the Windows-based server appliance to set up your printer on the network.

5. Select the manufacturer of your printer in the Manufacturers list.
6. Select the model of your printer in the Models list, and click Next.

Chapter 15: Setting Up a Microsoft Windows–Based Server Appliance

> **Tip**
>
> If your printer isn't listed, you can select a compatible printer or you can choose No, My Printer Is Not Listed Above and follow the instructions that appear.

7. Type a name for the printer, and click Next.

    Windows for Express Networks tries to print a test page and displays the options shown in Figure 15-4.

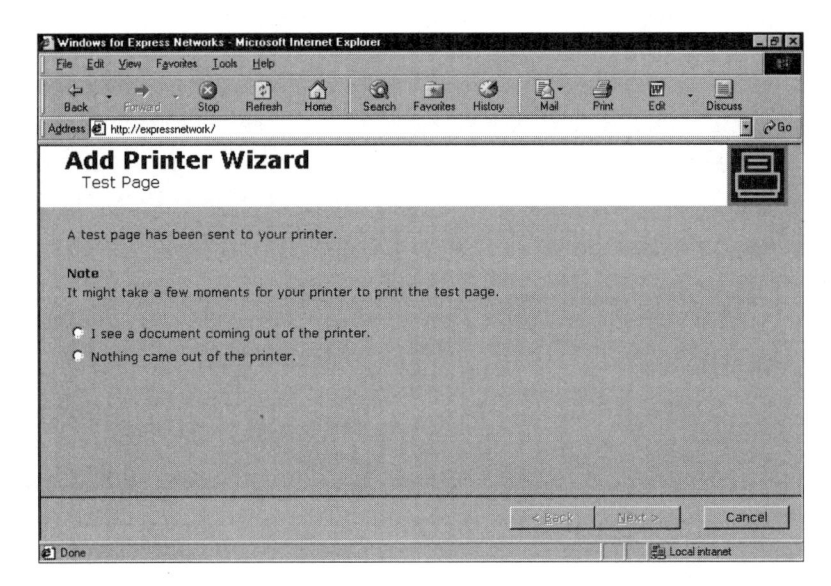

Figure 15-4
If Windows for Express Networks successfully prints a test page, choose the first option.

8. Select the appropriate option, and click Next and then Finish.

If you didn't get a printout, select the second option shown in Figure 15-4 and follow the resulting instructions to troubleshoot the printing problem. If you did get a printout, your printer will be listed on the Tasks tab. Your network printer is ready to be used. You can now set up your workstation to access the printer.

Setting Up Security

Users can share the hard disk drive on the appliance as soon as the appliance is communicating with your network. They can also share the modem

Part 3: Setting Up Computers on a Network

once the Internet connection is set up on the appliance. By enabling the security feature, you can control who has access to the shared modem and you can create individual user folders that only they can access.

Note

The printer and the public storage area of the appliance are available to all network users, even those without user accounts.

You enable security by creating a user account for yourself. You must then create separate accounts for each network user who will share the modem or will have access to his or her own private folder on the appliance. If you later want to disable security, remove all of the user accounts. The appliance turns off security when you delete the last user account.

To enable security and create your account, follow these steps:

1. Click Start, point to Programs and then to Windows For Express Networks, and click Manage Express Network.
2. Click the Security tab.
3. Click Enable Security Wizard to start the wizard.
4. Click Next to create your user account, as shown in Figure 15-5.

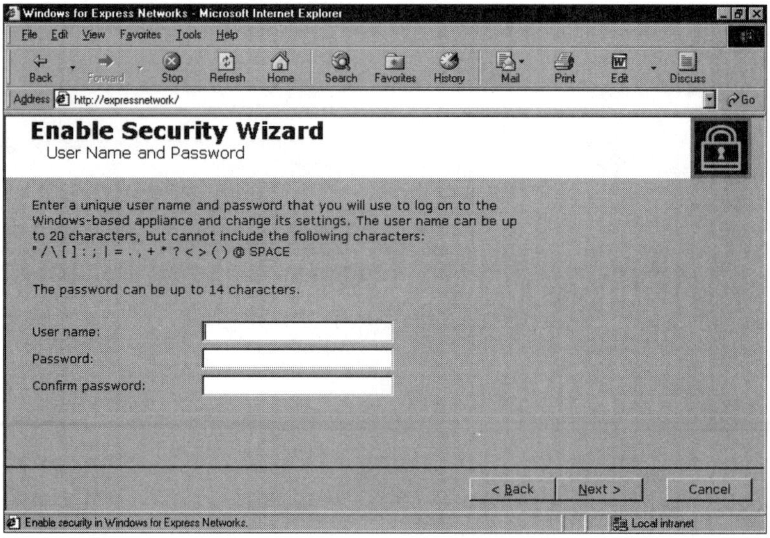

Figure 15-5

Create your user account to enable security on a Windows-based server appliance.

Chapter 15: Setting Up a Microsoft Windows–Based Server Appliance

5. Type your user name and password, and then confirm your password by typing it a second time.
6. Click Next.
7. Choose whether you want everyone to access the Internet or just users with accounts, and click Next and then Finish.

    When you click Finish, the Enter Network Password box appears.

8. Type your name and password, type workgroup as the network domain, and click OK.

    The Security tab appears with two options—Manage Users and Change Internet Access. Select Manage Users to add or delete user accounts from the network. Choose Change Internet Access to change who has access to the shared modem.

Setting Up Clients

Once your Windows-based server appliance is set up, you're ready to access it from your network workstations. You can access all of the appliance's features without installing any special software.

You can, however, set up workstations using software that came with the appliance. Insert the appliance's CD in your computer. When the setup program starts, choose the User option and follow the instructions that appear. If you've already run the setup program, you can change settings by clicking Start, pointing to Programs and then to Windows For Express Networks, and clicking Computer Setup Wizard.

At one point in the setup program, you'll see the options that you can choose, as shown in Figure 15-6. The options available depend on the services that are set up on the appliance. The Use Shared Internet Connection option, for example, appears only if Internet connection sharing is set up on the appliance. Select the features you want, and then click Next.

The options in Figure 15-6 do the following things:

- **Add Quick Access To Documents Disk** presents you with options for adding a shortcut to the appliance's hard disk drive on your desktop or mapping the hard disk so it appears as a drive in My Computer, such as drive Z.

- **Add Printer** adds the appliance's printer to the list of printers that your programs can access.

- **Use Shared Internet Connection** configures your Internet browser to dial the ISP through the modem connected to the appliance.

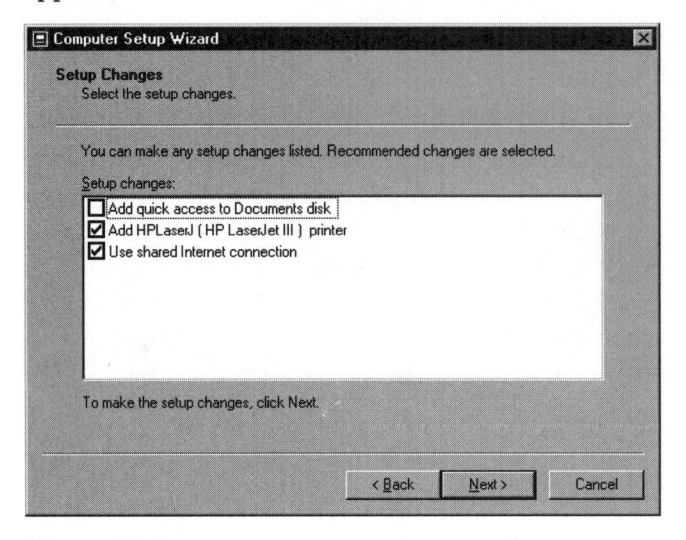

Figure 15-6
Select the appliance features you want to use.

Tip

If you want to turn off Internet sharing or you no longer use the printer, run the Computer Setup Wizard and clear the check boxes for the functions you no longer want to perform. You might have to reset your Web browser manually, however, to connect to the Internet through your computer's modem.

Manually Setting Up a Client

Instead of using the Computer Setup Wizard to set up your workstation, you can use standard Windows techniques.

To access the appliance's hard disk drive, for example, just navigate to it in Network Neighborhood. The appliance's hard disk drive is named Documents by default. You'll learn how to access files on networked computers in Chapter 17.

Chapter 15: Setting Up a Microsoft Windows–Based Server Appliance

> **Note**
>
> In "Accessing a Shared Printer" on page 310, you'll see how users can add the appliance's network printer to their workstations.

To set up your browser to connect to the Internet through the appliance, you need to configure it to use the appliance's proxy server. While the steps vary slightly with different browsers, here is how to set up Internet Explorer:

1. Right-click the Internet Explorer icon on your desktop, and choose Properties from the shortcut menu.
2. Click the Connections tab to see the options shown in Figure 15-7.

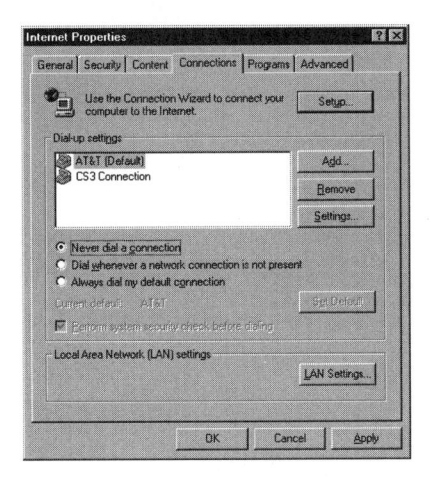

Figure 15-7

Set your browser for Internet sharing.

3. Choose the option Never Dial A Connection.
4. Click the LAN Settings button to see the options shown in Figure 15-8.

Part 3: Setting Up Computers on a Network

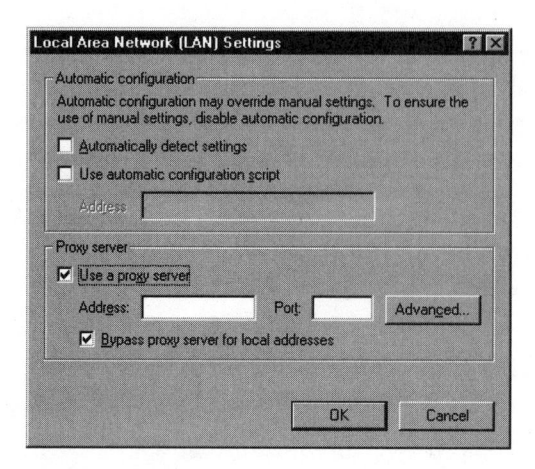

Figure 15-8
Set the LAN configuration in Internet Explorer to use the Proxy Server.

5. Select Use A Proxy Server in the Proxy Server area.
6. In the Address box, type the IP address or the HTTP address of the appliance.
7. Type *80* in the Port box.
8. Click OK twice.

    When you launch your Web browser, it'll dial your ISP using the modem in the Windows-based server appliance.

To disable Internet access through the modem for the whole network, you have to be the administrator and perform these steps:

1. Click Start, point to Programs and then to Windows For Express Network, and click Manage Express Network.
2. Click Internet Connection on the Status tab.
3. Click the Disconnect button.

In the next chapter, I'll cover setting up Microsoft BackOffice Small Business Server.

Chapter 16

Setting Up Clients on Microsoft BackOffice Small Business Server

To run Microsoft BackOffice Small Business Server (SBS) on your network, you have to create user accounts and then configure the workstations to access the server. You must create a user account for each person you want to access the server's resources. You can also set up and configure Microsoft Proxy Server to share the server's modem with other network users. You then must configure the workstations to connect to the network and install client software so it can access the various server features.

User Accounts

User accounts specify who can use the server's resources and how they can use them. With Microsoft Windows NT, for example, you can determine the days and hours a user can access the network and what actions he or she can perform.

Types of Accounts

When you install SBS, it creates four user accounts:

- The Guest account for users who only occasionally connect to the network
- The Administrator account for the person who manages the network
- The IUSR_Server account for an Internet guest account
- The IWAM_Server account for someone to launch IIS Process Account applications

Note

An explanation of the IUSR_Server and the IWAM_Server accounts is beyond the scope of this book. For more information on these accounts, see *Microsoft BackOffice Small Business Server 4.5 Resource Kit* published by Microsoft Press.

The person who installs SBS or Windows NT can log on to the network because he or she is assigned the Administrator user account. To allow other users to access the network, you have to create user accounts for them.

A wide range of activities and resources can be used on the network. Each user account needs to specify the activities and resources to which the user has access. Rather than assign individual permissions to each user, Windows defines a number of groups. Each group is assigned certain permissions. When you create a user account, you have to specify to which group the user belongs to declare their permission to use the network.

There are two types of groups—global and local.

A *global group* includes users from the same domain, and they can be granted permissions on the domain's servers and workstations. A *local group* can be granted permissions for only the computer on which it was created.

Chapter 16: Setting Up Clients on Microsoft BackOffice Small Business Server

A local group, however, can be defined to include all of the members of a global group. Windows NT has three default global groups and eight default local groups.

The default global groups are as follows:

- Domain Users
- Domain Guests
- Domain Admins

The default local groups are as follows:

- Guests
- Print Operators
- Replicator
- Server Operators
- Users
- Backup Operators
- Administrators
- Account Operators

By default, anyone assigned to the local group Guests is also part of the global group Domain Guests. The global group Domain Users contains all users in the local group Users, and the global group Domain Admins contains all users in the local group Administrators.

When you use SBS to create a user account, you'll be asked whether you want to assign the user full rights to the network. If you select yes, the user is placed in the global groups Domain Admins and Domain Users. If you select no, the user is assigned only to Domain Users.

Creating a User Account

If you're using SBS, you can create a user account from the SBS Console and the User Account Wizard. The wizard takes you through a number of dialog boxes that perform the following functions:

- Create the user account
- Determine the scope of the user's access
- Set the user's right to share printer, modems, and faxes
- Create a folder on the server for the user's files
- Create a floppy disk with a setup program for configuring the user's workstation

Part 3: Setting Up Computers on a Network

To see how easy setting up a user account for a client/server network is, let's go through the process of creating a user account.

1. Start by clicking Start and then SBS Console.
2. Click Small Business Server To Do List.
3. When the list appears, as shown in Figure 16-1, click Add A User to begin the User Account Wizard, which will help you add a user account in three steps:

    - **Create A User Account** lets you enter name and address information about the user and specify the password.

    - **Give Access To Network Resources** lets you assign the user permissions to access server resources.

    - **Set Up A User's Computer** lets you configure the user's computer to access the shared resources.

Figure 16-1
Use the To Do List to perform administrative tasks in SBS.

4. Click Next to display the User Account Information options.
5. Type the user's name, account name, and an optional description, and click Next.

    You now have the choice to specify the user's password yourself or to have the wizard generate a random password.

Chapter 16: Setting Up Clients on Microsoft BackOffice Small Business Server

6. Choose one of the options, and click Next.

    If you choose to let the wizard generate the password, it'll appear in place of the text boxes. Make a note of the password so you can tell it to the user.

7. Type and retype the password to confirm it.

8. Choose whether to allow the user to change the password at any time.

    If you select this option, the user must change the password the first time he or she logs on to the network.

9. Click Next.

10. Type the company information requested by the wizard, and click Next.

11. Type the name and address information requested, and then click Next.

12. Type the telephone and fax number information requested, and click Next.

    If you have created e-mail distribution lists on your network, you can now assign the user to one or more lists, as shown in Figure 16-2.

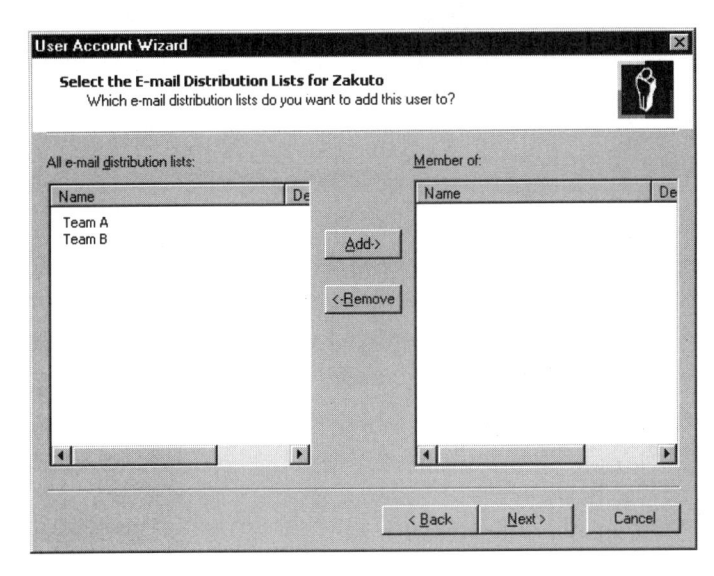

Figure 16-2
Assign the user to a distribution list through the User Account Wizard.

Part 3: Setting Up Computers on a Network

13. Select a list to which you want to assign the user, and click Add. Repeat the process for other lists to which you want to add the user, and click Next.

14. Click Finish to create the user account.

The next portion of the wizard lets you specify the permissions granted to the user to share server resources. Continue with these steps:

1. Click Next to display the options shown in Figure 16-3, which determine the shared folders the user can access.

    By default, the user is granted full access to every shared folder but is granted only read access to the folders of other users.

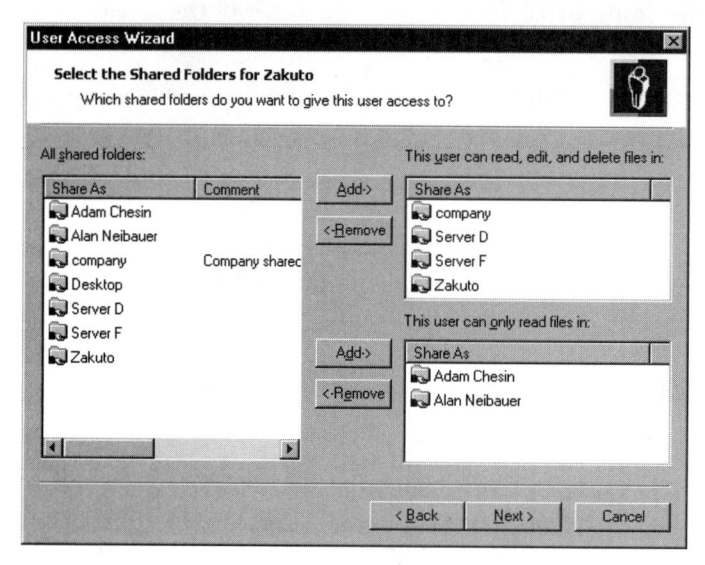

Figure 16-3
Set user permission to access shared folders through the User Access Wizard.

2. Add or remove folders from the two lists on the right, and click Next.

3. In the next dialog box, specify which shared printers you want the user to access, and then click Next.

4. Specify which shared fax modems you want the user to access, and click Next.

Chapter 16: Setting Up Clients on Microsoft BackOffice Small Business Server

5. In the next dialog box, choose whether you want the user to access the Internet over the server's modem or to have the ability to dial in to the server remotely, and click Next.

6. Select Yes if you want the user to have administrative privileges to the server, and then click Next.

7. Click Finish to complete that portion of the wizard, and click OK.

The final portion of the wizard creates a floppy disk with which the user can set up the workstation. The disk will configure the workstation to communicate with the server and install the necessary applications. You can skip this portion if you want to set up the workstation manually or if you want to set it up at a later time.

1. Click Next to begin the client setup portion of the wizard.

2. Choose whether you're setting up a new workstation or adding a user to a workstation that has already been set up for another user, and click Next.

3. The wizard will suggest a computer name. If the computer already has a name, type it in place of the suggested name, and click Next.

4. Specify the operating system installed on the client workstations—either Microsoft Windows 95/98 or Windows NT Workstation—and then click Next.

    You'll see the applications that can be installed on the client, as shown in Figure 16-4.

5. Select the first option button if you don't want to install any applications on the workstation at this time. You can always add applications from the server at a later time. If you want to install applications, choose the second option and select the applications from the list. Click Next.

6. Insert a blank formatted disk into the floppy drive, and click Next.

    The wizard will create a series of programs on the floppy disk that the user can run to set up his or her computer and install the selected applications from the server.

7. Click Finish.

Part 3: Setting Up Computers on a Network

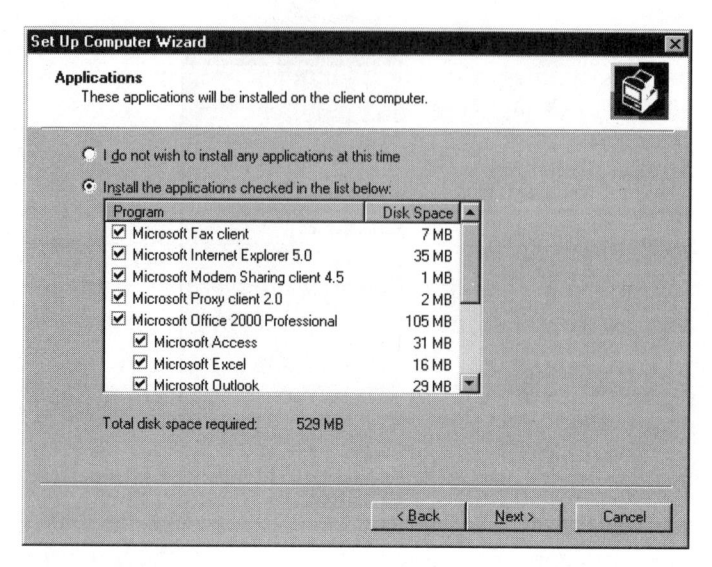

Figure 16-4

Select applications to install for the client.

Setting up the client computer will be covered in *"Configuring Client Computers" on page 255.*

User Manager For Domains

The User Account Wizard is just one way to set up a user account. You can also create an account from the User Manager For Domains program. In fact, you should be familiar with User Manager For Domains because it's the program you would use to change a user's account information.

> **Note**
>
> To use User Manager For Domains, you must be logged on as the Administrator.

1. Click Start, point to Programs and then Administrative Tools (Common), and click User Manager For Domains.
2. If you want to modify a user's account, double-click the user's name in the User Manager For Domains window. To add new users, choose New User from the User menu to open the User Properties dialog box shown in Figure 16-5.
3. Type the user's name and password information.

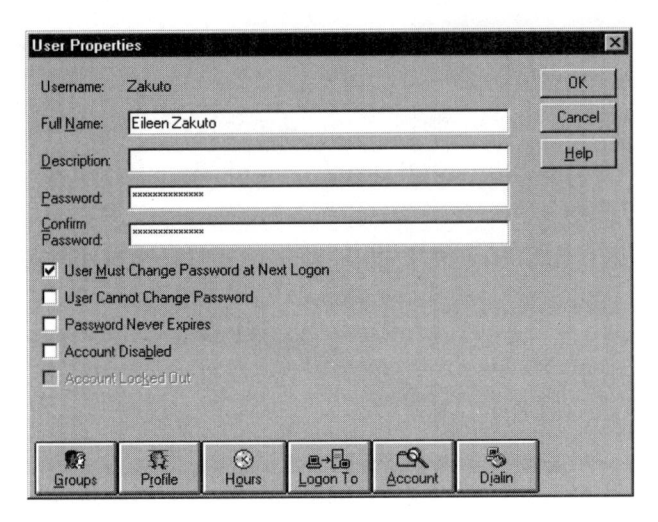

Chapter 16: Setting Up Clients on Microsoft BackOffice Small Business Server

Figure 16-5
Create a new user account in User Manager For Domains.

4. Select which of the following options you wish to enable for the user account, and click OK.

   - **User Must Change Password At Next Logon.** The user must choose a new password the first time he or she connects. This provides some extra security if the originally assigned password has been made known to other users or administrators.

   - **User Cannot Change Password.** The user is forced to keep the password you assign.

   - **Password Never Expires.** Windows NT can be configured so that passwords expire at a certain time. This is a security feature to ensure that passwords that might have been obtained by unauthorized persons will become invalid at a certain time. Choose this option if you don't want a password to expire.

   - **Account Disabled.** You can temporarily keep a user from logging on to the network. If an employee is out for an extended time, this option prevents another person from logging on to the network through the employee's workstation.

   - **Account Locked Out.** Windows NT can be set to lock an account if a number of unsuccessful attempts are made to access the network. This prevents a hacker from continually trying to log on by trying various passwords. This check box will be selected if the account is locked out so the administrator can unlock the account.

Part 3: Setting Up Computers on a Network

Use the buttons at the bottom of the User Properties dialog box to configure the other aspects of the accounts, as follows:

- **Groups.** Assign the user to and remove him or her from groups.
- **Profile.** Create a user profile and specify a home directory on the server for the user.
- **Hours.** Specify the times when the user is authorized to access the network. The default setting is no limitation.
- **Logon To.** Determine which workstations the user can log on to. By default, a user can log on to all workstations.
- **Account.** Set the expiration date of the account, if any.
- **Dialin.** Allow the user access to the server by dialing in. You can also determine whether the server will call the user back after an attempted log in to confirm the telephone number.

Roaming Profiles

As you learned in Chapter 14, a profile describes the environment in which the user works in Windows, which can include the items on the desktop. In Windows 95/98, the profile is always local—it's stored on the user's computer.

A person who uses Windows NT as the operating system can also maintain a profile on the server, a *roaming profile*. The user can then log on to the server from any Windows NT workstation to access his or her own desktop settings.

While users have the right to modify their roaming profiles, the network administrator can create mandatory roaming profiles that users can't change. In some cases, a mandatory roaming profile is assigned to a group of users to control their access to the server.

The administrator can also create a logon script as part of a user's profile. A *logon script* is a series of commands called a batch file that's run when the user logs on to the server. Logon scripts can connect a user to a specific folder, assign a shared printer to the user's printer port, or even synchronize the user's clock with the server's clock.

Creating roaming profiles and logon scripts are advanced tasks.

Chapter 16: Setting Up Clients on Microsoft BackOffice Small Business Server

Configuring Client Computers

In Chapter 13, you learned how to set up workstations to communicate with the network. On a client/server network, however, workstations also need software to use server resources, such as Proxy Server for sharing Internet access and Fax Service for sharing a fax modem. If you're using SBS, you can set up a workstation and install software using the floppy disk produced when you created a user account with SBS Console. The disk performs these steps:

- Determines and configures, if necessary, an IP address
- Installs the Proxy client to share the server's Internet connection
- Installs the Fax client to share the server's fax modem
- Installs Modem Sharing for access to the server's modem
- Installs Microsoft Internet Explorer
- Installs Microsoft Office applications

To use the floppy disk, insert the floppy disk in a client's workstation and run the setup program. With Windows 95/98, you don't have to be connected to the network when you run setup. A dialog box appears showing the user and computer name that'll be assigned to the workstation. If the names don't match those for the workstation you're on, you're using the wrong setup disk—click Cancel. Otherwise, click Begin to start the setup process. Setup configures the workstation to connect to the network and then restarts the computer.

Tip

Creating a new account through User Manager For Domains creates a Microsoft Exchange mailbox. Refer to Chapter 20 for more information on using Microsoft Exchange.

Once the computer restarts, it's able to connect to the server. The setup program continues by installing the applications that were selected when the user account was created.

If you selected not to install the applications when creating the user account, you can install them at any time. If you used the floppy disk to configure the workstation, you'll see a Microsoft BackOffice Small Business Server option on the Install/Uninstall tab of Control Panel's Add/Remove Programs applet. See Figure 16-6. You can double-click that option to select which client programs should be installed.

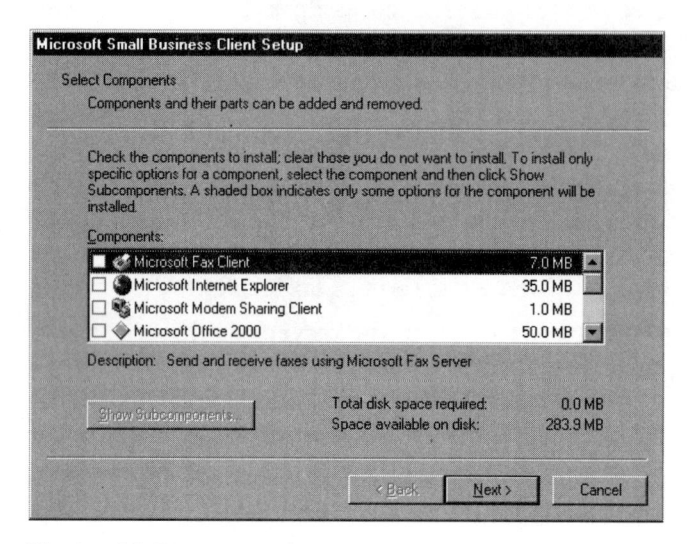

Figure 16-6

Choose applications to install on a client workstation in Control Panel.

You can also install client applications by connecting the workstation to the server and accessing the client setup programs on the server's hard disk. Most of the client software needed by workstations is stored in the server's \clientapps\ms folder. Connect to the server from the workstations, navigate to the folder, and then run the setup program from the appropriate subfolder:

- **Fax.** The fax client to share the server's fax modem
- **ModemShr.** The modem sharing client to share the server's modem
- **Office.** The Microsoft Office applications
- **SBSutil.** The programs used when installing Microsoft Outlook 2000
- **Winntsp4.** Windows NT Service Pack 4

To install the Proxy Server client for sharing the server's Internet account, run the setup program in the \mspclnt folder.

In the next chapter, I'll give more details on how to share files and programs on the network.

Part 4

Running Your Office on a Network

17	Learning to Share
18	Printing Anywhere on the Network
19	Communicating Over a Peer-to-Peer Network
20	Client/Server Communications with Exchange Server
21	Sharing Modems and Internet Accounts
22	Setting Up Servers for an Office Intranet Personal Web Server
23	Networking for Road Warriors Dialing In to Your ISP
24	Sharing Modems and Internet Accounts

Chapter 17

Learning to Share

One of the main advantages of networking is that you have the ability to share files, but sharing doesn't come automatically. You not only have to turn on the file sharing service when you configure your network, but you also have to specify which resources you want to share with other users. In this chapter, you'll learn how to share disks, folders, and files.

Turning On File Sharing

Before you can activate file and printer sharing, you must install the Microsoft Windows service that allows sharing. You probably installed this service along with your network drivers and software, as described in Chapter 13, but just in case you didn't, here's how to do it.

In Microsoft Windows 95 and Microsoft Windows 98, follow the steps on the next page.

Note

To share resources in Microsoft Windows 2000 Professional, see "Sharing with Microsoft Windows 2000 Professional" on page 284.

1. On the Start menu, point to Settings, and click Control Panel.
2. Double-click the Network icon to open the Network dialog box.
   In the list of network components that are installed, look for File And Printer Sharing For Microsoft Networks. If it's already listed, you can skip the rest of these steps. If the service isn't installed, continue with these steps:
3. In the Network dialog box, click Add.
4. In the Select Network Component Type dialog box, click Service.
5. Click Add.
6. In the Select Network Service dialog box, click File And Printer Sharing For Microsoft Networks.
7. Click OK.
8. Click OK again to close the Network dialog box.
9. When you're asked whether you want to restart your computer, click Yes.

Now that the service is installed, you're ready to turn on file and printer sharing.

1. On the Start menu, point to Settings, and click Control Panel.
2. Double-click the Network icon to open the Network dialog box.
3. Click the File And Printer Sharing button to open the File And Print Sharing dialog box.
4. Select both check boxes to allow access to your files and access to your printers.
5. Click OK.
6. Click OK again to close the Network dialog box.

Sharing and Accessing Network Resources

Installing the hardware and configuring Windows for sharing doesn't make the information on your computer instantly available to everyone. Before someone else can access a folder on your hard disk, you must first specify that the folder can be shared.

Chapter 17: Learning to Share

> **Note**
>
> Resources that are shared are called *shares*.

Windows organizes folders and files in the following hierarchical manner:

- Disks contain folders.
- Folders contain subfolders (and some files as well).
- Subfolders contain files.

When you specify what can be shared on a network, everything within it is also shared. For example, if you allow a hard disk drive to be shared, all folders and files on that hard disk are shared as well. If you allow only a folder to be shared rather than the whole hard disk, all subfolders and files within that folder can be shared, but not other folders on that hard disk. So if you do want everything in your hard disk drive to be available to the network, turn on sharing for your hard disk drive. You can also share a floppy disk, a CD, or a Zip disk. When you share a disk, an icon for its drive appears in the Network Neighborhood window for all users to see when they double-click the Network Neighborhood icon on their desktops. Once you share a disk, you don't have to turn on sharing for any of the individual folders contained on that disk—they're automatically shared across the network.

> **Note**
>
> A shared resource won't be available if the workstation containing it is turned off or not attached to the network. To provide full-time access to disks and CDs, see "Network-Attached Storage" on page 163.

Even though a folder on a shared disk is available to network users, it won't appear as a separate icon in Network Neighborhood unless you specifically share that particular folder and not just the disk on which the folder resides. If you want the folder to be seen on Network Neighborhood so that it can be easily accessed by network users, turn on sharing for the folder even if you've already turned on sharing for the disk.

Types of Access Controls

Two types of sharing are available—share-level access and user-level access.

On a peer-to-peer network, you can use only share-level access. This means that you control access by specifying how each resource can be shared and by providing a password if desired. Anyone with the password, however, can access the resource regardless of who they are or what computer they are using.

Share-level access has three levels of sharing:

- **Read-Only.** Users can open files in the shared folders and copy them to their own computers, but they can't change, delete, or add files.
- **Full.** Users can do anything to shared disks or folders.
- **Depends On Password.** The password a user types determines the level of sharing—full or read-only—granted to the user.

If you specify read-only access or full access to a disk or folder, a password is optional. You can do without one and allow all members of your staff to access a resource on your computer at whatever level of sharing you've specified for that resource. Or you can create a password and limit access—again, at the level of sharing you've specified—to staff members to whom you've given the password.

With the Depends On Password option, you can selectively grant read-only or full access to members of your staff. You create two passwords: a read-only password and a full password. Users to whom you give the read-only password can read and copy your files, but they can't change them, delete them, or add new ones. Users with the full password can do anything they want to your files.

When you're connected to a client/server network, you can choose between share-level and user-level access. With user-level access, you grant permissions to specific users or groups of users. For example, you can grant John permission to access your hard disk drive, but not Jill. All John has to do is log on to the network with his user name and password to be able to access your hard disk drive.

User-level access also has three levels of sharing: Read Only, Full, and Custom. The Custom level lets you specify which of the following permissions you want to grant a specific user:

- Read Files
- Write Files
- Create Files And Folders
- Delete Files
- Change File Attributes
- List Files
- Change Access Control

You can give Joan permission to read and write files on your disk but not to delete files. You can give Jim permission to delete files but not create new folders.

To select the type of access you want to use, follow these steps:

1. Open Network in Control Panel.
2. Click the Access Control tab.
3. Select either Share-Level Access Control or User-Level Access Control.
4. If you selected User-Level Access Control, you have to type the name of the server domain in which the user directory is stored.
5. Click OK.
6. Click Yes if you're asked to restart your computer.

Share-Level Access

Let's look at setting up share-level access first. Remember, you can choose share-level access on either a peer-to-peer or client/server network.

Sharing Drives

To turn on sharing for an entire drive and give only certain people access to it, follow these steps:

1. Double-click My Computer on the Windows desktop.
2. Right-click the drive that you want to share.
3. Select Sharing from the shortcut menu to open the Properties dialog box shown in Figure 17-1.

Part 4: Running Your Office on a Network

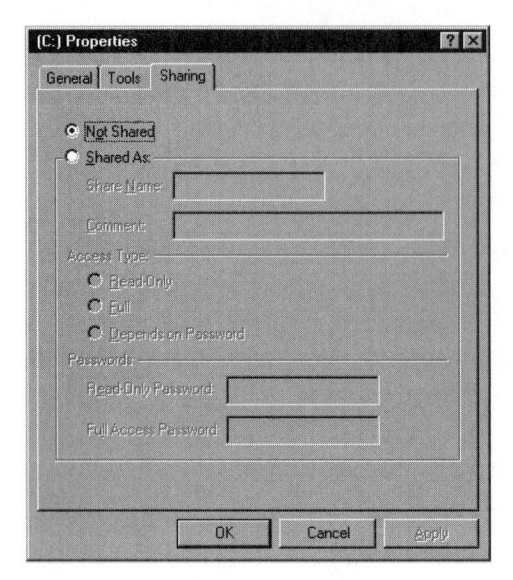

Figure 17-1
The Properties dialog box allows you to turn on sharing for a resource and limit access to it by password.

4. Click Shared As.

    Windows places a default name in the Share Name text box, which is usually the same letter as the drive.

5. Leave the Share Name as it is or change it to better identify the drive, as in *Alan's disk*.

    The Share Name is what appears when network users access your computer.

6. In the Comment text box, you can type an optional description of the drive.

7. Click one of the three access types—Read-Only, Full, or Depends On Password.

8. Type an optional password for Read-Only, Full Access, or both if you want the level of access to be determined by the password that the person types.

9. Click OK.

10. If you specified one or two passwords, retype each in the Confirm Passwords dialog box, and then click OK.

Chapter 17: Learning to Share

A cradling hand now appears on the icon for the shared drive, indicating that the drive is shared:

(C:)

When another member of your staff is connected to your computer and double-clicks the Network Neighborhood icon on the Windows desktop, an icon for your disk appears in the Network Neighborhood window the staff member sees. If you've granted full access without a password, that staff member can access your disk just as if it were a local hard disk rather than a disk in your computer.

> **Caution**
>
> If you turn on sharing for a floppy disk or a removable disk, such as a Zip disk, the drive is actually shared rather than a particular disk. Turning on sharing for a floppy disk, for example, means that any floppy disk in the drive is shared. You might want to think twice about sharing removable drives if some of your disks contain sensitive information.

More on Passwords

If you want to make a resource, such as a shared drive or folder, available to everyone on a network, you can leave the password for the resource blank. If you do enter a password, however, make sure you remember it. Let's say you're at a computer other than your own and you want to access your own files across the network. Your system won't know that it's you at the computer and will require the same password it requires from the computer's primary user.

If you do forget the password that you've assigned to a shared resource, you can easily change it as long as you log on to your own computer. Unlike some passwords, you can change a sharing password without knowing the current one. To change a password, right-click the shared disk or folder and choose Properties from the shortcut menu. Type the new password in place of the old one and click OK. You'll have to reenter the new password to confirm it.

> **Tip**
>
> To erase a password so that a shared disk or folder is no longer password-protected, just delete the asterisks in the password text boxes.

Sharing Folders

If you don't want to allow complete access to your disk, you can turn on sharing for only certain folders and not for the entire disk.

To turn on sharing for a folder, follow these steps:

1. Double-click My Computer on the Windows desktop.
2. Double-click the disk containing the folder you want to share.
3. Right-click the folder that you want to share.
   You might have to navigate through folders to display the subfolder you want to share.
4. Select Sharing from the shortcut menu to open the Properties dialog box.
5. Click Shared As.
6. Accept the default share name or type a new one.
7. Type an optional comment.
8. Choose an access type.
9. Type an optional password for Read-Only, Full Access, or both.
10. Click OK.
11. If you specified one or two passwords, retype each to confirm in the Confirm Passwords dialog box and click OK.

You can also turn on sharing from any window that displays the folder, such as Windows Explorer, the Find dialog box, or the File Save or File Open dialog box in an application such as Microsoft Word. To turn on sharing, right-click the folder icon, select Sharing from the shortcut menu, and follow steps 5 through 11 in the previous procedure.

> **Tip**
>
> You can't turn on sharing for the My Documents folder from the Windows desktop. If you want to share that folder, open My Computer, double-click the disk on which you've installed Windows, right-click the My Documents folder, and choose Sharing from the shortcut menu.

Chapter 17: Learning to Share

User-Level Access

When you select user-level access control, you have to turn on file sharing for the resource you want to share, such as a drive or a folder, and then designate who is allowed to access the resource and their permissions.

Sharing Drives and Folders

To grant permissions to use a drive or folder, follow these steps:

1. Double-click My Computer on the Windows desktop.
2. Right-click the drive or folder that you want to share.
3. Select Sharing from the shortcut menu to open the Sharing tab of the Properties dialog box.
4. Click the Add button to open the Add Users dialog box, shown in Figure 17-2.

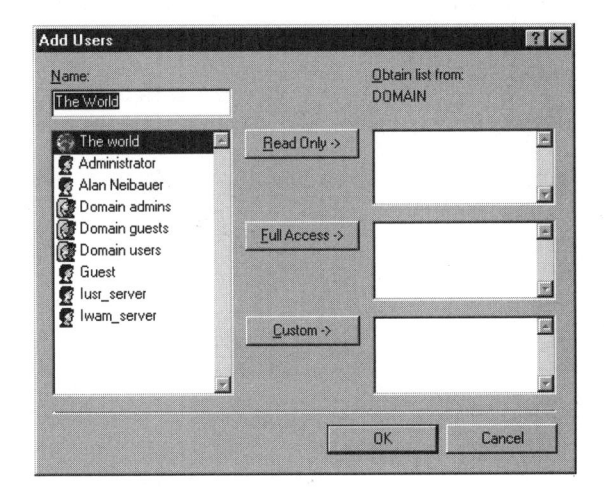

Figure 17-2
Grant user-level access permissions in the Add Users dialog box.

5. Select a user or group from the list. The group The World represents every network user.
6. Click Read Only, Full Access, or Custom.
7. Click OK. If you selected Custom, the Change Access Rights dialog box appears. (See Figure 17-3.)
8. Specify the permissions you want to allow the user, and click OK.

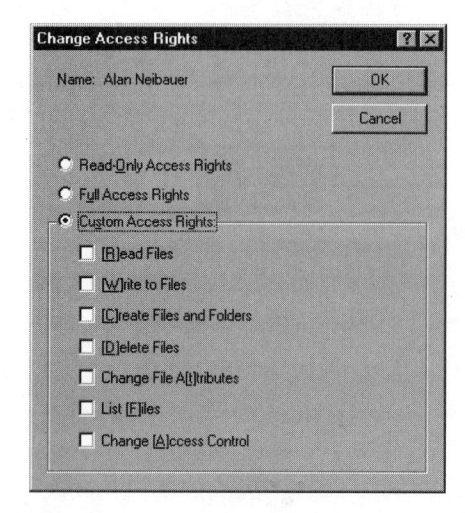

Figure 17-3

Give specific access permissions to a user in the Change Access Rights dialog box.

A list of users and their permissions appears in the Sharing tab. To change permissions, select the user and click Edit.

It only makes sense to grant rights to individuals or groups if you've removed full access from The World. Everyone is a member of The World and would therefore have complete access to the folder regardless of what other group or individual status you might give them. To limit access to the folder for specific users or groups of users, first select The World and do one of the following:

- Assign a low level of access (such as Read-Only Access Rights) to The World, suitable for everyone who has access to the network, and then selectively assign greater access levels to specific individuals or groups.
- Click the Remove button (on the Sharing tab) to remove The World, removing all access from the network except for those users you specifically add.

Accessing Shared Disks and Folders

Once disks and folders are shared, network users can access them in much the same way as they access disks and folders on their own computers. The trick is for them to locate the disk or folder on the remote computer.

Chapter 17: Learning to Share

> **Note**
>
> A *remote computer* is a computer on the network other than the one you're using.

You can always access remote computers using Network Neighborhood, so let's start there.

1. Double-click Network Neighborhood on your Windows desktop.
   Remember, it might take a few minutes after you turn on your computer for it to recognize the remote computers on the network. You'll see icons representing all the computers on your network, as well as an icon for the Entire Network.

> **Note**
>
> Clicking the Entire Network icon lets you access other workgroups and servers that might be connected to your network.

2. Double-click the icon for the computer you want to access.
   You'll see icons representing shared drives and printers as well as folders that you've shared.
3. Double-click the drive or folder you want to access.

Another way to access shared drives is from Windows Explorer or any Windows file management dialog box, such as the File Open dialog box in Word. Let's look at Windows Explorer.

1. On the Start menu, point to Programs, and click Windows Explorer.
2. Click the plus sign next to Network Neighborhood in the list of folders.
3. Click the plus sign next to the remote computer you want to access.
4. If the drive in the computer is shared, click the plus sign next to the drive to display its contents. You can then access any of the files as if they were on your computer.

> **Note**
>
> The Network Neighborhood icon appears in the Open and Save dialog boxes of most Windows programs that let you access disks and folders. You can always use it to access remote computers.

Once you access a shared folder in a remote computer, you can use the files in that folder just as if you were on that computer, but only at the level of sharing you've been granted. If you have read-only access, you'll be able only to open or copy files from the shared folder. You won't be able to change or delete files or add new files to the folder. If you attempt to do so, you'll see the following message:

Error Deleting File
Cannot remove folder Backup: Access is denied.
Make sure the disk is not full or write-protected and that the file is not currently in use.
[OK]

Accessing Resources with the Run and Find Commands

While Network Neighborhood and Windows Explorer are the most common ways to access a remote computer, Windows offers two other options: the Run and Find commands on the Start menu.

If you know the name of the remote computer, you can access a shared resource on it by choosing the Run command from the Start menu. This opens the Run dialog box.

To use a resource on a remote computer, you must enter the path to the resource by typing the *universal naming convention* (UNC) pathname. You start the UNC pathname with two backslashes (\\) followed by the name of the computer, as in *Joe*. Press Enter or click OK to open a window showing the shared resources on that computer. If you know the name of the specific drive and folder you're looking for on the remote computer, you can open it directly by adding its resource name to the pathname, as in *Joe\C\Budget*.

You can also search for a computer on the network using the Find command from the Start menu. Just follow these steps:

1. On the Start menu, point to Find, and click Computer.
2. In the Find Computer dialog box, type the remote computer's name, and press Enter or click Find Now.
3. When the computer is located and listed in the Find dialog box, double-click its icon to access its shared resources.

Accessing Resources with Passwords

When a resource requires a password in order to be shared, you must enter the password before you can open the disk or folder—or at least you must enter it the first time you try to access the resource. As you'll see, there's a way to save the password so that you don't have to type it each time you open a password-protected disk or folder.

When you first try to access a resource, you'll see the Enter Network Password dialog box. Before you type the password and click OK, you can select the check box labeled Save This Password In Your Password List. Windows maintains this password list in a file whose name is your user name plus the extension .pwl, as in alan.pwl. If you select this check box, the name of the shared resource and the password will be saved in your .pwl file. The next time you access the same disk or folder, Windows locates the password so that you don't have to type it again.

> **Caution**
>
> Don't select the check box if you want to prevent other network users from accessing shared resources with your password.

When the Enter Network Password dialog box opens, type your password and click OK. If the password you've typed is incorrect, a message appears telling you so. Click OK to clear the message, and then retype the correct password.

Making Sharing Easier

Navigating through Network Neighborhood to locate a folder or file can be time consuming. Fortunately Windows offers a number of ways to make network life easier.

Creating a Desktop Shortcut

The easiest way to access a remote disk, folder, or file is to add a shortcut for it to your Windows desktop, as shown here:

1. Use Network Neighborhood to locate the drive, folder, or file on the remote computer.
2. Right-click the drive, folder, or file and hold down the right mouse button while you drag the icon to your desktop.

Tip

To create a shortcut to the remote computer itself, drag the remote computer icon to your desktop.

3. Release the mouse button and select Create Shortcut(s) Here from the shortcut menu.

Windows 98 also allows you to drag the shortcut icon you placed on your desktop to the taskbar so that you can access it with a single click.

Adding Shared Resources to Favorites

If you're using Windows 98 (or Windows 95 with version 4 or later of Microsoft Internet Explorer), you can store frequently used folders and files in a Favorites folder, which is quickly accessible from the Start menu.

You'll also find a Favorites menu item in Windows Explorer, My Computer, Network Neighborhood, and other dialog boxes in Windows that let you manage files. After you've added a shortcut to a folder or file to your Favorites list, you can open Favorites and click the shortcut to open the folder or file.

To add a resource to the Favorites list, follow these steps:

1. Double-click the Network Neighborhood icon on the desktop and locate the folder or file in the Network Neighborhood window.
2. Double-click the folder or file so that its path appears in the Address field in the Address toolbar.
3. From the Favorites menu, choose Add To Favorites to open the Add Favorite dialog box.

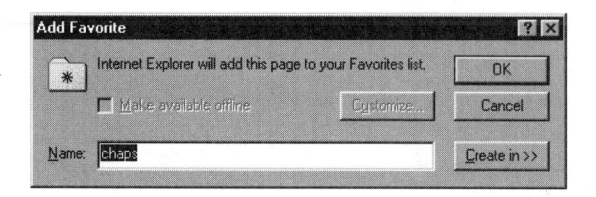

4. Click OK. You can also click the Create In button if you want to add the item to a folder within Favorites or to create a new subfolder of Favorites.

Mapping Network Drives and Folders

Another way to gain easy access to a drive on a remote computer is to assign it a drive letter on your own machine. This is called *mapping* the drive.

For example, suppose you have the following drives on your computer:

- A floppy disk drive, designated as A
- The hard disk drive, designated as C
- A CD or DVD drive, designated as D

If you frequently access a hard disk, CD, or other drive on a remote computer, you can map it so that it appears as drive E or F on your computer. Even better, you can map a specific folder on a remote computer to a drive letter, as long as the folder has been enabled for sharing. Let's say you often access a folder named Budget on a remote computer. You can map the folder so that it shows up in My Computer as drive F on your computer.

To map a disk or folder, follow these steps:

1. Double-click the Network Neighborhood icon on the desktop and double-click the icon for the remote computer in the Network Neighborhood window.

    You'll see icons for each of the disks and folders on the remote computer that have been shared.

2. Right-click the icon for the resource you want to map, and then choose Map Network Drive from the shortcut menu to see the Map Network Drive dialog box.

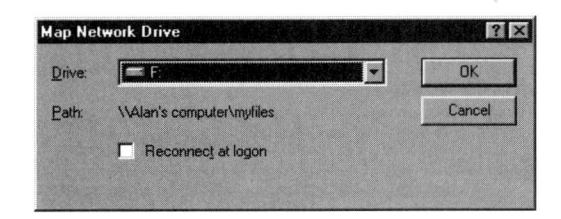

3. If you want to use a drive letter other than the one suggested, select it from the Drive list.

4. Select the Reconnect At Logon check box if you want Windows to map this resource every time you start your computer.

5. Click OK.

A window opens showing the contents of the drive or folder; the address box in the Address toolbar shows that the resource is now mapped to a drive on your computer.

If you close the window and open My Computer, you'll see the shared resource listed as a drive. Just double-click the icon as you would any actual disk drive to access its contents on the remote computer.

When you select Reconnect At Logon, Windows browses the network looking for the mapped disk or folder each time you start your computer. If the remote computer isn't turned on, Windows starts normally but doesn't map the shared resource. You'll have to remap it after the remote computer joins the network.

If you don't select Reconnect At Logon, the mapping is disconnected when you turn off your computer or restart Windows. You'll have to repeat the procedure above to map the drive again.

Browsing for mapped resources takes some time, and it'll slow down the logon process, so if you don't need to map the resource every time you use your computer, don't select the Reconnect At Logon option.

To speed up the process of mapping resources, use the Quick Logon feature so that Windows doesn't need to browse the network when your computer starts. When the Quick Logon feature is enabled, Windows displays the icons for mapped resources in Network Neighborhood, My Computer, and Windows Explorer without checking to see whether the resource is really available. Windows waits until you first try to use the resource before actually connecting to it. To enable the Quick Logon feature, follow these steps:

1. On the Start menu, point to Settings, and click Control Panel.

2. In the Control Panel window, double-click the Network icon to open the Network dialog box.

3. In the list of installed network components, select Client For Microsoft Networks.

4. Click Properties to open the Client For Microsoft Networks Properties dialog box shown in Figure 17-4.

Figure 17-4
You can change logon options in the Client For Microsoft Networks Properties dialog box.

5. Click Quick Logon.

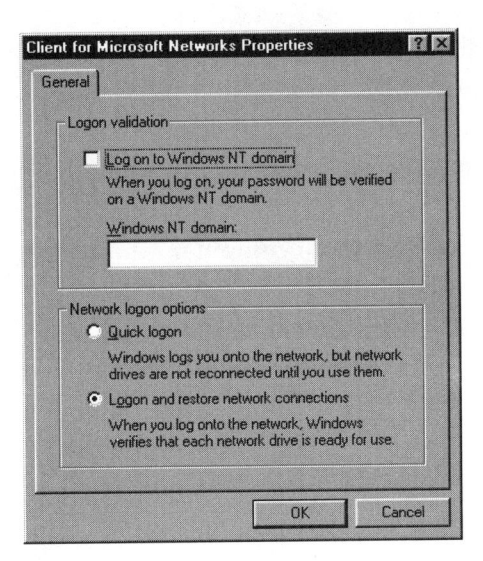

    The other option, Logon And Restore Network Connections, maps and connects to shared resources you've mapped every time Windows starts.

6. Click OK to close the Client For Microsoft Networks Properties dialog box.

7. Click OK to close the Network dialog box.

Working with Remote Files

After you've accessed a disk or folder on a remote computer, you can start working with its files in Network Neighborhood, My Computer, or Windows Explorer. Here's how to access a file with Network Neighborhood or My Computer:

1. Double-click the Network Neighborhood icon on the desktop, or double-click My Computer if the drive on the remote computer has been mapped.

2. Double-click the icon for the computer you want to access.

3. Double-click the drive or folder you want to open.

4. Select the file so you can work with it.

To access the file with Windows Explorer, follow these steps:

1. On the Start menu, point to Programs and click Windows Explorer.
2. Click the plus sign next to Network Neighborhood in the Folders list on the left.
3. Click the plus sign next to the remote computer you want to access.
4. Click the plus sign next to the drive you want to access on the remote computer.
5. Click the folder containing the file for which you're looking. If the folder contains subfolders, click the plus sign next to the folder to display its contents, and then select the subfolder containing the file.

After you've accessed a file, you can do anything with it that your level of sharing allows. If you have read-only access to the folder, you can open the file or copy it to another location, but you can't do anything else to it. If you have full access, you can also change, delete, or move the file.

Let's take a closer look at how to work with files on remote computers.

Opening Remote Files from Within Programs

On the network, you can open a file on a remote computer just as you would open it on your own computer. In Windows 95, you can locate the file in My Computer, Network Neighborhood, or Windows Explorer, and open it by double-clicking its icon.

You can also open files from within Windows applications, such as the programs in Microsoft Office. Because Network Neighborhood is an integrated part of the Windows file system, it shows up in all the lists you see whenever you try to access files. This means that you can treat a remote computer as you would any disk drive—locate it in the program's Open dialog box, choose the drive and the folder, and then choose the document you want to access.

For example, suppose you're working in Word and you need to open a file in the My Documents folder of a remote computer. Here's how you'd do it:

1. From the File menu, choose Open to display the Open dialog box.

2. In the Look In drop-down list, select Network Neighborhood.

   A list of computers on the network appears in the Open dialog box.

3. Double-click the icon for the computer whose disk contains the file you want.

   A list of shared resources on the remote computer appears in the Open dialog box.

4. Double-click the hard disk drive that contains Windows on the remote computer. It's usually the C drive.

5. Double-click My Documents.

6. Double-click the file you want to open.

Saving Remote Files from Within Programs

Saving a remote file from within a Windows application is even easier than opening it, as long as you have full access privileges. If you've made changes to an existing remote file, save it just as you would any other document by clicking the Save button on the program's Standard toolbar or by choosing Save from the program's File menu.

You can also use the Save As command on the program's File menu to save the document to another location or with a new file name. When the Save As dialog box opens, it shows the folder from which you opened the document. Choose another location from the Save In list in the Save As dialog box, such as a folder either on your own computer or on any other computer on the network.

If you're working on a new document and want to save it on a remote computer, use the Save In list in the Save As dialog box to select Network Neighborhood, choose the remote computer, and then select the destination folder.

Saving a Read-Only File   If you've made changes to a file that you opened from a read-only folder, you can't save it to the same location. If you try to do so, you'll see a message like this:

![Microsoft Word dialog box: Cannot save '\\Alan's computer\myfiles\Budget.doc'. The folder is marked as 'Read Only'. OK]

This isn't to say that you can't make changes to the file; you just can't replace the existing version in the shared folder with your edited version. (Remember that when a folder has been designated as read-only, you can't change its contents.) To save your changes, you must use the Save As command and save the file as a new document in a folder to which you have full access. The folder can be on your own hard disk or on a disk in a remote computer.

To save a file to a remote computer, navigate to the computer using Network Neighborhood in the program's Save As dialog box, using these steps:

1. From the File menu of the program, choose Save As to display the Save As dialog box.

Note

In some Windows programs, clicking Save when a file is read-only opens the Save As dialog box.

2. In the Save In drop-down list, choose Network Neighborhood.
   A list of computers on the network appears in the Save As dialog box.
3. Double-click the icon for the remote computer to which you want to save the file to see a list of its shared resources.
4. Double-click the disk drive.
5. Double-click the folder in which you want to save the file.
6. Click Save.

Avoiding Double Trouble

It doesn't make sense for two people to try to work on the same file at the same time. The result can be lost work and confusion.

Suppose, for example, that you and your partner want to work on the budget using two different computers. Here's what might happen:

1. You and your partner both open the document and see that Office Refreshments is set at $300 per month.
2. You change the category to $200.
3. Your partner changes the category to $500.

4. You save the document.

    The $200 amount for Office Refreshments is recorded on the disk.

5. Your partner saves the document after you do. The $500 figure is recorded on the disk, and your changes to the budget are lost!

If your partner had saved the document before you did, your $200 choice would have prevailed.

To avoid such situations, only one person at a time should work on a document in a folder to which full access has been granted. What happens, however, when one person opens a document that's already being used by another person depends on the version of Windows and the program you're both using.

For example, you might receive a message that the document you're trying to open is already in use and you might get the option to open it in read-only mode. Although this will allow you to make changes to the document, you won't be able to save it to the same location, using the same name.

Note

There are exceptions to the one-person-at-a-time rule. With a program such as Microsoft NetMeeting, two people can collaborate on a document at the same time and see each other's changes as they are made.

Some applications provide safeguards against opening a document in use. Word 2000, for example, displays this message if you try to open a file that's being used:

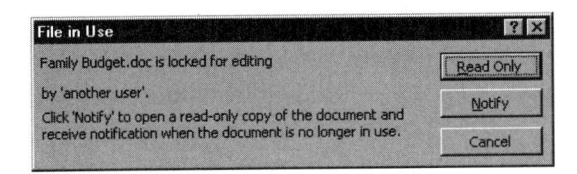

```
File in Use
Family Budget.doc is locked for editing    [ Read Only ]
by 'another user'.
Click 'Notify' to open a read-only copy of the document and   [ Notify ]
receive notification when the document is no longer in use.
                                            [ Cancel ]
```

In the File In Use message box, click Read Only to open the document in read-only mode. Clicking Notify also opens the document in read-only mode, but you'll also see a File Now Available message when the other user closes the file.

Click Read-Write to reopen the latest version of the document with the other user's changes. If you made any changes to the document, you'll see this message:

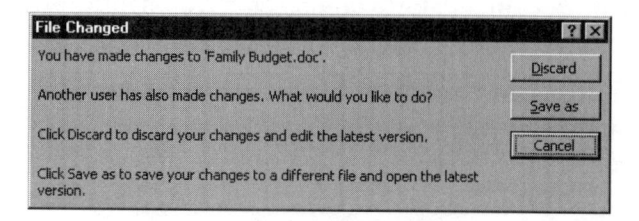

```
File Changed
You have made changes to 'Family Budget.doc'.                    Discard
Another user has also made changes. What would you like to do?   Save as
Click Discard to discard your changes and edit the latest version.  Cancel
Click Save as to save your changes to a different file and open the latest
version.
```

- Click Discard to ignore your changes and to reopen the latest version of the document.
- Click Save As to save your document under a new name and to open the latest version of the original file.

Copying and Moving Remote Files

You move or copy a file between computers on a network the same way you move or copy a file between folders on your own hard disk.

When you copy a file, you leave the original in its location and place a duplicate on another computer. Copying a file is a good idea when you want to make changes to a document without deleting the original version. Just remember that if someone changes one of the copies, two different versions of the same file will be on the network.

When you move a file, you delete the original from its location and place it on another computer. If you move a file that someone else might want to work with, let the other user know where you're placing it. You can't move a file from a read-only folder because moving it would be the same as deleting it from that folder, and read-only access doesn't permit deletion of files. If you try to move such a file, you'll get an error message.

You can move and copy files between a remote computer and your own, using either Windows Explorer or Network Neighborhood.

Copying Files Between Computers

Whether you're copying a file between your folders on your own hard disk or between computers on the network, you can use two basic methods. You can drag the file from one location to another, or you can use the copy and paste method.

Chapter 17: Learning to Share

Dragging Files To copy a file by dragging it, you need to have open both the folder that contains the file and the folder to which you want to copy it. This process is easiest with Windows Explorer, so let's start there.

Let's assume that you want to copy a file from a remote computer to your own computer. Here's how to do it:

1. On the Start menu, point to Programs and click Windows Explorer.
2. In the Folders list on the left, locate the folder in which you want to place the file.

    For example, if you want to place the file in the My Documents folder, make sure you see the folder in the list. If necessary, click the plus sign next to the C drive.
3. To locate the file you want to copy, click the plus sign next to Network Neighborhood in the list on the left.
4. Click the plus sign next to the remote computer you want to access.
5. Click the plus sign next to the drive on the remote computer that contains the file.
6. Click the folder containing the file for which you're looking.

    If the folder contains subfolders, click the plus sign next to the folder to display its contents, and then select the subfolder containing the file. You should see the file you want to copy in the list on the right.
7. Now scroll through the list on the left until you see the folder to which you want to copy the file, *but don't click it.*
8. Drag the icon of the file you want to copy from the list at the right to the destination folder in the Folder list on the left.

    As you drag, a small plus sign appears next to the mouse pointer indicating that you're copying, rather than moving, the file.

Note

It's also possible to drag a file by holding down the *right* mouse button as you drag rather than the left. This causes a shortcut menu to appear, from which you can choose Copy Here when you release the mouse button.

You can also copy a file using a combination of My Computer and Network Neighborhood. With this approach, you drag the file to be copied between two windows on your screen: one that shows the file's original location and another that shows its destination. This time, you'll copy a file from your computer to a remote one.

1. Double-click My Computer on the desktop and double-click the drive containing the file.
2. Double-click the folder containing the file.
3. If the folder window fills the screen, click the Restore button to make the window smaller.
4. Drag the window to the left side of the screen.
5. Double-click Network Neighborhood on the Windows desktop.
   Network Neighborhood appears in a new window. If the two windows overlap, drag the Network Neighborhood window to the right.
6. In the Network Neighborhood window, double-click the icon for the computer you want to access.
7. In the Network Neighborhood window, double-click the drive, and then double-click the folder in which you want to place the file.
8. Drag the file from the My Computer window on the left to the Network Neighborhood window on the right.

Copying and Pasting If copying a file by dragging seems too time consuming, you can always do it the old-fashioned Windows way, by using the Copy and Paste commands. You'll still need to open both a window showing the file in its original location and a window showing the new location, but you don't need to have both open at the same time.

You can copy and paste using Windows Explorer, Network Neighborhood, or My Computer. Here's how:

1. Open the folder containing the file you want to copy, and select the file.
2. Right-click the file and choose Copy from the shortcut menu. You can also click Copy on the Windows Explorer toolbar.
3. Open the folder to which you want to copy the file.
4. Right-click and choose Paste from the shortcut menu. You can also choose Paste from the Edit menu or from the toolbar.

Chapter 17: Learning to Share

Sending Files to Remote Drives

One very handy feature of Windows is the Send To list. If you need to save a file on a floppy disk, for example, you can right-click its icon on the desktop or in any folder, and then point to Send To to see a list of possible destinations. Click 3½ Floppy (A) at the top of the list to copy the file to the floppy disk drive, for example.

It's possible to add your own destinations to the Send To list so that you can copy files quickly to a remote computer of your choice. To do this, you first have to create a desktop shortcut to the drive or shared folder on the remote computer that you want to add to the Send To list. (*See "Creating a Desktop Shortcut" on page 271.*) Next, right-click the shortcut you've created to the remote computer and choose Rename from the shortcut menu. Type a name that you'd want to see in the Send To list and press Enter. Finally, drag the icon to the C:\Windows\Send To folder.

Now, whenever you want to copy a file to the remote location, right-click the file, point to Send To, and click the listing for the remote location.

Moving Remote Files

You move a file between computers in almost exactly the same way as you copy a file. To move a file by dragging, follow the steps for copying, but hold down the Shift key when you release the mouse button. While you hold down the Shift key, the small plus sign next to the pointer disappears, indicating that you're moving, rather than copying, the file. You don't have to hold down the Shift key while you're dragging the mouse, only when you release it.

If you prefer not to move a file by dragging it, you can move the file using Cut and Paste, rather than Copy and Paste. Right-click the file and choose Cut from the shortcut menu instead of Copy. Open the folder to which you want to move the file, right-click again, and choose Paste from the shortcut menu. When you paste the file into its new location, it's removed from its original folder.

Tip

As with copying, it's also possible to drag the file by holding down the *right* mouse button instead of the left. In this case, choose Move Here from the shortcut menu that appears when you release the mouse.

Deleting Remote Files

When you have full access to a remote folder, you can delete it or delete the files within it. But before you delete anything, you should be aware that Recycle Bin doesn't work across the network.

Recycle Bin, which is on the Windows desktop, is a holding tank for files or folders that you delete from your hard disk drive. If you change your mind about deleting an item, you can open Recycle Bin, select the deleted file or folder in the Recycle Bin window, and choose Restore from the File menu. If you're sure you don't need the files in Recycle Bin anymore, you can open Recycle Bin and choose Empty Recycle Bin from the File menu.

When you delete a file that's on another computer on the network, however, it's immediately deleted from the disk without making a protective stop at Recycle Bin on either computer. Even dragging the file to Recycle Bin on your computer erases it.

Note

Recycle Bin also doesn't work for files and folders deleted from floppy disks or removable-drive disks, such as Zip disks.

If you're sure you want to delete a remote file, just locate the file using Network Neighborhood, Windows Explorer, or any other method. Select the file and press the Delete key, or right-click the file and choose Delete from the shortcut menu. When you're asked whether you really want to delete the file, click Yes if you do or click No if you've changed your mind.

Note

You can delete an entire folder from a remote computer with this same procedure.

Sharing with Microsoft Windows 2000 Professional

The general concept of file sharing and accessing shared files is the same for Windows 2000 as it is in Windows 95 and Windows 98. However, Windows 2000 has inherited the file sharing capabilities from Microsoft Windows NT. With Windows 2000, you can set permissions for specific users and encrypt folders and files for added security.

Chapter 17: Learning to Share

In Windows 95 and Windows 98, for example, you could limit access to a folder by assigning it a password. Anyone who had the password could then access the folder. If an unauthorized user learned the password, he or she could access the folder from any computer on the network.

Windows 2000 doesn't use passwords because it offers user-level access. This means you can assign specific permissions to each user individually or in groups. To assign permissions to an individual, you would use the Users And Passwords feature in Control Panel to create a user account for the individual and then set his or her permissions. Users need to log on to the network with their user names and passwords to access the folders you have allowed.

The level of security that you choose depends on your network and office requirements.

Turning On File Sharing

Before you can activate file sharing, you must install the Windows service that allows sharing. You probably installed this service along with your network drivers and software, as described in Chapter 13, but just in case you didn't, here's how to do it.

1. On the Start menu, point to Settings, and then click Network And Dial-Up Connections.
2. Right-click Local Area Connection, and choose Properties from the shortcut menu.
3. In the list of network components that are installed, look for File And Printer Sharing For Microsoft Networks.
4. If it's installed, you can skip the rest of these steps. If not, continue as follows:
5. Click Install to open the Select Network Component Type dialog box.
6. Select Service, and then click Add to open the Select Network Service dialog box.
7. Select File And Printer Sharing For Microsoft Networks, and then click OK.
8. Click OK to close the Select Network Component Type dialog box.
9. Click Yes when you're asked whether you want to restart your computer.

Sharing Drives

To turn on sharing for an entire drive and give only certain people access to it, follow these steps:

1. Double-click My Computer on the Windows desktop.
2. Right-click the drive that you want to share, and select Sharing from the shortcut menu to see the Properties dialog box shown in Figure 17-5.

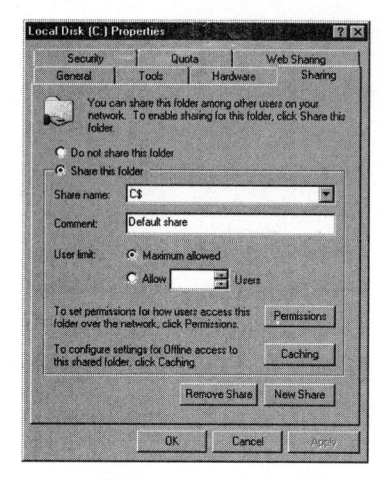

Figure 17-5
The Properties dialog box allows you to turn on sharing for a resource.

The Share This Folder option might already be enabled, in which case an entry with the $ sign appears in the Share Name box. The $ sign indicates a special shared resource that Windows needs for administrative purposes. You can't remove this type of sharing but network users won't be able to see it when they browse the network to access your computer.

3. If the drive is already assigned for sharing, click New Share, type the share name, and click OK. If the drive doesn't have a default name, click Share This Folder. Windows places a default name in the Share Name text box, which is usually the same letter as the drive.

Chapter 17: Learning to Share

4. In the User Limit section, choose either Maximum Allowed, or choose Allow and type the number of users allowed to access the drive at one time. The maximum is 10.

5. Click Permissions to see the dialog box shown in Figure 17-6.

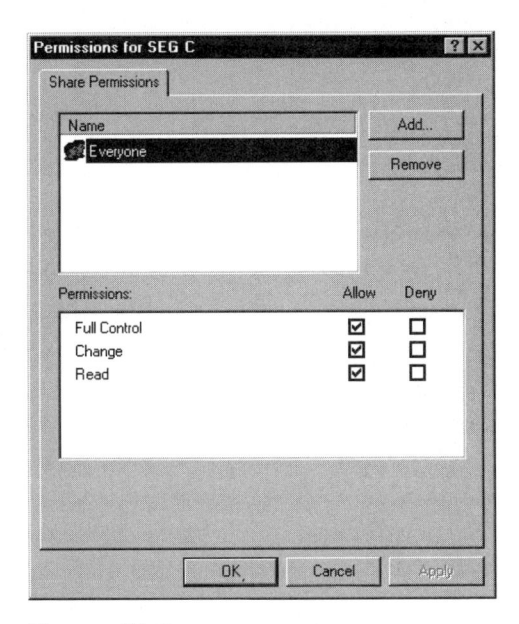

Figure 17-6
Set permissions for sharing a drive for all users on the network.

6. The default is set at Everyone, meaning permissions are granted to every network user accessing your computer. In the Permissions section, choose Allow or Deny for the specific permissions you want to grant to everyone: Full Control, Change, and Read.

    If you want to limit access to certain groups or users, you can remove Everyone and add specific users or groups. Click Add to open the dialog box shown in Figure 17-7. Double-click the user or group and click OK. Then set the permissions for the individual or group.

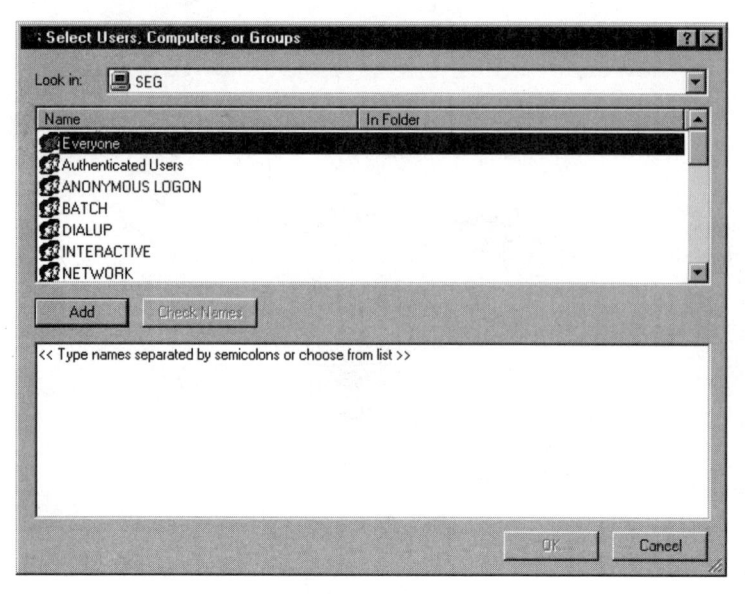

Part 4: Running Your Office on a Network

Figure 17-7
Set permissions for sharing a drive with specific users or groups.

For even more control over permissions, click the Security tab in a drive's Properties dialog box to set permission options.

Tip

If you want to change permissions, pull down the Share Name list and choose the new share you created. You can't set or change permissions for shares with the $ sign.

Sharing Folders

If you don't want to allow complete access to your drive, you can turn on sharing for only certain folders.

In fact, each user of the computer has a folder assigned to them in the Documents And Settings folder. Granting access to a drive on the computer doesn't grant access to these personal folders. If you want to grant access to a personal folder, which isn't recommended, you have to turn on sharing for it specifically.

Chapter 17: Learning to Share

To turn on sharing for a folder, follow these steps:
1. Double-click My Computer on the Windows desktop.
2. Double-click the drive containing the folder you want to share.
3. Right-click the folder that you want to share.
    You might have to navigate through folders to display the subfolder you want to share.
4. Select Sharing from the shortcut menu to open the Properties dialog box.
5. Click Share This Folder.
6. Click Permissions if you want to specify the rights and users, as you learned to do for drives.

Sharing Programs

So far, the chapter has covered rather generically how to share files, primarily documents, graphics, sounds, and other files that aren't programs. Sharing a program on a network is a slightly different matter.

What Can Be Shared?

Sharing programs on a network might have legal ramifications.

- It's not always legal to purchase one copy of a program and install it on each of the computers on your network.
- It's not always legal to purchase one copy of a program, install it on one computer, and then let more than one person on the network run the program at the same time.

Remember that software is usually licensed, and many software companies prohibit program sharing as part of their licensing agreements. By opening and using a piece of software, you're agreeing to abide by all of the small print and legal-sounding paragraphs that you're sure to find somewhere on the package or in the software itself.

Some licensing agreements require you to purchase a separate copy or license for every computer on which you want to run the software, even if you're using the software on just one computer at a time.

Some programs can't be shared at all. Many older MS-DOS (non-Windows) programs can be run only on the computer on which they were installed. These programs are designed to access additional files within the same computer. When you try to run such programs remotely, they can't find the other files they need and either display an error message or don't work at all.

Running a Program Remotely

Running a program on a remote computer is essentially the same as opening it on your own computer. You locate the program file and then open it by double-clicking it. When you run a program that's on a remote computer, the program runs in your computer, but its files remain on the remote computer.

Because some programs frequently draw information from the disk as they run, you might find that running a remote program uses up quite a bit of your network resources. You might also encounter problems with programs that won't run properly across a network. If you get error messages when you start the program or while you're using it, you won't be able to run it remotely. You'll have to either install the program on your computer (if the licensing agreement allows this) or go to the computer on which it's installed and run it from there.

Sharing a Data File

Sometimes you must share access to certain files, such as calendars and databases, on other computers. The shared data file might be a calendar, for example, that each member of the staff accesses to check for appointments and special events. You want only one copy of this calendar on the network so that everyone sees the same information and changes made to it are available to everyone.

You can open a data file by simply navigating to it and opening it, as you've learned in this chapter, or you can set up your application program to access the file on a remote computer.

Storing Shared Documents and Data Files on the Network

If you want to share a document or data file with other users in a peer-to-peer network, give some thought to the best location in which to keep the file. For example, storing it on the computer that is turned on most often increases the odds that the file will be available when someone needs to access it.

Chapter 17: Learning to Share

Security is another issue to consider. If you want to use a password to limit access to a file, you'll need to store the file in a folder that is password protected, which might limit your placement options. The computer on an assistant's desk might be on almost all of the time, for example, but you wouldn't want to store a personal file there. The trade-off for security might be to store the file on a computer that's used less frequently.

Another factor is that many programs expect to find files in specific places. They're set up to look in a default folder for the files they need to open. When you need to use this type of program, you have two choices: place the files where the program expects to see them or tell the program where you've chosen to keep the files.

Microsoft Money, for example, which lets you keep track of your bank accounts and even transfer funds and pay bills online, uses a data file named Mymoney.mny. The program stores this file in a specific folder on the hard disk.

To change where Money should look for Mymoney.mny, just copy the file to wherever you want to store it, and then double-click Mymoney.mny to start the program. Because Money always uses the last data file you opened, the new data file in its new location becomes the default.

You can share a Money file between computers on the network, so that anyone who runs the program can have access to the most current bank accounts. Just copy the Mymoney.mny file to the computer where you want the shared file to be located, and then have all network users start their copies of Money by navigating to the remote computer and opening the Mymoney.mny file.

Other applications let you set the default location for documents in a dialog box, such as Microsoft Word's Options dialog box, shown in Figure 17-8.

If you want Word to look for new documents on a remote computer or to save new documents to a remote computer, type the UNC path as the documents' location. Here's how to do it:

1. Start Word, and choose Options on the Tools menu.
2. In the Options dialog box, click the File Locations tab.
3. Click Documents in the File Types list, and then click Modify.
4. In the Modify Location dialog box, type the full path for the folder on the remote computer, such as \\Barbara\C\Myfiles.

    You can also browse for the location by choosing Network Neighborhood in the dialog box's Look In list.

5. Click OK to close the Modify Location dialog box.
6. Click OK to close the Options dialog box.

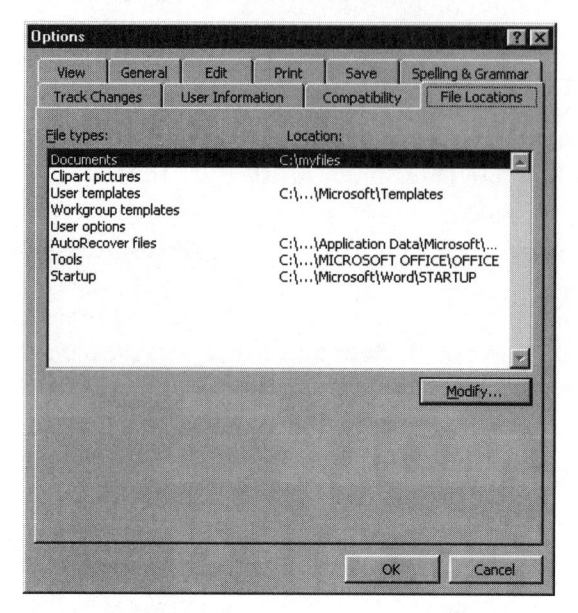

Figure 17-8
In Microsoft Word, the default location for documents is set in the Options dialog box.

Backing Up Important Files

When it comes to backing up, the best rule of thumb is: "Back up what you don't want to lose." Unfortunately, backing up is one of those things we all know we should do but too often don't.

Backing up means making a copy of important files in some location other than your hard disk drive. That way, if your hard disk decides it's had enough of your interference and departs to never-never land, your important files are safe and sound somewhere else. Sounds logical, only many of us forget to back up important files or we just get too lazy to do it.

When you're sharing files on a peer-to-peer network, backing up is even more important for two reasons:

- The more people who access your disk, the greater the chance an important file will be deleted or corrupted. This is especially true if you allow full access to your network's resources.

- More people are dependent on being able to use a given file and will be affected by its loss. It's not just you anymore.

All network users need to take some precautions to safeguard important files that would be difficult or impossible to recreate. Backing up programs isn't as critical because you can always reinstall them from their original disks. But your documents, database files, spreadsheets, banking files, and other data files might be unique and not easy to replace.

Some programs, such as MECA's Managing Your Money and Microsoft Money, create a backup file each time you exit. While the setup procedure varies from program to program, in most cases the backup option is available as a menu choice or in a dialog box that opens when you choose to exit the program. You can usually specify the backup location, including a drive on a remote computer.

Using Removable Disks

The best choice for quick and easy backups of files and folders is a Zip, Jaz, or other type of removable disk anywhere on your network. Removable disks hold at least 100 MB of information, the equivalent of about 70 floppy disks. That's not as much storage as you have on a hard disk or tape drive, but it can certainly accommodate a lot of files. Because the disk is removable, you can use multiple disks to store as much information as you like.

If the drive is attached to your computer, it'll appear as a drive icon in My Computer. Just drag the files or folders you want to back up to this icon. If your computer has a built-in removable disk or tape drive, it might appear in your Send To list. If it doesn't, create a shortcut to the drive on the desktop and add it to the SendTo folder yourself. *See "Sending Files to Remote Drives" on page 283.*

When the drive is attached to a remote computer, consider mapping the drive, so that you can access it from My Computer, or creating a shortcut to it in the SendTo folder.

Storing Files Remotely

Another option worth considering is backing up your files to the hard disk of a remote computer. One of the computers on the network might be newer and have a much larger hard disk than the disk in your own computer. Or it might not be used quite as much as other computers in the office, so it has extra hard disk space that can be shared around the office.

Create a folder on that computer with your name so you can easily identify it. Create a shortcut to the folder on your desktop, and then add the shortcut to the Send To folder. You'll now be able to back up folders and files to that remote disk quickly and easily.

> **Note**
>
> You can also contract with companies to let you store information on their computers through the Internet.

Using Tape Storage

If you want to store a large number of files or back up your entire hard disk to an external location, consider a tape drive. Tapes can store up to 24 gigabytes (or even more) of information, enough for complete system backups. Of course, the larger the storage capacity the higher the price. While 8-gigabyte tape drives start at about $300, 24-gigabyte drives can cost $1000 or more. The tapes themselves can cost between $50 and $100, although the cost per megabyte is still less than most removable disk options.

Tapes are sequential access devices, not designed to replace or serve as drives for everyday storage use. With a disk, for example, you can quickly access a file no matter where on the disk it's physically located. The drive mechanism can go directly to any location on the disk. If you need to reach a file at the end of a tape, however, the device has to fast-forward the entire tape to get to the file's location. However, tapes are an excellent choice when you want to back up entire disk drives, and most tape drives include their own backup software.

> **Caution**
>
> There are many different formats and types of tape drives, and most aren't compatible with each other. If you purchase a tape drive, make sure the vendor can also supply enough tapes for your anticipated needs.

Using RAID

If you use your computer for mission-critical tasks, consider installing a *redundant array of independent disks (RAID) system*. A RAID system consists of several disks across which data is spread to improve performance of a system and to avoid storing important data on one hard disk. RAID systems are classified into levels:

- **Level 0** uses a technique called *disk striping* in which the bytes that compose information are divided and stored across the multiple drives. Because more than one disk is being written to or read from at one time, disk access is much faster than writing to or reading from a single disk. This level increases only performance, not the security of your data.

- **Level 1** performs *disk mirroring* in which the entire contents of one disk are duplicated on another disk. If one disk fails, you can restore the information from the mirror disk without loss of data.

- **Level 2** performs disk striping but in a way that enables lost data to be restored. Error correction coding (ECC) is saved that can help the computer reconstruct data if the disk fails. The ECC information is stored on one of the disks.

- **Level 3** is similar to level 2 but saves parity information rather than ECC. Parity uses a binary system that stores data in less space than ECC but that also allows data to be restored. The parity information is stored on one of the disks.

- **Level 4** is similar to level 3 but stores information in larger blocks of data. This increases performance when you're working with large files, but decreases performance with smaller files.

- **Level 5** is also similar to level 3 but it stripes the parity information across the disks. This level provides optimum performance and data recovery.

A RAID system can be created with software or hardware. The software solutions are less efficient but can be implemented without any special hardware. The more efficient but costly hardware solution requires a special RAID disk controller and two or more regular disk drives.

Tip

If you're considering a RAID system and need to maintain important business data, look for a level 5 system.

Using Microsoft Backup

As an alternative to backing up individual files and folders, you can automate the backup process with Microsoft Backup. The program comes with Windows 95 and Windows 98, so you can't beat the price, and it works with floppy disks, tape backup drives, and most removable disks. It's great for a network because you can use it to back up files from your own or any other computer on the network and store the backup on a remote computer.

Backup isn't usually installed in Windows 95/98, so you'll have to do it yourself. But don't worry, it's easy. Just follow these steps:

1. Insert your Windows CD in the CD drive.
2. On the Start menu, point to Settings and click Control Panel.
3. In the Control Panel window, double-click Add/Remove Programs.
4. In the Add/Remove Programs Properties dialog box, click the Windows Setup tab.
   After a moment or two you'll see a list of Windows components.
5. Scroll through the list and click System Tools. Make sure you don't clear the check box on the left.
6. Click Details to see a list of items in the System Tools category.
7. In the System Tools dialog box, select the Backup check box.
8. Click OK to close the System Tools dialog box.
9. Click OK again to close the Add/Remove Programs Properties dialog box.
10. Click Yes when you're asked whether you want to restart your computer.

After your computer restarts, you're ready to configure and run Microsoft Backup. The process varies slightly, depending on the type of drive you're using for backup—tape, removable disk, or floppy disk.

Tip

If you don't have a tape backup drive or another device recognized by Backup as a backup device, you might be asked the first time you run the program whether you want it to search for a backup device. Click No.

Chapter 17: Learning to Share

Microsoft Windows 2000 Backup

The Backup program included with Windows 2000 is similar to the Windows 95/98 version discussed here but with a different look. To start the program, click Start, point to Programs, point to Accessories, point to System Tools, and click Backup. The Welcome menu appears with three choices, as shown in Figure 17-9.

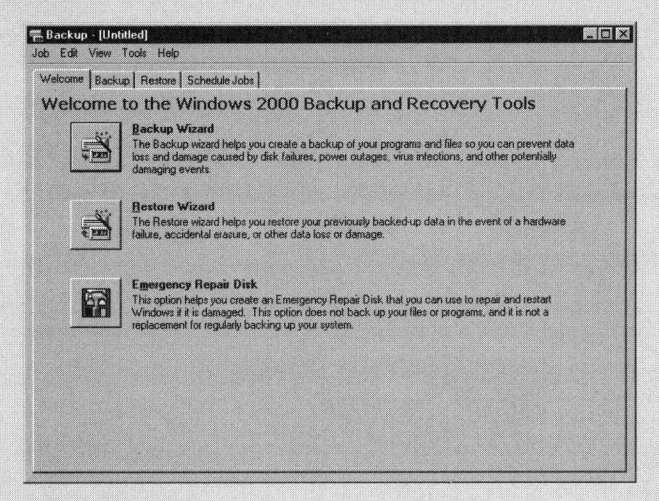

Figure 17-9
The Backup program in Microsoft Windows 2000 enables you to back up and restore data on your computer.

You can use the Backup Wizard to automate your backup, or click the Backup tab to specify the files you want to back up and their destination. Use the Restore Wizard or the Restore tab to restore files. The Emergency Repair Disk option creates a floppy disk that you can use to start your computer if Windows is damaged on your hard disk.
    The Schedule Jobs tab lets you schedule backup operations for specific dates and times.

Microsoft Backup lets you create a *backup job* that defines which files you want to back up and where you want them stored. It's possible to have any number of backup jobs defined, and you can easily repeat a backup to save updated files.

To start the program, follow these steps:

1. On the Start menu, point to Programs, point to Accessories, point to System Tools, and then click Backup.

    You'll see the Microsoft Backup dialog box shown in Figure 17-10.

2. Choose Create A New Backup Job to define a backup job, and then click OK to start the Backup Wizard.

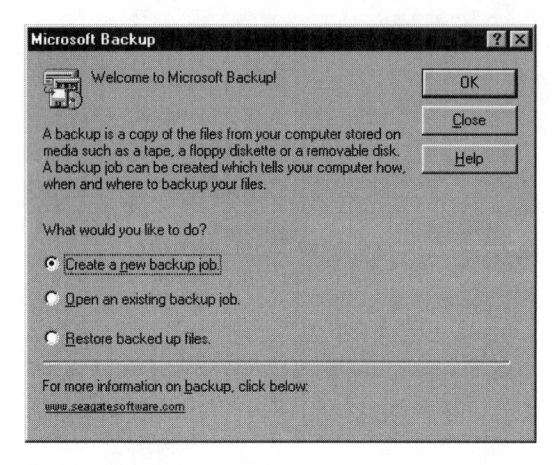

Figure 17-10

The Microsoft Backup dialog box prompts you to create a new backup job, which starts the Backup Wizard.

The wizard takes you step-by-step through the process of defining a backup job and performing the backup itself. You can choose options such as

- The name of the backup job
- Whether to back up your entire computer or only selected files
- The storage location for backup files
- Whether backups and originals are compared to verify their accuracy
- Whether backup files are compressed to save space

The Backup Wizard isn't the only way to define a backup job. You can also use the main Backup window, shown in Figure 17-11. This window allows you to specify what to back up, where to store it, and how to save it. Then you just click the Start button. To back up important files from a remote computer, for example, scroll through the What To Back Up list and click the plus sign next to Networks to access remote computers.

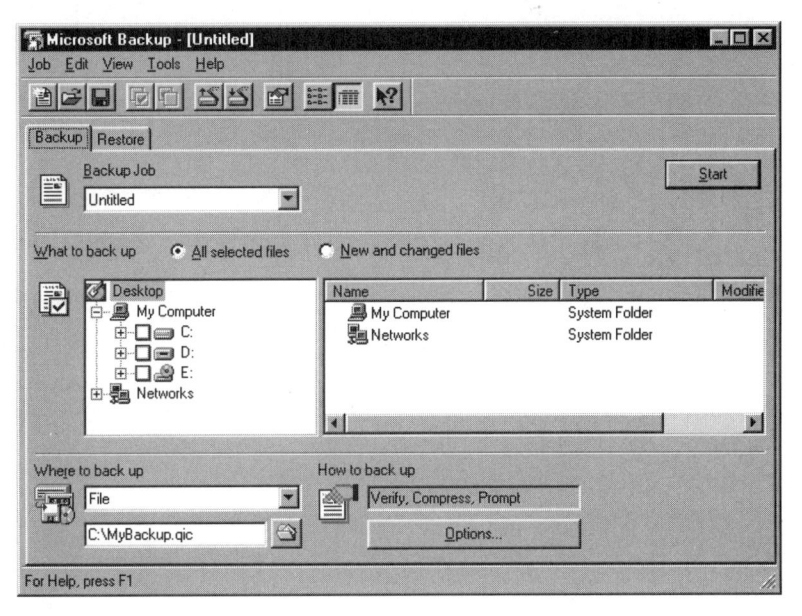

Figure 17-11

Using the controls in the Microsoft Backup window is an alternative to using the Backup Wizard.

Microsoft Backup doesn't store files individually. Instead, it combines them in one large file or a series of large files spread over several disks. For this reason, you can't use standard Windows or MS-DOS techniques to access individual files in a backup. If you want to retrieve files from the backup, you have to perform a *restore* operation.

To restore files, choose the Restore Backed Up Files option when you start Microsoft Backup. This opens the Restore Wizard. You can also click Close on the Microsoft Backup dialog box after you start Microsoft Backup and use the controls on the Restore tab to specify restore options. If you choose to restore selected files, you'll see a list of the individual files in the backup from which you can choose.

In the next chapter, you'll learn how to share another important resource on a network, the printers connected to the computers.

Chapter 18
Printing Anywhere on the Network

Sharing files and folders is one great advantage of connecting computers in a network; sharing printers is another. When you share printers, everyone on the network can access them. You might need to walk to the printer in another room to retrieve your printed documents, but the pages will be there, ready and waiting for you.

You should share printers if the following conditions are true:

- You don't have a printer for each computer.
- You want to use a feature on a printer that's connected to a remote computer.

Let's say you purchased printers for some but not all of the computers in the office. If your computers aren't connected to a network, you'll need to do one of two things to get a printout from a computer that doesn't have a printer:

- Save your documents on a disk and take the disk to a computer that's connected to a printer.
- Disconnect the printer from one computer and hook it up to the computer from which you want to print.

With a network, it doesn't matter whether all your computers have printers. You can send a document to printers connected to other computers on the network.

Even if you do have a printer for each computer, the printers might not all be of the same type. For example, you might have a laser printer connected to your computer for printing business documents, while someone else in the office has a color inkjet printer for reports and presentations. If your computers are connected in a network, you can get to the color printer whenever you want, and other folks in the office will be able to print with your laser printer—if you allow them.

There are two basic ways to link a printer to a network. The cheaper and easier method is simply to connect the printer to the parallel or USB port of one of the computers in the network. The other way is to connect the printer directly to the network. Although this second option is more expensive, connecting a printer directly has many advantages, as you'll learn later in *"Connecting Printers Directly to the Network" on page 312*.

Note

The Microsoft Windows–based server appliance lets everyone on a network share the printer that's attached to the appliance.

Sharing Printers

When you print a document on a printer connected to a remote computer, your print job travels over the network, through the remote computer, and then to the printer attached to it. It's the remote computer, rather than your own, that causes the printer to print the document.

Let the Printer Beware!

Sharing printers attached to computers connected in a network is a great time-saver, but there's one big gotcha: both the printer and the computer to which it's attached must be turned on, and the printer must be online, stocked with paper, and ready to go. Otherwise, it's no go!

This means that before you print on a printer connected to a remote computer, you have to check to make sure the printer is ready. If no one is using the computer that's attached to the printer, you might have to go to

Chapter 18: Printing Anywhere on the Network

the computer, turn on both the computer and the printer, and set up the printer for printing.

Even if the computer and printer are turned on and ready, they might be busy with someone else's print job. When the printer completes the job, it'll start printing your document and others that are waiting on a FIFO basis, old accounting talk for the phrase "First In, First Out," which means the first in line is processed first. Another problem can occur if the person using the remote computer to which the printer is attached shuts the computer down before the printer starts printing your work. A little coordination is clearly needed here.

You might suggest to everyone on the network that anyone who wants to print to someone else's shared printer should first send a short message to make sure the printer is on and ready. In Chapter 19 and Chapter 20, you'll learn how to send messages to other people on your network. You could also try yelling from room to room, but that's not always the best approach.

Setting Up Printer Sharing

Before you can share the printer connected to your computer on the network, you must have installed the File And Printer Sharing For Microsoft Networks service. Chances are, you already did this when you set up file sharing (see "Turning on File Sharing" on page 259). But to make sure that you've enabled the printer sharing part of the service, follow these steps:

1. On the Start menu, point to Settings and click Control Panel.
2. In the Control Panel window, double-click the Network icon to open the Network dialog box.
3. Click the File And Print Sharing button to open the File And Print Sharing dialog box.
4. Make sure the I Want To Be Able To Allow Others To Print To My Printer(s) check box is selected.
5. Click OK to close the File And Print Sharing dialog box.
6. Click OK to close the Network dialog box.

Installing a Printer

The next step in setting up a printer is to check that the printer is actually installed on your computer and working properly. If you can't use the printer directly attached to your computer, no one else will be able to use it over the network.

To make sure that your printer is installed in Windows, point to Settings on the Start menu and click Printers. If you see a listing for your printer, it's already installed and you can close the Printers window. If your printer isn't listed, you'll have to add the printer now.

If your printer came with a floppy disk or CD, your printer might have its own special printer drivers and installation program. Take a quick look at the documentation that came with the printer, and if the printer came with a CD, take a look at the CD too—sometimes you'll see instructions printed right on the CD.

Depending on the type of printer, running its special installation program can be as simple as inserting the CD in the computer and waiting for the installation program to start by itself. If nothing happens when you insert the CD, go to My Computer and double-click the icon for the CD. If that doesn't start the installation program, you might have to run the setup or install program on the CD. When the installation program starts, just follow the instructions that appear on the screen.

In many cases, however, setting up your printer doesn't require running a special installation program. Instead, you can set up the printer using the Add Printer Wizard in Windows. Here's how:

1. Insert your Windows CD in the CD drive.

    That might not be necessary depending on how your computer was set up, but it can't hurt.

2. On the Start menu, point to Settings and click Printers.

3. Double-click the Add Printer icon to start the Add Printer Wizard.

4. Click Next.

    The Add Printer Wizard appears and takes you through the steps of installing the printer.

5. When the wizard asks you whether you want to install a local printer or a network printer, click Local Printer and then click next.

    You should now see the dialog box shown in Figure 18-1, which contains lists of printer manufacturers and printer models.

Chapter 18: Printing Anywhere on the Network

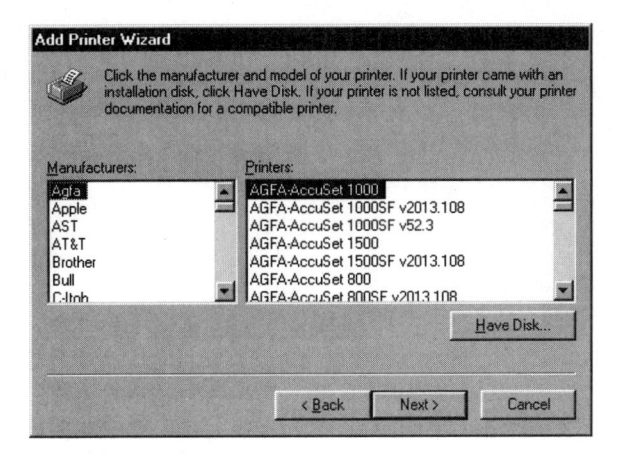

Figure 18-1
Select your printer's make and model in the Add Printer Wizard.

Note

If your printer model isn't listed, see "Handling Problem Printers" on page 306.

6. Click the manufacturer of the printer on the left, click the model of the printer on the right, and click Next.

    You'll now be asked to select the port to which the printer is attached. In most cases, your printer is attached to the LPT1 port, the standard parallel printing port on most PCs. If your computer has more than one printer port, the ports will be labeled LPT1, LPT2, and so on. If you have a USB or serial printer, it might be connected to the USB or a serial (COM) port instead.

7. Click the port that your printer is attached to, and click Next.

8. Type a new name for the printer if you want, such as *Laser printer*, or leave the default name.

9. Click Yes if you want the printer to be the default printer in all Windows programs. Click No if you want to leave another printer as the default. If you choose No, you can still select the printer you just installed when you're ready to print. *See "Selecting a Different Printer on the Network" on page 311* for more information on how to do this.

10. Click Next.

11. Make sure your printer is turned on and loaded with paper, and click Yes.

    Printing a test page isn't really necessary, but it's a good idea to confirm that everything is working properly now rather than waiting until you have an important document to print.

12. Click Finish.

    Windows loads the appropriate printer drivers and prints the test page. A dialog box opens to ask whether the page printed correctly.

13. Click Yes if the page printed without a problem. If the page didn't print correctly, click No to start the Print Troubleshooter. Follow the dialog boxes that appear, selecting the answers that best explain the problem you're having.

Handling Problem Printers

If you run the Add Printer Wizard and your printer's model doesn't appear on the list, don't give up hope. Many new printer models and many very old ones might not be listed.

If your printer is new, insert the floppy disk or CD that came with it in the appropriate drive before you start the Add Printer Wizard. When you see the dialog box in the Add Printer Wizard that prompts you to select the printer's manufacturer and model, click the Have Disk button. In the dialog box that appears next, specify the location of the disk and then continue following the prompts. You might have to specify a subfolder on the disk that contains the proper drivers for your printer or browse the disk in order to locate the drivers.

If your printer is older, it might not be listed in the Add Printer Wizard, and you might no longer have its installation disk. If this is your case, try selecting the same manufacturer as your printer's and choosing one of the older models listed for that manufacturer. If that doesn't work, look for information in the printer's manual about other printers that yours can emulate. Many laser printers, for example, use the same drivers as some Hewlett-Packard (HP) printers. If you have an older laser printer with no documentation or software, try selecting the LaserJet Plus, LaserJet II, or LaserJet III model from the HP list.

If you still can't get the printer to work, hit the Web. You might be able to download the drivers you need to install the printer. On the Web, look for the printer manufacturer's home page. If the manufacturer is out of business, search the Microsoft Web site for driver information or do general searches using your printer's make and model as search words. You might be able to find someone at some site to help you.

Enabling Printer Sharing

The last step you must take to share your printer is to tell Windows that the printer can be shared. This is similar to turning on sharing for a drive or folder.

In this section, I'll look at printer sharing in Microsoft Windows 95 and Microsoft Windows 98. *See the sidebar, "Sharing in Microsoft Windows 2000 and Microsoft Windows NT," on page 309* for those operating systems.

1. On the Start menu, point to Settings and click Printers.
2. In the Printers window, right-click the printer you want to share.
3. Select Sharing from the shortcut menu.
4. On the Sharing tab of the Properties dialog box, click Shared As.
5. In the Share Name text box, type a name for the printer that'll identify it to other network users.

    You also have the option of entering an identifying description of the printer in the Comment text box. To make it easier for other users to select the printer, include its type, such as Canon Color Bubble Jet or HP LaserJet, in the description. You might want to include the printer's location, such as an office number.

6. If you want to allow sharing only for users with a password, type a password.
7. Click OK.
8. If you entered a password, type it again to confirm it, and then click OK.

The printer's icon now shows that it's a shared resource.

HP LaserJet
1100

The check mark next to the printer icon in the Printers window indicates that the printer is the default in all Windows applications. To make a different printer the default, right-click its icon and choose Set As Default from the shortcut menu.

Separating Print Jobs

Once other folks start using your printer, don't be surprised if it starts churning out pages that you're not expecting. Windows will print documents in the order they're received, so if another network user starts a job before you do, you'll have to wait a bit for your document to print.

If you're not careful, you might wind up with several documents in the printer's output tray at one time. And you certainly wouldn't want to grab your quarterly report and your shopping list and distribute both to the board members later in the morning. You also wouldn't want your document to disappear with someone else's job.

To help prevent this, you can have Windows print a separator page between documents. The page prints at the start of each job and shows the name of the person who printed it.

Here's how to enable the separator page feature:

1. On the computer to which the printer is attached, click Start, point to Settings, and click Printers.

2. Right-click the printer that's being shared, and select Properties from the shortcut menu.

    The General tab of the printer's Properties dialog box appears, as shown in Figure 18-2.

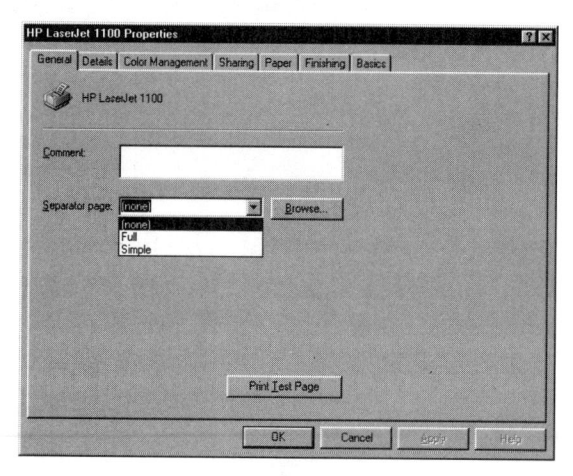

Figure 18-2
You can enable separator pages on the General tab of the printer's Properties dialog box.

Chapter 18: Printing Anywhere on the Network

3. Pull down the Separator Page list and select Full or Simple. Both options print the user's name, document name, and current date and time. The Full option just prints it larger.

Note

Choose None from the Separator Page list if you no longer want to print separator pages.

4. Click OK.

Sharing in Microsoft Windows 2000 and Microsoft Windows NT

The concepts you learned for sharing printers in Windows 95/98 apply to Windows NT and Windows 2000, although the dialog boxes in which you enable sharing have some differences.

In Windows 2000, if you're sharing your printer with computers that are using another version of Windows, click Additional Drivers on the Sharing tab to select and install the drivers for their systems. In Windows NT, select from a list of operating systems on the Sharing tab.

After you enable sharing, you have to set the permissions. In Windows 2000, click the Security tab to display the permission options. As with sharing files, you can choose the users or groups to which you want to assign permissions. The three levels of permissions are as follows:

- **Print** allows users to print documents.
- **Manage Printers** allows users to change printer properties.
- **Manage Documents** lets users delete print jobs and manage the printer queue.

In Windows NT, click the Permissions button on the Security tab to select users and assign these permissions:

- No Access
- Full Control
- Print
- Manage Documents

Part 4: Running Your Office on a Network

Accessing a Shared Printer

The printer you have set up and shared is now available to everyone on the network. But to access it, each person must first install the printer as a remote network printer rather than a directly connected local printer. The procedure for installing a network printer is similar to that for a local printer, but with a few twists along the way. And you must be sure that everyone who wants to add the network printer to a computer has access to the printer drivers.

To install a network printer, each person on the network must follow these steps:

1. Insert the Windows CD in the CD drive.
    Again, that might not be necessary because the drivers might already be on the computer's hard disk, but it can't hurt.
2. Double-click Network Neighborhood, and then double-click the computer connected to the shared printer.
3. Right-click the icon for the shared printer, and choose Install to start the Add Printer Wizard.

You now have to specify whether you want MS-DOS programs, such as an older version of WordPerfect or dBASE, to be able to print to the network printer. Normally, MS-DOS programs can't use printers across the network. They can print to local printers only. But when you tell Windows to provide network printing capability to MS-DOS programs, Windows captures the information the MS-DOS program is trying to print and then channels it to the network printer.

4. If you want to be able to print from MS-DOS programs to network printers, click Yes. If you don't use MS-DOS programs or you want to print with them only to a local printer, click No.
5. Click Next.
6. If you chose to capture MS-DOS printing, you'll be asked to select a port. Click the button labeled Capture Printer Port, select LPT1, and then click OK.
7. Type a name for the printer if you want, such as *Marketing's color printer*, or leave the default name, which is usually the printer's model name.
8. Select Yes if you want the printer to be the default printer in all Windows programs. Select No if you want to leave another printer as the default. You can still select the printer when you're ready to print (see "Selecting a Different Printer on the Network" on page 311).

9. Click Next.
10. When you're asked whether you want to print a test page, make sure the printer is turned on and loaded with paper, and then click Yes.
11. Click Finish.
12. When a message box appears to ask whether the page printed correctly, click Yes. If the page didn't print, click No to start the Print Troubleshooter. Follow the dialog boxes that appear, selecting the answers that best explain the problem you're having.

Selecting a Different Printer on the Network

When you set a printer as the default—either your local printer or one of the printers on the network—all your documents are directed to that printer unless you choose a different printer. To change which printer is the Windows default, double-click the Printers icon to open the Printers window, right-click the printer you want as the default, and then choose Set As Default from the shortcut menu.

You can also choose to print a particular document on a printer other than the default printer. How you do this depends on the application you're using. In many programs, such as Microsoft Word, clicking the Print button on the toolbar prints the document on the default printer. If you want to choose a different printer, you must select the printer in the Print dialog box.

For example, suppose your own monochrome laser printer is the current default, but you want to print a document in color. Someone else in the office has a color printer that's been set up as a network printer. Here's how you'd print a document on the color printer:

1. Select Print from your application's File menu.
2. Click the drop-down arrow next to the Name box, which shows the default printer, and choose the network color printer from the drop-down list.
3. Click OK.

Using Printer Shortcuts

Normally, you start an application and then print a document. But with Windows, you can use several shortcuts for printing documents.

In My Computer or Windows Explorer, you can right-click a document's icon and choose Print from the shortcut menu. Windows opens the application used to create the document, sends the document to the printer, and then closes the application.

You can also drag a document onto a printer icon that you've placed on the Windows desktop. To place a printer icon on the desktop, follow these steps:

1. On the Start menu, point to Settings, and then click Printers.
2. In the Printers window, right-click a printer and choose Create Shortcut from the shortcut menu.
3. When a message tells you that you can't place a shortcut in the Printers folder and asks if you want to place the shortcut on the desktop instead, click Yes.

Connecting Printers Directly to the Network

Because a printer that's connected to a computer on the network works only when the computer is on, you might want to use an alternative: connecting the printer directly to the network.

Connecting a printer directly to the network also frees up a computer's printer port so that you can hook up an external Zip drive, scanner, or other parallel device without conflict.

In a twisted-pair network, you use twisted-pair cable to connect a printer to the hub. In a Thin Ethernet network, you use coaxial cable to connect the printer to the network interface card (NIC) of the nearest networked device. Because the printer isn't connected to the printer port of a computer, anyone on the network can access it directly as long as the printer is turned on.

The disadvantage to connecting printers directly to the network is expense. Most printers are designed for standard parallel or USB connections only. To connect them directly to the network, you'll need to purchase either a network-ready printer or a device, called a *print server*, that makes your printer network ready.

Network-ready printers have an NIC built in. They cost more than standard printers and can be a little harder to find. An alternative is to purchase a print server, which is equipped with an Ethernet connection on one side and a parallel connection on the other.

Chapter 18: Printing Anywhere on the Network

The least expensive printer servers are called *pocket servers*. About the size of a pack of cigarettes, a pocket server plugs directly into a printer's parallel port. The twisted-pair cable from the network hub or the coaxial cable from another networked device plugs into the other end of the server.

Another type of print server connects to a printer with a cable. These external servers are usually more expensive than pocket servers, but they might include additional features. Some models, for example, have more than one parallel port, allowing them to connect several printers to the network at the same time.

Note
For some HP LaserJet printers, you can purchase an internal print server that fits inside the printer, similar to the way NICs fit inside a computer.

When selecting a print server, make sure it matches your cable type—either twisted-pair or coaxial. Some print servers, but not all, can accommodate both types.

The print server must also support the protocol you're using on your network. Some print servers support only IPX/SPX; others require either TCP/IP or NetBEUI.

Finally, while most printers have a standard-sized parallel port, called a *Centronics* port, some models, like the LaserJet 1100, have a smaller mini-Centronics port. The standard-sized connection on a pocket print server won't fit a mini-Centronics port. If you're using such a printer, you'll need an adapter for the print server.

Note
To install an external print server to a mini-Centronics port, just connect the cable that came with the printer to the server's parallel connection. Connect the network cable to the server's network connection.

Setting Up a Pocket Print Server

There are many different models of pocket print servers. While they all operate in about the same way, their setup procedures vary. Most servers are sold with software that helps them connect to the network, but the process really depends on the type of protocol the server supports.

A TCP/IP server needs to be assigned an IP address. On a Windows peer-to-peer network, you'll probably have to assign the server a static IP address that isn't used by any computer on the network. This means that you might have to assign static IP addresses to every computer on the network as well, rather than have Windows assign them for you. Check the literature that came with your server for step-by-step directions for assigning it an IP address.

> **Note**
>
> In a Windows NT client/server network, you can assign dynamic IP addresses to most print servers as well.

Most manufacturers provide programs to help you through the process of installing their printer servers, which includes assigning IP addresses. The Microplex Ethernet Pocket Print Server, for example, offers two programs for configuring the print server—IPAssign and Waldo. Once you assign an IP address to your print server, you configure Windows to communicate with the printer. You have to associate the server with a printer port first. The default port used by most printers is called LPT1, the parallel connector into which the printer cable plugs. When you configure a printer *as you learned in "Installing a Printer" on page 303,* you associate the printer with the port, so Windows knows where to send the information to be printed—through the LPT1 port to the printer.

When you connect a print server to the network, you need to create a port with which the IP address is linked. When you associate a print server with that port, Windows sends the information through the network to the Ethernet address of the print server.

How you associate a printer port to the print server depends on the print server itself. With Microplex servers, for example, the server appears as a device in Network Neighborhood and has four ports associated with it. When you configure the printer, you browse until you find the port you want to use, in the same way you would browse to find a workstation *as explained in "Accessing a Shared Printer" on page 310.*

Other manufacturers handle port assignments. The pocket print servers from Axis Communications, for instance, don't appear in Network Neighborhood. Instead, you use the NetPilot program that comes with an Axis pocket server to associate the server with a port, and then you use a program called Axis Print System to add the printer to Windows.

Microplex and Axis certainly aren't the only makers of pocket print servers. Table 18-1, on pages 315–16, lists other print server makes and models.

Chapter 18: Printing Anywhere on the Network

Setting Up an External Print Server

External print servers, an alternative to pocket print servers, connect to a printer by cable rather than plugging directly into the printer itself. External servers work in the same way and are set up the same way as pocket print servers, although they're more expensive than pocket print servers. Many models also come with two or more parallel connections that allow you to place multiple printers on the network so you can use different printers for different documents.

Hewlett-Packard's JetDirect print servers, for example, work with virtually any printer equipped with a parallel port—not just HP's own brand. The line includes two models that have three parallel connections and a one-printer model. Setting up an HP print server is easy. After you connect the server both to the printer and to your network hub, you press a small button on the back of the server to print a page of configuration information, including the Ethernet address that's built into the device.

You then install the JetAdmin program supplied with the server and use the HP JetDirect Printer Wizard to configure the device.

There are many manufacturers of print servers, so you have plenty of choices. Table 18-1 lists print server makes and models and each manufacturer's Web address.

Table 18-1 Print Server Manufacturers and Models

Manufacturer	Models	Web site
Axis Communications	Pocket, one-port, and two-port models, some with both parallel and serial ports	*www.axis.com*
NETGEAR	One-port and two-port models, some with built-in four-port hub	*netgear.baynetworks.com*
Emulex	Pocket, two-port, and three-port models	*www.emulex.com*
Extended Systems	One-port and two-port models, some with both parallel and serial ports	*www.extendedsystems.com*
Hewlett-Packard JetDirect	One-port and three-port models, external and internal	*www.hp.com*

(continued)

Table 18-1 *(continued)*

Manufacturer	Models	Web site
Intel NetportExpress	One-port and three-port models	www.intel.com
Lantronix	Pocket and external print servers, up to six-port models (four parallel and two serial)	www.lantronix.com
Linksys EtherFast	Pocket, one-port, and three-port models	www.linksys.com
Microplex	Pocket and a four-port model (two parallel and two serial)	www.microplex.com

Sharing printers on a network can be a great time-saver and step-saver. You'll no longer need to carry a disk to another computer to print a document or carry a printer to another computer. With Windows, you don't have to purchase any additional software or hardware, unless you want to connect your printer directly to the network.

Sharing files and printers isn't the only benefit of connecting computers in a network, however. You'll learn in the next chapter that you can use your network to create an e-mail system for sending and receiving messages within the office.

Chapter 19

Communicating over Your Peer-to-Peer Network

You've seen how a network is great for sharing files and printers, but it's also a convenient way to communicate with other members of your staff. Why yell across the office or leave scribbled notes, when you can transmit messages over your network?

In this chapter, you'll learn three ways to communicate via a peer-to-peer network, ranging from the easiest to the most advanced. You'll learn how to

- Send and receive short messages that appear on the recipient's screen
- Send and receive e-mail messages just as you can over the Internet
- Set up Microsoft Outlook to communicate over your network

> **Note**
>
> You can also communicate over the network with the program Microsoft NetMeeting. You can use NetMeeting like an intercom system to speak with other staff members and even see them, if your computers are equipped with cameras.

Sending and Receiving Pop-Up Messages

The easiest and least formal way to communicate over the network is to send and receive pop-up messages. You can send a message to a specific family member or "broadcast" it to everyone on the network.

With a program called WinPopup, which comes with Microsoft Windows 95, Microsoft Windows 98, and Microsoft Windows 98 Second Edition, you can send out a quick question, reminder, or other message to someone else on the network. Your message simply appears in a window on the recipient's screen.

> **Note**
>
> WinPopup isn't included with Microsoft Windows NT or Microsoft Windows 2000. You can download shareware programs over the Internet, however, that let Windows NT send and receive pop-up messages to Windows 95/98 computers that are using WinPopup.

Starting WinPopup

WinPopup is usually installed when you set up Windows, but it's not listed with other programs on the Start menu. If you plan to use WinPopup regularly, you can add it to the Start menu, to your desktop, or to your Windows taskbar.

To locate WinPopup and add it as a shortcut on your Windows desktop, follow these steps:

1. On the Start menu, point to Find and click Files Or Folders.
2. In the Named text box, type *winpopup.exe* and click Find Now.
   Windows searches your hard disk drive and locates the WinPopup program. If Windows doesn't locate the program, *see* "Installing WinPopup," on page 319.
3. In the list of files in the Find dialog box, right-click WinPopup and choose Create Shortcut from the shortcut menu.

Chapter 19: Communicating over Your Peer-to-Peer Network

4. Click Yes when a message appears reporting that you can't add the shortcut to the current location and asking if you want to add the shortcut to your desktop.

5. Close the Find window.

You now have a shortcut to the program on your desktop.

Shortcut to WinPopup

If you're using Windows 98, you can add the WinPopup shortcut to your Quick Launch toolbar on the taskbar so that you can access it from within any application. To do this, drag the shortcut icon to the Quick Launch toolbar, which is just to the right of the Start button. You can now delete the shortcut from the desktop, if you want, by right-clicking it and choosing Delete from the shortcut menu.

Note

If the Quick Launch toolbar is now too short to fit all the icons it needs to display, you can bring them all back into view by dragging the vertical line on the right of the last icon farther to the right.

Because WinPopup must be running for someone to send or receive messages, you should have everyone on the network copy the WinPopup shortcut to the StartUp folder located at C:\Windows\Start Menu\Programs\StartUp. When the shortcut is in that folder, it starts whenever Windows is started.

Installing WinPopup

If the WinPopup program isn't already installed on your computer, you'll have to install it yourself. Insert the Windows CD in your CD drive, and then follow these steps:

1. On the Start menu, point to Settings and click Control Panel.

2. In the Control Panel window, double-click Add/Remove Programs.

3. On the Add/Remove Programs Properties dialog box, click the Windows Setup tab.

4. In the list of components, click System Tools, but be careful not to clear the check box to its left.

5. Click Details.
6. In the System Tools dialog box, scroll through the components list and select the check box next to WinPopup.
7. Click OK to close the System Tools dialog box.
8. Click OK again to close the Add/Remove Programs Properties dialog box.

At this point, you might need the Windows CD. On some computers, the files that Windows needs are already stored on the hard disk. If that's the case, WinPopup will be installed and you're ready for the next stage. If the programs aren't on your hard disk, you'll be asked to insert the CD in the drive and click OK.

Using WinPopup

WinPopup must be running in order for you to send or receive a message. If the WinPopup shortcut isn't in the StartUp folder on your machine, you must open WinPopup by double-clicking the icon you placed on the desktop. If you're not ready to send a message, just minimize the window so that WinPopup appears on the taskbar.

Here's how to send a message:

1. Click the WinPopup button on the taskbar to open the WinPopup window.
2. Click the Send button on the toolbar, which shows a picture of an envelope, or choose Send from the Messages menu to open the Send Message dialog box.
3. To send a message to everyone on the network, click Workgroup. To send a message to a specific person on the network, click User Or Computer.
4. If you want to send a message to everyone and the workgroup name isn't listed, type the name of the workgroup in the text box in the To area of the Send Message dialog box. If you want to send a message to one person, type that person's user name or computer name.
5. Type the message (up to 128 characters) in the Message box, and then click OK.

A complete message might look like Figure 19-1.

Chapter 19: Communicating over Your Peer-to-Peer Network

Figure 19-1
The WinPopup Send Message dialog box allows you to send messages on the network.

Note

To paste text into the message from the clipboard, right-click in the Message text box and choose Paste from the shortcut menu.

6. A message box reports that the message was sent successfully.
7. Click OK.

If the window is minimized, click its button on the taskbar to display the message. The WinPopup icon in the taskbar, by the way, indicates whether or not you have pop-up messages to read. When you have no messages, the icon looks like this:

Here's what the icon looks like when you've received a message:

If you want the WinPopup window to open when a message arrives, choose Options from the Messages menu and select the check box for Pop Up Dialog On Message Receipt. Other options allow you to turn off the beep that sounds when a message arrives and to keep the WinPopup window in the foreground in front of other program windows.

When you have more than one message, click the Previous and Next buttons in the WinPopup toolbar to switch from one message to the next. Click the Delete button in the toolbar to delete a displayed message.

When you close the WinPopup window, a message box appears to remind you that you can't send or receive any more messages. If you still have undeleted messages, the message box also reminds you that all of them will be discarded when you close WinPopup because the program doesn't save messages from session to session. Click OK to close the WinPopup window.

Creating Your Own Post Office

While WinPopup is free with Windows, quick, and convenient, it does have its limitations. A pop-up message can be no longer than 128 characters, and the message is available only while WinPopup is open. When you exit WinPopup, all messages you've received are erased. It certainly would be better if you could send and receive e-mail over the network, just as you can over the Internet. Well, as it happens, Windows allows you to do just that.

In order to send and receive e-mail on your peer-to-peer network, you must set up a network mail server. The mail server lets you create mailboxes in which messages are stored until they are read by the recipient.

Note

Creating an office e-mail system in a client/server environment is discussed in Chapter 20.

Windows includes a mail server program called Microsoft Post Office. You can also download shareware mail server programs from the Internet. I'll look at Microsoft Post Office in this chapter.

Using Mail Servers and E-Mail Clients

To understand how e-mail works, you should understand the different roles played by the mail server and an e-mail program, such as Microsoft Outlook Express.

A mail server, such as the mail server at your Internet service provider (ISP) or the mail server you set up on your network, receives incoming e-mail, transmits outgoing messages, and organizes and stores messages

Chapter 19: Communicating over Your Peer-to-Peer Network

that have been received in mailboxes. Your ISP's mail server, for example, maintains a mailbox for each member and stores incoming messages until you retrieve them. Similarly, programs for creating a post office on your network let you create a mailbox for each user, and they handle the transfer of messages between the sender and the recipient.

An e-mail program, called the *e-mail client,* on the other hand, is the software that you run on your computer to read and write messages. It also transfers the messages you send to the mail server and picks up from the mail server messages that are waiting for you.

Most ISP mail servers on the Internet use the Post Office Protocol (POP). This means that you can communicate with them using any e-mail program that can handle POP e-mail. Outlook Express, Microsoft Outlook, Eudora, and Netscape Messenger are all POP e-mail programs. The abbreviation POP3, which you'll often see referenced in the online help for these programs, indicates version 3 of the Post Office Protocol.

Note

Some mail servers, such as the one used by America Online (AOL), are designed to communicate only with the e-mail programs built into their own software.

When you install Microsoft Post Office to add e-mail capabilities to your network, Microsoft Windows Messaging is installed at the same time. Windows Messaging works with the Microsoft Post Office as well as Internet e-mail.

Microsoft Exchange

When Windows 95 was first released, it included a program called Microsoft Exchange. Exchange was an e-mail client for sending and receiving mail through Microsoft Post Office on a network, but it didn't support Internet mail.

To use Exchange for Internet mail, you had to install Internet mail services, which were available in three ways: in a product called Microsoft Plus!, with versions of Microsoft Internet Explorer starting with 2.0, or as a separate update from Microsoft.

The name of the product was later changed from Microsoft Exchange to Microsoft Windows Messaging to distinguish it from Microsoft Exchange Server, the network messaging program.

You can use Outlook as your e-mail client because it can communicate with both Internet POP e-mail servers and Microsoft Post Office. Outlook has more features than Windows Messaging, but you must purchase it separately because it isn't included with Windows. *See "Setting Up Microsoft Outlook," on page 334,* if you want to use Outlook for your network e-mail.

Using Microsoft Post Office

Just like an Internet mail server, your network post office can handle messages of any length, including attachments. Messages you send are stored in your Sent Items folder, so you can keep a record of your communications. Messages you receive are stored in an Inbox until you decide to delete them. You can reply to messages and forward them to others on the network with a single click.

You do all this by installing Microsoft Post Office to create a post office on one of the computers on the network. The post office acts as a central station for channeling mail from senders to receivers. If you send a message to someone whose computer isn't turned on and ready to receive the message, the post office stores it until it can be received.

The person who sets up the post office has to specify who will be using it. Each user gets a post office mailbox, in which messages are stored, and a password for accessing the messages.

If you create a message and the post office is closed—the computer storing the post office is turned off or disconnected from the network—your message is held in the Outbox folder on your own computer until it can be sent. To ensure that messages won't sit in a sender's Outbox folder for too long, it's a good idea to set up the post office on the computer that's turned on most often.

Installing Microsoft Mail Postoffice

The first step in creating your postal system is to make sure the Microsoft Mail Postoffice program, a client program that comes with Windows, is installed on each computer on the network. To install the program, open each computer's Control Panel and look for two icons labeled Mail and Microsoft Mail Postoffice on each computer.

If you're running the original version of Windows 95, Microsoft Mail Postoffice was installed with Exchange. If your computer is running one of the updates to Windows 95, Microsoft Mail Postoffice was installed along with Windows Messaging.

Chapter 19: Communicating over Your Peer-to-Peer Network

> **Note**
>
> With Windows NT, Microsoft Mail Postoffice is installed with the Microsoft Mail components. If you don't see the Microsoft Mail Postoffice icon in Control Panel, you have to copy all of the files that are part of Microsoft Mail Postoffice on the Windows NT CD, those that have filenames beginning with *wgpo* (wgpo*.*), and place them in the \WINNT\SYSTEM32 folder.

If you don't see the Microsoft Mail Postoffice icon in Control Panel, use the Add/Remove Programs option in Control Panel to install either Exchange or Windows Messaging. When you look in the list of components that you can install, one or the other will be available.

Windows 98 and Windows 98 Second Edition don't install Microsoft Mail Postoffice. If you installed either version of Windows 98 over Windows 95, Windows 98 will leave the existing version of Microsoft Mail Postoffice on your computer, though.

> ### Fixing Microsoft Office 2000
>
> If you have Microsoft Office 2000 installed at the time you install Microsoft Mail Postoffice, the WMS program might replace some Office 2000 files on your hard disk, making Office 2000 unstable or unusable. If you run WMS after installing Microsoft Office 2000, you should repair the Office installation by following these steps:
>
> 1. Insert the Office CD in your CD drive.
>
>   The Office setup program should start. If it doesn't, open Add/Remove Programs in Control Panel, select Office 2000, and click Add/Remove.
>
> 2. In the Microsoft Office 2000 Maintenance Mode window, click the large Repair Office button.
>
> 3. In the Reinstall/Repair Microsoft Office 2000 window, choose Repair Errors In My Office Installation.
>
> 4. Click Finish, and then wait until the process is completed. This might take some time.
>
>   Repairing Microsoft Office won't cause any harm to the files installed by WMS.

Part 4: Running Your Office on a Network

To install Microsoft Mail Postoffice in either version of Windows 98, run the WMS program, which you'll find on your Windows CD in the \tools\oldwin95\message\us folder. If you have an international installation, choose the \intl directory instead of \us. Restart your computer after running the program, even if you aren't prompted to do so.

Creating the Post Office

Now that each computer on the network has Microsoft Mail Postoffice installed, you're ready to create the post office itself on one of them. Be sure to pick a computer that'll be on frequently, and then create and share a folder on that computer's hard disk, in which you'll store the post office files. Here's how it's done:

1. On the Windows desktop, double-click My Computer.
2. Double-click the C drive icon.
3. Right-click in the C window, point to New, and click Folder.
   The new folder is created, and its default name is highlighted.
4. Type *POFFICE* to replace the default name of the folder, and press Enter.
5. Right-click the POFFICE folder, and choose Sharing from the shortcut menu.
6. In the Properties dialog box, click Shared As.
7. Click Full.
8. Click OK.

You now have to create the post office itself, along with your own mailbox.

1. In the Control Panel window, double-click the Microsoft Mail Postoffice icon.
2. In the Microsoft Workgroup Postoffice Admin window, click Create A New Workgroup Postoffice, and then click Next to see the dialog box shown in Figure 19-2.
3. Type the path of the folder you created to store the post office (*c:\poffice*), and then click Next.
4. The Microsoft Mail Postoffice program creates a folder within the c:\poffice folder named Wgpo0000 that contains numerous files and subfolders, and the program asks you to confirm the folder's location.

Chapter 19: Communicating over Your Peer-to-Peer Network

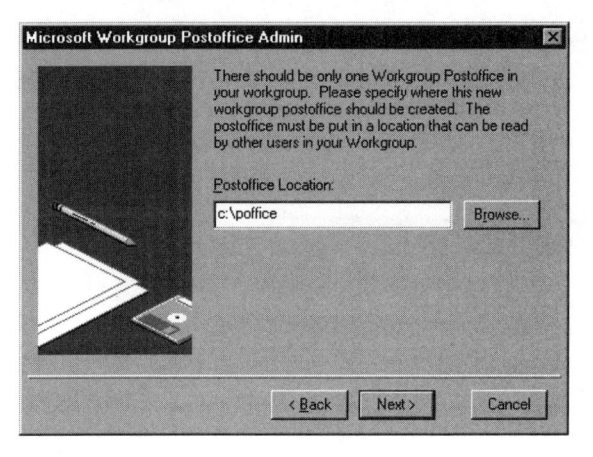

Figure 19-2
Create a folder for your post office in the Microsoft Workgroup Postoffice Admin dialog box.

5. Click Next.
6. In the Enter Your Administrator Account Details dialog box, type your name in the Name text box.
7. Make a note of the Mailbox name in the Mailbox text box. You'll need to know it later.
8. Press Tab twice, and type a replacement password in the Password text box.
9. Click OK.
10. Click OK in the Mail dialog box.

Adding Post Office Users

When you set up Microsoft Mail Postoffice, a mailbox is created for you. For other post office users, you'll need to create additional mailboxes. To add a user and create a mailbox, follow these steps:

1. In the Control Panel window, double-click the Microsoft Mail Postoffice icon.
2. In the Microsoft Workgroup Postoffice Admin dialog box, click Administer An Existing Workgroup Postoffice, and then click Next.
3. Click Next to accept the path to your post office.
4. Type your mailbox name as the post office administrator.

5. Type the password you entered earlier.
6. Click Next to open the Postoffice Manager dialog box, which lists all current users.
7. Click Add User to see the dialog box shown in Figure 19-3.

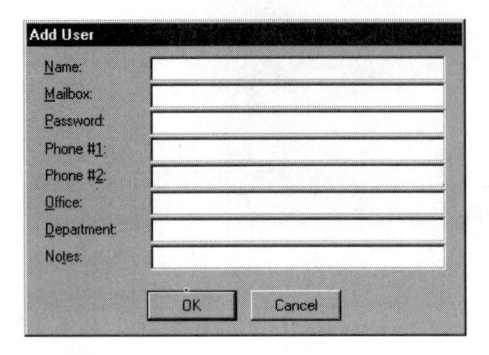

Figure 19-3
The Add User dialog box allows you to add new users to your post office.

8. Type the user's name.
9. Type the name for the user's mailbox.
10. Click OK.
11. Give to the user the path and name of the post office, the name of the mailbox, and the password.
12. Repeat steps 7 through 11 for each additional user, and then click Close.

Setting Up Windows Messaging

Each user must set up an e-mail program in order to be able to send and receive files through the Microsoft Mail Postoffice. Once a user has done this, he or she should have an Inbox icon on the desktop. Double-clicking this icon starts an e-mail program called Windows Messaging or Exchange, depending on the version of Windows, through which a user can send and receive information over the network. Outlook can also be used to send and receive mail through the network. Because Windows Messaging is included with Windows, I'll look at this program in some detail. You'll learn how to set up Outlook for network e-mail later in this chapter.

Chapter 19: Communicating over Your Peer-to-Peer Network

> ### Fixing Windows 98 Second Edition
>
> If you have Windows 98 Second Edition, you might get the following error message when you start Windows Messaging:
>
> ```
> MAPISP32 caused an invalid page fault in module KERNEL32.DLL
> ```
>
> If this happens to you, you'll need to take a few extra steps to get Windows Messaging working. Here's how to fix the problem:
>
> 1. Restart your computer.
> 2. Locate mapi32.dll in your Windows\System directory.
> 3. Rename the file to mapi32.lld.
> 4. Reinstall Windows Messaging from your Windows 98 Second Edition CD.
> 5. Restart your computer.

The first time you open the Inbox, you must create a profile. A profile lists the mail services that Windows Messaging can use. To create a profile, follow these steps:

1. Double-click the Inbox icon on the desktop to start the Inbox Setup Wizard.
2. Make sure the Use The Following Information Services button is selected and the Microsoft Mail check box is selected, and then click Next.

    You'll be asked to provide the path to the post office folder.

3. Click Browse to open the Browse For Postoffice dialog box.
4. Double-click Network Neighborhood, and locate the post office folder you created earlier.
5. Click OK to return to the Inbox Setup Wizard, and then click Next.

    The wizard displays a list of mailboxes in the post office.

6. Click your mailbox, and then click Next.
7. In the box that appears, type your mailbox password, and then click Next.

The wizard now shows you the default location of your personal address book. This is where you can store e-mail addresses.

8. Click Next to accept the default location.
9. The wizard now shows you the default location of your personal folder, in which your messages are stored.
10. Click Next to accept the default location and to see a summary of your profile.
11. Click Finish.

Adding Mail to Your Profile

If you're already using Windows Messaging or Exchange for your Internet e-mail, you can add Microsoft Mail to your profile to send and receive mail over the network. Here's how:

1. In the Control Panel window, double-click Mail.
2. If the profile to which you want to add Microsoft Mail isn't displayed, click the Show Profiles button to display the Mail dialog box, select the profile you want to change, and then click Properties.
3. In the Properties dialog box, click Add to display a list of services that can be installed in Windows Messaging.
4. Click Microsoft Mail in the list of information services.
5. Click Properties.
6. On the Connection tab of the Microsoft Mail dialog box, shown in Figure 19-4, type the name of the post office folder or browse for it. The name contains the path to the computer on the network. If the post office is on your computer, it might appear as C:\poffice\wgpo0000. If the post office is on another network computer, the path might be something like \\JoesComputer\C\poffice\wpgo0000.
7. On the Log On page, type your mailbox name and password.
8. Click OK.

Note

To set up Microsoft Messaging for Internet e-mail, you have to add Internet Mail to the profile. See "Working with Profiles" on page 336.

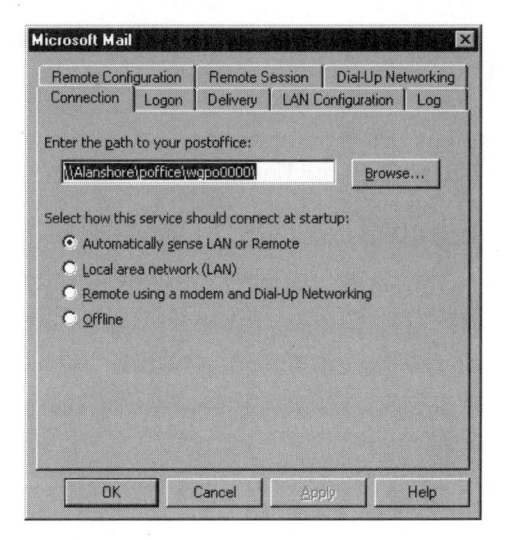

Chapter 19: Communicating over Your Peer-to-Peer Network

Figure 19-4

Type the path to your post office in the Microsoft Mail dialog box.

Sending and Receiving E-Mail

After you create a profile, opening the Inbox opens the Windows Messaging window shown in Figure 19-5. The window shows the Inbox, which displays the messages you've received. An initial welcoming message from Microsoft appears in the Inbox the first time you use Windows Messaging.

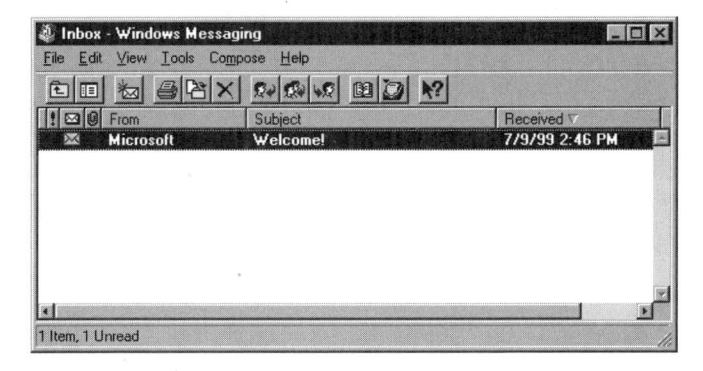

Figure 19-5

The Windows Messaging Inbox displays your incoming messages.

Creating and Addressing a Message To create a message, click the New Message button in the toolbar. A new message window opens. Click the To box to view a list of post office mailboxes. In the list of mailboxes, click

331

each person to whom you want to send a message, and then click the To button. When you've selected all the intended recipients, click OK.

Instead of clicking the To button to select recipients' names, for example, you can just type a recipient's user name in the To text box rather than look up the recipient in the address book. But if you type a name, click the Check Names button on the toolbar before you send the message. This feature makes sure that each name you've entered belongs to a person who actually has a mailbox in the post office and warns you if that's not the case.

Next, type the subject of the message and press Tab to move the cursor to the main message area, in which you type the message.

Attaching a File To send a file along with your message, click the Attach button, select the file you want to send, and then click OK. The file becomes an attachment that's transmitted along with the message.

Using Special Message Options If you click the Read Receipt button before sending a message, Microsoft Mail Postoffice will send you an e-mail message when the recipient opens the message. This confirms that the message was at least opened, if not necessarily read.

The three Importance options allow you to assign a level of importance to your message. If you click either High or Low, the message will be flagged in the recipient's Inbox with an icon indicating its level of importance. If you don't click either of these buttons, the Importance level is set at the default normal, which has no identifying icon.

Clicking the Properties button on the toolbar displays information about the selected message and offers you additional delivery options, as shown in Figure 19-6. It also allows you to assign your message one of four sensitivity levels—*Normal, Personal, Private,* or *Confidential.* When you designate a message as Private, for example, the recipient can't modify it when replying or when forwarding it to someone else. The other options merely display an icon next to the message in the Inbox showing the message's sensitivity level.

Note

Using the Columns command on the View menu, you can add a column to the Inbox that shows the sensitivity level of a message.

In addition to a read receipt, you can also request a delivery receipt—an e-mail message that Windows Messaging sends you when your message is delivered. To request a delivery receipt, select the check box for The Item Has Been Delivered on the Send tab of the Options dialog box.

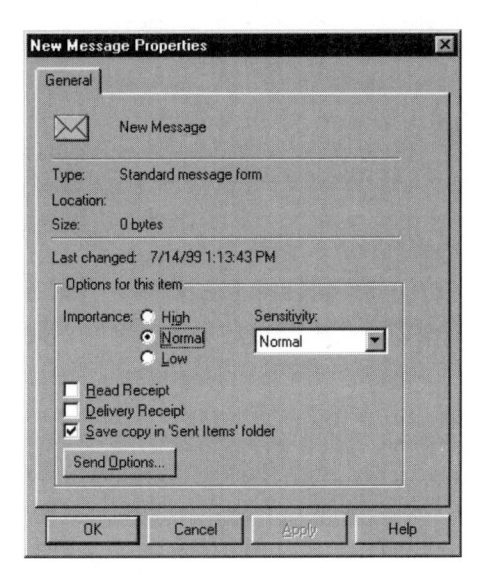

Chapter 19: Communicating over Your Peer-to-Peer Network

Figure 19-6
Message properties include several useful delivery options.

Sending the Message When your message is ready to go, click the Send button on the toolbar to move the message to the Outbox, where it's temporarily stored until it's sent to the post office. To make sure that all of your messages are actually sent to and received from the post office, on the Tools menu click Deliver Now, which sends and also collects all e-mail.

Reading Messages from Others When you receive mail through the post office, its header appears in your Inbox. The header shows the sender, subject, and the date and time the message was received. Double-click a message header to read the message.

If the message has an attachment, you'll see a paper clip icon to the left of its header. Open the message and then double-click the icon representing the attachment that appears in the body of the message. Depending on the format of the attachment, its contents might appear immediately or you might be prompted to save the attachment to your hard disk.

After you read a message, you can close it and do nothing (to leave it in your Inbox) or delete it. The headers of messages you haven't read appear in bold text. To reply to a message, click the Reply To Sender button. You'll see a message window addressed to the sender and containing the text of the original message. If the sender sent the message to more than one person, you can click Reply To All to send your reply to all recipients of the original message.

Click the Forward button to send a copy of the message on to someone else, without responding to the original sender.

Filing Messages in Folders   In addition to an Inbox, Windows Messaging has an Outbox, a Sent Items folder, and a Deleted Items folder. To display the entire list of folders when you have one of the folders open, click the Up One Level button.

Double-click the folder you want to open. You can also display the list of folders by clicking the Folder List button in the toolbar. Click a folder in the folder list to display its contents.

The Deleted Items folder stores the messages that you delete from the other folders, just in case you change your mind. By default, these messages are permanently deleted when you exit Windows Messaging. To keep the messages in the Deleted Items folder, choose Options from the Tools menu, and clear the Empty The Deleted Items Folder Upon Exiting option. Then if you really want to erase the messages, you can always open the Deleted Items folder and delete the messages you find there.

Setting Up Microsoft Outlook

Outlook is an e-mail program that's a component of Microsoft Office. If you're using Office and Outlook is installed on your computer, you can use it to send and receive mail through your network as well as through the Internet.

Note

Outlook Express, which comes with Internet Explorer 4.0 or later, is designed for Internet e-mail. With Microsoft Post Office, only Outlook is capable of sending and receiving e-mail over a network. While using Outlook for all your e-mail needs is a good solution, you might want to use Outlook Express or some other e-mail program for both Internet e-mail and e-mail on your network. If so, you'll need a mail server other than Microsoft Post Office, such as the shareware program VPOP3, which is available for download on the Internet.

To use Outlook for your network e-mail, you have to install the Microsoft Mail Postoffice program, as described earlier in this chapter. You can then install Outlook in its Corporate/Workgroup configuration and create or choose a profile. A profile tells Outlook how to connect to your e-mail server, your network, or the Internet.

Selecting the Mail Service

When you first start Outlook, you'll be given three options: Corporate Or Workgroup, Internet Only, and No E-Mail. Choose Corporate Or Workgroup to send and receive e-mail messages either through the network or over the Internet. The other two options are:

- **Internet Only.** This option lets you exchange e-mail only through the Internet. When you choose Internet Only, you won't be able to use Outlook on a network to send and receive e-mail. But you'll be able to send and receive e-mail through the Internet, check schedules, assign tasks, and perform other Outlook functions.

- **No E-Mail.** This option lets you use Outlook's record-keeping and time-management tools but not its communications capabilities. You won't be able to use Outlook to send or receive e-mail through your network or the Internet.

If you've already set up a profile, such as a profile that was set up for a previous version of Outlook, Outlook will use that profile. If you haven't yet set up a profile when you choose the Corporate/Workgroup installation, Outlook begins the Inbox Setup Wizard that guides you through the process. You set up Outlook to use your Microsoft Mail Postoffice for network e-mail by using the Inbox Setup Wizard *as described in "Setting Up Windows Messaging," on page 328*. If you already have a profile, you can add your post office to your Outlook Profile, *as described in "Adding Mail to Your Profile," on page 330*.

> **Note**
>
> If you have already installed Outlook in its Internet Only or No E-Mail configuration, you can change it to Corporate Or Workgroup without reinstalling the entire program. Start Outlook, choose Options from the Tools menu, and click the Mail Delivery tab. Click the Reconfigure Mail Support button, and choose the Corporate Or Workgroup option in the dialog box that appears.

Working with Profiles

After you create a profile, it's not too late to create a new profile, or to add, remove, or modify the properties of the services within a profile. If you use your computer at more than one location, for example, you might need a separate profile for each location. You might also want a separate profile to send faxes from your computer over a telephone line that you also use for connecting to an Internet e-mail server. Just be cautious when you make changes. An incorrect profile could prevent Outlook from starting or connecting to your network or ISP, or you could potentially lose the information you've stored in Outlook.

Creating a Profile

You can set up, change, and remove a profile with the Mail option in the Control Panel. After you've set up Outlook, you can add services to a profile or remove them from within Outlook.

To create a new profile, follow these steps:

1. Double-click the Mail icon in the Control Panel window.
2. If one or more profiles have been set up, click the Show Profiles button in the Properties dialog box for the currently active profile. This displays the Mail dialog box. If no profiles have been set up on your system, the Mail dialog box opens.
3. Click the Add button in the Mail dialog box to create a new profile using the Inbox Setup Wizard.
4. After completing all the steps of the wizard, click Finish to return to the Mail dialog box.
5. In the Mail dialog box, you can choose a default profile in the box labeled When Starting Microsoft Outlook, Use This Profile.
6. Click Close.

You can use the Inbox Setup Wizard to create profiles specific to each location from which you use Outlook: office, home, and on the road.

Modifying a Profile

Suppose you signed up for a new online service. At the same time, you also bailed out of an online service that wasn't giving you what you wanted. Your profile is now out of date, so you want to update the online service information. Here's how you do it.

Chapter 19: Communicating over Your Peer-to-Peer Network

1. Double-click the Mail icon in the Control Panel window to open the Properties dialog box.
2. If the profile you want to change isn't displayed, click the Show Profiles button to display the Mail dialog box, select the profile you want to change, and then click Properties.

    The Services tab of the Properties dialog box lists all of the services in the profile you've selected.
3. On the Services tab of the Properties dialog box, you can:
    - Click Add to install a new service to the current profile. Fill in the text boxes in the dialog boxes that appear to help you configure the service.
    - Click Copy to copy the selected service to another profile.
    - Select a service and click Properties to view or edit its settings.
    - Select a service and click Remove to delete the service from the profile.

Click OK when you're finished modifying the profile. If you want to make changes to another profile, click Show Profiles and repeat the process. Click the Close button in the Mail dialog box when you've finished.

Using a Different Profile

If you have more than one profile set up, you can select which profile to use when you start Outlook.

1. Double-click the Mail icon in the Control Panel window.
2. Click Show Profiles, and then open the list labeled When Starting Microsoft Outlook, Use This Profile.
3. Choose the profile you want to use by default, and then click Close.

You can set Outlook to always use a particular profile or to let you choose a profile each time you start the program.

To use the same profile every time, do this:

1. In Outlook, choose Options from the Tools menu, and then click the Mail Services tab, if it isn't already displayed.
2. Enable the Always Use This Profile option, and then select the profile you want to use from the drop-down list.
3. Click OK.

Part 4: Running Your Office on a Network

If you prefer, you can choose a profile at the start of each Outlook session. For this option, follow these steps:

1. In Outlook, choose Options from the Tools menu, and then click the Mail Services tab if it isn't already displayed.
2. Click the Prompt For A Profile To Be Used option.
3. Click OK.

Once the Prompt For A Profile To Be Used option is selected, you'll need to select a profile in the Choose Profile dialog box each time you start Outlook.

Removing a Profile

Now suppose that your situation changes and you no longer need all the profiles that you created. Perhaps you no longer have access to a corporate network and you want to delete the profile that includes the Exchange service. To simplify your Outlook life, you can remove the unwanted or unnecessary profiles.

To remove a profile from Control Panel, follow these steps:

1. Double-click the Mail icon in the Control Panel window.
2. In the Properties dialog box, click the Show Profiles button.
3. Select the profile you want to remove.
4. Click the Remove button, and then click Yes when you're asked whether you want to remove this profile.
5. Click the Close button.

Using the Microsoft Outlook Address Book

Outlook maintains its own address book, separate from addresses you might have in Windows Messaging, Outlook Express, and other mail programs.

Network users will have more than one address list within the address book. On a peer-to-peer network using Microsoft Mail Postoffice, you have the post office address list of other network users. You'll also have a personal address book for e-mail addresses of people not on the network, and maybe an offline address book so you can address messages when you aren't connected to the network. You'll also probably have an Outlook address book, which is created from entries in your Contacts folder. And finally, you can have separate address lists for each online service you use to send and receive e-mail.

Chapter 19: Communicating over Your Peer-to-Peer Network

When you open the Outlook Address Book, you have to select the address list that contains the names to which you want to send your e-mail.

Opening the Address Book

To open the Address Book, choose Address Book from the Tools menu or click the Address Book button on the Standard toolbar—the button is displayed when the Inbox, Outbox, Outlook Today, Sent Items, Drafts, or other mail folder is open. If you're creating an e-mail message, click To in the new e-mail message. The Address Book opens and displays the names from the address list that's set up as the default, as shown in Figure 19-7.

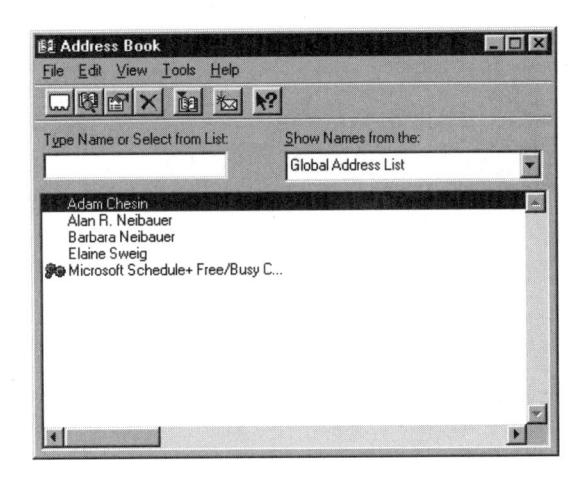

Figure 19-7
Choose a name from the Outlook Address Book.

Note

You can change the default address list using the Services dialog box. To open this dialog box, choose Services from the Tools menu. Click the Addressing tab and select the list you want to see first from the Show This Address List First list.

If the list of names in the Address Book that appears isn't the one with the information you need, do the following:

1. Click the arrow next to the Show Names From The list to display the available address lists.
2. Select the list you want to open, such as Postoffice Address List for addresses on your peer-to-peer network.

Adding a Personal Address Book to Your Profile

You can't add names to the Postoffice Address list of the Address Book. The names in this list are taken directly from the Postoffice mailbox names that you've set up as the Postoffice administrator.

If you want to use the Address Book for Internet e-mail as well, you can add a personal address list to the Address Book by adding it to your profile. To add a personal address list, follow these steps:

1. Start Outlook, and choose Services from the Tools menu.
2. On the Services tab, click the Add button.
3. In the Add Service To Profile dialog box, select Personal Address Book, and then click OK.
4. In the Personal Address Book dialog box, type a name for the personal address book in the Name box.
5. In the Path text box, type the path of the personal address book file, or click the Browse button to locate a personal address book file that already exists. Personal address books are maintained in files with a .pab extension.
6. Click OK in the Personal Address Book dialog box, and then click OK again in the message box that appears.
7. Click OK in the Services dialog box, and then exit and restart Outlook.

To add a personal address book to a profile other than the one you're currently using, double-click the Mail icon in the Control Panel window. On the Services tab, click Show Profiles. On the General tab, click the profile you want in the Profile box, click Properties, and then follow steps 2 through 7 in the previous procedure.

To add a name and address to your personal address book, do the following:

1. Choose Address Book from the Tools menu, or click the Address Book button on the Standard toolbar.
2. Click the New Entry button on the Address Book toolbar to open the New Entry dialog box, shown in Figure 19-8.
3. Click the arrow next to the Put This Entry In The list, and choose Personal Address Book in the list.
4. In the Select The Entry Type list, select the type of address you want to enter.

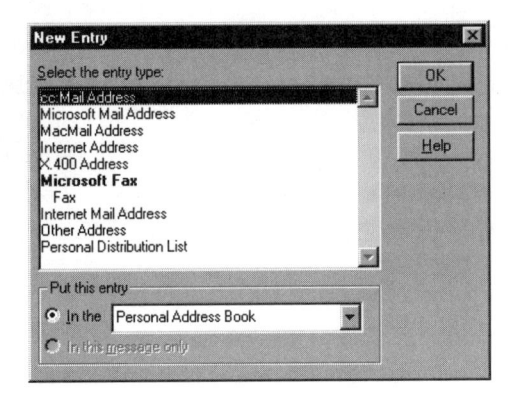

Chapter 19: Communicating over Your Peer-to-Peer Network

Figure 19-8
You can choose a new entry type and destination in the New Entry dialog box.

5. Click OK.

    The next dialog box you see varies according to the type of entry you've selected. For most new entries, you'll type information to display in the address book and the e-mail address.

6. In the Display Name text box, type the name as you want it to appear in the address book.

7. In the E-Mail Address text box, type the e-mail address, such as *alan@neibauer.net*.

8. In the E-mail Type text box, type the designation for the recipient's e-mail system, such as *SMTP*, a common format for Internet e-mail.

9. Select the check box labeled Always Send To This Recipient In Microsoft Outlook Rich-Text Format if you want to send meeting requests and tasks to other Outlook users.

10. Fill in the text boxes on the other tabs with as much information as you want. For example, the Business tab provides text boxes for a mailing address and phone number. The Phone Numbers tab contains text boxes for multiple phone numbers, including a text box for a fax number. If you want to send a fax to this person, be sure to enter the fax telephone number.

    When you add a name and address, Outlook requires only that you fill in the text boxes on the New Address tab. You can leave the other tabs blank and fill them in later by double-clicking the name in the Address Book window or by using the Properties button on the Address Book toolbar.

11. Click OK.

> **Note**
>
> If you communicate with other Outlook users over the Internet, make sure you select the Always Send To This Recipient In Microsoft Outlook Rich-Text Format check box. Then you can send Outlook items, such as meeting requests and tasks, which will be properly formatted when opened by others in their Calendar or Tasks folders.

Sending a Message

The fastest and easiest way to send a message is simply to type the text and click the Send button.

> **Note**
>
> You can create a new message from any folder in Outlook. From the Inbox, Outbox, or Drafts folder, click the New Mail Message button. From another folder, click the down arrow on the Standard toolbar's New button and select Mail Message.

To send a simple message from a mail folder, do the following:

1. Click the New Mail Message button at the left end of the Standard toolbar to open a message window.
2. In the new message window, click the To button to display the Select Names dialog box.
3. Select the address book you want to use from the Show Names From The list box.
4. In the Type Name Or Select From List text box, type part of the name of a recipient, type the full name, or select a name from the list below.

   When you type the beginning of a name in the Type Name Or Select From List box, Outlook scrolls through the list of addresses to the first name that matches the letters you've typed. You can then scroll further, if you need to, to find the name you want.

   You can also select a distribution list from either the personal address book or from the Contacts list to send the message to a group of people. To select more than one addressee, hold down the Ctrl key and click each name.

Chapter 19: Communicating over Your Peer-to-Peer Network

5. Click the To button to enter the main addressees, and click the Cc or Bcc box to send copies to others.

    The name or names you've selected appear in the boxes to the right of each button.

6. Click OK when you've chosen all the addressees.

7. In the message window, click in the Subject box and type a brief description of the subject of your message.

8. Click the message area or press the Tab key to move to the message text area, and then type your message.

9. When your message is ready to send, click the Send button.

> **Note**
>
> If you don't complete your message or aren't ready to send it, choose Save from the File menu. Outlook stores the message in the Drafts folder. To complete the message, open the Drafts folder, and then double-click the message in the message list. Click Send when you're ready to send the message.

What happens when you click the Send button depends on how your system is set up and to whom the mail is addressed. E-mail messages that you've sent to recipients on your network (those people who have mailboxes in your Microsoft Mail Postoffice) are transmitted immediately. E-mail messages to Internet recipients, however, are stored in the Outbox folder until you're ready to dial in and connect. To actually send the messages, click the Send And Receive button on the Standard toolbar. Outlook sends any messages in the Outbox folder and checks for new messages waiting for you.

When you send a message, Outlook saves a copy of it in the Sent Items folder. To check your sent messages, click the Sent Items folder.

Reading a Message

When e-mail arrives in your Inbox, you can read it, respond to it, and forward it to others. You can read a message in the preview pane or in a separate window. The preview pane is an area at the lower right of the Inbox that displays the contents of the selected message. If the preview pane isn't displayed, on the View menu click Preview Pane.

> **Note**
>
> Once you've opened a message in its own window, you can use the Previous Item and Next Item buttons (the buttons with the large up and down arrows) on the Standard toolbar in the message window to move from message to message. Next to each of these buttons is a small down arrow that you can click to see a list of commands that let you move more quickly to the messages you want to read. For example, you can move to the next or previous message from the same sender or to the next or previous unread message.

To quickly read e-mail text when the preview pane is displayed, click the message header in the Inbox message list. If part of a long message falls below the bottom of the preview pane, scroll through the message window to read the remainder of the message. To see the first three lines of messages directly in the message list, choose AutoPreview from the View menu.

To read the message in its own window, simply double-click the message line in your Inbox's message list. If you want to add the sender's name to your address book, right-click the person's name in the open message, and then choose Add To Personal Address Book. Choose Properties from the shortcut menu if you just want to see the sender's e-mail address.

> **Note**
>
> For more information on using Outlook for network and Internet e-mail, see *Running Microsoft Outlook 2000,* published by Microsoft Press.

In the next chapter, you'll learn how to set up an e-mail system on a client/server network using Microsoft Exchange Server.

Chapter 20

Client/Server Communications with Exchange Server

In Chapter 19, you learned how to communicate over a peer-to-peer network using WinPopup, Microsoft Post Office, and e-mail clients, such as the Microsoft Exchange client and Microsoft Outlook. If you have a client/server network that's running Microsoft BackOffice Small Business Server (SBS) or Microsoft Windows NT, you can use Microsoft Exchange Server for your interoffice, remote, and Internet e-mail. Exchange Server is a powerful messaging system with which you can even host your own Internet mail server. In this chapter, you'll learn how Exchange Server can be used for network communications and Internet e-mail.

Exchange Server needs two major elements for your office e-mail—user mailboxes and e-mail clients. A *user mailbox* is a file on the server in which messages to and from the users are stored. Someone acting as a network or Exchange Server administrator must create the mailbox and set its parameters. As with peer-to-peer networking, workstations can use the Exchange client or Outlook as their e-mail client.

Creating Mailboxes

The first step to using Exchange Server is to create a mailbox for each user. If you installed Exchange Server as part of SBS, mailboxes are created when you create user accounts.

If you're using Windows NT and you didn't install it as part of SBS, you might have to create a mailbox separately. Here's how to get started:

1. Click Start, point to Programs and Microsoft Exchange, and then click Microsoft Exchange Administrator. The Exchange Administrator window opens as shown in Figure 20-1.

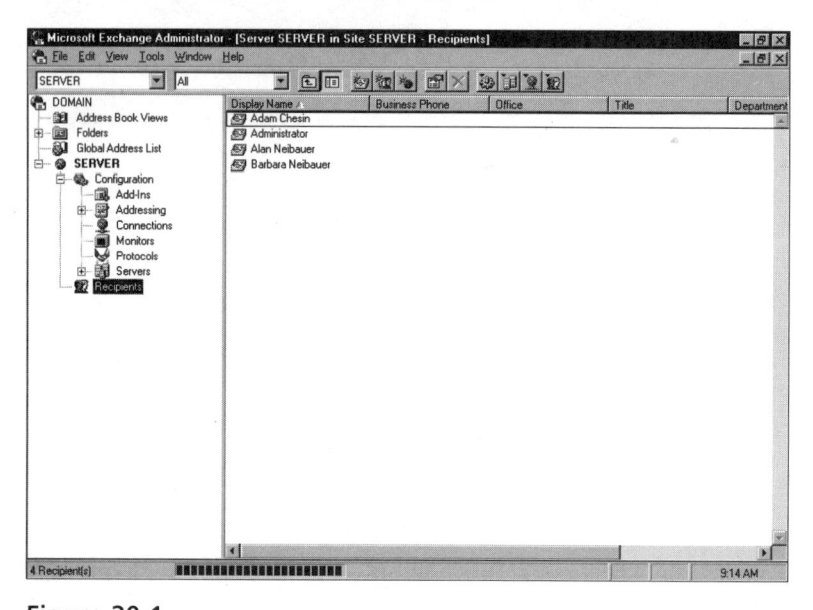

Figure 20-1
Create user mailboxes with Microsoft Exchange Administrator.

2. Click Recipients in the list on the left under Server. If Recipients isn't shown, click the plus sign in front of Server.
3. Select New Mailbox from the File menu to open the Properties box.
4. If the user already has an NT user account, or you want to create a new NT account, click Primary Windows NT Account.
5. Choose either Select An Existing Windows NT Account or Create A New Windows NT Account, and then click OK.
6. If you chose to select an existing account, choose the user in the box that appears, and click Add and then OK.

7. If you chose to create a new user account, type the account name in the box that appears and then click OK. Click OK again in the box that reports that you'll need to assign a user password later in User Manager For Domains.

8. Enter the information on the General tab of the Properties dialog box.

9. On the Organization tab, you can enter the user's manager and to whom the user reports.

10. On the Phone/Notes tab, enter up to 8 telephone numbers and notes.

11. On the Delivery Restrictions tab, you can specify to accept or reject messages from specific users.

Offline Address Book

Network users can address mail to other network recipients using the address book created by Exchange Server. The address book, however, is normally available only when the user is logged on to the network because it's maintained on the server.

If you want users to be able to address mail when they aren't connected to the network, such as when the server is down or they're away from the office, you have to create an offline address book. Users can download copies of this address book to their own computer. They can then address messages to network users offline and send the messages when they next connect to the network.

To generate an offline address book, follow these steps:

1. Open Exchange Administrator, and click Configuration under Server in the left-hand list.

2. Double-click DS Site Configuration on the right of the window to open the DS Site Configuration Properties dialog box.

3. Click the Offline Address Book tab and then the Generate All button.

4. Click OK when the message appears reporting that the offline address book has been created.

If you add or delete network users' accounts, you have to regenerate the offline address book in the same way you update the list of recipients.

Instead of generating the book manually, however, click the Offline Address Book Schedule tab to see the options shown in Figure 20-2. Use this dialog box to schedule automatic generation of the address book.

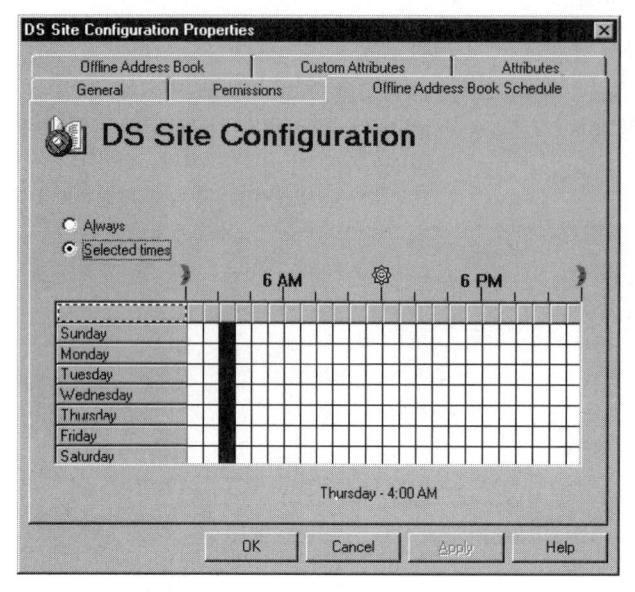

Figure 20-2

Use the Offline Address Book Schedule tab to schedule when the Outlook address book will be generated.

You select a time for the book to be generated by clicking a block in the time grid so it appears highlighted. In Figure 20-2, for example, the schedule is set to generate the book at 2 A.M. every day.

To generate the book every 15 minutes starting at the highlighted time, select the Always option. To generate the book only at the specific times set, select the Selected Times option.

Security

There are two ways to secure mail—encryption and digital signing.

- Encryption ensures that only someone who logs on to the e-mail server as a valid recipient can read your message. Without encryption, your messages are sent as readable text.

- A digital signature assures the recipient that you're really the person who sent the message—in other words, that the message

Chapter 20: Client/Server Communications with Exchange Server

isn't some bogus transmission sent by a pernicious computer hacker—and that the message hasn't been altered along the way.

With Exchange Server, you perform both encryption and digital signing using Key Management Server (KMS). The system administrator has to install KMS, which assigns a special randomly generated startup password that'll be required to start KMS on the server. The administrator can choose to type the password each time KMS is started or save the password on a floppy disk that must be inserted into the disk drive when KMS starts. The KMS installation process also lets the administrator specify a logon password, which is needed to enable user security or change KMS settings.

KMS can be set up as a manual or automatic service. The administrator must turn on a manual service after the server is started. An automatic service is started when Windows NT Server is started.

The administrator then determines whether a user should be allowed to secure mail. KMS generates a random security code called a *token*, which the administrator sends to the user. The user has to apply for security by returning the token to KMS. The token verifies that the person requesting security is indeed the authorized user.

When KMS is installed, follow these steps to begin the service:

1. Double-click Services in the Control Panel window.

2. In the list of services that appears, double-click Microsoft Exchange Key Management Server to see the Service dialog box shown in Figure 20-3.

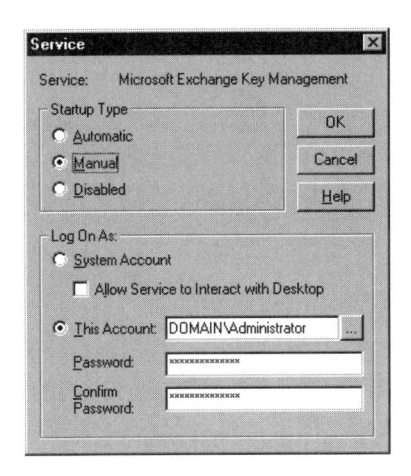

Figure 20-3
You must enable Key Management Server after you install it.

Part 4: Running Your Office on a Network

3. If you want KMS to start the next time you start the server, choose Automatic in the Startup Type section. Otherwise, leave the option set to Manual.
4. Click OK to return to the Services dialog box.
5. Insert the startup password disk into your floppy disk drive.
6. With Microsoft Exchange Key Management Server still selected, click Start. Windows will read the startup password from the floppy disk and begin the service. If you chose to enter the startup password rather than save it on a floppy disk, type the password in the box that appears and then click OK.
7. Click Close.

When you want to assign a user a token for his or her e-mail, follow these steps:

1. Open the Exchange Administrator and double-click the user's name in the recipients list.
2. Click the Security tab to see a dialog box asking for your KMS password.
3. Type the password, and then click OK.
4. Click Enable Advanced Security to be prompted for your password.
5. Type your KMS password again, and click OK. A box appears reporting the user's token.
6. Copy down the token so you can give it to the user, and click OK.
7. Click OK.

> **Note**
>
> The Valid From and Valid To fields aren't filled in until the key is assigned to the user.

Setting Up Exchange Clients

Once Exchange is set up and running on the server, clients can be configured to access their Exchange Mailboxes. The process is similar to setting up a profile in a peer-to-peer environment and using the Exchange client or Outlook as the e-mail client.

Chapter 20: Client/Server Communications with Exchange Server

The first step, however, is to add Exchange Server to your mail profile. To do this, you must have a user account and an Exchange Server mailbox on your server. Then follow these steps:

1. Double-click Mail in the Control Panel window to see the Properties list for your profile.
2. Click Add to open the Add Service To Profile dialog box.
3. Click Microsoft Exchange Server and then OK to open the dialog box shown in Figure 20-4.

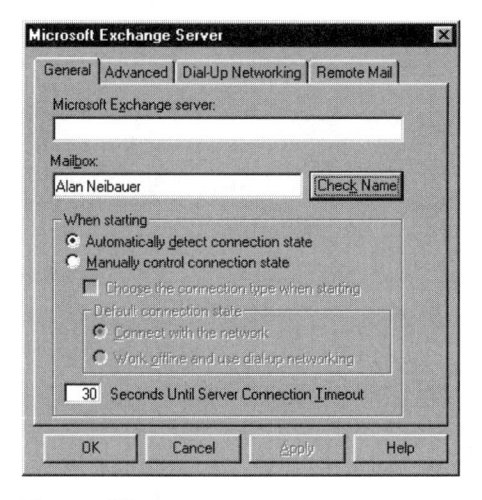

Figure 20-4
Add Exchange Server to your mail profile.

4. Type the name of your server.
5. Type your mailbox name if it's not correct.
6. Click Check Name.
   An underline should appear under your mailbox name and the name of the server verifying that they match your actual mailbox and server names. If you get an error message, check with the administrator for the correct mailbox name.
7. Click OK to return to the Properties dialog box.

Setting the Delivery Point

When you use Outlook with Exchange Server, you can have your messages and other information stored primarily on the server or on your own computer.

Part 4: Running Your Office on a Network

Your decision really doesn't matter if you're *always* connected to the server. But if you use your computer primarily offline or if you sometimes connect to a peer-to-peer network, it's probably best to store your information on the computer itself. For this you'll use *personal folders,* a special set of files on your computer that are used for your mailbox.

The Delivery tab of the Properties dialog box for your profile is where you'll set the location to which your mail and network messages are delivered. Click the Delivery tab of the Properties box to see the options.

Storing Information on the Server

If you want all mail sent to you to be stored in your mailbox on the server, follow these steps:

1. Click the Delivery tab of the Properties dialog box for your profile.
2. Pull down the Deliver New Mail To The Following Location list and choose the item labeled Mailbox followed by your mailbox name.

All of your incoming mail and other Outlook information will be stored in folders on the server.

Storing Information Locally

If you want to store your information on your own computer, you'll have to add the Personal Folders service to your profile and then choose personal folders as the delivery point for new messages.

First, check to see if the Personal Folders service already exists. Open the Properties box for your profile and see whether Personal Folders is included in the list of services. If not, follow these steps to create personal folders:

1. On the Services tab of the Properties dialog box for your profile, click Add to display the Add Service To Profile dialog box.
2. Select Personal Folders.
3. Click OK.
4. In the dialog box that appears, select the location for the new or existing folder.
5. In the File Name box, type the name for the new folder or select an existing file.
6. Click Open to display the dialog box shown in Figure 20-5.

Chapter 20: Client/Server Communications with Exchange Server

Figure 20-5
Set up folders to store your mail in the Create Microsoft Personal Folders dialog box.

7. Type a name for your personal folders in the Name box as you want it to appear in Outlook.
8. Choose an encryption setting.
9. Type an optional password.
10. Type the same password again for verification.
11. Select the Save This Password In Your Password List check box if you don't want to be prompted for the password when you use the folder.
12. Click OK.

Now that your profile contains the Personal Folders service, you can designate this as the delivery point. This means that mail from the Exchange Server will be sent to your personal folders inbox even when you're connected to the network.

1. Click the Delivery tab of the Properties dialog box.
2. In the Deliver New Mail To The Following Location list, click Personal Folders.

Communicating with Microsoft Outlook

When you first start Outlook, you'll be given three options: Corporate Or Workgroup, Internet Only, and No E-Mail. Choose Corporate Or Workgroup to send and receive e-mail messages either through the network or over the Internet.

Part 4: Running Your Office on a Network

If you've already set up a profile, such as a profile that was set up for a previous version of Outlook, Outlook will use that profile. If you haven't yet set up a profile when you choose the Corporate Or Workgroup installation, Outlook begins the Inbox Setup Wizard that guides you through the process, as described in Chapter 19, and you can add Exchange Server *as described in "Setting Up Exchange Clients" on page 350.*

> **Note**
>
> If you have already installed Outlook in its Internet Only or No E-Mail configuration, you can change it to Corporate Or Workgroup without reinstalling the entire program. Start Outlook, choose Options from the Tools menu, and click the Mail Delivery tab. Click the Reconfigure Mail Support button and choose the Corporate Or Workgroup option in the dialog box that appears.

Using Exchange Security

Before you can send and receive encrypted and signed messages, you have to configure Outlook for security. While in Outlook, select Options from the Tools menu, and then click the Security tab to see the options in Figure 20-6. You'll find options for encrypting your messages, adding your digital signature to messages, setting your security file, changing your security password, setting up advanced security, logging off advanced security, and sending security keys.

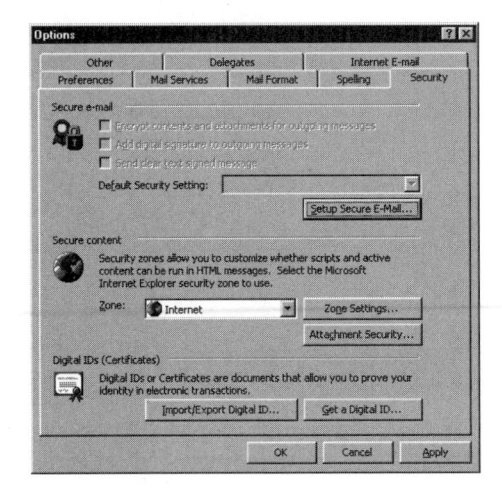

Figure 20-6
Provide a layer of protection for your e-mail on the Security tab of the Options dialog box.

In order to use encryption and digital signatures, you must have a security certificate that verifies who you are to others. Two types of certificates are available in Outlook—an Exchange certificate to use over the network and a S/MIME certificate to use on the Internet.

Getting a Digital Certificate

To get a digital certificate, follow these steps:

1. Choose Options from the Tools menu, and click the Security tab.
2. Click Get A Digital ID.
3. If you're not connected to a security-enabled Exchange Server network, you can obtain a digital ID only over the Internet. Clicking Get A Digital ID will launch your Web browser and connect you to a site that provides information on security certificates.
4. If the Get A Digital ID dialog box appears, choose Get A S/MIME Certificate From An External Certification Authority if you want to get a security certificate for use over the Internet. Select Set Up Security For Me On The Exchange Server if you want an Exchange Key Management Server to assign you a digital ID for your network.

Exchange Server Security

To get an Exchange certificate, your network administrator must have security running on the server and must give you a token. When you choose Exchange security in step 3 above, the Set Up Advanced Security dialog box should appear.

Now follow these steps:

1. Type a name for your digital ID.
2. Type the token given to you by the network administrator in the Token text box.
3. Click OK to close the Setup Advanced Security dialog box and process your request for a digital ID.
4. When a message appears telling you that your request for security has been sent to Exchange Server, click OK.
5. Click OK again on the Security tab.

In a few moments (depending on how busy the server is), Exchange Server will send you an e-mail message verifying your token. When you open the message, a dialog box appears reporting that Outlook is writing the Exchange signing key to your system. Click OK to display a box reporting that Outlook is writing the encryption key to your system. Click OK again. A message appears reporting that you're now security enabled. This means that the certificate has been added to Outlook and you can now send and receive encrypted and digitally signed messages.

> **Note**
>
> Once you enroll in Exchange security, you don't have to do it again, unless you're notified by your system administrator that you need to obtain a new token.

S/MIME Internet Security

To use Internet security, known as S/MIME, you have to get a certificate from a third-party company by registering on their Web site. Most companies charge a small fee for their certificate services, although many offer a free trial period.

When you select Get A S/MIME Certificate From An External Authority in the Get A Digital ID dialog box, Outlook launches your Web browser and connects you to the appropriate site. Follow the instructions on the screen to apply for a digital certificate. In most cases, after you apply you'll be notified by e-mail that your certificate is ready, and you'll have to connect to a Web site to accept it. When the site verifies your certificate, it'll download and install it on your system so you're ready to send and receive secure messages.

Changing Security Settings

If you're on a network and connected to the Internet, you can have both types of security certificates. In the Security tab of the Options dialog box, choose the setting to use as the default from the Default Security Setting list.

If you have problems using security procedures, something might not be set up properly. On the Security tab of the Options dialog box, click the Change Settings button to display the Change Security Settings dialog box. Generally, the settings in the Security Settings Name and Secure Message Format boxes should match. That is, if you're using the Exchange security setting, you should also use the Exchange secure message format.

The following options in the Change Security Settings dialog box determine which type of security is used:

Send These Certificates With Signed Messages. Choose this option to send a copy of your certificate with secure messages. The recipient will be able to use the certificate to send you encrypted messages. You can't clear this check box when you're using Exchange Server security.

Default Security Setting For This Secure Message Format. If you select this check box, these settings will be used by default for the format listed above in the Secure Message Format text box. If you chose the S/MIME format, for example, the settings will be used when you send a secure message using S/MIME. Select this check box if you want to use different settings when sending S/MIME and Exchange Security secure messages.

Default Security Setting For All Secure Messages. Selecting this check box will apply these settings to all types of secure messages.

Tip

You can obtain more than one certificate. Click the Choose buttons in the Change Security Settings dialog box to select the certificate to use for your digital signature and for encrypted messages. You can also click the Choose buttons to display information about the certificate.

Securing Contents

E-mail messages using HTML formatting can also contain active content—elements that have the potential to run programs and perform operations on your computer. While it's unlikely that you'll receive such a message, it pays to be careful. The Zone setting in the Secure Content area of the Security tab lets you control how active content is handled in both e-mail messages and attachments.

Selecting and Changing Zones

In the Zone list, you can select from two zones: Internet Zone and Restricted Sites Zone. The Internet Zone offers a medium level of security that'll warn you before active content is accepted and run. The Restricted Sites Zone offers a high level of security that simply excludes any active content. To change the degree of security in a zone, click the Zone Settings button to see the dialog box shown in Figure 20-7, and follow the steps on the next page.

Part 4: Running Your Office on a Network

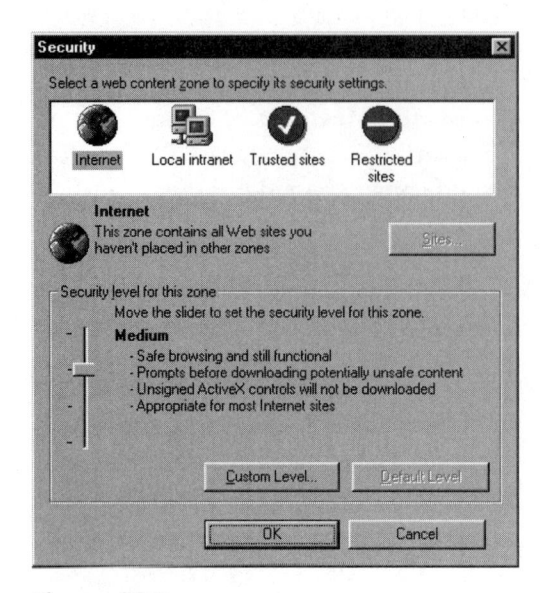

Figure 20-7

Configure security for a zone in the Security dialog box.

1. Choose the zone you want to change.
2. If you chose Restricted Sites in step 1, click Sites to enter specific Web sites to restrict.
3. Select the level of security for the zone you selected.
4. Click OK.

If you choose the Custom level of security, you can click Settings and choose to enable or disable security or warn about potential security issues for each of a list of specific types of content.

Securing Attachments

Active content can also be found in message attachments. Again you probably won't receive an attachment with dangerous content, but by default, you'll be warned of the potential problem when you save or open some attachments. If you don't want to receive this warning, click the Attachment Security button, choose None in the dialog box that appears, and then click OK.

Using Security

To use security with all messages, select the encryption and digital signature check boxes on the Security tab of the Options dialog box.

Chapter 20: Client/Server Communications with Exchange Server

- Select the Encrypt Contents And Attachments For Outgoing Messages check box to encrypt your messages. Without encryption, your messages are sent as readable text.

- Select the Add Digital Signature To Outgoing Messages check box to add a digital signature to each message you send so your recipient can be sure that the message originated from you.

- Select the Send Clear Text Signed Message check box if you want recipients who can't read S/MIME signatures to be able to read your message.

You can, of course, clear the encryption and digital signature check boxes on the Security tab, as explained earlier. If you do so, you can encrypt a single message or add your digital signature to a single message by clicking the Options button on the Standard toolbar when composing a message, and then selecting the Encrypt Message Contents And Attachments check box or the Add Digital Signature To Outgoing Message check box. You can also clear these check boxes to turn off security for an individual message. When you're sending an encrypted message over the Internet, you must have the recipient's public key stored with the recipient's address in your address book. If you don't have this information or if an Exchange recipient doesn't have security set up, you'll see a message box telling you so. You then have two choices for delivering the message:

- Click the Don't Encrypt Message button to send the message anyway. When encryption is turned on, this is the only way to send a message to a recipient who does not have advanced security.

- Click the Cancel Send button if you decide not to send the message to someone who doesn't have advanced security.

Coordinating Calendars on Your Network

In addition to sending and receiving e-mail over the network, you can use Outlook to coordinate your calendar with other network users. You can schedule meetings, for example, checking to see whether other staff members are available, and then placing the meeting on their online calendars to reserve the time.

To Outlook, a *meeting* is an activity for which you use Outlook to invite other participants, either in or out of your office, who also use Outlook.

A meeting can also require you to reserve a resource, such as a meeting room or piece of equipment, which is controlled by another person who uses Outlook.

An Outlook *appointment,* on the other hand, is an activity that you put on your calendar as a reminder or to reserve the time. While the appointment can be with another individual, you don't use Outlook to send the meeting request and check participant's schedules.

You would create a meeting, for example, to schedule a staff meeting and to use Outlook to notify your staff of the date, time, and location. You would create an appointment to set aside a block of time to meet with a prospective employee or to attend a meeting that has been called by someone outside of the office who didn't schedule it with Outlook.

Appointments and meetings have fixed starting and ending times. An event, on the other hand, is an activity that occurs on one or more days that does not have a fixed time. You would create an event, for instance, to remind yourself of a birthday or anniversary or to set aside an entire day for a conference. You can also use Outlook to invite other Outlook users to an event.

The Calendar Folder

In Outlook, you work with meetings, appointments, and events in the Calendar folder, shown in Figure 20-8. To display the Calendar folder, click Calendar on the Outlook Bar on the left side of the Outlook window.

The *time bar* shows the hours of the day in half-hour increments, with working hours shown in a lighter color than nonworking hours. Next to the time bar are the *time slots* where information about appointments and meetings appear. Icons indicate whether the entry is a group meeting, a one-time or a recurring event, a private activity and whether you've set a reminder for it. To see more details, just position the mouse pointer on the appointment for a moment to see a message box with the subject, location, and duration of the appointment.

Use the *Date Navigator* to see appointments on other dates, even months and years in advance. To display appointments for a certain date, just click the date in the Date Navigator. You can also scroll the Date Navigator to jump months ahead or back. Dates that contain appointments are shown in boldface, today's date has a red box around it, and dates that are currently visible in the Calendar window are highlighted in the Date Navigator.

Chapter 20: Client/Server Communications with Exchange Server

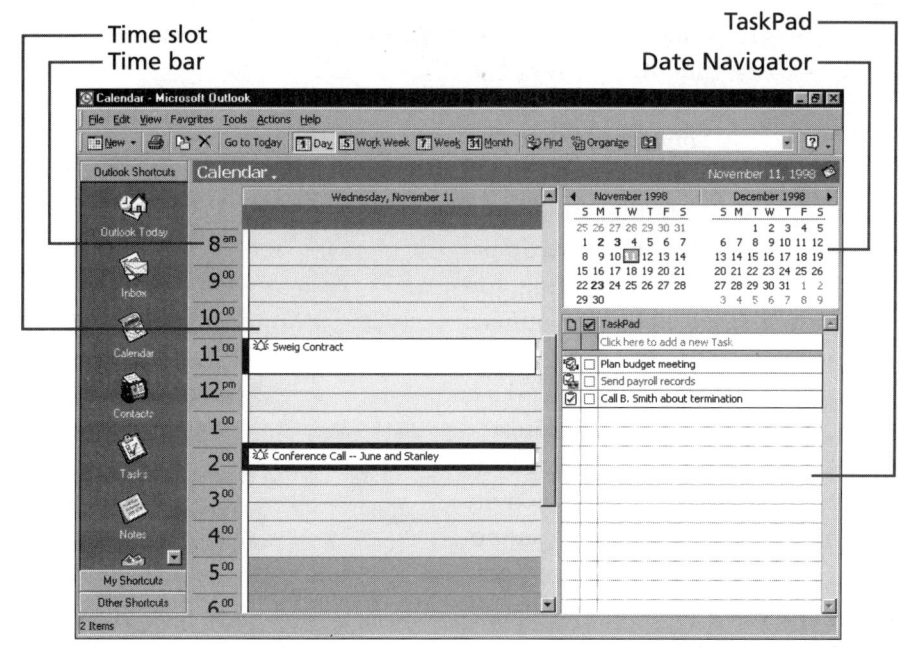

Figure 20-8
Use the Calendar folder to schedule meetings, appointments, and events.

The *TaskPad* shows a summary of the items in Outlook's Tasks folder. Icons to the left of each task indicate one-time, recurring, or assigned tasks. Typically, the TaskPad shows your currently active tasks, including tasks that are overdue (shown in red instead of black) and tasks without a due date.

Updating Free/Busy Time

A record of your available time is maintained on the network server for all users to access. If you're on a peer-to-peer network, the schedule is maintained by Outlook in the post office folder. To cut down on network access and overhead, just a few months of your free/busy time, as your schedule is called, is updated to the server periodically.

To set the number of months of your calendar and the interval at which the information is updated, follow these steps from within Outlook:

1. Choose Options from the Tools menu.
2. Click the Preferences tab if it's not already displayed.
3. Click Calendar Options.

4. In the box that appears, click Free/Busy Options.
5. Set the number of months from your calendar that you want to publish on the network.
6. Set the interval at which the information is updated on the network.
7. Click OK.

Tip

Depending on your Outlook setup, you might also be able to store and update free/busy time over the Internet, but you'll need a URL where the information can be saved, such as a page on a Web site you might have. Your colleagues or clients can store this URL as part of the address book entry they have for you so that the Internet site is checked for your availability when they want to schedule a meeting or appointment.

Setting Up an Appointment

While you don't use Outlook to invite others to an appointment, you should place your appointments on the Outlook calendar. This way, staff members who are scheduling meetings can check your calendar to see when you're busy. If you have an appointment set for a certain time, they'll be able to reschedule the meeting so all participants are able to attend.

You can schedule an appointment quickly by typing it in the appropriate time slot or in more detail in a separate window.

To quickly set up an appointment without worrying about the finer points, take these steps:

1. Display the date for the appointment.
2. Click and hold the mouse on the time slot for the starting time and drag the cursor down to the ending time.
3. Type a name for the appointment.
4. Press Enter or click outside the appointment box.

To change any of the information you typed, just click in the appointment's time slot, and then edit the information as you would any other text. Double-click an appointment to see details. Enter or edit the information describing the appointment, such as its subject, location, and start and ending dates and times.

Outlook is set up to remind you of the appointment 15 minutes before its starting time. To change the reminder time, click the down arrow on the right side of the Reminder box, and select a new time from the list. You can also type the reminder time you want directly in the Reminder box.

If you don't want a reminder for a calendar item, clear the Reminder check box. You can quickly turn off the reminder by right-clicking the appointment in the time slot, and then clicking Reminder from the shortcut menu.

Describing Your Availability

Other Outlook users in your company will be able to access your schedule to see whether you're free to attend a meeting. When you schedule an appointment, that time period is designated as "busy" so your schedule shows that you're unavailable. You might have times, however, when you don't want to lock out that time period, just in case a meeting is being planned.

To designate how you want the appointment time categorized, select one of these options from the Show Time As list box in the Appointment window:

- **Free.** Even though you have an appointment scheduled, you might want to be available for an important meeting—your appointment can be moved or canceled.

- **Tentative.** Sometimes you pencil in an appointment, either because you're not sure it will happen or because you want to be available for other engagements that might be more important.

- **Busy.** You have an appointment scheduled that can't be changed.

- **Out Of Office.** If you're going to be away from the office for an appointment, you might want to make it clear to anyone planning a meeting that you can't be reached.

Tip

To quickly change the availability setting, right-click the appointment on the Appointments page, point to Show Time As, and choose Free, Tentative, Busy, or Out Of Office.

In the time slot, the color line to the left of the appointment and the border that surrounds the appointment when it is selected indicate the availability. Busy is dark blue, Free is white, Tentative is light blue, and Out Of Office is purple.

Saving the Appointment

When you're done adding or editing the details of your appointment, you have to save it. To save your information, click the Save And Close button. This saves the appointment and closes its window, returning you to the Calendar window. You can also choose Save from the File menu to save the information without closing its window.

To close the appointment without saving it or any changes you've made, click the Close box in the upper-right corner of the window, or select Close from the File menu. If you made any changes to the appointment since you last saved it, you'll be asked if you want to save it at this time.

Note

A recurring appointment is one that'll be repeated at some regular interval. After filling out the information in the appointment window, click the Recurrence button on the appointment window's Standard toolbar, or choose Recurrence from its Actions menu to open the Appointment Recurrence dialog box and define the occurrence pattern.

Setting Up a Meeting

When you use Outlook to set up a meeting, Outlook checks the schedules of other network users and sends each person an e-mail notification about the meeting. It then keeps track of their responses so you know who will be attending.

You can create a meeting in several ways with Outlook, but in this chapter, I'll look at the Plan A Meeting option as an example. Use the Plan A Meeting command when you want to find a time that fits the schedules of those you're inviting. Specify the date and time of the meeting, select who is invited, and check their schedules before completing the other details.

Chapter 20: Client/Server Communications with Exchange Server

To plan a meeting, take these steps:

1. Drag your cursor over the time slots to select the time for the meeting.
2. Choose Plan A Meeting from the Actions menu to display the Plan A Meeting dialog box.
3. Click the Invite Others button.
    You'll see the Select Attendees And Resources dialog box.
4. In the Show Names list, select the address list containing the name of an invitee.
5. Select the invitee's name from the list, or select a distribution list to invite a group.
6. Click Required or Optional, based on the person's attendance. Use the Resource button to add meeting rooms, transportation, meals, equipment, or other materials that need to be available at the meeting.
7. Click OK to return to the Plan A Meeting dialog box. Outlook will check the schedule of other users on the network for their free/busy time. The Plan A Meeting dialog box now shows the schedules of those you invited, as shown in Figure 20-9.

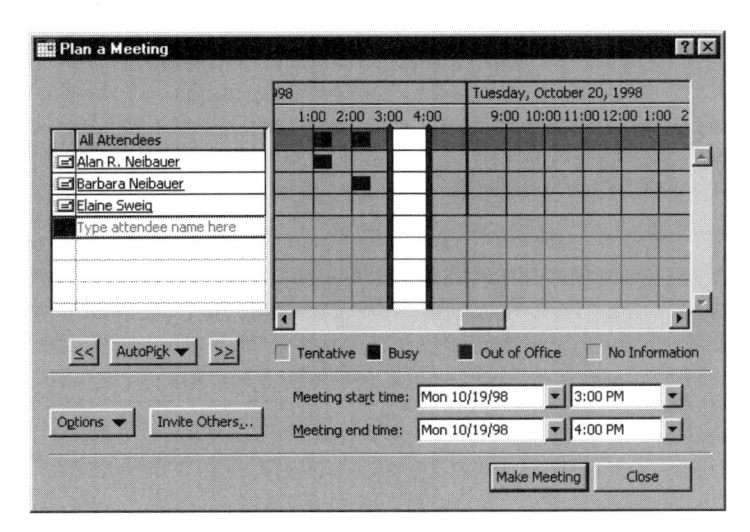

Figure 20-9
The Plan A Meeting dialog box shows attendee availability.

Part 4: Running Your Office on a Network

> When you select a distribution list in the Select Attendees And Resources dialog box, its name appears preceded by a plus sign. If you don't want to invite certain persons from the list, or want to check their individual schedules, click the plus sign and then click OK in the dialog box that appears. Outlook replaces the distribution list name with individual listings for each of the group's members.

8. Now review the schedules for attendees. Horizontal bars indicate when invitees are busy. The top dark-gray line labeled All Attendees shows the consolidated schedules of all the invitees—a bar on this line means that at least one invitee is busy for that time period. Individual lines appear next to each busy invitee's name. You can adjust the time of the meeting by dragging the vertical bars that mark the start and end times or by entering new dates and times in the Meeting Start Time and Meeting End Time boxes. You can also click AutoPick or its arrow buttons to look for an earlier or later time when all recipients are available. Click and hold the mouse on the AutoPick button and choose from the menu to specify which schedules are checked.

Note

The term *One Resource* means that Outlook 2000 will find a common time when all the invitees is available and *one* of the resources you've picked, such as a meeting room, is available. For example, you usually don't want Outlook to find a time when six potential conference rooms and six invitees are available—instead, you want to know when the six invitees can meet in any *one* of the six potential conference rooms.

9. Click Make Meeting when you've selected all of the invitees and chosen a time to see the window shown in Figure 20-10.
10. Complete the other details of the meeting just as you did for appointments, including setting a reminder, creating recurring events, applying categories, designating the item as private, and attaching items such as agendas and background materials.

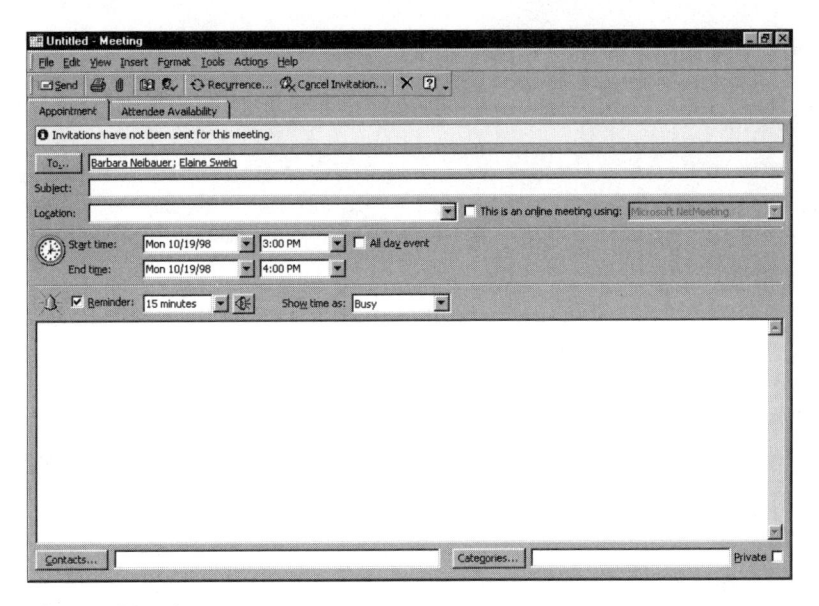

Chapter 20: Client/Server Communications with Exchange Server

Figure 20-10
Use the Meeting window to set up the details of a meeting before sending invitations to invitees.

11. If you want to check meeting details again, click the Attendee Availability tab in the Meeting window. This tab displays the information you set up in the Plan A Meeting dialog box. On this tab, you can review and change the details of the meeting, review the schedules of the invited attendees, adjust the display of the schedule, and invite other attendees if necessary.

12. When you've finished reviewing the meeting details in the meeting window, click the Send button. Outlook then sends messages to the people and resources you invited.

Including but Not Inviting Others

Sometimes you want to include in a meeting people you've already invited or who don't have e-mail addresses. You can list them as invitees to let others know that they'll be at the meeting but not send them an invitation.

To not send an invitation, click the envelope icon to the left of the person's name in the Plan A Meeting dialog box or the Attendee Availability tab and choose Don't Send Meeting To This Attendee.

Inviting Resources to Your Meeting

Meeting resources include conference rooms, audio/visual equipment, and other equipment or material you need for a meeting. You might want to include a resource in the list of meeting invitees so that the attendees know that such equipment will be available. When using Outlook over a Windows NT network, the server administrator can set up rooms and equipment in the global address list, so you can "invite" the resource to a meeting by choosing it as you would an invited guest. When you invite a resource to a meeting, a message is delivered to the inbox for the resource, which is usually handled by a staff person.

Receiving and Responding to a Meeting Request

When someone invites you to a meeting or an event, you receive an e-mail message with the meeting request icon next to it. To properly respond to such messages, you should open the message in its own window, rather than using the preview pane.

> **Note**
>
> In order to process the meeting request, you must receive it using Outlook. The meeting request format isn't compatible with Outlook Express.

If you click Accept, Tentative, or Decline, Outlook asks whether you want to send your response and whether you want to add comments to it. If the meeting conflicts with something already on your calendar, you'll see a notice to that effect above the sender's name in the message window. In any case, before responding to the invitation, you might want to check your schedule. If you click the Calendar button on the message window's Standard toolbar, a separate calendar window appears with the item shown at the proposed date and time. If an activity is already on your calendar for that time, the two items will appear side-by-side in the appointment pane. In this calendar window, you can review the details of the meeting and any conflicting items to determine how you want to respond. Close the calendar window to return to the meeting request window and click the appropriate button on the Standard toolbar to accept, tentatively accept, decline, or forward the invitation. You can also choose to simply delete the invitation, which doesn't send back any response at all.

Chapter 20: Client/Server Communications with Exchange Server

Checking Attendees

If you organized the meeting, you'll receive e-mail messages when invitees accept or decline the invitation. The Subject column of your Inbox's message list shows the general response of Accept, Tentative, or Declined. You can also look at the meeting request icon next to each message header to see whether it shows a check mark (accepted), a question mark (tentative), or an *X* (declined). Open the messages to see whether they contain more detailed responses.

For a summary of responses and to check availability, open the meeting in the Calendar. A note on the Appointment tab summarizes the responses. For more details, click the Attendee Availability tab. You can select one of two options to determine how you view the information—Show Attendee Availability and Show Attendee Status.

If you select Show Attendee Availability, you'll see who is invited and their free/busy time, as shown in Figure 20-11.

If you select Show Attendee Status, the tab shows the responses you've received so far to your meeting request. Both tabs allow you to invite additional persons by clicking the Invite Others button at the bottom of the tab.

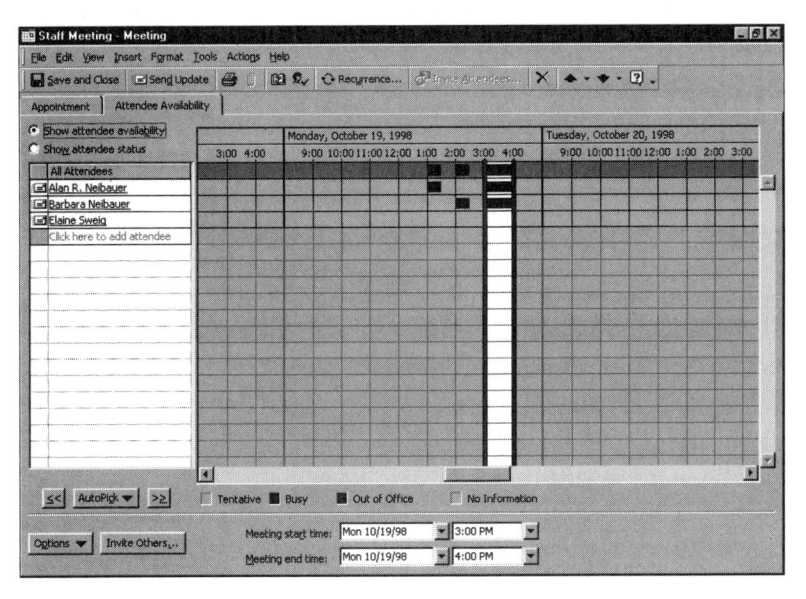

Figure 20-11

The Attendee Availability tab shows the availability of other people.

Part 4:   Running Your Office on a Network

If you're an invited participant to the meeting, you can also open the meeting item to check the availability of other participants. When you select Show Attendee Status, you'll see who is invited and whether each is a required or optional participant. Select Show Attendee Availability to check the free/busy time of guests. Once you accept an invitation, your time will appear as busy on the tab. Other invitees' times won't appear as busy until their free/busy time has been updated on the server.

The next chapter covers how to share modems and Internet accounts across a network.

Chapter 21

Sharing Modems and Internet Accounts

Chances are if you have more than one computer in the office, you have more than one modem. If you have a small business, especially a home-based operation, then you might have only a limited number of phone lines. Even if you have several phone lines, most Internet service providers (ISPs) won't allow more than one person at a time to access the Internet using the same account. If you try, you'll get a message telling you that the account is already in use.

However, connecting your computers through a network allows you to share a phone line and one Internet account with everyone in the office. You could be looking up suppliers for the best prices on supplies, for example, while another staff member is downloading software or just surfing the Net.

Sharing a phone line is especially useful when one computer on the network has a connection that's faster than the others, such as a 56-Kbps modem, a DSL line, or an ultra-fast cable modem. In fact, when you're connected on a network, you don't even need a modem on more than one machine. All the computers on the network can share the high-speed modem connected to one computer.

When a modem is shared on a network, only one user—the first to dial in to the ISP—is actually logged on, and that user can be anyone on the network. Other users who want to access the Internet just piggyback onto the existing connection through the network. Their modems don't need to dial in because the connection has already been made by the first computer. As far as the ISP is concerned, only one person is logged on.

> **Caution**
>
> With modem sharing now so easy and popular, many ISPs have fine-tuned the small print in their customer agreements to discourage simultaneous sharing of an account. You shouldn't share an ISP account if the membership agreement forbids it.

Internet Sharing Alternatives

There are two basic ways to share a modem and an Internet account—by using software or by using hardware.

When you use software to share a modem, you have to designate one computer on the network as the host. That computer's modem will then be shared by the other computers on the network, called the clients. A modem-sharing program, such as Microsoft Windows Internet Connection Sharing or others described in this chapter, reconfigures the network to accept Internet requests from the client computers and channels them to the shared modem on the host computer. The host computer's modem dials the ISP directly; the client computers are reconfigured to connect to the ISP through the network rather than through their own dial-up connections and modems.

If the host computer is already online, a client computer can go online without dialing. If the host computer is turned on but isn't online, the client computer dials in to the ISP through the modem connected to the host computer.

The shared modem can be any of the following types:

- A standard modem
- An Integrated Services Digital Network (ISDN) modem

Chapter 21: Sharing Modems and Internet Accounts

- A digital subscriber line (DSL) modem
- A cable modem

Table 21-1 summarizes the advantages and disadvantages of each type.

Table 21-1 Sharing Different Modem Types: Advantages and Disadvantages

Modem Type	Advantages	Disadvantages
Standard modem	Connects to a standard telephone line. Usually included with PCs, but inexpensive to purchase and upgrade.	Connects at the slowest speeds, with a maximum of 56 Kbps.
ISDN	Connects at a high speed, up to 128 Kbps. Uses a dedicated connection so you can use your regular phone line at the same time.	More expensive than a standard modem and requires special telephone service that costs more than a regular phone line. Most ISPs charge more for ISDN service.
DSL	Connects at a very high speed, up to 1.5 Mbps. Uses a dedicated connection so you can use your regular phone line at the same time.	More expensive than standard modems and requires special telephone service that costs more than a regular phone line. DSL service might not be available everywhere, and your ISP might not support it.
Cable	Connects at an ultra-high speed, up to 10 Mbps. Uses cable TV service instead of your phone line.	Not all cable companies offer modem service. You'll have to pay a setup and installation fee, as well as monthly ISP charges that are usually higher than regular dial-up ISP charges.

Whatever the type of modem you have in your office, just select the one that's fastest or most reliable and designate the computer connected to it as the host.

The main disadvantage of using software to share a modem is that the host computer must be turned on for its modem to be shared. If the computer is turned off, a client computer will get an error message when it tries to connect to the Internet through the host on the network.

There are ways around this problem, however. The fastest solution is to just go to the room with the shared modem and turn on the computer. An alternative to sharing a modem with software is to buy and install a LAN modem, which is connected directly to the network. A LAN modem (LAN stands for local area network) is directly connected to the network in the same way a printer can be connected to a network, which you learned to do in Chapter 9. As long as the modem and network hub are turned on, anyone on the network can access the Internet at any time.

The downside to a LAN modem is its cost. LAN modems are more expensive than standard modems, and they can be difficult to set up.

Getting Ready to Share a Modem

If you're considering Internet connection sharing with software, make sure that the modem on the host computer works and that you can use the host computer to connect to the Internet. The network connections between computers must also be working properly. Each computer should be able to communicate with other computes on the network. One way to test this is to make sure that each computer is listed in Network Neighborhood.

Making Sure TCP/IP Is Installed

Almost all Internet connection sharing requires that you have the TCP/IP protocol installed on each computer connected to the network. You'll need TCP/IP installed even if it's not the primary protocol you use for the network.

To determine whether TCP/IP drivers are installed on computers running Microsoft Windows 95 or Microsoft Windows 98, follow these steps:

1. On the Start menu, point to Settings, and then click Control Panel.
2. In the Control Panel window, double-click the Network icon.
3. On the Configuration tab of the Network dialog box, look in the installed network components list for an entry showing TCP/IP followed by your network card.

If the listing isn't present, you'll need to install the TCP/IP protocol. For instructions for setting up a network protocol, see "Installing Protocols" on page 196.

You'll have to configure TCP/IP, but how you do it depends on the particular software you're using for Internet connection sharing and whether or not you're using TCP/IP as your network protocol. For more information, *see "Configuring TCP/IP" on page 204.*

Using Modem-Sharing Software

Many programs let you share a modem and Internet connection over a network. One such modem-sharing program is built into Microsoft Windows 98 Second Edition and Microsoft Windows 2000 Professional. If you have one of those versions of Windows, you don't need to download or purchase any additional modem-sharing software.

You'll find modem-sharing software in most network starter kits, although the programs vary in the way they're set up. Some modem-sharing programs are also available as shareware. This means that you can download them from the Internet and try them out for free during a short trial period. If you like the program, you can then register it for a fee. When you register, you'll get a password or serial number that enables the program to continue working beyond the trial period.

Installing Windows Internet Connection Sharing

Here's a look at the Internet Connection Sharing feature in Windows 98 Second Edition. For information on using this feature in Windows 2000 Professional, *see "Internet Connection Sharing with Microsoft Windows 2000" on page 382.*

Because Internet connection sharing isn't installed automatically when you install or upgrade to Windows 98 Second Edition, you'll need to add it as an additional component to the Windows installation on the computer you plan to use as the host. Here's how to do it:

1. Make sure the Windows 98 Second Edition CD is in your CD drive.
2. On the Start menu, point to Settings, and then click Control Panel.
3. In the Control Panel window, double-click the Add/Remove Programs icon.

Part 4: Running Your Office on a Network

4. In the list of components on the Windows Setup tab, click Internet Tools to select it. Don't click the check box to the left of Internet Tools or that will clear the check mark.
5. Click the Details button to see a list of the items in the Internet Tools category, shown in Figure 21-1.

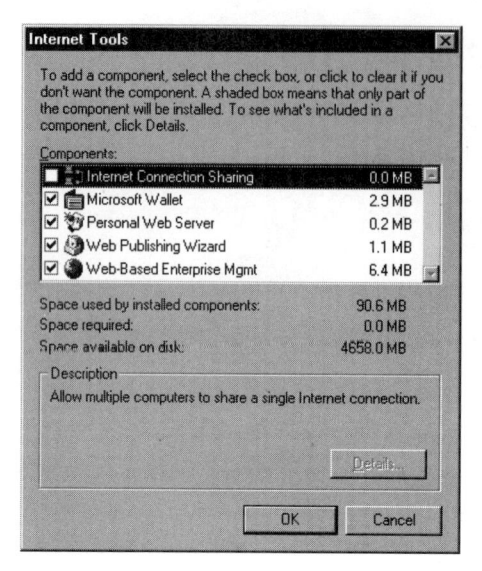

Figure 21-1
Select Internet Connection Sharing from the list of components in the Internet Tools dialog box.

6. In the list of components, select Internet Connection Sharing.
7. Click OK to close the Internet Tools dialog box.
8. Click OK in the Add/Remove Programs Properties dialog box.

Windows installs the Internet connection sharing feature and then displays the Internet Connection Sharing Wizard dialog box, which starts the process of setting up the feature:

1. Read the information in the dialog box, and click Next.
2. Click Next in the next dialog box.
    The wizard explains that it will create a floppy disk to set up the client computers for Internet sharing through the host computer.
3. Click Next.
4. Insert a formatted floppy disk that has at least 200 KB of free space into your floppy disk drive, and then click OK.

Chapter 21: Sharing Modems and Internet Accounts

5. When the wizard tells you to do so, remove the disk, and then click OK.
6. Click Finish.
7. Click Yes when you are asked whether you want to restart the computer.

The wizard makes some changes to the network settings in Control Panel. It adds a binding for Internet connection sharing to each of the installed protocols, and it sets or changes the IP address and subnet mask of the network card to a special address.

Changing Internet Connection Sharing Options

After you install Internet connection sharing, you can make the following adjustments to its settings:

- Turn Internet sharing on or off.
- Place an icon for changing Internet connection sharing in the *system tray,* the area of the taskbar adjacent to the clock.
- Select which connection the host will use to access the Internet, if you have more than one Internet account.
- Choose which network interface card (NIC) to use for the network, if you have more than one.

To change any of these Internet connection sharing settings, follow these steps:

1. On the Start menu, point to Settings, and then click Control Panel.
2. In the Control Panel window, double-click the Internet Options icon.
3. In the Internet Properties dialog box, click the Connections tab.
4. Click Sharing in the Local Area Network (LAN) Settings section of the dialog box.
5. Change options in the Internet Connection Sharing dialog box and click OK.

If you choose to show the Internet Connection Sharing icon in the taskbar in the Internet Connection Sharing Wizard, you can right-click the taskbar icon to see the following options:

- **Status** displays which computers are sharing the connection.

- **Options** shows information about your connection and the NIC you're using.
- **Disable Internet Connection Sharing** turns off the feature. If you find that sharing your connection slows down Web surfing or program downloading significantly, you might want to choose this option.

Setting Up the Client Computers for Internet Connection Sharing

After you've installed Internet Sharing on the host computer, the next step is to configure each client computer to access the Internet through the network rather than through its own dial-up connection and modem. But first you need to set up each client computer so it gets an IP address. Here's how to do this:

1. On the Start menu of the client computer, point to Settings, and then click Control Panel.
2. In the Control Panel window, double-click the Network icon.
3. On the Configuration tab of the Network dialog box, select the TCP/IP listing for the client computer's NIC.
4. Click Properties.
5. On the IP Address tab of the TCP/IP Properties dialog box, select Obtain An IP Address Automatically.
6. Click the WINS Configuration tab, shown in Figure 21-2.
7. Make sure the Use DHCP For WINS Resolution option is selected.
8. Click the Gateway tab.
9. Make sure the Installed Gateways list is empty. If you see entries in the Installed Gateways list, select each entry, and then click Remove.
10. Click the DNS Configuration tab.
11. Make sure the Disable DNS option is selected.
12. Click OK.
13. Click OK to close the Network dialog box.
14. Click Yes when you're asked whether you want to restart your computer.

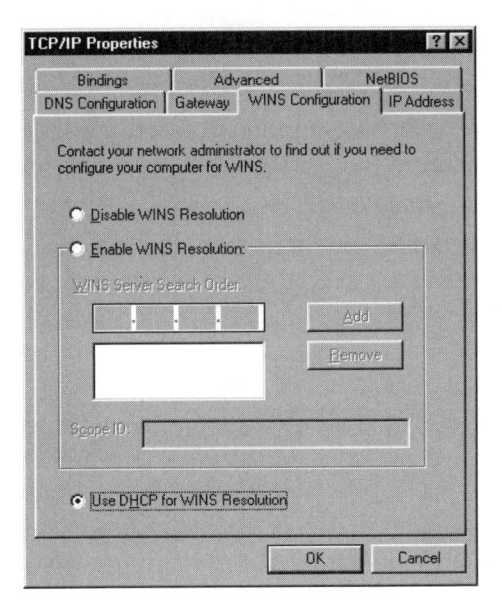

Chapter 21: Sharing Modems and Internet Accounts

Figure 21-2
Enable DHCP on the WINS Configuration tab of the TCP/IP Properties dialog box.

Static IP Addressing

To use Internet Connection Sharing with a TCP/IP network, your network should be configured for automatic IP addresses rather than static IP addresses. The Internet Connection Sharing Wizard will change the IP address of the computer being used as the server to 192.168.0.1.

If you set up your network so the workstations obtain their TCP/IP addresses automatically, the workstations will all be able to communicate with each other after you install Internet Connection Sharing. If you're using static TCP/IP addresses that you entered yourself, however, the Internet connection server might no longer be able to communicate with the other computers on the network.

If you really want to specify IP addresses yourself, assign IP address to the other computers in the range 192.168.0.2 to 192.168.0.253. You don't need to make any changes to the host computer's TCP/IP settings.

Running the Browser Connection Setup Wizard

When you installed Internet connection sharing on the host computer, you created a floppy disk containing the Browser Connection Setup Wizard. You now need to use this disk to configure each of the client computers so that they access the Internet through the network.

1. Start the host computer, and use it to connect to the Internet.
2. Insert the disk in the floppy drive of a client computer.
3. On the Start menu, click Run.
4. In the Run dialog box, type *A:\Icsclset.exe* and click OK.
5. Click Next until the last wizard page appears, and then click Finish.
6. Repeat the process on each client computer.

Once you've configured the client computers, you'll be able to access the Internet from any of them through the host computer's modem. If, however, you try to connect to the Internet from a client computer and receive an error message, the host computer might be turned off. In this case, you can change the client computer's settings to connect through its own modem rather than through the host's. How you do this depends on your browser. With Microsoft Internet Explorer, follow these steps:

1. Right-click the Internet Explorer icon on the client's desktop and choose Properties from the shortcut menu. If there's no icon, double-click the Internet Options icon in Control Panel.
2. Click the Connections tab.
3. With Internet Explorer 5.0, select Always Dial My Default Connection. You can also click Setup and use the Internet Connection Wizard to select your dial-up connection.

    With Internet Explorer 4, select Connect To The Internet Using A Modem on the Connections tab, or click Connect to start the wizard.

The Browser Connection Setup Wizard doesn't change the settings of other programs that access your ISP, including e-mail programs such as Microsoft Outlook Express. If you want these programs to connect through the network as well, you have to change their setup yourself. Most of these programs have a dialog box or menu option that allows you to specify a type of connection. As an example, let's run through the process for Outlook Express.

Chapter 21: Sharing Modems and Internet Accounts

Click the Outlook Express icon in the taskbar, or start the program as you would normally, and then follow these steps:

1. On the Tools menu, click Accounts.
2. In the Internet Accounts dialog box, click your account, and then click Properties.
3. On the Connection tab of the Properties dialog box, click Always Connect To This Account Using.
4. Click the down arrow next to the drop-down list and choose Local Area Network.
5. Click OK.
6. Repeat the process for each account, and then click Close to close the Internet Accounts dialog box.

Note

Versions of Outlook Express earlier than 5.0 have an option button on the Connection tab that you can click to connect through the network.

Connecting to the Internet Through Internet Connection Sharing

When you're ready to connect to the Internet, just start your browser as you would normally. If you're on a client computer, it will connect through the network, dialing the modem on the host computer if the host isn't already connected. If you're on the host computer, don't disconnect from the Internet unless you're certain no one else is connected through the network.

Note

To learn how to put the Internet Connection Sharing icon in the system tray, see "Changing Internet Connection Sharing Options" on page 377.

To determine whether anyone is online, right-click the Internet Connection Sharing icon in the system tray, and choose Status. A box appears reporting the number of computers using the connection. The number includes your own computer even if you aren't connected, so don't disconnect if the number is greater than one. If you do, you'll disconnect other staff members who are connected.

If no one else is connected to the Internet, you can disconnect. If you're used to seeing a message asking if you want to disconnect when you close your browser, don't be surprised if it no longer appears. The message is turned off to avoid disconnecting when someone else is using the modem.

Internet Connection Sharing with Microsoft Windows 2000

Internet connection sharing is installed when you install Windows 2000 on your computer. You have to enable sharing, however, before other network users can access the modem and Internet account.

To use Internet connection sharing, your network can't use static IP addresses. When you enable Internet Connection Sharing, your host computer is assigned an address by the program. If other computers are set for static addressing, they might no longer be able to connect to the host computer. To enable Internet connection sharing on the host computer, you must be a member of the Administrators group.

To enable Internet sharing, follow these steps:

1. Open Control Panel and double-click Network And Dial-Up Connections.
2. Right-click your dial-up connection and choose Properties from the shortcut menu.
3. Click the Sharing tab and select Enable Internet Connection Sharing For This Connection.
4. Select Enable On-Demand Dialing if you want network computers to use this connection for all of their dial-up needs.

You then have to set the Internet browsers in the other workstations to access the Internet through your LAN. You do this by configuring your Internet browser to connect to the Internet through the computer acting as the host computer.

Using Microsoft BackOffice Small Business Server

Microsoft BackOffice Small Business Server (SBS) includes two ways to share modems that are quite different—Modem Sharing Service and Microsoft Proxy Server. Modem Sharing Service lets other users access the server's modem, but restricts the number of users to one at a time. Proxy Server lets user share a modem and Internet account simultaneously.

Chapter 21: Sharing Modems and Internet Accounts

Using Modem Sharing Service

With Modem Sharing Service, anyone on the network can use the modem attached to the server as if it were connected to his or her own computer. However, only one person can use the modem at a time, so it's best used to take advantage of a high-speed access connected to the server or when a workstation's modem fails to work. If the server has more than one modem attached, modems are made available as a pool. When a user connects to the modem pool, it will find a modem that isn't currently being used.

To set up modem sharing, you have to install the Modem Sharing Service in SBS. The installation adds Modem Sharing Service to the Control Panel, a client installation program to the server's hard disk, and a Manage Modems function to the SBS Console.

On the server, use the Configuration tab in the Modem Sharing dialog box to create a pool of modems on the server that contains one or more modems. Use the General tab of the dialog box to turn on or off the service and to disable any new connections.

You then run the modem sharing client installation on each of the workstations. You can find the client installation program on the server in the \Clientapps\MS\ModemShr folder. The installation adds communication ports to the workstation system, such as those shown in Figure 21-3.

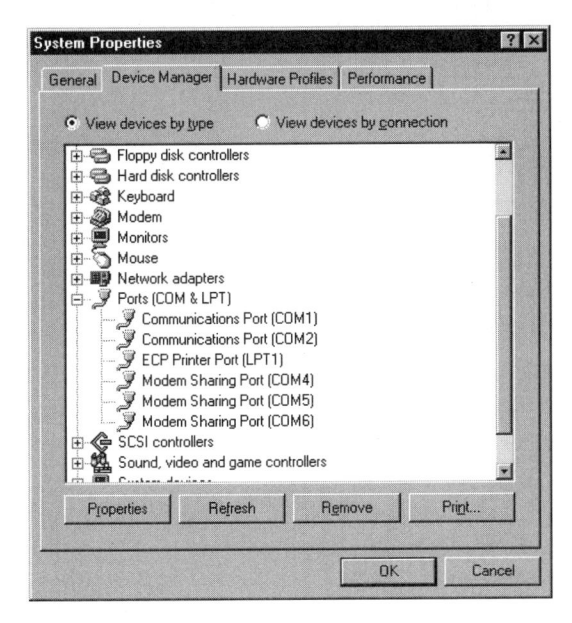

Figure 21-3

Shared modems are available through communication ports.

383

These ports, which aren't physically installed in the workstation, each represent a modem on the server. You then use the Modems program in the Control Panel to install a new modem on the workstation and assign it to one of the modem-sharing ports. Finally, select the modem in your Dial-Up Networking program. When you use the program to connect to the Internet, your workstation dials through the modem connected to the modem-sharing port on the server.

Using Microsoft Proxy Server

With Proxy Server, more than one workstation can use the server's modem at the same time, sharing a single phone line and Internet account. After installing Proxy Server with SBS, you specify the range of IP address that you authorize to access the Internet. Figure 21-4, for example, shows three ranges of IP addresses that are permitted to access the Internet. These are the groups of IP addresses used on local area networks rather than the Internet.

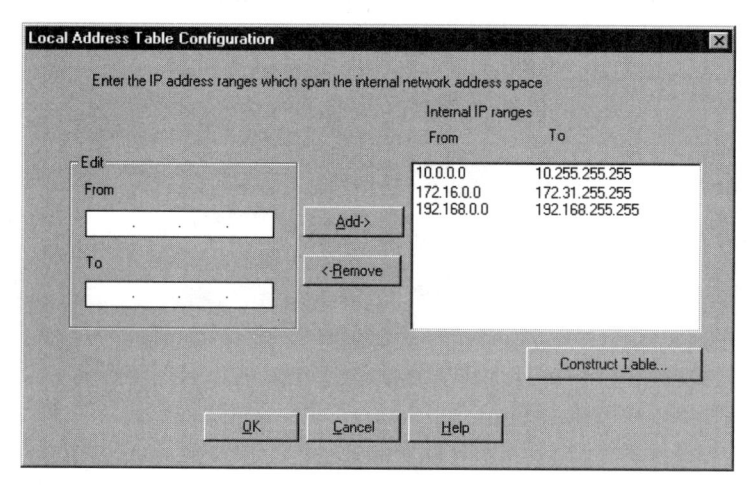

Figure 21-4

Specify the ranges of IP address for modem sharing.

You can then configure your Internet browser and Dial-Up Networking settings to connect to the Internet through Proxy Server. In Figure 21-5, for example, Microsoft Internet Explorer is set to make the connection using a proxy server, which can be found on the computer named Server and at

Chapter 21: Sharing Modems and Internet Accounts

the default port 80. When you start Internet Explorer, it connects to your server and then through the Proxy Server firewall to the Internet.

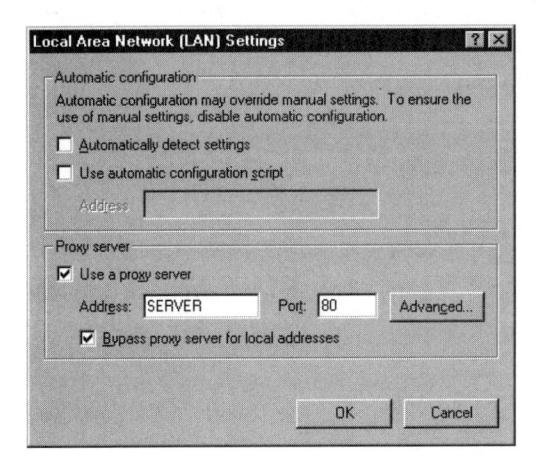

Figure 21-5
Set Internet Explorer to connect to the Internet through a proxy server.

Other Software Solutions for Internet Connection Sharing

Other software solutions for sharing an Internet connection are similar in concept to Internet connection sharing in Windows 98 Second Edition, but they're set up differently. Table 21-2 lists some of the Internet connection sharing programs you can download from the Internet.

Table 21-2 Other Internet Connection Sharing Software

Software	Internet Address
Avirt Gateway	www.avirt.com
MaccaSoft Internet Gate	www.maccasoft.com
Artisoft i.Share	www.artisoft.com
Acotec Internet LanBridge	www.acotec.com
MidPoint Companion	www.midcore.com
PPPindia PPPshar	www.pppindia.com
ITServ RideWay	www.itserv.com
ShareTheNet	www.sharethenet.com
Sybergen SyGate	www.sybergen.com
Deerfield.com WinGate	wingate.deerfield.com

385

Each of these programs requires that the TCP/IP protocol be installed on the computers on the network and that you install the Internet sharing program on the host computer. The main difference among the programs is how the client computers are configured to access the shared modem.

Using Internet Routers

As an alternative to using software to share an Internet connection, you can purchase a router that provides a modem-sharing solution. Some routers have built-in modems and hubs that connect directly to the phone line and network computers, while other routers must be connected to an external analog (56 Kbps), ISDN, DSL, or cable modem. Some routers have one or more internal modems and a connection for an external modem as well.

When you use a router, you set up your hardware so that the router is turned on whenever your network hub or switch is turned on. That way, the modem will be available to everyone on the network all the time regardless of which computers on the network are turned on.

In addition, many routers let you create a firewall between your network and the Internet. The router can prevent unauthorized access into your network by hackers and can control the type of access allowed to each network user. You can limit a user to just sending and receiving e-mail, for example, without allowing the user to surf the Internet. Through Web content filtering, some models also let you control the types of sites accessed by users. These are ideal if you'd like to limit access to gaming, auction, and other sites that you don't feel are appropriate for your office staff during work hours.

Routers can be expensive, though. While you can purchase an internal 56-Kbps modem card for under $50, a router can cost $250 or more. Routers also require quite a few steps to set up, sometimes involving complex protocol configurations. Still, if you have a few extra dollars to spend and the time to set it up and configure it, a router can be a very useful addition to your office network.

The OfficeConnect LAN-Modem from 3Com, for example, includes its own analog or ISDN modem and a four-port hub, which allows it to serve as the network's modem and hub at the same time. After connecting the device, you can set it up just by starting your browser and connecting to a configuration Web page that's stored within the modem. Use the information on the Web page to set up the modem for your ISP. At the time of this book's printing, the 56-Kbps version of the LAN modem cost less than $300; the ISDN version was less than $400.

Seven models are in the WebRamp series of routers, ranging from less than $300 to more than $800. Some models have built-in 56-Kbps modems; others have ISDN modems with enhanced features for business users. For small offices, the model 200i, available for less than $300, contains a built-in 56-Kbps modem and 4-port hub, and you can connect to it another external 56-Kbps or ISDN modem.

Note

Some routers are also *remote access servers*, letting users dial into your network when they're away from the office. You'll learn more about remote access servers in Chapter 23.

Companies such as ATronics, Lantronix, NETGEAR, Netopia, Perle Systems, and others make a variety of models of routers. In choosing the model for your office, make sure it can accommodate the type of modem or phone line you have. If you have a cable modem, for example, you'll need a router that has an Ethernet connection; you can't use a router that has a serial connection intended for an external analog modem or a router that has only a built-in analog modem. Decide whether you want firewall protection and control over the Internet sites accessed by your network users, and purchase a router that can accommodate these features. Some routers limit access to a specific number of connections at one time, so make sure you choose one that's appropriate for your Internet traffic.

Sharing Fax Modems

When you have a network, you can also share a modem to manage faxes in your company. By using one modem for all faxes, you can keep track of fax traffic and long-distance telephone usage.

Sharing a modem for sending and receiving faxes on a network is actually easier than sharing a modem for the Internet. The software for sharing a fax modem is built into Windows Messaging and Microsoft Exchange in Windows 95 and Windows 98. SBS has its own fax-sharing feature that you can use in a client/server network.

Part 4: Running Your Office on a Network

Sharing Faxes Peer to Peer

If you are using a peer-to-peer network, you need to select one computer that will function as a fax server. Choose a computer with a high-speed fax modem that's available most of the time. You'll then need to install the Fax service on the computer and choose to share it across the network.

Installing Fax Service

If you use Windows 95, the fax service is installed when you install Exchange or Windows Messaging. If you don't install Exchange, you have to install Microsoft Fax from the Windows CD. To do that, follow these steps:

1. Insert the Windows CD into your CD drive.
2. Point to Settings on the Start menu, and click Control Panel.
3. In the Control Panel window, double-click the Add/Remove Programs icon.
4. On the Windows Setup tab, select Microsoft Fax, and click Have Disk. Follow the instructions on the screen.

Windows 98 doesn't install fax service by default and doesn't offer it as a regular setup option. (Windows 98 does leave an existing Windows 95 version of Microsoft Fax on your computer if you installed Windows 98 over your Windows 95 installation.) To install the fax service, you have to run a program called Awfax.exe. You can find it on your Windows 98 CD, in the folder \tools\oldwin95\message\us. (For international installations choose the \intl directory instead of \us.)

I strongly recommended that you install the fax service, regardless of the version of Windows you use, *before* installing Microsoft Office 2000. If you've already installed Microsoft Outlook as a separate program, not as part of Office, rerun the Outlook installation program after installing the fax software. If you've already installed Office 2000, follow these steps after you run Awfax.exe to update any Office files that might have been affected:

1. Insert the Office CD into your CD drive.
2. Point to Settings on the Start menu, and click Control Panel.
3. In the Control Panel window, double-click the Add/Remove Programs icon.
4. Click Microsoft Office 2000, and then click Add/Repair.

Chapter 21: Sharing Modems and Internet Accounts

5. Click the Repair Office button.
6. Choose Repair Errors In My Office Installation.
7. Click Repair, and then wait until the process is completed—it could take some time.

Setting Up a Fax Profile

You now need to add the fax service to your mail profile before you can send or receive faxes. Just follow these steps:

1. Insert the Office CD into your CD drive.
2. Point to Settings on the Start menu and click Control Panel.
3. In the Control Panel window, double-click the Mail icon, and then click the Show Profiles button.
4. Select the profile you want to change and click the Properties button.
    When the Properties dialog box appears, be sure that the Services tab is showing and that the name of the profile you want to change appears in the title bar.
5. Click the Add button on the Services tab.
6. In the Add Service To Profile dialog box, select Microsoft Fax, and then click OK.
7. A message asks whether you are ready to supply your name and fax number. Click Yes.
8. When the User tab of the Microsoft Fax Properties dialog box appears, fill in as much of the information as you can. You *must* provide your fax number on the User tab.
9. Fill in the other information as required, and select options.
10. Click the Modem tab.
11. If more than one modem is available to you, select the modem you'll be using, and then click the Set As Active Fax Modem button.
12. Select Let Other People On The Network Use My Modem To Send Faxes.

13. If the Select Drive dialog box appears, select the drive on your local machine that you want the network fax service to use, and then click OK.

14. Click the Properties button to display the NetFax dialog box shown in Figure 21-6.

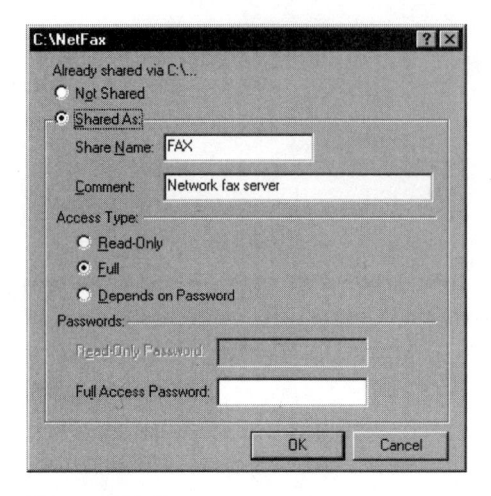

Figure 21-6
Share a fax modem on the network.

15. Make sure that Shared As is selected, and change the share name if needed.

16. Select Full in the Access Type section. You might choose Depends On Password if you want to require users to have a password to send and receive faxes. The Read-Only option shouldn't be selected.

17. If you want to restrict access to those with a password, type the password in the Full Access Password text box.

18. Click OK.

Setting Up a Workstation

All users who want to use the fax server for sending and receiving faxes must now choose it as their fax modem. They must have the fax service installed on their computers, along with Windows Messaging or Exchange. They can then use the Exchange client or Outlook to send faxes through the fax server.

To specify the fax server as the fax modem for a specific user, follow these steps:

1. If necessary, add the fax service as described on the previous pages to the user's profile.
2. Once the fax service is installed, point to Settings on the Start menu, and click Control Panel.
3. In the Control Panel window, double-click the Mail icon, click Microsoft Fax, and then click Properties.
4. Click the Modem tab, and then click Add.
5. Select Network Fax Server.
6. Click OK.
7. Type the network address and share name of the shared fax modem, such as \\FAXSERVER\FAX, and then click OK.
8. Choose the shared fax modem, and then click the Set As Active Fax Modem button.
9. Click OK to close all of the dialog boxes.

Using SBS Fax Service

SBS includes a feature called Fax Service. Using Fax Service, you set up a fax modem on the server and allow other network users to access it. The server can be set up in a user profile for sending and receiving faxes through Outlook, and it can be used as a fax printer from within any Windows application. When you want to fax a Microsoft Word document, for example, prepare the document and then choose the fax printer from the Print dialog box. Rather than actually printing the document, Word will send it to the fax modem for transmission.

After installing Fax Service on the server, install the Fax Service client, which is in the \Clientapps\MS\Fax folder of the server. The client setup program asks you to enter some information, such as the path of the fax server and your name, and then adds the Fax Mail Transport to your mail profile and the Fax On Server printer driver. You can then use the Fax Mail Transport for sending and receiving mail with the Exchange client or Outlook or the fax printer for faxing from within applications.

Clicking on the Fax Client icon in Control Panel will let you select or design a cover page, set your user information, and specify other fax details, shown in Figure 21-7.

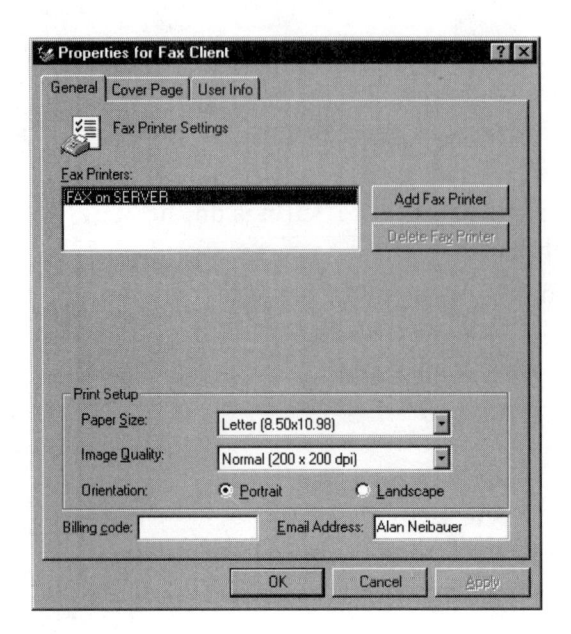

Figure 21-7

Set up the fax client in Control Panel.

The next chapter covers setting up an intranet for your office.

Chapter 22

Setting Up Servers for an Office Intranet

Now that your computers are connected on a network, you can easily set up your own intranet. Staff members can set up their own Web sites on the intranet with their own home pages that everyone else on the network can see in their Web browsers. *Web sites,* whether on the Internet or on your own intranet, consist of one or more pages of text, specially formatted to enable Web browsers to display them on the screen. The formatting instructions for Web pages are called HTML (Hypertext Markup Language) tags. The pages are connected by hyperlinks, which are usually called links. You click a link to jump to another page of the Web site, to send e-mail, or to go to another Web site on the Internet or intranet.

The first page that you encounter when you go to a Web site is called the site's *home page*. The other pages of the site are separate files that are retrieved and displayed on the screen when you click their associated hyperlinks.

Part 4: Running Your Office on a Network

Figure 22-1 shows how one company Web site might look on the office intranet. It includes information that a workgroup project manager wants to share with workgroup members and other company personnel. The page also provides links to other pages that make up the Web site. Anyone viewing the home page can click a link to see more information about the project or to return to the home page.

Other members of the office can have their own Web sites on the office intranet as well. For example, the personnel department can advertise job opportunities within the company, which staff members can respond to by leaving a message. As you can see from these examples, an office intranet is a great way for everyone to share information.

In order to let a Web browser access a Web site over the network, the computer on which the site is located must be set up as a Web server. The

Tip

If you have a company Web site with your Internet service provider (ISP), you can also use your intranet to fine-tune and test your Web pages before uploading them to the ISP. This way you can be sure your Web site looks right and works correctly before you expose it to the world.

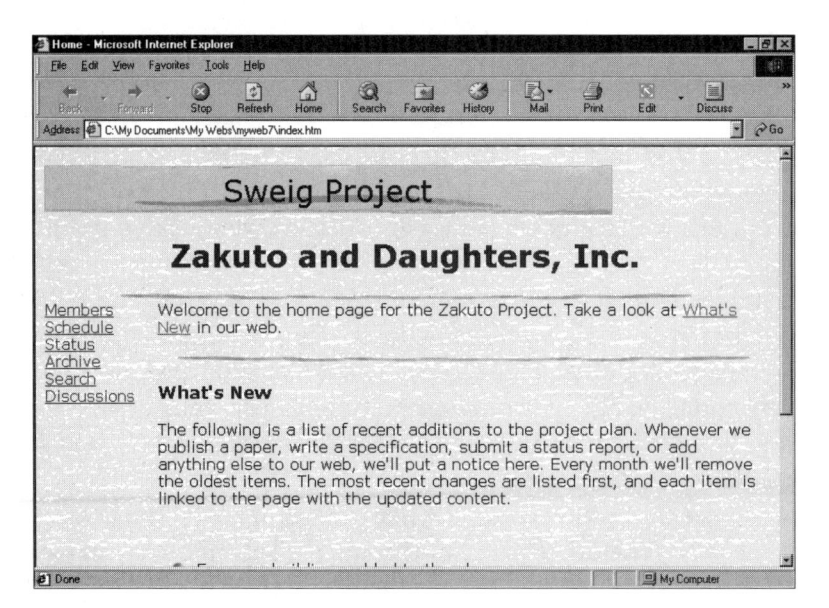

Figure 22-1

This is one example of a home page on a company intranet.

Chapter 22: Setting Up Servers for an Office Intranet

Web server software handles communications with Web browsers used by intranet surfers, displaying the Web pages requested by the browser. So any person on your network who wants to have a Web site on the intranet must install Web server software.

Users who don't install Web server software can access Web sites on the intranet using their Web browsers. They cannot, however, make their own Web pages available to other users.

Creating a Web Site with Microsoft Windows 98

The only software you need to set up an intranet on your office network is a program called Microsoft Personal Web Server (PWS), which comes with Microsoft Windows 98 and Microsoft Windows 98 Second Edition.

PWS lets you set up and maintain a Web site on any computer on the network. In fact, each computer on the network can host its own Web site, as long as it has PWS installed. If you have three computers connected on a network, for example, you can have three separate personal Web sites, any of which can be viewed by the entire office.

Staff members can then access everyone's pages using their Web browsers in much the same way as they access Web pages on the Internet. Instead of dialing in to an ISP to connect to the worldwide Internet, however, a user's browser connects to a personal Web server on the network. The personal Web server delivers the Web pages to the viewer's screen. As far as that browser is concerned, it's connected to a Web server just as if it were actually on the Internet.

Installing PWS

PWS is included on your Windows CD, but it isn't installed as part of Windows. You have to install it yourself, directly from the CD, on the computer that you plan to use to create a Web site. Each person on the network who wants to set up a Web site must install PWS.

Note

If you use PWS to create a home page, it creates a file with the ASP (Active Server Pages) extension. Some computers on the network might not be able to access ASP Web pages unless you install PWS on those computers as well.

Part 4: Running Your Office on a Network

Follow these steps to install PWS:

1. Insert the Windows CD in your computer. If the Windows installation menu appears, click the Close button.
2. On the Start menu, click Run.
3. Type *D:\add-ons\pws\setup.exe* (where *D* is the letter of your CD drive), and then press Enter.
4. When the setup program begins, click Next.

    You'll see three setup options: Minimum, Typical, and Advanced.

5. Click Typical, which supplies all the services you'll probably need.

    The next screen, shown in Figure 22-2, lets you set the location for the WWW Service (your Web site).

6. Accept the default for the location of the WWW Service by clicking Next.

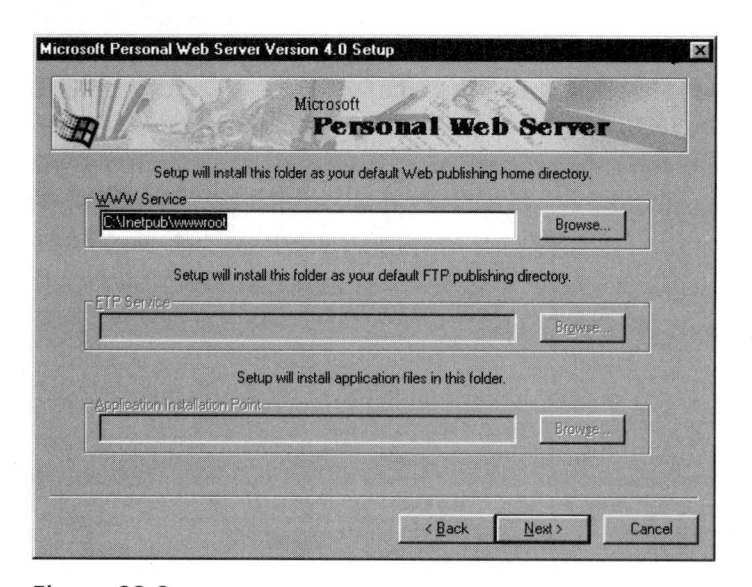

Figure 22-2
This PWS screen lets you set your Web site's location.

Chapter 22: Setting Up Servers for an Office Intranet

> **Note**
>
> When you install PWS on a small office network, you can ignore any error messages you encounter during setup that report problems with MTS, Transaction Server Core Components, or Microsoft Transaction Server, and just click OK. These messages might appear if your Windows registry is full and the setup program is unable to add the necessary entries for Microsoft Transaction Server in your registry. If you want to learn more about these messages and how to correct the error, use your Web browser to visit *support.microsoft.com/support/kb/articles/q214/6/44.ASP.*

7. Click Finish after Windows installs PWS and displays a final dialog box.
8. Click Yes when you're asked whether you want to restart your computer.

Now that PWS is installed, you're ready to create a home page and make it available to others in your company.

Using the Personal Web Manager

When you restart your computer after installing PWS, you'll see a Publish icon on your desktop and a new icon in the system tray next to the clock. Double-clicking either of these icons opens the Personal Web Manager. If you right-click the icon in the system tray, you'll see Start Service and Stop Service options on a shortcut menu; these options allow you to turn PWS on or off or to pause or continue the service. You can also open the Personal Web Manager window by selecting Programs from the Start menu, pointing to Accessories and then Internet Tools and finally Personal Web Server, and clicking Personal Web Manager.

The Tip Of The Day window appears first. You can click Close to close this window, or click Next to read another tip. You can also clear the Show Tips At Startup check box if you want to skip seeing tips each time you start the program. After closing the Tip Of The Day, you'll see the Personal Web Manager window, shown in Figure 22-3.

Part 4: Running Your Office on a Network

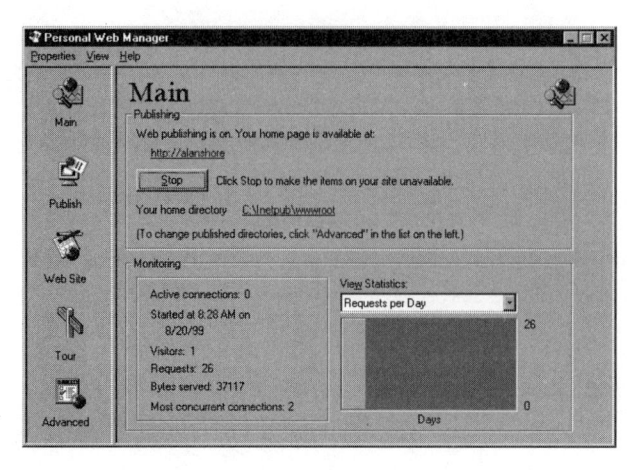

Figure 22-3
The Personal Web Manager helps you create and manage your home page.

Along the left side of the window is a sidebar with five icons:

- **Main** displays the initial window that you now see.
- **Publish** lets you add documents to your Web site that you want to share over the intranet.
- **Web Site** runs the Home Page Wizard, which lets you create a personal home page.
- **Tour** takes you through a PWS tutorial.
- **Advanced** lets you change the directories in which your Web site is stored and the default home page document.

In the Personal Web Manager window, you'll see your home page address, which is *http://* followed by your computer's name, such as alanshore, and the name of the home directory in which the new Web site will be stored, such as C:\Inetpub\wwwroot. You'll also see a Stop button, which allows you to disable your Web server temporarily. Once you click the Stop button, the button changes to Start to allow you to turn the Web server back on. The number of times your Web site has been accessed over the intranet is listed at the bottom of the window along with other useful information, such as the number of people who are currently connected.

To access your Web site, just click the link to your home page. Until you create your own home page, you'll see a default home page in its place. Click the Home directory link to display the subfolders and files in that location. To go to your site from My Computer or Windows Explorer, type

Chapter 22: Setting Up Servers for an Office Intranet

your home page address in the Address text box, such as *http://alanshore*, and press Enter.

Note

When it creates an http address, PWS substitutes dashes for the spaces and apostrophes in your computer's name. For example, the computer named Barb's Room becomes *http://barb-s-room*.

Creating Your Home Page

Your next step is to create a home page on your server. You can do this manually, using a Web page creation program such as Microsoft FrontPage or Microsoft FrontPage Express, or you can use the Home Page Wizard in PWS.

Although it offers only a limited number of Web site design options, the Home Page Wizard is still great for creating a Web site because it's easy to use and it lets you add two very handy features to your site: a guest book and a drop box. A guest book displays messages from network users that all visitors to your site can view. You can use the guest book to hold discussions and to leave messages for other people on the network.

A drop box contains private messages that only you can view. To read drop box messages, you have to log on to your computer with your own user name and start PWS.

To create a home page with the Home Page Wizard, follow these steps:

1. In the Personal Web Manager, click the Web Site icon to start the wizard.

    A dialog box appears, along with a small, animated figure of a wizard.

2. Click the animated wizard or the >> button.

    On the next page of the Home Page Wizard, you can select from a list of templates to set the design of your home page.

3. Select one of the templates, and then click the >> button.

    You'll now be asked whether you want a guest book for public messages.

4. Click the >> button to accept the default response of Yes.

    You'll now be asked whether you want a drop box for private messages.

5. Again, click the >> button to accept the default response of Yes.
   A message appears in the Home Page Wizard reporting that you're ready to personalize your home page.

6. Click the >> button to open the PWS Quick Setup page in Windows Explorer, as shown in Figure 22-4.

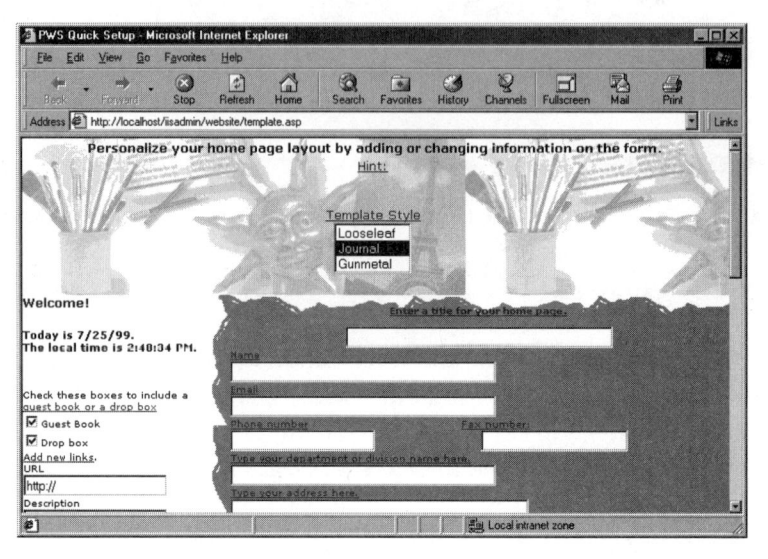

Figure 22-4

By filling in the text boxes on the PWS Quick Setup page, you can personalize your home page.

Use the PWS Quick Setup window, which is actually a window in your Web browser, to create and edit your home page. Notice that the page contains an underlined link above each text box. To get help for the text box, click the link.

The PWS Quick Setup window shows the template you've selected and whether you've included a guest book and drop box. You can change these settings here, such as choosing a guest book if you didn't do so in the Home Page Wizard. Each of the templates you can select contains the same items; only their arrangement and background graphics differ.

In the PWS Quick Setup window, you can enter the following elements on your home page:

- A page title
- Your name

Chapter 22: Setting Up Servers for an Office Intranet

- Your e-mail address
- A phone and fax number
- Your department or division name
- Address
- Four headings and a paragraph of text under each heading

You can also enter links to favorite Web sites and documents on your computer. In the URL and Description text boxes type the URL or path of a site, enter a brief description, and click Add Link. After you add your first link, it'll be shown in a list box along with the Remove Link button.

After you've entered information in as many text boxes as you'd like, click the Enter New Changes button near the bottom of the page. The Web page appears. Close the browser window when you finish reviewing the page.

Note

If you want to change the information on your home page, click Web Site in the Personal Web Manager window, and then click Edit Your Home Page. After you make your changes, click Enter New Changes.

Accessing Your Home Page

When you want to access your home page to see how it looks, enter its address in your Internet browser's address box or as the address in Windows Explorer. You can also choose Run from the Start menu, type your home page address (*http://* followed by your computer's name), and then click OK.

Other staff members on the network can access your home page in the same ways—using the Run box, their Web browser, or Windows Explorer. In some cases, however, a browser might try to dial in to the ISP rather than access the intranet. If this happens, the browser has to be set to access the intranet using the local area network (LAN) rather than the dial-up connection. Here's how it's done with Microsoft Internet Explorer:

1. Right-click the Internet Explorer icon on your desktop, and choose Properties.

    You can also double-click the Internet Options icon in the Windows Control Panel.

2. Click the Connections tab.

3. With Internet Explorer 5, select Dial Whenever A Network Connection Is Not Present or Never Dial A Connection. With earlier versions of Internet Explorer, select Connect Through A Local Area Network.

4. Click OK.

Using Your Guest Book and Drop Box

The guest book serves as a bulletin board on which staff members can leave their names, a short message, or even a favorite link. It's a great place to post important announcements or everyday information that you or another staff member wants to share with everyone else on the network. Placing a message in the guest book is like sending e-mail, except that the guest book message can be viewed by anyone who visits your site.

To leave a message in someone's guest book, go to the home page on that person's computer and click the Read My Guest Book link. The guest book appears, formatted in three columns. Click a column heading to sort the list. To read a message, click its link.

Leave a message by clicking Click Here To Sign The Guest Book. Type the information you want in the message window, and then click Send Message. To clear the message window and start again, click Clear Fields.

If you want to leave a private message that only the owner of the home page can read, click Leave A Private Message. Type the message text, and then click Send Message. The message is stored in the drop box.

Once your guest book and drop box contain messages, you can view, sort, and delete messages. Open Personal Web Manager and click Web Site to see three options: Edit Your Home Page, View Your Guest Book, and Open Your Drop Box.

Use the options in this window to construct a query that will find certain messages to display according to the criteria you supply. You can display messages by the date they were written, the person who sent them, their subject, or any combination of these categories. By default, the search is set to display all messages written before the current date and time. To view these messages, just click the Submit Query button.

By using the drop-down lists and text boxes, however, you can fine-tune your search for specific messages. Next to the MessageDate option, you can choose Less Than, Equal To, or Greater Than, and then enter a certain date as the criterion. To display messages written after a certain date, for example, you'd choose Greater Than from the drop-down list and type the date in the text box to its right.

With the From option, you can choose to list messages from persons whose names begin with, contain, end with, or are equal to the text you enter in the box. The Subject option works the same way, except that it searches the Subject field of messages. For example, to look for messages whose subject contains the word "vacation," select Contains from the Subject drop-down list and type *vacation* in the text box to its right.

> **Note**
> To update the time in a query to the current time, click the Web Site link, and then click View Your Guest Book again.

When you click Submit Query, you'll see a list of messages in the Home Page Wizard that meet the criteria you've entered. You can sort the messages by date, author, or subject by clicking the appropriate column heading. To read a message, click its link. Click Delete Message to erase the message from your guest book. You can also click New Query to change the search criteria or you can click Web Site to return to the Web Site options.

The drop box is similar to the guest book, except it contains messages that only you can see and you don't have the opportunity to create a query. When you click Web Site in the Personal Web Manager window and then click Open Your Drop Box, all the messages in your drop box appear.

Publishing Documents on Your Site

In addition to adding a home page, you can place all sorts of documents on your Web site and share them with staff members. You can post Microsoft PowerPoint presentations, meeting notes, or instructions on how staff members can reach you when you're away on business.

One way to place a file on your Web site is simply to copy the file to the C:\Inetpub\Webpub folder. Or you can let the Publishing Wizard do it for you. The Publishing Wizard lets you select one or more files from any location on your hard disk to copy to the Web site folder. Here's how this wizard works:

1. Click the Publish icon on the left side of the Personal Web Manager window.

    If you haven't yet used the wizard to publish a file on your Web site, the animated wizard figure appears.

2. Click the wizard figure or the >> button.

Part 4: Running Your Office on a Network

3. Enter the file's path and name or click Browse and locate the file using this dialog box:

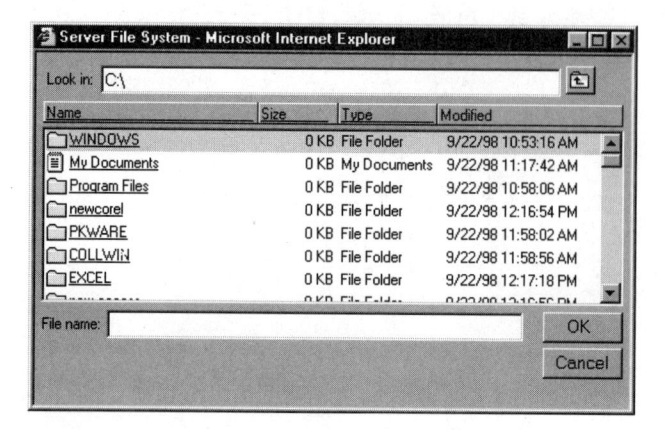

4. To locate a file, click the underlined link for the folder or subfolder containing the file, and then click the file itself.
5. Enter a description of the file in the Description text box.
6. Click Add.
7. Repeat the process for other files you'd like to add.
8. When you've added all the files you want, click the >> button.

Personal Web Manager copies the files to the C:\Inetpub\Webpub folder. Now they're available to anyone who clicks View My Published Documents on your home page.

> **Note**
>
> As a shortcut, you can drag the file name to the Publish icon on the Windows desktop or to the Personal Web Manager sidebar to start the Publishing Wizard. You can also right-click a file, click Send To, and then click Personal Web Server to publish a file.

Once you publish the first file on your Web site, clicking Publish displays these options rather than the animated wizard:

- ⦿ Add a file to the published list
- ○ Remove from the list of published files
- ○ Refresh published files from their originals
- ○ Change a file description

Make your selection, and then click the >> button to add the new file or files to your published file list.

Chapter 22: Setting Up Servers for an Office Intranet

Creating a Web Site with Microsoft Windows 2000

Microsoft Windows 2000 provides Microsoft Internet Information Services for creating and managing an intranet. Internet Information Services is similar to PWS in that it handles requests from Web browsers to display Web site pages.

In addition to Web services, Internet Information Services includes a File Transfer Protocol (FTP) server. FTP lets users access folders for uploading and downloading files. You can use FTP, for example, to make collections of shareware available for users or to provide access to project files and documents.

You can select which features of Internet Information Services you want to install during setup or by accessing the Add/Remove Programs feature in Windows Control Panel. See Figure 22-5.

Installing the services creates the Inetpub folder with your intranet site in the \inetpub\wwwroot folder. Users can access your site in their browser by going to your computer, as in http://Adam, where your computer is named Adam. You can access your site and then folders on your site by choosing Administrative Tools in Control Panel and selecting Personal Web Manager.

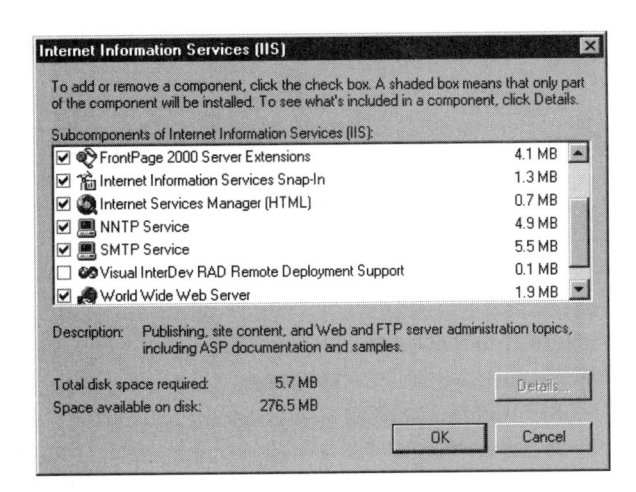

Figure 22-5
Select which features you want to install for Internet Information Services.

Click the Website link to open your site in the browser, or click the folder link to display the folder contents. Click Stop to turn off the Web server or Start to later restart it. Advanced users can manage their site using the Internet Services Manager option in Administrative Tools.

Creating a Web Site with Small Business Server

Small Business Server (SBS) provides a Web server called Internet Information Server (IIS). Installing IIS with Small Business Server creates two Web site locations on your hard disk. One location, \inetpub\wwwroot, is a staging area where you can test your Web site before you actually place it on the Internet. Design your site using FrontPage or any other development program, and place it in the staging area. You can then access the site with a Web browser to see how it appears and to test it out. When the site is ready, transfer the files to your Web hosting company to make the site available on the Internet. The other location, \inetpub\wwwroot\intranet, is an area where you can keep files for a local intranet.

Tip

You can use both \inetpub\wwwroot and \inetpub\wwwroot\intranet for your intranet, depending on how users access your site.

Publishing Web Pages

To make it easy to publish a Web site on an intranet or an Internet staging area, use the Web Publishing Wizard in SBS. The Wizard takes you step-by-step through choosing the files you want to publish and the location where you want to publish them. Access the Wizard by choosing Programs from the Start menu, pointing to Accessories and then Internet Tools, and then clicking Web Publishing Wizard.

Click Next in the first dialog box in the wizard. Use the Browse Folders button to locate entire folders that you want to publish or use the Browse Files button to locate specific files. After you select the files you want to publish, click Next.

The next dialog box asks for the name of a Web server. This isn't the actual address of the Web site or the server but a "friendly name" that you

Chapter 22: Setting Up Servers for an Office Intranet

can use to identify the site, such as My Intranet. Web Publishing Wizard will remember the names, and the actual Web servers that they refer to, so you can choose one quickly from a list. Now enter the URL that you use to access the Web site. To publish to your intranet, for example, enter http://Server (assuming your computer is named Server). To publish to your Internet staging area, enter http://Server/intranet.

Click Next, and then type the actual URL of the site. For your intranet, it'll be the same address you entered in the previous box—either http://Server or http://Server/intranet. Select the Use Local Area Network option if you're publishing the files to your intranet or to your Internet staging area. The dial-up networking option is used to connect to your ISP for uploading files to your Internet site. Finally, click Next and then Finish. Click OK when the message appears reporting that the files have been published.

Accessing Your Site

A user can access either your Internet staging area or intranet site on the network by typing your server's address into the browser. If your server is called Server, for example, the address http://Server opens the Web site in the Internet staging area, while http://Server/intranet accesses the Web page in the intranet folder.

Users can also type these addresses in the Run dialog box. They type either http://Server or http://Server/intranet, depending on the site they want to see, and then click OK.

> **Note**
>
> If your browser tries to dial your ISP when accessing the intranet, you have to set it so it doesn't dial automatically.

On your computer, you can access your sites using two bookmarks that IIS adds to your browser's Favorites menu—My Internet Home Page and My Intranet Home Page. You can also use the SBS Console to access your sites by following these steps:

1. Choose SBS Console from the Start menu.
2. Click More Tasks.
3. Click Publish On The Internet.
4. Select Intranet Web Site or Staging Internet Web Site.

> **Note**
>
> Advanced users can manage Web sites using Internet Services Manager. With SBS, choose Programs from the Start menu, point to Windows NT 4.0 Option Pack and then Microsoft Internet Information Server, and click either Internet Services Manager or Internet Services Manager (HTML).

Creating a Web Site with Microsoft Office

The Home Page Wizard is fast and fun, but it generates only one type of home page, even if it does come in three designs. Whether you're dealing with the Internet or your own office intranet, what makes creating pages for a Web enjoyable is that you can let your imagination go wild and create really personalized Web sites.

When you use the Home Page Wizard to create a home page, it adds the HTML tags to the information that you enter. You don't see the tags in a Web browser; you just see the finished result in the form of a formatted Web page. If you want to, you can learn how to add the HTML tags yourself and create a Web page with even the simplest of text editors, such as Windows Notepad.

To create more personalized Web pages, however, you don't have to rush out and take a course on writing HTML code. You can use any of the dozens of programs that write the tags for you as you design Web pages. Programs such as FrontPage and FrontPage Express are specifically designed to create Web pages and manage all the pages that make up a Web site. But you can also create Web pages with most of today's major applications, such as those that come with Microsoft Office 2000. Using programs included in Office, you can write documents, create spreadsheets and databases, and design slide shows. The programs then convert the formats in your document, spreadsheet, database, or slide show into HTML so that you can publish the content on the Internet or on your intranet.

Creating Web Pages with Microsoft Word

Microsoft Word offers you two ways to create a Web page. You can use Word's Web Page Wizard to design a Web page in much the same way you use the Home Page Wizard in PWS to design a Web page. You follow a series

Chapter 22: Setting Up Servers for an Office Intranet

of dialog boxes to select the format and enter the content of the page. Word then displays the resulting Web page so that you can further personalize it. You can also write and format a document using all of Word's formatting features and then have Word convert the document into a Web page for you. Word will convert the formatting you've set up, such as boldfaced headings, into the HTML tags that your Web browser can understand.

Using the Web Page Wizard

The Web Page Wizard creates a small Web site of one or more Web pages with links that you can click to navigate between the pages. One of the first things you'll have to do with the Web Page Wizard is decide where you want the Web page to be stored. If you choose to save it on C:\Inetpub\Webpub, network users can then access the Web page and any other files you have stored in that folder by selecting View My Published Documents on your home page. You don't have to use the Publish command in Personal Web Manager.

If you want to use your Word Web page as the PWS home page, the page that people see when they enter the address of your computer into their browsers, you can delete all the files in the C:\Inetpub\wwwroot folder and select that folder as the location of your Word home page. However, this will also delete your guest book and drop box, and your PWS home page will have only the features you've added in Word.

Now let's go through the process of creating a Web page in Word using the Web Page Wizard to see how it's done. You'll go step by step through creating your own Web page and placing it in the C:\Inetpub\Webpub folder to publish it.

Here are the generic steps for using the Web Page Wizard to create a Web site:

1. From the File menu in Word, choose New.
2. In the New dialog box, click the Web Pages tab.
3. On the Web Pages tab, double-click the Web Page Wizard icon.
4. Read the information on the first page of the wizard, and then click Next.
5. Type the title for the Web page, and specify the location where you want it stored—usually C:\Inetpub\Webpub.
6. Click Next to see the options shown in Figure 22-6.

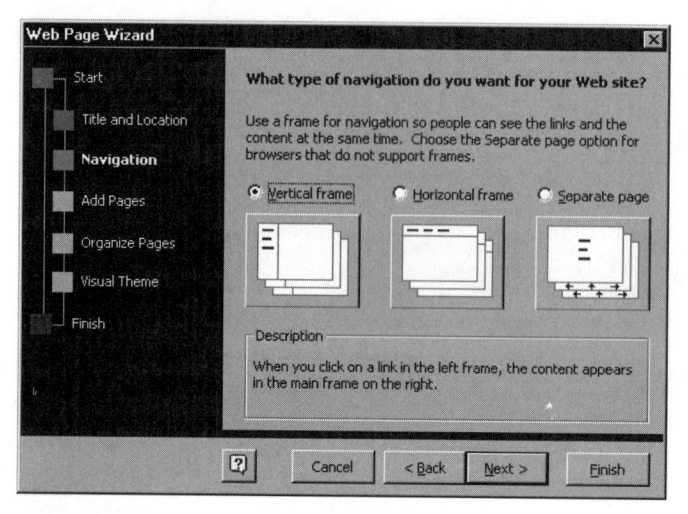

Figure 22-6

Select the layout of your Web page from the options in this window.

You can select one of three navigation methods for the pages in your Web site. A page can have hyperlinks in a vertical or horizontal frame, or it can have navigation buttons that link to other pages you add.

7. Select a navigation method, and click Next.

   The wizard gives you the option of adding more pages to the Web site. The default option is a Personal Web Page and two blank pages—Page 1 and Page 2. You can add more blank pages or pages that are designed according to templates provided by the wizard.

8. Clicking Add Blank Page immediately adds a blank page to the Web site, but if you want to add a template page, click Add Template Page to see a list of templates. When you click a template in this list, a sample of the page appears in the background.

9. When you are finished adding pages, click Next. You can now change the sequence of pages by selecting a page and then clicking the Move Up or Move Down button.

10. Click Next to display the next page of the wizard, which allows you to add a theme to your Web site.

11. To add a theme, click the Add A Visual Theme button, and then click Browse Theme to choose the theme.

Chapter 22: Setting Up Servers for an Office Intranet

Only some of the themes are installed with Office 2000 when you perform the typical installation. If you select a theme that wasn't installed, a message appears asking whether you want to install the theme at this time. Insert your Office 2000 CD in the CD drive and click Install.

12. From the list of themes, select a theme, such as Artsy or Blends, and then click OK.
13. Click Finish to display the Web page on the screen.

Word adds sample text as a placeholder until you enter your own text on the Web page. Now you only need to fill in the sample text areas. You can click a link to another page or topic to move to that page.

Working with Web Pages Your Web page appears in Word's Web Layout view. In Web Layout view, your document appears just as it will when it's displayed in a Web browser. To actually use a browser to view your Word document, you can select Web Page Preview from the File menu. Office launches your Web browser without connecting you to the Internet and displays the document. Just close the browser to return to Word.

In Web Layout view, you also see the Frames toolbar. You can use this toolbar to change the way your page is divided into frames. A frame is a separate section of the page that contains its own text and hyperlinks, and it scrolls independently of the text in other frames. You won't be using the Frames toolbar in this example because your page already contains two frames, so click the toolbar's Close button to remove it from the screen.

When you're working in Web Layout view, you can continue formatting the document using Word's formatting commands. To change the theme, for example, choose Theme from the Format menu to see the Theme dialog box, shown in Figure 22-7. Choose the theme you want to apply, and then click OK.

In the Theme dialog box, you can also apply various templates to format your text. Click the Style Gallery button in the Theme dialog box to display the Style Gallery dialog box.

Each template listed in the Style Gallery dialog box contains a collection of text formats that will be applied to certain areas of the documents, such as titles, subtitles, and body text. To see how a template will affect your document, click a template in the list of templates, and then select the

Document option in the Preview section. Your document will appear in the Preview Of panel. You can also select Example to see a sample document that uses most of the styles, or you can select Style Samples to see the name of each style set in that style. Click OK in the dialog box to apply the template to your document.

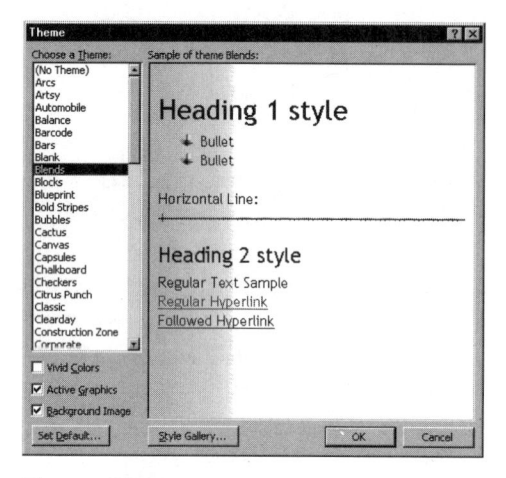

Figure 22-7

Choose a theme in the Theme dialog box to give your Web page a certain look.

Of course, the sample text on the Web page isn't exactly what you'd like for your own home page. You can modify the text, beginning with the headlines and then adjusting the hyperlinks.

1. Select the headline Main Heading Goes Here, and type *Get All of the News Here!*
2. Select the headline Work Information, not the underlined link, and type Meeting Notes.
3. Select the next six lines, between Meeting Notes and Back To Top, and replace them with information about recent staff meetings.
   You can leave the Favorite Links section as it is for now. You'll add several hyperlinks later.
4. Select the heading Contact Information, and type *How to Reach Me*.
5. Select the next six lines, between How to Reach Me and Back To Top, and replace them with your daytime telephone number.
6. Now for the sake of brevity, delete the remainder of the text, from the heading Current Projects to the end of the document.

Chapter 22: Setting Up Servers for an Office Intranet

Working with Hyperlinks   It's now time to tackle the hyperlinks on the page. Go back to the top of the page where you see a series of six underlined hyperlinks, from Work Information to Personal Interest. You want to adjust the links for the new text.

1. Select the last three links, and press the Delete key to remove them.

    You can't click a link to select its text because clicking a link actually goes to its associated location in the document or Web page.

2. To change the text of the Work Information link, right-click it, point to Hyperlink on the shortcut menu that appears, and select Edit Hyperlink to see the Edit Hyperlink dialog box shown in Figure 22-8.

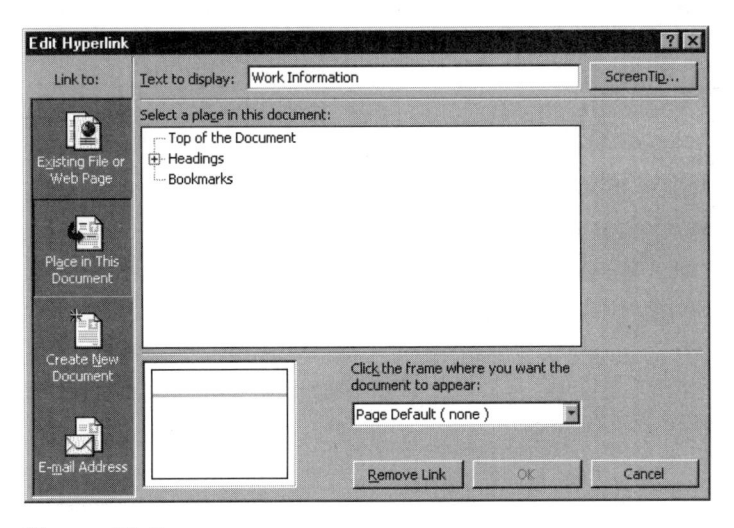

Figure 22-8
Editing a hyperlink is easy.

3. Change the text in the Text To Display text box from Work Information to Project Status.

    Because you deleted the original heading, Work Information, you now have to specify which heading in the document you'll jump to when the link is clicked.

4. Click the plus sign next to Headings to see the headline Get All of the News Here!

Part 4: Running Your Office on a Network

5. Click the plus sign next to Get All of the News Here! to see a list of the subheadings on the page.
6. Click Project Status, and then click OK.
   When someone clicks the Project Status link in a browser, the browser will display the section of the page starting with the heading Project Status. Clicking the Back To Top link will cause the browser to display the top of the page.
7. Change the Contact Information link so it reads How to Reach Me, and link it to the How to Reach Me heading.

Now it's time to add your favorite Web pages to the Favorite Links section.

1. Scroll to the Favorite Links section of the page.
2. Select the first line, Insert A Hyperlink Here, and then click the Hyperlink button on the toolbar, which looks like a globe with a length of chain.
3. In the Insert Hyperlink dialog box, click Existing File Or Web Page.
   The Web site addresses shown in the list depend on the links you last inserted using Office.
4. In the Text To Display text box, type the text that will be the link.
5. In the Type The File Or Web Page Name text box, enter the address of a favorite Web site, such as *http://www.westerns.com*. If you don't know the address of the site, you can click Web Page in the Browse For section to go online and locate the site.
6. Click OK to close the Insert Hyperlink dialog box. Now let's add a link to a document that you've already created and saved on your disk.
7. Select the second line, Insert A Hyperlink Here, and then click the Hyperlink button on the toolbar.
8. In the Insert Hyperlink dialog box, click the Recent Files button to display a list of recently opened files. If the document you want to link to isn't shown, you can type its path and name or click File in the Browse For section to locate the document.
9. In the Text To Display text box, type the name of a document.

Chapter 22: Setting Up Servers for an Office Intranet

10. Click one of the documents in the list of recent files, and then click OK.

    When someone clicks this hyperlink, the linked document will open.

Now let's add a link to a Web site that you've recently visited with your Web browser.

1. Select the third line, Insert A Hyperlink Here, and then click the Hyperlink button on the toolbar.
2. In the Insert Hyperlink dialog box, click the Browsed Pages button to display a list of recently visited Web sites.
3. In the Text To Display box, type the name of the Web site.
4. Click the site you want in the list of browsed pages, and then click OK.

Tip

To add additional hyperlinks to your Web page, just type text where you want the link to appear. Select the text, click the Hyperlink button in the toolbar, and create the link the way you've just learned.

The Web page also has hyperlinks in the top frame. These links jump to the pages of the Web site and return to the page that serves as the site's home page, Personal Web Page. Let's change the text of these links and then look at one of these other pages.

1. Right-click the link Blank Page 1, point to Hyperlink in the shortcut menu, and click Edit Hyperlink to open the Edit Hyperlink dialog box.
2. In the Text To Display text box, change the text from Blank Page 1 to Personnel, and then click OK.
3. Now click the Personnel link to open the Web page.

The Personnel page has the same upper frame as the Personal Web Page, but the lower frame contains only the text This Web Page Is Blank Page 1. The actual name of the file in which the page is stored is Blank Page 1.htm. You can leave the file name the same because it's the content of the page that you're interested in.

You can now add and format any text and hyperlinks that you want to appear on the Personnel page. When you're done designing the page, click the link Personal Web Page to return to the site's home page.

Using the same procedure, you can change the text of the link Blank Page 2 and the contents of that page.

To view the Web page you created in Word and access all its links, click the View My Published Documents link on your PWS home page, and then click the link for default.htm.

Converting a Word Document to a Web Page

If you already created a document that you'd like to add to your Web site but it isn't in HTML format, you can easily convert it to a Web page. Just follow these steps:

1. Open a document that you've typed and formatted.
2. From the File menu, choose Save As Web Page.
3. In the Save As dialog box, click in the Save In box and locate the C:\Inetpub\Webpub folder.
4. In the File Name text box, type the file name you want for the Web page.
5. Click Save.

    Word converts the document to Web page format and displays it in Web Layout view. A message appears if a Word format in the document doesn't have an HTML equivalent. Click OK to convert the document anyway, displaying the formatted text as plain text. The file will be stored in the C:\Inetpub\Webpub folder so it can be accessed using the View My Published Documents link on your PWS home page.

Web pages are a great way to share information and opinions over your computer network. But when you're not in the office, such as when you're on a business trip or on vacation, you can still keep in touch with the network remotely, as you'll learn in the next chapter.

Creating Web Pages with Microsoft Excel

To save a Microsoft Excel worksheet as a Web page, choose Save As Web Page from the File menu to open the Save As dialog box. You can then

Chapter 22: Setting Up Servers for an Office Intranet

choose the Entire Workbook option button, type a filename, and then click Save. When you open the file in your browser, all the workbook pages will be available. You'll see sheet tabs at the bottom of the window—just click the tab to open the Web page for that sheet.

If you choose the Selection: Sheet option, only the current worksheet is saved as an HTML file. However, you can also enable the Add Interactivity check box. With this option, the worksheet appears with an Excel toolbar to perform some basic Excel operations on the Web when the worksheet is displayed in a Web browser, as shown in Figure 22-9.

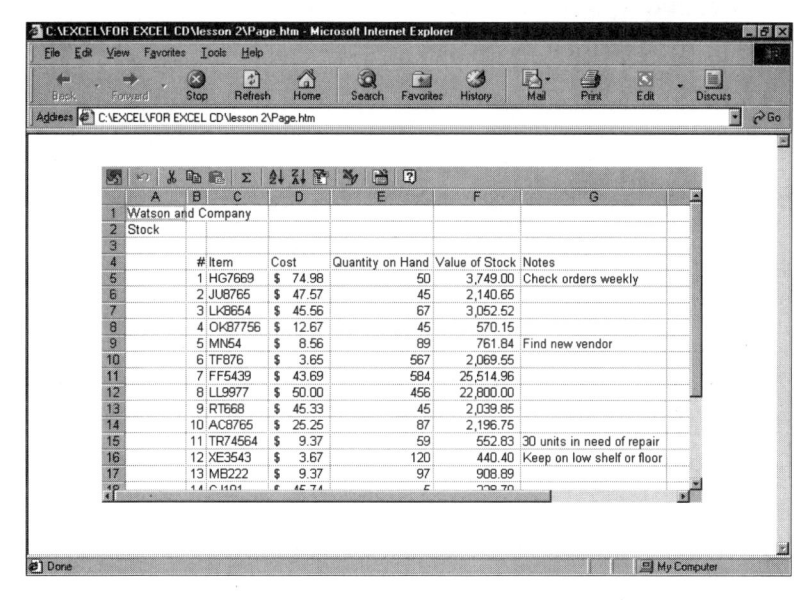

Figure 22-9
You can create an Excel Web page that allows the user to modify the information it contains.

Creating Web Pages with Microsoft Access

With Microsoft Access you can create Web pages in two ways. You can use the Export command to select the type of Web page you want to create, or you can construct a data access page. When you use the Export command, Access creates a page that can be opened and accessed by your Web browser. As an alternative, you can create a data access page that can be used both from within Access and on the Internet.

A data access page contains fields with text boxes in which you can view, edit, and add information. At the bottom of the form is a special toolbar containing the Access navigation buttons, Add Record, and Delete Record buttons as well as buttons to save and undo record changes, sort the table, and create and apply a filter. When you open a data access page from within Access, you're actually looking at a Web page. Right-click the page, for example, to display your browser's shortcut menu rather then Access's shortcut menu.

To create a data access page, follow these steps:

1. Double-click Create Data Access Page By Using Wizard on the Pages tab of the Database window.
2. In the first wizard dialog box, shown in Figure 22-10, select the fields that you want to add to the Web page, and then click Next.

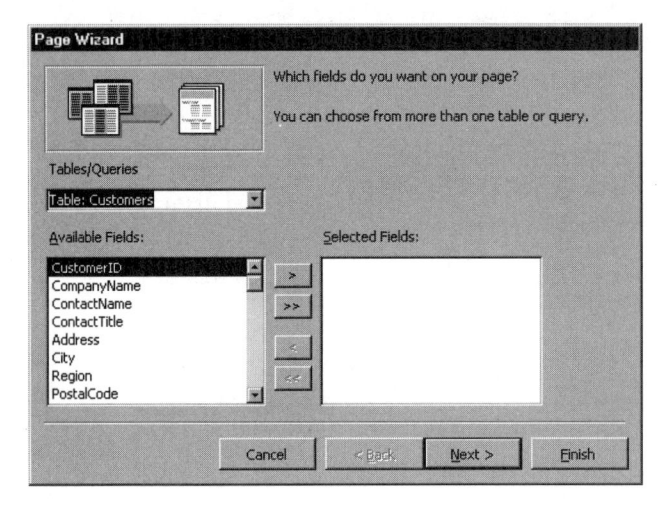

Figure 22-10
Select fields for the data access page.

3. A box now appears in which you can group the fields. Grouping the information makes the page read-only, so the information can't be changed using the data access page. Click Next.
4. You can now choose to sort the database records. Choose a field to sort the information, and click Next.
5. Type a name for the page, select whether you want to choose a theme, and then click Finish.

Chapter 22: Setting Up Servers for an Office Intranet

Rather than create a data access page, you can use the Export command from the File menu. Click the name of the table you want to save in the Access database window, and then choose Export from the File menu. In the Save As Type list, choose one of these formats:

- HTML Document
- Microsoft IIS 1-2
- Microsoft Active Server Pages

The HTML Document format has no link between the HTML page and the data itself. Once you create the page and upload it to a Web site, any changes to the information in the database won't be reflected in the Web page.

The other two options create dynamic pages so users will always see the most current information in the database. The information on the page will be updated each time it's accessed. The dynamic options are designed for users of IIS.

IIS (also known as HTX/IDC) creates two files: an IDC file and an HTX file. The IDC file contains Open Database Connectivity (ODBC) information, which tells the server the names of both the data source and the HTX file and includes an SQL statement so the server can access the information from the file. The HTX file serves as a template to specify how to format the data as an HTML document. When a user accesses the Web page, the server uses the files to retrieve the information from the database and display it on the screen.

The Microsoft Active Server Pages option is for use with the ActiveX component of IIS 3.0 or later. The ASP file contains HTML formatting commands as well as SQL statements needed to access the information, along with Microsoft Visual Basic code that references ActiveX Server Controls.

If you selected a dynamic type of Web page, the next dialog box asks you to specify information the server needs to access and update the information. You'll need to enter the Data Source Name, User Name, and Password. If you choose the ASP type, you'll also have to specify the Server URL and the Session Timeout options.

Creating Web Pages with Microsoft PowerPoint

One of the easiest ways to create a Web site is to do so as a Microsoft PowerPoint presentation. Create the slide show as you would any other

Part 4: Running Your Office on a Network

presentation, and then choose Save As Web Page from the File menu. In the dialog box that appears, enter a filename, and click Save. PowerPoint creates an HTML file with the name you designate as well as a separate folder of supporting files. The folder has the same name as the Web page but with "_files" appended to the name.

When you open the resulting HTML file in your browser, you'll see an index frame on the left showing the presentation outline, as shown in Figure 22-11. The entries in the outline serve as hyperlinks to move from slide to slide, with each slide serving as another Web page.

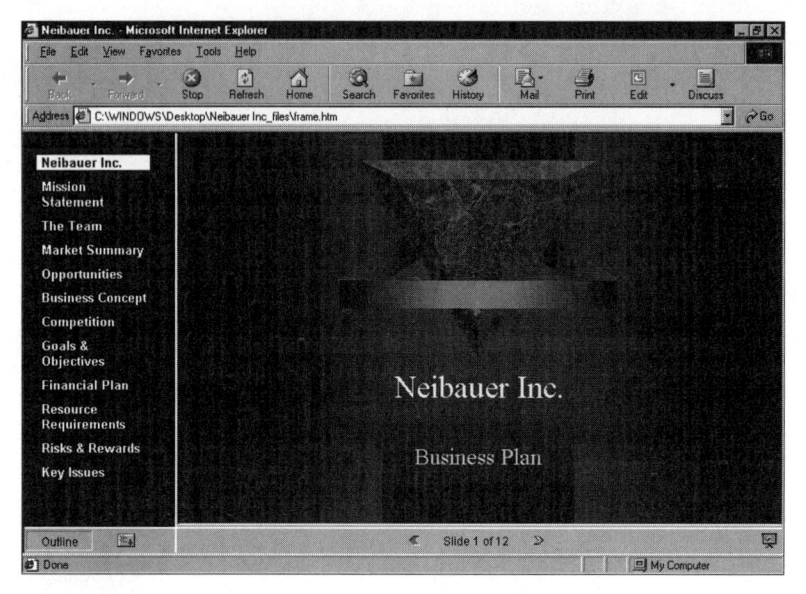

Figure 22-11
You can navigate to a slide in a Microsoft PowerPoint presentation by clicking an entry in the left frame.

The next chapter covers setting up Remote Access Server.

Chapter 23
Networking for Road Warriors

Whether you work in an office or out of the home, at some point you'll probably hit the road for business. As you'll learn in this chapter, even when you're traveling you can still communicate with the folks at the office or back home on the network and take advantage of all the benefits the network offers, such as sharing files and printing documents.

As countless computer-toting business travelers—road warriors—already know, it's easy to stay in touch with a home or office computer from any place that's within reach of a telephone. In this chapter, you'll learn how to set up and use a process called remote computing to dial in to your network to access its resources the same way you dial in to an Internet service provider (ISP) to access the Internet.

You'll also learn how to use Microsoft NetMeeting, a program that allows you to talk to and even see another person on your network or at a remote location, as long as both computers are equipped with video cameras (which can be inexpensive and are easily added) and microphones.

NetMeeting not only allows you to hold long-distance meetings, it also provides a handy feature called remote desktop sharing that allows you to take over another computer on the network and actually operate it from your keyboard and screen, no matter where you are. As you'll see later in this chapter, remote desktop sharing gives you the opportunity to troubleshoot problems someone might be having with a computer on the network or even show someone how to perform a specific task on the computer.

Packing for the Road

Suppose you're on a business trip away from the office and you're relaxing in your hotel room going over the day's events. You'd like to dial in to your network to check e-mail messages, send a file, or perhaps print a document on one of your network printers. At the office, your modem is probably already plugged into the phone jack, so going online is simple. But when you're away from the office, connecting to a phone line isn't always that easy. Even if your hotel room or a conference center has a standard, modular phone jack, the jack might not be conveniently located or close enough to the spot at which you'd like to use your computer.

To avoid some potential hassles, you should start by packing a few essentials along with your laptop:

- Two 6-foot or longer telephone extension cables
- A telephone cable coupler
- A two-to-one or three-to-one telephone adapter

The telephone cables, coupler, and adapter weigh practically nothing and take up little space in your computer case or briefcase, but they can be lifesavers when you want to connect to a home network or to the Internet. You can purchase all of these items at a hardware store, your local Radio Shack, or your local "Nothing more than $1.00" store. They'll allow you to reach a phone jack—even one that's in an out-of-the-way place.

The coupler lets you connect two lengths of telephone cable to lengthen your reach even further. If a telephone is already connected to the phone jack, the two-to-one adapter lets you plug in both the phone and your modem.

> **Note**
>
> In a pinch, the adapter can also be used as a coupler—just plug both extension cables into the adapter and plug one end of the cable, rather than the adapter, into the jack.

Chapter 23: Networking for Road Warriors

Most hotels cater to business travelers, who are now, more than ever, equipped with laptop computers. But not every hotel you stay in will be set up to facilitate remote computing.

The first hurdle you might encounter, especially if you are traveling abroad, is the lack of a standard RJ-11 modular phone jack in your room. This is the standard type of receptacle that's used as a phone jack in the United States. Even with the extra cables, couplers, and adapters that you've packed, you'll be stuck if there's no place to plug in your modem.

The second hurdle might be the phone line itself. The telephone lines in your home are regular analog lines. Your modem converts the digital information in your computer to analog signals that these regular phone lines can carry. But many hotels and offices have special, digital telephone systems. In a digital system, voice and fax communications are transmitted through the system as digital information, so your analog modem won't work. What's worse is that if you connect your laptop to a digital network, the voltage from the digital lines might damage your laptop's analog modem permanently.

With a little preparation before your trip, however, you can overcome both these hurdles. When you make hotel reservations, find out whether the hotel's telephone system is analog or digital. Even if it's digital, you might be able to request a room with an analog phone connection and an RJ-11 jack that you can use with your laptop. Such rooms are frequently available to business travelers.

You can also purchase an *acoustic coupler,* a device that fits over the telephone handset and connects to your modem. Instead of plugging the modem directly into the phone system, you connect it to the acoustic coupler, which sends and receives signals through the telephone handset. Another device that you can use with a digital system allows you to connect your modem to the jack into which the phone's handset is plugged. Both of these devices overcome the problems of not having access to a jack and to an analog phone system. Devices such as these are sold by Road Warrior (*www.warrior.com*). These devices enable you to connect easily and safely to digital phone lines when you're on the road.

If you are traveling abroad, you can purchase jack adapters, which let you connect your modem to the type of jack used in the country you are visiting. To order the correct adapter, you'll have to find out what type of jack you'll be using, but most mail-order companies that specialize in remote computing hardware, such as Hello Direct (*www.hello-direct.com*) and Road Warrior, can help you with that.

For maximum protection, you might want to consider buying a *line tester*, a device that indicates whether a line is analog or digital, and a *surge protector*, which protects a modem against power surges while you're connected. Road Warrior, for example, offers a product called the Modem Saver Plus. You plug this device into the phone jack before plugging in your modem. A green light indicates that the jack is safe to use; a red light indicates that it could damage your modem. A surge protector is also built into the Modem Saver Plus.

Dialing In to Your ISP

One other important item you should have for your trip is a local phone number for your Internet service provider in the area in which you'll be staying.

You've probably set up your computer to dial in to your ISP from home or the office using the local number that's available where you live. You could use that same number when you travel, but you'd have to do two things first:

- Adjust Microsoft Windows so that it dials the area code as well as the number.
- Take out a loan to pay the long distance charges, especially at hotel rates.

Note

Some ISPs require that you install special software to connect to them. If that's the case with your ISP, you'll need to follow the instructions that came with the software to change the access number for your ISP that your modem dials.

Fortunately, large ISPs that are nationwide have local phone numbers in or near most major cities, so you should find out from your ISP ahead of time the local phone numbers for the areas in which you'll be staying. Call the ISP's support number and request the local access numbers, or connect on line before you leave and look for the numbers on the ISP's Web site. When you arrive at your destination, you can change the phone number that your system dials to connect to the ISP. Be sure to make a note of the original number so you'll be able to restore it when you return home.

Chapter 23: Networking for Road Warriors

> **Tip**
>
> If you use a program such as Microsoft Outlook Express to check your e-mail, you'll need to change the connection it uses to dial in to your ISP to send and receive mail.

You can change the telephone number your computer dials by following these steps:

1. Double-click My Computer on the Windows desktop.
2. In the My Computer window, double-click the Dial-Up Networking icon. In Windows 2000, double-click Control Panel and then double-click Network And Dial-Up Connections.
3. Right-click the connection you normally use, and choose Properties from the shortcut menu.
4. On the General tab, replace the existing area code and telephone number with the new numbers.
5. If you must dial 9 or some other number to get an outside line, add the number and a comma before the phone number, as in *9,5551212*. The comma causes the modem to pause after dialing the number 9 so the outside dial tone can be obtained.
6. Click OK.

> **Note**
>
> Remember to change the phone number again when you return home.

Creating an Additional Dial-Up Networking Connection

If you travel frequently to the same location, such as a branch office in a different city, changing and restoring the telephone number of your ISP can be an annoyance. So instead of changing the number in your dial-up connection, you can create a new connection. The new connection will have all the settings required to dial into your ISP from the road. You can choose to use that connection when traveling and then switch back to the original when you get home.

First, you need to check your existing settings. If you're using Microsoft Windows 2000, *see "Using Microsoft Windows 2000" on page 427*.

Part 4: Running Your Office on a Network

If you're using Microsoft Windows 95, Microsoft Windows 98, or Microsoft Windows NT, just follow these steps:

1. Double-click My Computer on the Windows desktop.
2. In the My Computer window, double-click the Dial-Up Networking icon.
3. Right-click the connection you use to dial in to your ISP, and then choose Properties.
4. Click the Server Types tab in the Properties dialog box for the new connection.
5. Make a note of the settings on the Server Types tab, including the Type Of Dial-Up Server setting and the check boxes that are selected in the Advanced Options and Allowed Network Protocols sections.
6. Click the TCP/IP Settings button.
7. In the TCP/IP Settings dialog box, write down any numbers that appear in the Primary DNS and Secondary DNS text boxes. You should also make a note about the other settings in the box, although these are usually already set for you by default when you make a new connection.
8. Click Cancel to return to the Dial-Up Networking window, and click Cancel again to close the dialog box for the connection.

Now you can make a new connection by following these steps:

1. In the Dial-Up Networking window, double-click Make New Connection to open the Make New Connection dialog box.
2. Type a name for the connection, such as *Branch Office*.
3. If you have more than one modem, click the down arrow next to the Select A Device drop-down list, and choose the modem you'll use to connect to the ISP.
4. Click Next.
5. Enter the ISP's local phone number at the remote location.
6. Click Next, and then click Finish.

While the Dial-Up Networking window is still open, you need to configure the connection for the proper protocol. Here's how to do it:

Chapter 23: Networking for Road Warriors

1. Right-click the connection you've just created, and choose Properties.
2. In the connection dialog box, click the Server Types tab.
3. Set the options on the Server Types tab so that they match the settings you made a note of earlier. Be sure to check that you've matched the Type Of Dial-Up Server, Advanced Options, and Allowed Network Protocols settings.
4. Click the TCP/IP Settings button.
5. In the TCP/IP Settings dialog box, enter the Primary DNS and Secondary DNS numbers that you copied down earlier. Take a look at the other settings to make sure they're the same as your main ISP connection.
6. Click OK to close the TCP/IP Settings dialog box.
7. Click OK to return to the Dial-Up Networking window.

Now when you're away from home and want to dial in to your ISP, you can choose the new connection you've just made. When you want to connect to the Internet, you can open the Dial-Up Networking window and double-click the connection to dial in to your ISP. The first time you connect with the new connection, you'll have to enter your user name and password. Select the Save Password check box so that Windows will remember the password for later connections. When you see a message reporting that the connection has been made, you can start your Web browser.

Using Microsoft Windows 2000

If you're using Microsoft Windows 2000, follow these steps to create a dial-up connection for your ISP:

1. On the Start menu, point to Settings and then Click Network And Dial-Up Connections.
2. Right-click the connection you use to dial in to your ISP, and then choose Properties.
3. Click the Networking tab in the dialog box for the connection.
4. Make a note of the settings on the Networking tab, including the setting for Type Of Dial-Up Server I Am Calling and the check boxes that are selected in the Components Checked Are Used By This Connection section.

5. Select Internet Protocol (TCP/IP), and click the Properties button.
6. In the Internet Protocol (TCP/IP) Properties dialog box, write down any numbers that appear in the Preferred DNS Server and Alternate DNS Server text boxes.
7. Click Cancel to return to the connection Properties dialog box, and click Cancel again to close the Properties dialog box.

Now you can make a new connection by following these steps:

1. In the Network And Dial-Up Connections window, double-click Make New Connection to open the Network Connection Wizard.
2. Click Next.
3. Select Dial-Up To Private Network, and click Next.
4. Type the ISP's local phone number at the remote location, and click Next.
5. Select Only For Myself, and click Next.
6. Type a name for the connection, and click Finish.

While the Network And Dial-Up Connections window is still open, you need to configure the connection for the proper protocol. Here's how to do it:

1. Right-click the connection you've just created, and choose Properties.
2. On the General tab, select your modem from the Connect box.
3. Click the Networking tab.
4. Set the options so that they match the settings you made a note of earlier. Be sure to check that you've matched the settings for Type Of Dial-Up Server I Am Calling and Components Checked Are Used By This Connection sections.
5. Select Internet Protocol (TCP/IP), and click the Properties button.
6. In the Internet Protocol (TCP/IP) dialog box, type the Preferred DNS and Alternate DNS numbers that you copied down earlier.
7. Click OK to close the Internet Protocol (TCP/IP) dialog box.
8. Click OK to return to the Dial-Up Networking window.

Now when you're away from home and want to dial in to your ISP, you can choose the new connection you've just made. When you want to connect to the Internet, you can open the Network And Dial-Up Connections window and double-click the connection to dial in to your ISP. The first time you connect with the new connection, you'll have to enter your user name and password. Select the Save Password check box so that Windows will remember the password for later connections. When you see a message reporting that the connection has been made, you can start your Web browser.

> ### Checking Your Connection in Microsoft Internet Explorer 5
>
> If you're using Microsoft Internet Explorer 5, you can easily change the default connection.
>
> 1. Right-click the Internet Explorer icon on the desktop.
> 2. Choose Properties from the shortcut menu.
> 3. On the Connections tab of the Internet Options dialog box, click the connection you want to use, and then click the Set Default button.
> 4. Click OK.
>
> Now whenever you start your browser, it'll dial into the ISP using the new connection. Using this technique means you'll need to change the connection again when you get home.

Dialing In to Your Network

As long as you can connect your modem to a phone line, you can dial in to your network to transfer files or print documents when you're away.

In order to connect to your network from the road, you have to take two steps:

- Prepare your laptop computer to dial in to your network.
- Prepare a network workstation or server to accept the call.

Preparing Your Laptop

Set up your laptop by creating a connection to call your office network. If you're using Windows 2000, *see "Preparing Your Microsoft Windows 2000 Laptop" on page 431.* If you're using Windows 95, Windows 98, or Windows NT, just follow the steps shown on the following page.

Part 4: Running Your Office on a Network

1. Double-click My Computer on the Windows desktop.
2. In the My Computer window, double-click the Dial-Up Networking icon.
3. Double-click Make New Connection to open the Make New Connection dialog box.
4. Type a name for your connection, such as *Road Warrior*.
5. If you have more than one modem, click the down arrow next to the Select A Device drop-down list, and choose the modem you'll use to connect to your computer.
6. Click Next.
7. Type your computer's area code and telephone number.
8. Click Next, and then click Finish.

While the Dial-Up Networking window is still open, you need to configure the connection for the proper protocol. Here's how to do it:

1. Right-click the connection you've just created, and choose Properties.
2. In the connection dialog box, click the Server Types tab to see the options shown in Figure 23-1.

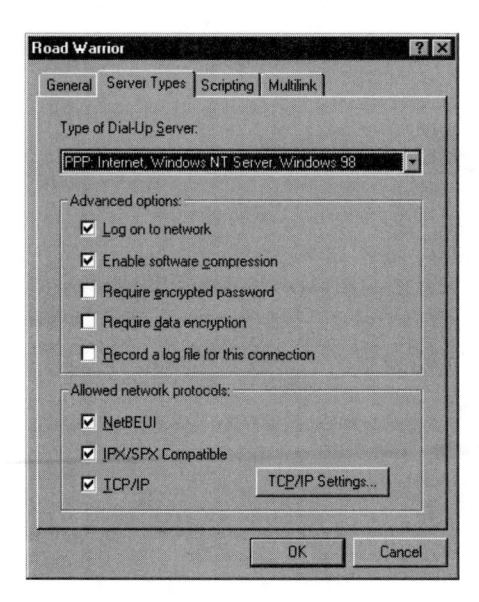

Figure 23-1

Configure your dial-up connection from this set of options.

3. Make sure the Type Of Dial-Up Server option is set to PPP: Internet, Windows NT Server, Windows 98. If you're using Windows 95, make sure the option is set to PPP: Windows 95, Windows NT, Internet.
4. Select the Log On To Network check box.
5. Select all three protocols listed in the Allowed Network Protocols area of the dialog box: NetBEUI, IPX/SPX Compatible, and TCP/IP.
6. Click OK.

> **Note**
>
> You don't need to configure an IP address or set any other TCP/IP options.

Preparing Your Microsoft Windows 2000 Laptop

If you're using Microsoft Windows 2000 on your laptop, follow these steps to create a dial-up connection to use when you travel:

1. On the Start menu, point to Settings and then click Network And Dial-Up Connections.
2. Double-click Make New Connection to start the Network Connection Wizard.
3. Select Dial-Up To Private Network, and click Next.
4. Type the phone number of your office network, and click Next.
5. Select Only For Myself, and click Next.
6. Type the name of your dial-up connection, and click Finish.

While the Network Dial-Up Connections window is still open, you need to configure the connection for the proper protocols. Here's how to do it:

1. Right-click the connection you've just created, and choose Properties.
2. In the connection Properties dialog box, click the Networking tab.
3. Make sure the Type Of Dial-Up Server I Am Calling option is set to PPP: Windows 95/98/NT 4/2000, Internet.
4. In the Components Checked Are Used By This Connection box, make sure that all of these protocols are present: Internet Protocol (TCP/IP), NetBEUI Protocol, and NWLink IPX/SPX/NetBIOS Compatible Transport Protocol. If all three are present,

click OK. If one or more of the three protocols aren't present, you'll need to install them.

5. Click Install.
6. Select Protocol, and click Add.
7. Select the protocol you want to install in the Network Protocol Box, and click OK.
8. If you need to install another protocol, follow steps 5 through 7 again.
9. Once you've installed all of the necessary protocols, click Close.

Using Dial-Up Server

Whether you want to connect to your network to share or print files or just access your computer to pick up messages, you need to set up your computer so that it will allow you to dial in from the road. You do this by installing Dial-Up Server, a Windows feature that sets up a computer on the network so that its modem answers the phone when you call in from a remote location, such as from a hotel room when you're traveling with a laptop computer.

Note

To dial in to a Microsoft Windows NT Server or Microsoft Windows 2000 Server computer, see "Using Remote Access Service" on page 436.

When you set up your computers for dial-up networking, you can choose to password-protect your system so that only authorized persons can access your files. Password protection is optional but it's highly recommended. You should also consider using password protection to restrict access to sensitive folders, *as explained in "Types of Access Controls," on page 262.*

Installing Dial-Up Server

Although it comes with Windows 98 and it's part of the Microsoft Plus! add-on for Windows 95, Dial-Up Server isn't installed by default. Installing Dial-Up Server, though, requires only a few simple steps.

Your first step is to make sure that all three network protocols are installed and that your hard disk is shared. If you haven't done this already, see *"Installing Protocols" on page 196* and *"Accessing Shared Disks and Folders" on page 268.*

Chapter 23: Networking for Road Warriors

You'll need to install TCP/IP because Microsoft's Dial-Up Server software requires TCP/IP to connect to the remote computer. If your network uses TCP/IP as its protocol, you can dial in to the dial-up server and access its files, but you won't be able to access the other computers on the network. In order to dial in to your dial-up server and access your entire network, you must have installed either IPX/SPX or NetBEUI as a network protocol. In other words, you should install all three of the protocols—IPX/SPX, NetBEUI, and TCP/IP—on the computer you want to use as a dial-up server, but only IPX/SPX and NetBEUI on the other computers on the network.

You also need to set the Primary Network Logon to Windows Logon and turn on file sharing through the dial-up adapter (usually a modem). If you just use your modem to connect to the Internet, file and printer sharing over the modem will be turned off. This helps prevent Internet hackers from accessing your files when you are connected to the Internet. In order to access your own files when you dial into the network, however, you have to turn on file sharing. Here's how you do this:

1. On the Start menu, point to Settings, and then click Control Panel.
2. In the Control Panel window, double-click the Network icon.
3. From the Primary Network Logon drop-down list, shown in Figure 23-2, choose Windows Logon.

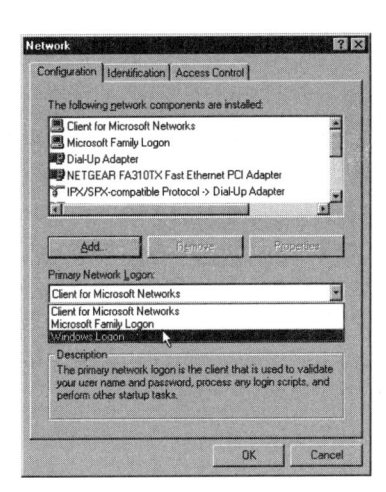

Figure 23-2
Choose Windows Logon from the Primary Network Logon drop-down list.

433

4. Scroll the network components list, and click on the setting TCP/IP -> Dial-Up Adapter.
5. Click Properties, and then click OK to the message that appears.
6. Click the Bindings tab.
7. Select the check box labeled File And Printer Sharing For Microsoft Networks.
8. Click OK.
9. Click OK again to close the Network dialog box.
10. Click Yes when you're asked whether to restart your computer.

Installing the Dial-Up Server Software

To install the Dial-Up Server software, follow these steps:

1. If you're using Windows 95, you must first install Microsoft Plus! before you can set up and configure Dial-Up Server.
2. On the Start menu, point to Settings, and then click Control Panel.
3. In the Control Panel window, double-click the Add/Remove Programs icon.
4. In the Add/Remove Programs Properties dialog box, click the Windows Setup tab.
5. In the list of components, click Communications, but be careful not to remove the check mark in the check box to its left.
6. Click Details.
7. In the Communications dialog box, shown in Figure 23-3, select the Dial-Up Server check box.
8. Click OK.
9. Click OK again to close the Add/Remove Programs Properties dialog box.

At this point, you might need to insert the Windows CD. On some computers, the files that Windows needs are already stored on the hard disk. In either case, Dial-Up Server will be installed and you'll be ready for the next stage of the setup process.

Chapter 23: Networking for Road Warriors

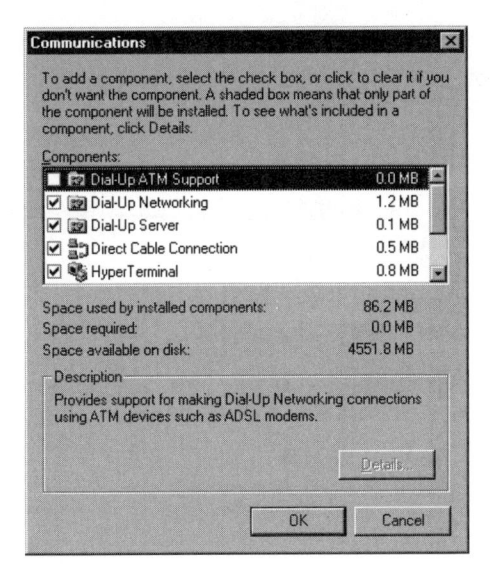

Figure 23-3

If the component's check box is selected, the component, such as Dial-Up Server, is installed.

Activating Dial-Up Server

Now that Dial-Up Server is installed, you have to activate it. This sets up your computer to answer the telephone when it rings and establish the connection to the remote computer. Follow these steps to activate Dial-Up Server:

1. Double-click My Computer on the Windows desktop.
2. In the My Computer window, double-click the Dial-Up Networking icon.
3. From the Connections menu, choose Dial-Up Server to open the Dial-Up Server dialog box.

    If you have more than one modem, you'll see a tab for each modem in or connected to your computer. Click the tab for the modem you want to use to answer incoming calls.

4. Select Allow Caller Access.
5. To password-protect your system so that only authorized persons can connect to the network, click Change Password to open the Dial-Up Networking Password dialog box.

6. If you haven't yet set a password, leave the Old Password text box blank. Type your password in both the New Password and Confirm New Password text boxes, and click OK.

7. Click Apply.

You'll now see an icon next to the clock in your Windows system tray, indicating that Dial-Up Server is running.

Using Remote Access Service

Windows NT Server and Windows 2000 Server include a dial-in feature called Remote Access Service (RAS). Setting up RAS lets authorized network users access the network from the road. To provide security, RAS includes an optional callback feature with two choices:

- Specific callback number
- Requested callback number

Tip

Windows 2000 Server also allows you to authenticate users by their Caller-ID.

You can associate each user with a specific phone number. After the user dials in to the network and is authenticated, the server disconnects the line and calls the user back at the specified number. This not only ensures that the dialer is at the authorized location, but it reduces long-distance charges for the user by placing the call by the server.

The other choice is to have the server request the callback number from the user. After the user dials in to the network and is authenticated, the server asks for the number it should use for the callback. The phone number is retained on the RAS log so that it can be later checked by the administrator. This allows the user to call in from various locations.

Setting up RAS requires quite a few steps that vary based on the way your server is set up. In this chapter, I'll look at setting up and using RAS as a manual service with Windows NT Server and as an automatic service with Windows 2000 Server. A manual service is turned off by default and must be manually started when you want to provide access to your network over the modem. An automatic service is turned on each time you start your server.

Configuring RAS in Microsoft Windows NT Server

The first step in setting up RAS for Windows NT Server is to allow your modem to answer incoming phone calls. Here's how to do that:

1. On the Start menu, point to Settings, and then click Control Panel.
2. In the Control Panel window, double-click Network.
3. Click the Services tab, and select Remote Access Service.
4. Click Properties to open the Remote Access Setup dialog box that lists the modems installed in your computer.
5. Click the modem you want to use for incoming calls, and click Configure.
6. Select Dial Out And Receive Calls if you want to use the modem for both making calls and receiving them. Choose Receive Calls Only if you only want the modem to receive incoming calls.
7. Click OK to return to the Remote Access Setup dialog box.
8. Click Continue to display the dialog box shown in Figure 23-4.

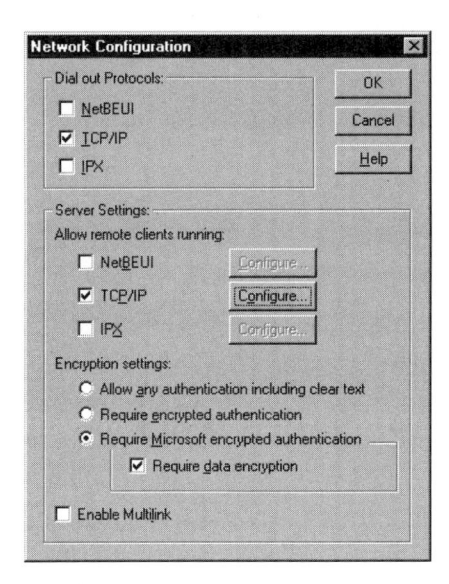

Figure 23-4
Select protocols for dial-out connections in the Network Configuration dialog box.

Part 4: Running Your Office on a Network

9. In the Server Settings section of the dialog box, select the protocols you want to use for dial-in connections.

   You'll now need to configure all of the protocols. For each protocol, you can choose to allow access to just the computer you're using or to the entire network. For each protocol, click the Configure button to display another dialog box, choose options from the box, and then click OK. The NetBEUI and IPX protocols require very little setup. TCP\IP is more complex, so I'll look at that option in detail.

10. Click the Configure button that's next to the TCP/IP protocol to see the options in Figure 23-5.

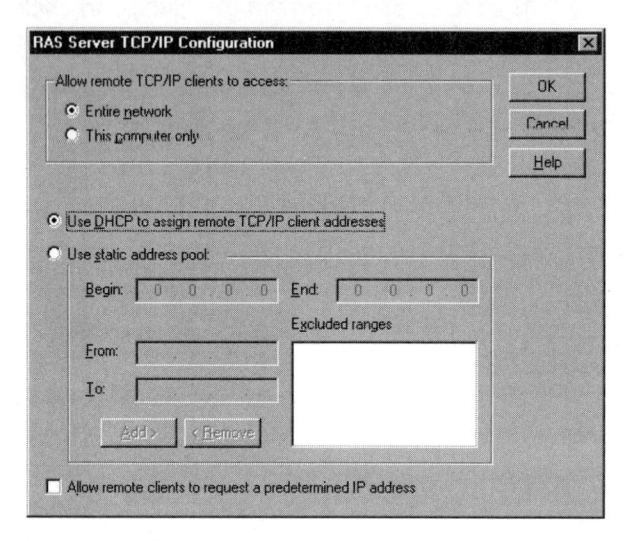

Figure 23-5
Configure TCP/IP to permit remote access to the network or to just the server.

12. Choose either Entire Network or This Computer Only.

13. If your server is using DHCP to assign IP addresses to workstations, choose Use DHCP To Assign Remote TCP/IP Client Addresses.

14. If you aren't using DHCP on your server, you need to specify a range of IP addresses that RAS can assign to clients when users dial in. Select Use Static Address Pool, and enter the beginning and ending IP addresses in the appropriate boxes. You can exclude certain addresses that you wouldn't want RAS to assign to dial-in clients. You'll need to get these IP addresses from your system administrator.

15. If you want the dial-in client to request a specific address whether you're using DHCP or not, select the check box labeled Allow Remote Clients To Request A Predetermined IP Address.

16. Click OK, and then restart your computer.

Activating RAS

The next step is to turn on RAS so that your server will be able to actually receive incoming calls. Follow these steps.

1. On the Start menu, point to Settings, and then click Control Panel.
2. In the Control Panel window, double-click Services.
3. Scroll the Service list, and choose Remote Access Server.
4. Click Start. Windows will begin the service.
5. Click Close.

Setting Dial-In Permissions

Finally, you have to give permission to the users whom you want to be able to dial in to the server. Follow these steps.

1. Click Start, point to Administrative Tools (Common), and click Remote Access Admin.
2. Select Permissions from the Users menu to display a list of domain users as shown in Figure 23-6. For each user you want to access the system, continue with the rest of the steps.

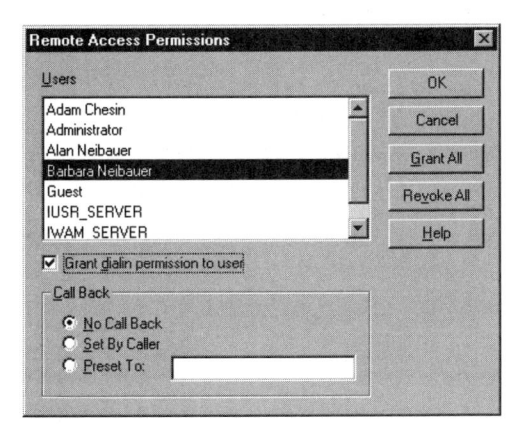

Figure 23-6

Grant permissions to specific users for RAS connections.

3. Select the user's name.
4. Select Grant Dialin Permission To User.
5. Choose a callback option.
6. Click OK.

Configuring RAS in Microsoft Windows 2000 Server

When you use Windows 2000 Server, you have to set up remote access as an automatic service using the Routing And Remote Access feature. Follow these steps.

1. Click Start, point to Programs, Administrative Tools, and then click Routing And Remote Access.
2. From the Action menu, select Configure And Enable Routing And Remote Access to start the Routing And Remote Access Wizard.
3. Click Next to see a list of services that you can install.
4. Select Remote Access Server and then click Next.
   You'll see a list of protocols.
5. Click Next.
   You'll now be asked if you want to provide remote access for IP addresses automatically or select from a range of addresses.
6. If you're using DHCP, select the Automatically option and then click Next. If you're assigning static IP addresses to computers on your network, select From A Specified Range Of Addresses and click Next.
7. In the box that appears, click New, enter the range of IP addresses you want to assign to workstations, and then click OK.
   You'll then be asked if you want to use Remote Authentication Dial-In User Server (RADIUS), a special database of users who are authenticated to access your network remotely. Using RADIUS is for advanced network administrators.
8. Select No, click Next, and then click Finished.

Tip

If you want to change any of the remote access settings later, open the Routing And Remote Access window, click Action, and choose Properties.

Remote access is now an automatic service. If you want to turn it off, open the Routing And Remote Access window, click Action, choose Disable Routing And Remote Access, and then click Yes. To activate the feature again, you'll need to repeat the configuration process.

Setting Dial-In Permissions

You now have to give permission to users to access your network remotely. Here's how.

1. If the server is part of a Windows 2000 domain, click Start on the taskbar, point to Programs, Administrative Tools, and then click Active Directory Users And Computers. If the remote access server is a stand-alone server, click Start on the taskbar, point to Programs, Administrative Tools, and then click Computer Management.

2. On the left side of the window, click the name of the server, so all of the users are listed on the right.

3. Right-click the name of the user you want to dial in, and click Properties.

4. Click the Dial-In tab, and select Allow Access.

5. If you want to authenticate users by their Caller-ID and you have Caller-ID service set up on your phone system, select Verify Caller-ID and then type the phone number from which the user calls the network.

6. To use a callback feature, select either of these options:
   - Set By Caller (Routing And Remote Access Service Only) to have the caller specify the callback number.
   - Always Callback To. You'll need to enter the specific number for the user.

7. Click OK.

Accessing an Office Computer Remotely

You're now ready to dial in to your computer from the road. In Windows NT, open the Dial-Up Networking window and double-click the remote dial-up connection. Click Connect to make the connection In Windows 2000, open the Network And Dial-Up Connections window and click the remote connection. Click Dial.

Part 4: Running Your Office on a Network

Windows will dial in and make the connection to your computer. Enter your password if you're asked for it.

To access the files on a computer on your network, you must enter its name, as follows:

1. On the Start menu, click Run.
2. In the Run dialog box, type two backslashes followed by the name of the computer you are dialing in to, and then click OK.

   If the computer is named adam, for example, you'd enter *adam*.

After you enter the computer name, you can access the computer just as if you were at the office and connected to the network. You'll see a window showing all the shared resources on the computer.

To access a file, double-click the shared drive and navigate to the file just as if you were using the My Computer window on your office computer. Copy and move files by dragging them between windows. For example, to get a copy of a file from the office onto your laptop, locate the file on your office computer and drag it to your laptop's desktop.

Printing a document on a shared printer that's connected to the network is just as easy. Locate the document using My Computer or Windows Explorer on your laptop, and drag it to the icon for the shared printer. The document will be waiting for you when you return to the office.

Virtual Private Network

Even if you don't want to allow your network to receive calls, you still might be able to connect to your network from the road by using a virtual private network (VPN) over the Internet. With VPN, you dial in to your ISP from any location and then create a private secure link to your network using the Point-to-Point Tunneling Protocol (PPTP).

Both your ISP and network must support the PPTP protocol, and your network must be set up and online as a VPN server. To use VPN, you create two dialup networking connections—one to your ISP using its telephone number and a second to your network using its IP address or VPN server name. After connecting to your ISP, you run the VPN connection to link into your network. The PPTP protocol creates a secure "tunnel" through the Internet that connects you to your network.

For more information about creating and using VPN, consult your ISP and network administrator.

Chapter 23: Networking for Road Warriors

Keeping in Touch Using Microsoft NetMeeting

NetMeeting allows you to communicate in a variety of ways when you're traveling and away. It's also a good way to keep in touch with other staff members who are at remote locations.

Let's say you're on a business trip. Instead of simply sending and receiving e-mail, you can use NetMeeting to talk to each other just as you would over the telephone. You can also send and receive files, work on programs together, and share drawings, as shown in Figure 23-7. If your computers are equipped with video cameras, you can even see each other at the same time you talk.

If you have version 4 or later of Internet Explorer, NetMeeting will be already installed on your system. If NetMeeting isn't installed, you can download a free copy of it from the Microsoft Web site at this address: *www.microsoft.com/windows/netmeeting/*

The information in this chapter is based on NetMeeting 3.0, the version of the program that's installed with Internet Explorer 5 or later. If you

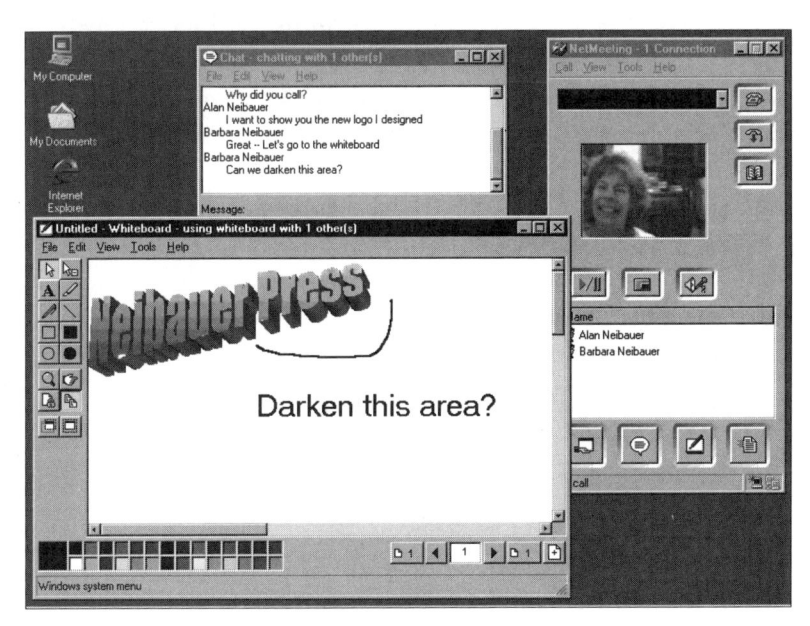

Figure 23-7
Use NetMeeting to see the person to whom you're talking and to collaborate on projects.

have an earlier version of NetMeeting, you should download the newest version from the Microsoft Web site to obtain all the latest features.

To start NetMeeting, point to Programs on the Start menu, and click Microsoft NetMeeting. The program might also be listed in the submenu that appears when you point to Internet Explorer on the Programs menu or when you point to Accessories and then point to Internet Tools.

The first time you run NetMeeting, you'll see a series of dialog boxes that help you set up the program on your system. Depending on your system's configuration and on the version of NetMeeting that you're using, the order and content of these dialog boxes might be somewhat different from the following description, which is based on NetMeeting 3.0:

1. Click Next in the first dialog box, which explains the features available in NetMeeting.

2. Type your name, e-mail address, city, state, and country and a brief comment about yourself that will identify you on-screen to other NetMeeting users, and click Next.

3. Choose whether you want to log on to a server whenever NetMeeting starts, and select the default server.

    The server is a Microsoft computer or an Internet service provider's computer that handles communications among NetMeeting users over the Internet. The server acts like a gigantic telephone switchboard, maintaining a directory of everyone who is logged on and ready to accept calls. The people that you plan to contact over the Internet with NetMeeting should choose the same server.

Note

When you're in the office, you can also use NetMeeting directly over your network. Since you don't need to log on to a server if you'll be using NetMeeting over your network, don't choose to log on to a server when NetMeeting starts.

4. Click Next to continue.

5. If you have a video capture board installed in your computer, you'll see a dialog box that asks you to confirm its use. Click Next.

Chapter 23: Networking for Road Warriors

6. If a dialog box appears asking for the speed of your connection, select the speed of your modem, and click Next.

7. To make NetMeeting easier to start, select both check boxes in the next dialog box to place shortcuts for NetMeeting on your Windows desktop and on the Quick Launch toolbar, and click Next.

    NetMeeting informs you that the Audio Tuning Wizard is about to help you tune your audio settings. It also instructs you to close all other programs that play or record sound.

8. Click Next.

    You might now see a dialog box that asks you to select the devices that will record and play back sound on your system. Generally, your sound card performs both functions.

9. Select the sound card you have, and click Next.

10. Test the volume of your speakers by clicking the Test button in the Audio Tuning Wizard dialog box and adjusting the slider to set a comfortable listening level. Click Stop to stop the sound, and then click Next.

11. To set the sensitivity of your microphone, speak into the microphone and watch the color bar that indicates the volume of your voice. Adjust the Record Volume slider so that the bar reaches about the halfway mark, and click Next.

12. Click Finish when the Audio Tuning Wizard reports that you have successfully tuned your settings.

Tip

After you start NetMeeting, you can change all of the setup options and fine-tune calling, audio, and video settings by choosing Options on the NetMeeting Tools menu.

When you click Finish, you'll see the NetMeeting window, shown in Figure 23-8.

Part 4: Running Your Office on a Network

Figure 23-8
The NetMeeting program allows you to call other network users.

Starting a Meeting

If NetMeeting is set to log on to a directory server automatically, it will dial in to your ISP each time it's started. If it doesn't dial, choose Log On To from the Call menu, which is followed by the name of the server, such as ils.Microsoft.com.

To place a call, choose Directory from the Call menu to open a dialog box listing the people logged on to the server. If many people are logged on, the list might take a few moments to appear while their names are downloaded. Scroll the list to locate the person you want to speak with and double-click that person's name.

NetMeeting on a Network

Although NetMeeting is initially set to work across the Internet, you can call someone on your office network by adjusting the program so that it places the call through the network instead of through the Internet.

> **Note**
>
> If your computer tries to dial in to the Internet when you're placing a network call, just close the Dial-Up Networking box in Windows 9x and Windows NT or close the Dial-Up Connection box in Windows 2000 to stop the call.

Chapter 23: Networking for Road Warriors

1. Find out the IP address or name of the network computer you want to dial.

    You must be using the TCP/IP protocol on the network to make NetMeeting calls across the network.

2. Click the Place Call button or choose New Call from the Call menu to see the Place A Call dialog box.

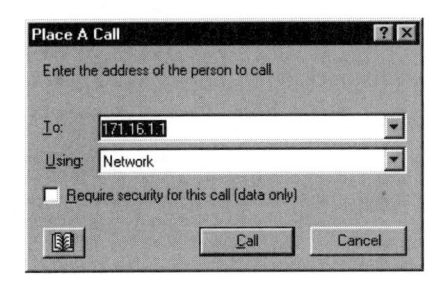

    [Place A Call dialog box showing To: 171.16.1.1, Using: Network, with Call and Cancel buttons]

3. From the Using drop-down list, choose Network.
4. In the To box, enter the IP address or the name of the computer you're trying to reach, and then click Call.

    The person at the computer you're calling will hear a sound like a telephone ring, and a message box will appear to ask whether the user wants to accept or ignore your call.

If the person chooses to ignore the call, a message appears on your screen reporting that the other user didn't accept your call.

Note

NetMeeting might also display a message reporting that the person you've called is currently in another meeting and can't accept your call, or it might inform you that the person is in a meeting and ask if you would like to join.

When your call is accepted, the names of the people in the meeting are displayed in the NetMeeting window, and you can start communicating. If each computer has a microphone and speakers, you can each speak into the microphone to talk to one another. If your computer is equipped with a camera, the person you're talking to will also able to see you, as shown in Figure 23-9.

Part 4: Running Your Office on a Network

Figure 23-9
In NetMeeting, you can see the people to whom you're talking.

To end the meeting, click the End Call button or choose Hang Up from the Call menu.

Using the Microsoft Internet Directory

Rather than log on to a directory server, you can connect to the Microsoft Internet Directory and search for the person you want to contact.

1. In NetMeeting, choose Options from the Tools menu to see the Options dialog box.
2. On the General tab of the dialog box, click the Directory drop-down arrow, choose Microsoft Internet Directory from the list, and click OK.
3. Select Log On To Microsoft Internet Directory from the Call menu.
   The search form appears.
4. Enter the name or e-mail address of the person you want to contact and click Search.

You'll see a list of persons who meet your search criteria. To place a NetMeeting call, click the person you want to contact.

Note

You can talk (speak) and chat (write) at the same time.

Chatting in NetMeeting

Even with the proper equipment, the audio quality of a NetMeeting call can be poor. Instead of actually speaking over the network, you might want to open a chat window and type messages to the other participants in the meeting. Follow these steps to open a chat window:

1. Click the Chat button or choose Chat from the Tools menu to open the chat window.

    The Chat window also opens on the other participants' screens.

2. Read the chat messages as they appear in the large text box, as shown in Figure 23-10.

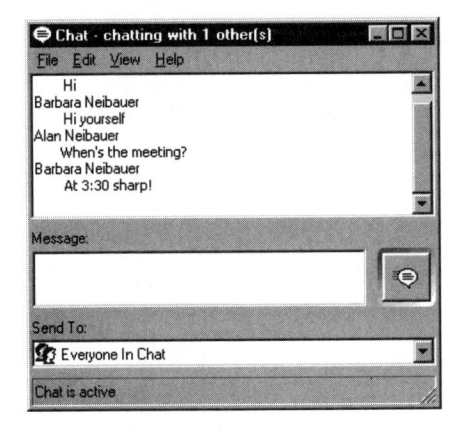

Figure 23-10
With NetMeeting, you can create your own chat room on the network.

3. Type your messages in the Message text box, and press Enter to send them.

If you want to send a private message to a particular chat participant, select the participant's name from the Send To drop-down list before clicking the Send Message button.

To resume sending public messages to everyone in the chat, choose Everyone In Chat from the Send To drop-down list.

To exit a chat, simply close the Chat window, or choose Exit from the File menu.

Using the Whiteboard

Sometimes you might need to communicate about something online that you can't easily express in words. Suppose, for example, that you want the participants in the meeting to review a drawing. You'd like to give each participant the opportunity to comment on the drawing or even make changes to it as the meeting progresses. The solution in such situations is a handy NetMeeting feature called the Whiteboard.

The Whiteboard is a drawing window that you can share with everyone at the meeting. Whatever you draw on the Whiteboard appears on the Whiteboards of all the other participants in the meeting. They, in turn, can use their Whiteboards to add to your drawing, as long as you permit it. A NetMeeting Whiteboard is shown in Figure 23-11.

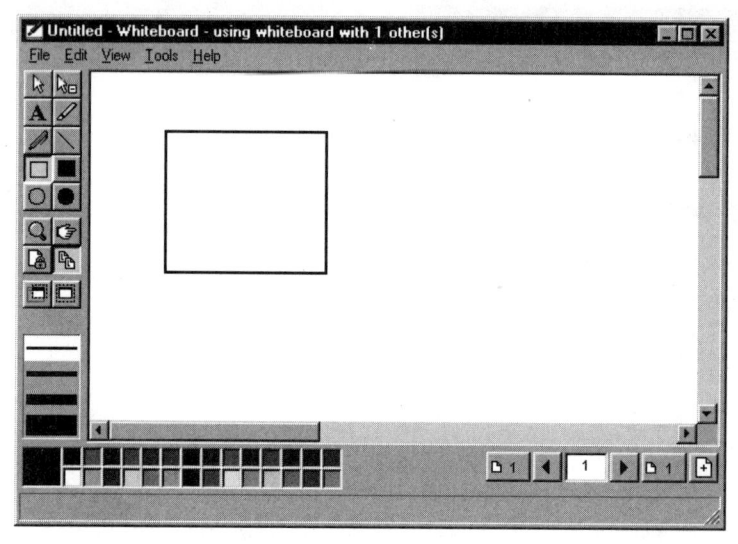

Figure 23-11
The Whiteboard feature in NetMeeting allows meeting participants to view and make changes to drawings.

To use the Whiteboard, follow these steps:

1. Click the Whiteboard button, or choose Whiteboard from the Tools menu.
2. Draw on the Whiteboard using tools from the Whiteboard tool palette, shown in Figure 23-12.

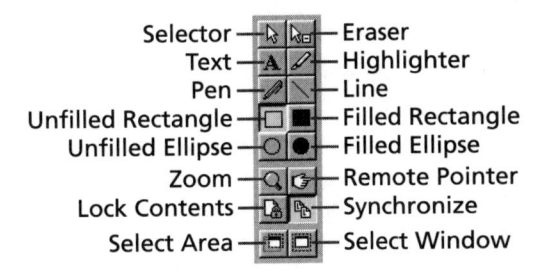

Chapter 23: Networking for Road Warriors

```
Selector ─────┐  ┌───── Eraser
Text ─────────┤  ├───── Highlighter
Pen ──────────┤  ├───── Line
Unfilled Rectangle ──┤  ├── Filled Rectangle
Unfilled Ellipse ────┤  ├── Filled Ellipse
Zoom ─────────┤  ├───── Remote Pointer
Lock Contents ┤  ├───── Synchronize
Select Area ──┘  └───── Select Window
```

Figure 23-12
The items in the Whiteboard tool palette allow you to work on shared graphics and text.

The tool palette contains everything you need to create and edit drawings and text on the Whiteboard. The same features are also available on the Tools menu.

Here's how to use the Whiteboard tools:

- **Selector.** Click this button, and then click an object you want to select. Choose Delete, Copy, or Cut from the Edit menu, or drag the selected object to move it on the screen.

- **Eraser.** Click this button, and then click an object you want to erase. You can also drag a rectangle around an area, and all objects even partially within the rectangle will be deleted.

- **Text.** Click this button to use your keyboard to type on the Whiteboard. Choose a color from the color palette, or click the Font Options button that appears when you select the tool to change the font, font size, and font style. The Colors and Font commands on the Options menu also allow you to change the color, size, and style of your type.

- **Highlighter.** Choose a line width and a color, and then click this button and drag it over the area you want to highlight.

- **Pen.** Click this button, and then drag it in the Whiteboard area to draw freehand on the screen.

- **Line.** Click this button to draw straight lines by dragging the mouse pointer from one point to the next. Select a line width and choose a color from the color palette shown in the Whiteboard window. You can also use the Colors and Line Width commands on the Options menu.

> **Note**
>
> You can use the Bring To Front or Send To Back commands on the Edit menu to change how objects overlap.

- **Rectangle.** Choose a line width and color from the palette, and then click the Unfilled Rectangle button and draw the outline of a rectangle by dragging, or click the Filled Rectangle button and draw a solid rectangle of the selected color.
- **Ellipse.** Click one of the two ellipse buttons, and then drag it on the Whiteboard to draw filled or unfilled circles or ellipses in the line width and color of your choice.
- **Zoom.** Click this button or use the Zoom command on the View menu to switch between normal and enlarged views.
- **Remote Pointer.** Click this button to display a pointer, and then move it to the area of the Whiteboard you want others to look at.
- **Lock Contents.** Click this button to prevent others from changing the Whiteboard contents. Click it again to allow others to change the Whiteboard.
- **Synchronize.** This button lets you determine whether other Whiteboard users can see the same pages you are viewing. To synchronize the pages, click the button so that it appears pressed down. To unsynchronize the pages, click the button so that it appears released.
- **Select Area.** Click this button to drag a rectangle over an area of the screen outside of the Whiteboard that you want to copy to the Whiteboard.
- **Select Window.** This button works in much the same way as the Windows Clipboard. Click any window on your screen, even a partially obscured one, to copy the contents of the window to the Whiteboard. The Whiteboard will show the contents of the window inserted as a graphic.

Adding and Changing Whiteboard Pages

If a meeting you were conducting was held in person, you might use a flip chart to draw images and highlight important points. When you fill up one page, you just flip it over and start a fresh sheet. You can use the Whiteboard in the same way, adding pages and changing them as needed.

Use the buttons at the lower-right corner of the Whiteboard window to insert a page and to switch from page to page.

Choose Clear Page from the Edit menu to erase the current page, or choose Delete Page from the Edit menu to delete the page. Erasing a page removes the page's contents on the screens of all NetMeeting participants but leaves the page in place. Deleting a page actually removes it from your Whiteboard and from those of other participants as well.

Saving and Printing the Whiteboard

When your meeting is over, you don't have to lose the contents of the Whiteboard. While the Whiteboard is still displayed, each participant in the meeting can print a copy of the whiteboard by choosing Print from the File menu. Each participant can also save the Whiteboard by choosing Save from the File menu. Whiteboards are saved in a special format, with an .nmw extension (.wht in earlier versions of NetMeeting). To reopen saved Whiteboard files, choose Open from the File menu.

> **Note**
>
> Closing your own Whiteboard doesn't close the Whiteboards of other participants, who can continue to draw on theirs. If you open the Whiteboard again, NetMeeting will locate and display the same Whiteboard the other participants see. If you try to close a Whiteboard before saving it, NetMeeting asks if you want to save it.

Working Together on Programs

In addition to sharing a drawing on the Whiteboard, you might want meeting participants to share a program as well. When you share a program with others, the meeting participants can see the program, but they can't control it unless you specifically allow them to do so. The person running the program is called the *owner,* and only the owner has control over who can work with the program. Here's how to use NetMeeting to share a program:

1. Start the program you want to share, and then switch back to NetMeeting.
2. Click the Share Program button, or choose Sharing from the Tools menu to see the dialog box in Figure 23-13.

Part 4: Running Your Office on a Network

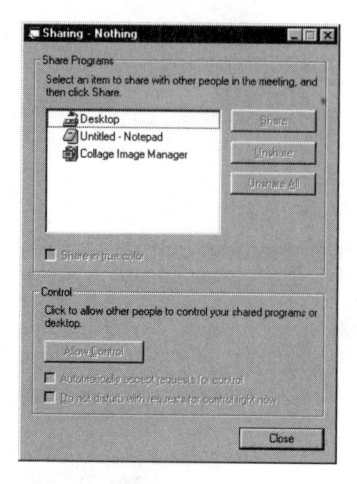

Figure 23-13
The Sharing dialog box allows you to share programs with other meeting participants.

3. In the list of programs that are running, select the program you want to share, and then click Share.

    Other meeting participants will now be able to see exactly what you are doing with the shared program.

If you want to allow meeting participants to use the shared program, rather than just view it, click the Allow Control button in the Sharing dialog box. You'll be offered these two options:

- **Automatically Accept Requests For Control** lets a meeting participant use the program without your express permission.

- **Do Not Disturb With Requests For Control Right Now** prevents requests for sharing from appearing on your screen.

To gain control of a program, a meeting participant must double-click the program window on the screen. This either takes control of the program or, if you haven't turned on automatic acceptance in the Sharing dialog box, displays a dialog box asking whether you want to Reject or Accept the request.

By clicking Accept, you transfer control of the program to the participant, and you'll no longer be able to use your pointer on screen.

To regain control over the program and your cursor and to stop any participant who is currently working with the shared program, press Esc or click the mouse button.

To stop sharing the program, click Unshare or Unshare All in the Sharing dialog box.

Sending and Receiving Files

While you're in a meeting, you can exchange files with other participants. Click the Transfer Files button or choose File Transfer from the Tools menu to view the File Transfer dialog box shown in Figure 23-14.

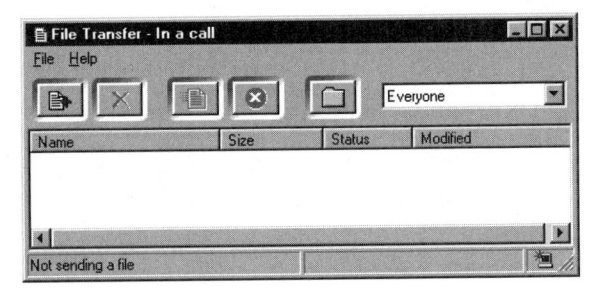

Figure 23-14
The File Transfer dialog box shows the files that you're sending to other meeting participants.

Click Add Files and, in the Choose Files To Send dialog box, choose the files you want to transfer. Then click Send All to send the files to everyone or, from the drop-down list of meeting participants in the File Transfer dialog box, choose the participant to whom you want the files sent, and then click Send All.

When you receive a file from someone else, you'll see a dialog box giving you the option to close the dialog box, open the file, or delete the file.

Files that you receive are stored in the C:\Program Files\NetMeeting\Received Files folder. Click the View Received Files button—the one that shows an icon of a folder—to open that folder.

Controlling an Office Computer Remotely

NetMeeting includes a powerful feature that lets you actually control one of the other computers on the network. For example, suppose a staff member is having trouble changing a setting in Control Panel or needs help performing some Windows task. You can take control of another person's computer from your own system and perform tasks as though you were sitting in front of the other computer.

To set up a computer to accept remote control, you have to use the Remote Desktop Sharing Wizard on that computer. Follow these steps:

1. Start NetMeeting on the computer you want to be able to control, and choose Remote Desktop Sharing from the Tools menu.
2. Click Next after reading the first Remote Desktop Sharing Wizard page.
3. Type a password of at least seven characters that will allow access from the controlling computer.
4. Retype the password to confirm it, and then click Next.
5. You can now choose to password-protect a screen saver as an extra security feature. Make your choice and click Next.
6. Click Finish.
7. Close NetMeeting.
   The Remote Desktop Sharing icon will appear in the computer's system tray, to the left of the clock on the Windows taskbar.
8. Right-click the Remote Desktop Sharing icon, and select Activate Remote Desktop Sharing from the shortcut menu.
9. Start NetMeeting on the computer that will be in control, and call the computer you want to share.
10. In the Place A Call dialog box that appears, select the Require Security For This Call (Data Only) check box, and then click Call.
    You'll be asked to type the password.
11. Type the password, and click OK.

You'll see a window that contains the other computer's desktop. You can now control the remote computer just as if you were sitting at its keyboard.

To stop sharing, right-click the Remote Desktop Sharing icon on the desktop of the computer you are sharing, and select Exit.

Dialing in from the road, remotely controlling a computer, and seeing the folks you are talking to over the Internet—it all seems like something out of the future, but these options are available to you today.

Index

Page numbers appearing in italics refer to figures and tables

Numbers

10Base2coaxial cable. *See* ThinNet coaxial cable
10Base-T cable. *See* twisted-pair cable
4800 Turbo DS, wireless system, 55

A

access controls, 34
   overview, 262–63
   share-level access, 263–66
   user-level access, 267–68
accessibility features, in Microsoft Windows 2000, 107–9
Accessibility Wizard, 107, *108*
access points, 51– 52
account databases, 77–78
acoustic couplers, 423
ACPI, 107
Active Directory, 115, 170
active hubs, 145
Add Printer option, 241
Add Printer Wizard, *238*, 304–6
Add Quick Access To Documents Disk option, 241
address books
   Microsoft Outlook, 338–39, 340-42
   offline, 347–48
addresses
   Ethernet, 207
   HTTP, creating, 399
   IP, 161
      assigning, 231–32
      assigning using Windows–based server appliances, 234–35
      configuring TCP/IP in Microsoft Windows, 205–8
      Ethernet addresses and, 207
      setting up client computers to get, 378
      specifying using Microsoft Proxy Server, 384
      TCP/IP and, 204–5
      TCP/IP pocket print servers and, 313–14
      using server-assigned, 208–9

addresses, *continued*
   IRQ
      adding non-plug-and-play NIC drivers and, 191–92
      changing, 133–35
      full, 191
   static, 204, 234
addressing, e-mail messages, 331–32
Administrators group, 226
Administrator user account, 246
Advanced icon, 398
AGP (Accelerated Graphics Port) slots, *124, 125*
AGP video hardware, 106
applications, controlling 454. *See also* software; *specific applications*
   creating/running Web-based, 84
   opening remote files from within, 276–77
   running/loading from server, 28–29
   running remotely, 290
   saving remote files from within, 277–78
   sharing, legal issues, 289–90
   specifying for network printers, 310
   working together on, 453–55
appointments, 360
   recurring, 364
   setting up, 362–64
ASP (Active Server Pages) Web pages, 395
Audio Tuning Wizard, 445

B

backing up. *See also* storage
   files, 6, 292–93
      with Microsoft Backup, 296–99
      with RAID system, 294–95
      with removable disks, 293
      with tape storage, 294
Backup Operators group, 226
Backup Wizard, 297–98
barrel connectors, *154*
BDC (Backup Domain Controller), 168–69
bindings, 199
blocks. *See* connect blocks
BNC connectors, 152–54

Index

booted-end cable, 150
bridges, 146–47
Browser Connection Setup Wizard, 380–81
browsers. *See also specific browsers*
   accessing home page with, 401
   accessing network Web sites, 394–95
   misdialing when accessing intranets, 407
   setting, 243
bulk cable, buying, 150–51
bus, fitting NIC to, 124–26
bus topology, 42

C

cabinets, 177
cable modem, advantages and disadvantages of, 373
cables. *See also specific types*
   bending, 155–56
   buying bulk, 150–51
   coaxial, *120*, 154
   connecting hubs with, 142–44
   connecting printers directly to networks with, 312
   connecting thin servers and, 160–61
   crossover, 139–41, *140*
   distinguishing crossover from patch, 141
   Ethernet networks and, 38–45
   fiberoptic, 43–45, 154–55
   grades of, 39
   keeping tidy, 156
   network, comparing with other network connections, *35*
   organizing, 177–79
   patch, 138, 141
   premises wiring, 139
   STP (shielded twisted-pair), 39
   ThickNet, 42
   ThinNet, 41–43, *42*, 144
   twisted-pair, 38–41, *120*
   UTP (unshielded twisted-pair), 39, 40
caching, 87
calendars
   coordinating network, 359–60
   describing availability on, 363–64
   setting up appointments on, 362–64
   setting up meetings on, 364–70
   updating free/busy time on, 361–62
callback service, 70
category (cat) cable. *See* twisted-pair cable, grades of

CD drives
   as NAS server, 65, *66*
   NAS servers with multiple, 66
CDs
   installing printers with, 304, 306
   sharing, 6–7
cells, 51–52
central processing system, 179
Centronics ports, 313
chatting, in Microsoft NetMeeting, 449
Client for Microsoft Windows, 194, 195
client licenses, for Microsoft Windows NT Server, 82
clients
   configuring, 255–56
   configuring for Internet access, 380–81
   e-mail, 322–24
   setting up for Internet Connection Sharing, 378
   setting up Microsoft Exchange, 350–51
   setting up on Microsoft BackOffice Small Business Server, 245–56
   setting up on Microsoft Windows–based server appliances, 241–44
   thin, 179–81
client/server networks. *See also* combination networks; peer-to-peer networks
   access controls on, 262–63
   advantages of, over thin server networks, 75
   domain controllers and, 168–71
   ease of setting up, 76
   hardware for, 167–68, 171–79
   hubs and, *40*
   network control and, 27–30
   network operating systems for, 77
   vs. peer-to-peer networks, *24*
   personnel for, 23
   reasons for selecting, 33
   small business and, 63
   using thin servers to balance workload on, 174, *175*
client software
   Microsoft Exchange client, 99–100
   with Microsoft Exchange Server, 98–99
   Microsoft Outlook, 100–102
coaxial cable. *See also* ThinNet coaxial cable
   connector for, *120*
   making your own, 154
combination networks, 32–33
combo cards, 123
commercial-quality wireless systems, 51–53, 55

Index

communication. *See also* e-mail; messages
    on client/server networks, 27, *28*
    infrared, 107
    on peer-to-peer networks, *25*
    pop-up messages, 318–22
    using Microsoft Outlook, 353–59
computer rooms, 175–76
computers. *See also* hardware; laptop computers; remote computers
    accessing office, remotely, 441–42
    accommodating more than 50, 82
    checking for network readiness, 119–20
    configurations for connecting to wireless networks, 50
    configuring for Microsoft Windows NT, 82
    configuring to modem server, 69
    connecting, 34–36
    connecting to hubs, 143
    connecting with ThinNet coaxial cable, 152–54
    controlling office, remotely, 455–56
    copying remote files between, 280–82
    finding others on network, 209–11
    identification changes, *203*
    identifying on networks, 201–3
    installing network software on, 185–86
    installing NIC in, 122
    linking with telephone cables, *57*
    NOS accommodating varieties of, 80–81
    opening, 129-31
    proximity of, wireless networks and, *51*
    removing cover plate, *131*
    requirements for server, 173
    running cables to/from, 147–48
    selecting correct NIC for, 123–24
    setting up/configuring with Set Up Computer Wizard, 89–90
    sharing, 215
    storing e-mail on local, 352–53
Computer Setup Wizard, 241–42
computer shows, shopping at, 128
computer superstores, shopping at, 127–28
configurations
    for client/server networks, 167
    for client/server vs. peer-to-peer networks, 76
    for connecting computers to wireless networks, 50
    of Microsoft Windows–based server appliances, 161
    Microsoft Windows 2000 server options, *105*

connect blocks, 178–79
connections
    comparing, *35*
    determining, 34–36
    planning hardware, 18
connectors. *See also* couplers
    barrel, *154*
    BNC, 152–54
    for coaxial cable, *120*
    damaging, 156
    RJ-45, 149
    T, 152–54
    for twisted-pair cable, 38–39, *120*
Control Panel
    adding user profiles through, 219–20
    changing passwords with, 223
cookies, 216
copying, remote files, 280
    between computers, 280–82
    and pasting, 282
couplers, *149, 155. See also* connectors
crimpers, 150
crossover cable, 139, *140*
cross-pinned cable, 139–41, *140*

D

data access pages, 417–18
databases
    PDC, 168–69
    SAM, 168–69
    user, group, network resource information, 115
database systems, using Microsoft SQL Server as backend to, 86, *87*
data-centric networks, 164–66, *165*
Date Navigator, 360
deleting, remote files, 284
delivery receipts, 332
Depends On Password sharing, 262
desktop shortcuts, facilitating sharing with, 271–72
devices, hot swappable, 106–7. *See also specific devices*
DHCP (Dynamic Host Configuration Protocol) servers, 209
    Microsoft Windows–based server appliances as, 234
    thin servers as, 232
dial-up connections
    creating additional Internet, 425–29
    creating network, 430–32

459

Index

Dial-Up Server, 432
    activating, 435–36
    installing, 432–34
    installing software, 434, *435*
digital certificates, getting, 355–56
digital phone systems, 423
digital signatures, 104–5, 348–50, 354–55. *See also* security
direct-sequence spread spectrum radio technologies, 53
discussion groups, Internet servers and, 71
disk mirroring, 295
disks. *See also* resources, shared
    floppy, 4–5
    removable
        backing up files with, 293
        sharing, 7–8
    shared, accessing, 268–84
    sharing drives and, 265
disk stripping, 295
distributed processing system, 179
DLL (dynamic-link library) files, 105–6
DNS (Domain Name System), 209
documents. *See* files
domain controllers, 168
    in Microsoft Windows 2000, 170
    in Microsoft Windows NT, 168–69
    multiple domains, 169–70
domains
    administrating, 171
    multiple, 169-170
drivers
    appropriate for peripherals, 173
    digitally signed, 104–5
    installing network, 186–90
drives. *See also* hard disk drives; removable disks/disk drives; resources, shared
    mapping, 273–75
    remote, sending files to, 283
    sharing, 263–68, 286–88
    tape, 294
drop boxes, 399, 402–3
DSL modem, advantages and disadvantages of, 373
dual-boot configurations, 29
DVD players, 106

E

ECC (error correction coding), 295
e-commerce Web sites, technical knowledge for, 76
EFS (Encrypting File System), 110
EISA (Extended ISA) slots, 125
e-mail. *See also* address books; public folders
    active content in, 357–58
    attaching files to, 332
    on client/server network, 29
    creating and addressing messages, 331–32
    filing in folders, 334
    formatted in Microsoft Outlook, 342
    keeping private, 217
    Microsoft Outlook options, 335
    navigating through, in Outlook, 344
    network vs. Internet, 334
    from other systems, 96
    receiving, in Outlook, 343–44
    receiving in Microsoft Mail, 333–34
    securing attachments, 358
    sending
        in Microsoft Mail, 331–33
        in Outlook, 342–43
    setting security to use with all, 358–59
    special message options, 332
    storing, using Microsoft Outlook and Microsoft Exchange server, 351–53
    using Microsoft Outlook for, 86, 100–102
e-mail clients, 322–24
e-mail service, Internet servers and, 71
e-mail systems
    Microsoft Exchange Server and, 85, 93–95
    on peer-to-peer networks, 26, 93
Enable Security Wizard, *240*
encryption, 110–11, 348, 349–50, 354–55. *See also* security
Entire Network icon, 269
error messages
    for Microsoft Windows Messaging in Microsoft Windows 98, 329
    MTS, Transaction Server Core Components, or Microsoft Transaction Server problems, 397
Ethernet Addresses, 207
Ethernet cards, connecting to Ethernet networks with, *80*
Ethernet hubs. *See* hubs
Ethernet networks. *See also* non-Ethernet networks; WLANS (wireless networks)
    advantages and disadvantages, 47–49
    alternatives to, phone line networks, 56–58
    cables and, 38
    comparing with other network connections, 35
    connecting printers directly to, 312
    fiberoptic cable and, 43–45
    gigabit, 43

Index

Ethernet networks, *continued*
   migration to, 48
   need for hubs and, 141
   overview, 37
   selecting network speed, 123–24
   ThinNet coaxial cable and, 41–43
   twisted-pair cable and, 38–41
Ethernet network starter kits, 126
Ethernet sockets, 139
evaluation, need for, 24
expansion, cabling and, 157
expansion slots
   fitting NIC to, 124–26
   types of, *124*
external print servers, 315–16

F

faceplates, *151*
Family Logon. *See* Microsoft Family Logon
fault tolerance, 115
Favorite Links section, adding favorite Web pages to, 414–15
Favorites list, 216–17, 272–73
faxing, with Microsoft Fax Service, 87–88
fax modems, sharing, 387, 388–91
fax server, selecting as fax modem, 390–91
fiberoptic cable, 43–45, 154–55
File And Printer Sharing For Microsoft Networks service, 303
file encryption, 110–11
files. *See also* resources, shared
   attaching to e-mail messages, 332
   backing up, 6, 292–93
      with Microsoft Backup, 296–99
      with removable disks, 293
      with tape storage, 294
   controlling access to, 78, 109–10
   DLL (dynamic-link library), 105–6
   hierarchical organization of, 261
   locating easily, 5
   maintaining as current, 5
   Microsoft Word, converting to Web pages, 416
   password-protected, 28
   publishing on Web sites, 403–4, 406–7
   read-only, saving, 277–78
   receiving, with Microsoft NetMeeting, 455
   remote, 275–78, 280, 283–84
   saving to remote computers, 291–92
   searching for on Web sites, *84*
   securing e-mail attached, 358

files, *continued*
   sending, with Microsoft NetMeeting, 455
   sending to remote drives, 283
   setting default locations for, 291
   sharing, 4–5, 25–26, 61–62
   storing remotely, 293–94
   tracking revisions on, 15
   working simultaneously on, 278–80
   working with offline, 111–14
file servers, of Microsoft Windows–based server appliance, 161
Find command, accessing shared resources with, 270
firewalls, 59
   Microsoft Proxy Server and, 87
   technical knowledge for, 76
FireWire, 106–7
floor cable covers, 138
floppy disks. *See also* disks
   keeping files current and, 5
   sharing files/folders and, 4
folders. *See also* resources, shared
   configuring client computers from, 256
   deleting remote, 284
   filing e-mail messages in, 334
   hierarchical organization of, 261
   locating profile, 222–23
   mapping, 273–75
   My Documents, sharing, 266
   offline, 101, 111–14
   private storage, 72
   public, 97–98
   public storage, 72
   read-only rights to, 25
   read/write access to, 25–26
   shared, accessing, 268–84
   sharing, 4–5
      access control and, 288–89
      adding service, 200–201
      availability, 261
      on peer-to-peer networks, 25–26
      problems with, 61–62
      with share-level access, 266
      with user-level access, 267–68
   storing e-mail drafts in, 343
formal sharing, 20
formatting
   HTML Document, 419
   Microsoft Outlook e-mail messages, 342
   web page text, 411–12
frames, 37, 411

461

Index

frequency-hopping spread spectrum radio technologies, 53
FTP (File Transfer Protocol) servers, 405
Full Control permissions, 309
Full sharing, 262

G

gateways, 147
gigabit Ethernet networks, 43
global groups, 246–47
GPS satellites, 70, 71
group policies, 115
groups. *See also* users
    assigning permissions to, 229
    SBS user, 246–47
    user in Microsoft Windows 2000, 226
guest books, 399, 402–3
Guests group, 226
Guest user account, 246

H

hard disk drives. *See also* resources, shared
    network, 65
    sharing, 261
hardware. *See also specific hardware*
    checking for conflicts, 192–93
    for client/server networks, setting up, 175–79
    diagnosing conflicts, 212–13
    Microsoft Windows 2000 supporting new, 106–7
    non-Ethernet, 49
    planning for, 18–19
    proprietary, 48
    recovering from failures, 115
    selecting for client/server networks, 171–75
    shopping for, 127–28
HCL (Hardware Compatibility List), selecting client/server network hardware for, 171–75
home pages, 393, *394*. *See also* Web pages; Web sites
    accessing, 401–2
    address, 398
    changing information on, 401
    creating, 399–401
    personalizing, *400*
    using Microsoft Personal Web Server to create, 395
Home Page Wizard, 399–401, 408
hotels, remote computing from, packing for, 422–24
HTML (Hyptertext Markup Language) tags, 393
HTTP addresses, creating, 399
hubs, 139
    alternatives to, 145–47
    connecting, 142–44
    in Ethernet networks, 40–41
    need for, 141–42
    placing, 144
    star bus topology, *143*
    thin server networks and, 160
hyperlinks. *See* links

I

icons
    Entire Network, 269
    Internet Connection Sharing, 377–78
    on Microsoft Windows–based server appliance LCD panel, 161
    Network Neighborhood, 269
    printer, *307*
    shared drive, *265*
    viewing on Quick Launch toolbar, 319
    WinPopup, *319*, *321*
IEEE 802.3. *See* Ethernet networks
IEEE (Institute of Electrical and Electronics Engineers), 802.11 standard, 53
IMAP (Internet Messaging Access Protocol), 85
Inbox. *See* Windows Messaging Inbox
Inbox Setup Wizard, 329–30
information
    analyzing current system and, 20
    planning for flow of, 19–20
    planning improved processing of, 21
information store, 95, *96*
Information Systems, 19
infrared communication, 107
infrastructure, 19, 21–24
installing
    Dial-Up Server, 432–34
    Dial-Up Server software, 434, *435*
    Microsoft Fax, 388–89
    Microsoft Mail Postoffice, 324–26
    Microsoft Personal Web Server (PWS), 395–97
    Microsoft Windows 2000, ease of, 104–7
    Microsoft Windows–based server appliances, 233–36
    Microsoft WinPopup, 319–20
    network drivers, 186–90
    network software on computers, 185–86

installing, *continued*
   NICs (network interface cards), 121–22, 130–35
   non-plug-and-play NIC drivers on Microsoft Windows 95/98, 191
   non-plug-and-play NIC drivers on Microsoft Windows 2000, 192
   plug-and-play NIC drivers on Microsoft Windows 95/98, 188–89
   plug-and-play NIC drivers on Microsoft Windows 2000, 189–90
   printers, 303–6, 310–11
   protocols, 196–99
instant messages, 14
Intel, phone line networks kits by, 57
intelligent hubs, 145
IntelliMirror, 114–16
interference
   power line networks and, 59
   wireless network systems and, 51
Internet
   alternative connection-sharing software, *385*
   configuring clients for access to, 380–81
   connecting to, through Internet Connection Sharing, 381–82
   contracting to store files through, 294
   handling printer problems with, 306–7
   security, 356
   selecting connection to, 377–78
   sending e-mail through, 334
   setting browser to connect through Microsoft Windows–based server appliances, 243–44
   setting up connection to, 236–37
   sharing, 10–13
Internet Connection Sharing icon, 377–78
Internet Connection Sharing Wizard, 376–78
Internet Connection Wizard, 236–37
Internet Mail Service, 96
Internet servers, 71
Internet Service Manager, 408
Internet Service Providers. *See* ISPs (Internet Service Providers)
interoperability, 53
intranets, 83. *See also* Web sites
   creating Web sites on, 394–95
   home page on, *394*
   setting browsers to access, 401–2
invitations. *See* meetings
I/O address, 133–35
IP addresses, 161
   assigning, 231–34, *235*
   configuring TCP/IP in Microsoft Windows, 205–8

IP addresses, *continued*
   Ethernet Addresses and, 207
   setting up client computers to get, 378
   specifying using Microsoft Proxy Server, 384
   TCP/IP and, 204–5
   TCP/IP pocket print servers and, 313–14
   using server-assigned, 208–9
IPX/SPX (Internet Package Exchange), 196–97
IrDA, 107
IRQ addresses
   adding non-plug-and-play NIC drivers and, 191–92
   changing, 133–35
   full, 191
ISA devices, 54
ISA (Industry Standard Architecture) slots, 124, 126, 133–35
ISDN modem, advantages and disadvantages of, 373
ISPs (Internet Service Providers)
   accounts, 10–11, 371–74
   changing access number, 425
   creating additional dial-up networking connections, 425–29
   dialing into, from remote locations, 424–25
   hosting mail servers through, *94*
   mail servers, 322–23
   modem servers and, 69
   overview, 11–12
   usage limits, 13

J

jack adapters, 423
jacks
   for patch cable, 151
   phone, testing, 424
   RJ-11 modular phone, in hotel rooms, 423
jumper, *133*

K

keyboards, On-Screen, 108
Key Management Server, 96
KMS (Key Management Server), 349–50

L

LAN modems, 374
laptop computers. *See also* remote computers; remote computing
   connecting, 126
   preparing for dialing in to networks, 429–32

Index

LDAP (Lightweight Directory Access Protocol), 98
Line tool, 451
links, 393, 401, 413–16, *413*
load balancing, 115
local groups, 246–47
Lock Contents tool, 452
logging on
  adding user profiles when, 218
  as different users, 221–23
logon script, 254

M

Magnifier, 108
mailboxes
  accessing through Web site browser windows, 96
  accessing with Microsoft Exchange client, *99*
  creating, 346–47
  Microsoft Exchange Server and, 94–95
  Microsoft Exchange Server directory and, 95–96
mail order retailers, shopping with, 122, 128
mail servers, *94,* 322–24
mainframes, 179
Main icon, 398
managed hubs, 145
Manage Documents permissions, 309
Manage Printers permissions, 309
mandatory profiles, 228
mapping, network drives/folders, 273–75
master replication, 170
MAU (multistation access unit), 146
meeting resources, 366, 368
meetings, 359–60
  checking attendees, 369–70
  with Microsoft NetMeeting, 446–48
  responding to request for, 368
  setting up, 364–70
  starting with Microsoft NetMeeting, 446
messages. *See also* chatting, in Microsoft NetMeeting; e-mail; Microsoft Windows Messaging
  assigning level of importance to, 332
  creating and addressing e-mail, 331–32
  in guest books/drop boxes, 402–3
  sending through Microsoft NetMeeting, 449
Microsoft Access, creating Web pages with, 417–19
Microsoft Active Server Pages format, 419

Microsoft BackOffice Small Business Server (SBS), 75
  company-wide access to Internet and, 11
  configuring clients in, 255–56
  creating a Web site with, 406–8
  creating user accounts in, 247–52
  as DHCP server, 209
  Fax Service, 391–92
  overview, 81–82
  SBS Console with, 88–90
  setting up clients on, 245–56
  sharing modems using, 382
  types of user accounts in, 246–47
  varieties of, 90–91
Microsoft Backup, 296–99
Microsoft/3Com HomeConnect network kit, 127
Microsoft Exchange, 323. *See also* Microsoft Windows Messaging
  getting security enabled on, 355–56
  Microsoft Fax and, 387–89
Microsoft Exchange Chat Service, 96
Microsoft Exchange clients, 99–100, 350–51
Microsoft Exchange Server, 345
  client software with, 98–99
  creating mailboxes with, 346–47
  creating offline address books with, 347–48
  directory, 95–96, 98
  Microsoft BackOffice Small Business Server with, 85
  overview, 93–95
  using Microsoft Outlook with, 351–52
Microsoft Exchange Service, creating/managing public folders in, 97–98
Microsoft Family Logon, 194
  on Microsoft Windows 95/98, 195
  setting as default logon option, 222
Microsoft Fax Service, 87–88, 388–89
Microsoft FrontPage, 86
Microsoft IIS 1-2 format, 419
Microsoft Index Server, with Microsoft BackOffice Small Business Server, 84–85
Microsoft Internet Directory, using with Microsoft NetMeeting, 448
Microsoft Internet Explorer
  setting LAN configuration in, *244*
  setting to access intranet, 401–2
  version 5, changing default connection in, 429
Microsoft Internet Information Services, 405–6

Index

Microsoft Mail Postoffice
  adding to Microsoft Windows Messaging profile, 330–31
  adding users to, 327–28
  creating post offices, 326–27
  installing, 324–26
Microsoft Modem Sharing Service, 86–87, 383–84
Microsoft NetMeeting, 14, 421–22
  chatting in, 449
  overview, 443–45
  using Microsoft Internet Directory with, 448
  using on office network, 446–48
  Whiteboard feature, 450–53
  working simultaneously on files and, 279
  working together on programs on, 453–55
Microsoft Office, 88, 408–20. *See also specific applications*
Microsoft Outlook, 14, 86
  address book, 338–39, 340–42
  changing security settings in, 356–57
  coordinating network calendars, 359–64
  creating profiles in, 335
  as e-mail client, 324
  indicating availability with, 362–64
  mail service options, 335
  modifying profiles in, 335–36
  overview, 334–35
  reconfiguring, 354
  removing profiles in, 338
  sending e-mail messages in, 331–34
  setting up meetings with, 364–70
  using different profiles in, 337–38
  using with Microsoft Exchange Server, 100–102, 351–52
  voting buttons features, 102
Microsoft Outlook Express, 334
  configuring clients for Internet access and, 381
  using remotely, 425
Microsoft Outlook Web Access, 96
Microsoft Personal Web Server (PWS), 395
  accessing home pages in, 401–2
  creating home pages in, 399–401
  guest books and drop boxes in, 402–3
  installing, 395–97
  Personal Web Manager, 397–98
  publishing files on Web sites with, 403–4
  Quick Setup window, 400–401
  screen, *396*
Microsoft Post Office, 323, 324

Microsoft PowerPoint, creating Web pages with, 419–20
Microsoft Proxy Server, 87, 384–85
Microsoft SBS Console, 88–90
Microsoft Schedule +, *100*
Microsoft Site Server 3.0, 91
Microsoft SNA Server 4.0, 90
Microsoft SQL Server, 86, *87*
Microsoft Systems Management Sever 2.0, 91
Microsoft Transaction Server, with Microsoft BackOffice Small Business Server, 84
Microsoft Windows 95/98
  activating sharing service, 259–60
  adding network services in, 200–201
  configuring network clients, 194–95
  configuring TCP/IP in, 205–7
  creating additional dial-up networking connections, 426–27
  creating Web sites with, 395–404
  enabling printer sharing in, 307
  finding other computers on network in, 210
  fixing Microsoft Windows Messaging in Win 98 2/e, 329
  identifying computers on networks in, 202
  installing non-plug-and-play NIC drivers on, 191
  installing plug-and-play NIC drivers on, 188–89
  installing protocols in, 197–98
  Microsoft Exchange, 323
  Microsoft Mail Postoffice in, 325
  preparing laptops for dialing in to networks, 429–31
  sharing in, 259–60
  switching profiles in, 221–22
  System Information program, 212
  WinPopup in, 318–22
Microsoft Windows 2000, 103–4
  accessibility features, 107–9
  activating sharing service, 285
  adding network services in, 201
  Backup program, 297
  configuring network clients, 196
  configuring TCP/IP in, 207–8
  creating additional dial-up networking connections, 427–29
  creating the Web site with, 405–6
  creating user groups in, 78
  domain controllers in, 170
  ease of installation, 104–7

Index

Microsoft Windows 2000, *continued*
  finding other computers on network in, 210–11
  identifying computers on networks in, 203
  installing non-plug-and-play NIC drivers on, 192
  installing plug-and-play NIC drivers on, 189–90
  installing protocols in, 198–99
  IntelliMirror, 114–16
  Internet Connection Sharing with, 382
  network licenses, 79
  preparing laptops for dialing in to networks, 431–32
  profiles in, 226–29
  RAS (Remote Access Service), 440–41
  security in, 109–11
  sharing in, 284–85
  sharing printers in, 309
  WBTs (Microsoft Windows–based terminals) and, 180–81
  working remotely and, 111–14
Microsoft Windows–based server appliances, 30–31, 161–63
  installing, 233–36
  reasons for selecting, 33
  setting up clients on, 241–44
  setting up printer sharing on, 237–39
  setting up security on, 239–41
  sharing printers and, 302
Microsoft Windows Explorer, accessing home page with, 401
Microsoft Windows Internet Connection Sharing, 375–77
  changing options in, 377–78
  connecting to Internet with, 381–82
  setting up client computers for, 378
  using with TCP/IP networks, 379
Microsoft Windows Messaging, 323. *See also* Microsoft Exchange
  Microsoft Fax and, 387–89
  setting up, 328–30
Microsoft Windows NT
  accommodating multiple platforms, 80–81
  creating additional dial-up networking connections, 426–27
  creating user groups in, 78
  domain controllers in, 168–69
  Microsoft Mail Postoffice in, 325
  network licenses, 79
  part of SBS package, 82

Microsoft Windows NT, *continued*
  preparing laptops for dialing in to networks, 429–31
  RAS (Remote Access Service), 436–40
  sharing printers in, 309
  WBTs (Microsoft Windows–based terminals) and, 180–81
Microsoft WinPopup
  installing, 319–20
  sending/receiving messages in, 320–22
  starting, 318–19
Microsoft Word
  creating Web pages with, 408–16
  files, converting to Web pages, 416
  working with links in, 413–16
mini-Centronics ports, 313
modems
  fax, 387–92
  LAN, 374
  remote access servers and, 70
  selecting, 173
  sharing, 12–13, 371–74, 382–87
Modem Saver Plus, 424
modem servers, 68–69
  of Microsoft Windows–based server appliance, 161
  selecting, 160
modem-sharing software, 372–74, 375–86
moderated public folders, 98
molded-end cable, 150
monitors, using multiple, 107
moving, remote files, 283
MS-DOS programs, network printers and, 310
MTA (message transfer agent), 95, *96*
multiple domains, 169–70
multipurpose thin servers, 159
My Computer, accessing remote files with, 275–76
My Documents folder, sharing, 266
My Internet Home Page bookmark, 407
My Intranet Home Page bookmark, 407
My Network Places icon, 211–12

N

Narrator, 108
NAS (network-attached storage) servers, 65–67, 160, 163–66
navigation methods, for web pages, 410
neighborhood. *See* Network Neighborhood

Index

NetBEUI (NetBIOS Extended User Interface), 196–97
network administrators, 23, 77, 162–163
network appliances, 72–73
network clients, adding, 194–96
network collisions, 145
network control, 24
   client/server networks and, 27–30
   peer-to-peer networks and, 25–27
network hard disk drives, 65
Network ID button, 203
networking, defined, 3
networking scheme, planning for, 23
network licenses, 79
Network Neighborhood
   accessing hard disk drive through, 242
   accessing network without, 211
   accessing remote files with, 275–76
   seeing other computers with, 210
Network Neighborhood icon, 269
network PCs. *See* thin clients
network services, 200–201. *See also* sharing
network settings, checking, 211–12
network starter kits, 126–27
NICs (network interface cards), 48
   checking for hardware conflicts after installing, 192–93
   connecting cable to, 152–54
   fitting in slot, 132
   installing, 121–22, 130–35
   installing drivers for non-plug-and-play, 190–92
   installing drivers for plug-and-play, 186–90
   need for, 119–20
   for power line networks, 58
   preparing to install, 129–30
   professional installation, 122–23
   selecting, 123–24
   selecting which to use for network, 377–78
   working without, 120–21
NNTP (Network News Transport Protocol), 85
No Access permissions, 309
non-Ethernet networks. *See also specific networks*
   advantages/disadvantages to, 47–49
   phone line networks, 56–58
   power line networks, 58–60
   wireless networks, 49–55
NOS (network operating systems), 77, 80–81
NTFS (NT File System), 110
NTP (Network Time Protocol) standards, 70

O

offices, layout and cabling situations, 137
offline files. *See* files, working with offline
Offline Files Wizard, 112
offline folders, 101. *See also* folders, offline
OneResource, 366
one-way trust, 169–70
online retailers, shopping with, 128
On-Screen keyboard, 108
operating systems, dual-boot configurations, 29

P

packets, 37, 145, 146
parallel ports, 54
   multiple devices on, 63
   parallel overload and, 10
   using for removable disk drives, 8
passwords. *See also* security
   accessing shared resources with, 271
   adding user profiles and 218–220
   changing, 223
   client/server network and, 28
   computer access and, 25
   erasing, 266
   forgetting, 224, 265
   share-level access and, 262
   user account, 77–78
pasting
   remote files, 282
   text into popup messages, 321
patch cables, 138
   distinguishing from crossover, 141
   jacks for, 151
patch panels, 177–78
PC Cards, 126
PCI interface, 54
PCI (Peripheral Component Interconnect) slots, 124, 125
PDC (Primary Domain Controller) database, 168–69
peer-to-peer networks. *See also* client/server networks; combination networks; phone line networks
   access controls on, 262
   accessing files on other workstations on, 169
   adding Microsoft Windows–based server appliances to, 161–63
   adding Microsoft Windows–based server appliance to, 30–31
   vs. client/server networks, 24

Index

peer-to-peer networks, *continued*
  communicating over, 317
  computer communication on, 25
  disadvantages of, 61–63
  e-mail systems on, 93
  hubless, 139–41
  hubs and, *40*
  need for backing up on, 292–93
  network control and, 25–27
  network operating systems for, 77
  personnel for, 23
  reasons for selecting, 33
  sharing fax modems on, 388–91
permissions, 78. *See also* access controls
  assigning group, 229
  assigning user, 115
  setting dial-in, 439–40, 441
  setting for drive sharing, 287–88
  setting for printer sharing, 309
  setting up in Microsoft BackOffice Small Business Server, 250–51
  user-level, 109–10
Personal Web Manager, 397–98
Personal Web Server. *See* Microsoft Personal Web Server (PWS)
personnel, planning for network, 23
phone extension cables, packing, 422
phone jacks. *See* jacks
phone line network connections, comparing with other network connections, 35
phone line networks, 56
  advantages/disadvantages of, 56–57
  selecting, 57–58
phone lines
  in hotels, 423
  Internet access and, 12
  sharing, 371–72
PLC networks. *See* power line networks
plenum-grade cable, 150–51
plug-and-play devices, NICs, installing drivers for, 186–90
plug-and-play support, in network operating systems, 104
Plug and Play thin servers, setting up, 160
Plug & Store NAS servers, 165
pocket print servers, 313–14
pocket servers, 68
POP (Post Office Protocol), ISP mail servers and, 323
POP3 (Post Office Protocol 3), 85, 96
pop-up messages, 318–22

ports
  attaching printers to, 305
  modem sharing, 383–84
  parallel, 8, 10, 54, 63
  pocket print servers and, 314
  printer, print servers and, 313
  standard and uplink, 142
  uplink, 142–43
  USB, *121*
power line network connections, comparing with other network connections, 35
power line networks, 58–60
Power Users group, 226
PPTP (Point-to-Point Tunneling Protocol), 442
premises wiring, 139
printer port network devices, 121
printers
  availability of, 240
  connecting directly to network, 312–16
  connecting to network, 67–68
  installing, 303–6, 310–11
  network ready, 67–68
  network-ready, 312
  problems with, 306–7
  Properties dialog box, *308*
  selecting, 173–74
  sharing, 8–9, 301–3
  using shortcuts, 312–13
printing
  Microsoft NetMeeting Whiteboard, 453
  from non-network computers, 301
  queuing for, 303
  removable disk drives and, 8
  separating print jobs, 308–9
  shortcuts for, 312–13
Print permissions, 309
print servers, 67–68
  connecting printers directly to networks with, 312–13
  external, 315–16
  manufacturers and models, *315–16*
  of Microsoft Windows–based server appliance, 161
  pocket, 313–14
  selecting, 160
profiles
  adding Microsoft Exchange server to, 351
  adding users, 218–21
  changing, 220–21
  creating, 217–18
  defined, 215

profiles, *continued*
    deleting, 221, 224–25
    information contained in, 216–17
    Microsoft Outlook, 335–38, 340–42
    in Microsoft Windows 2000, 226–29
    Microsoft Windows Messaging
        adding Microsoft Mail to, 330, *331*
    roaming, 254
    setting up fax, 389–91
    switching, 221–23
    user, 114
    using Microsoft Outlook and, 354
program documentation, sharing and, 7
projects, collaborating on, 14–15
proprietary hardware, 48
protocols, 147. *See also specific protocols*
    configuring RAS in Microsoft Windows NT
        Server, 438
    installing, 196–99
    installing Dial-Up Server and, 432–33
    listing existing, *197*
    troubleshooting, 212
public folders, 97–98
Publisher icon, 398
Publishing Wizard, 403–4
PVC plastic cable, 150–51
PWS. *See* Microsoft Personal Web Server (PWS)

Q–R

Quick Launch toolbar, viewing icons on, 319
Quick Logon feature, mapping and, 274–75
raceways, 138
racks, 176–77
RadioLAN wireless system, 55
radio waves
    interfering with power line networks, 59
    radio technologies and, 53
    wireless networks and, 49– 50
RAID (redundant array of independent disks)
    system, 294–95
RAS (Remote Access Service), 436
    activating, 439
    configuring in Microsoft Windows NT Server,
        437–40
    configuring in Microsoft Windows 2000
        Server, 440–41
    setting dial-in permissions, 439–40, 441
read only rights, 25
read receipts, 332
read/write access, 25–26
receipts, read and delivery, 332

Rectangle tool, 452
recurring appointments, 364
Recycle Bin, 284
remote access servers, 69–70, 387
remote computers, 269–70. *See also* laptop
        computers; resources, shared
    accessing resources on, with Run/Find
        commands, 270
    creating shortcut to, 272
    saving documents to, 291–92
    sharing printers and, 302–3
remote computing, 421–22. *See also*
        telecommuting
    accessing office computers, 441–42
    controlling office computers remotely,
        455–56
    creating additional dial-up networking
        connections, 425–29
    dialing in to ISPs, 424–25
    dialing in to a network, 429–32
    Dial-Up Server and, 432–36
    Microsoft NetMeeting, 14, 421–22
        chatting in, 449
        overview, 443–45
        using Microsoft Internet Directory with,
            448
        using on office network, 446–48
        Whiteboard feature, 450–53, *451*
        working simultaneously on files and, 279
        working together on programs on, 453–55
    packing for, 422–24
remote connections, planning for, 18
remote files. *See* files, remote
Remote Pointer tool, 452
remote users, 76, 111–14
removable disks/disk drives
    backing up files with, 293
    sharing, 7–8
repeaters, 146
Replicator group, 226
resources, shared. *See also* access controls;
        specific shared resources
    accessing with passwords, 271
    accessing with Run/Find commands, 270
    adding to Favorites list, 272–73
    specifying, 261
revisions, tracking document, 15
RJ-11 modular phone jacks, in hotel rooms, 423
roaming profiles, 228, 254
rooms, running cables within/between, 148
routers, 147, 386–87
Run command, accessing shared resources with,
        270

Index

S

SAM (Security Accounts Manager) database, 168–69
saving, Microsoft NetMeeting Whiteboard, 453
SBS. *See* Microsoft BackOffice Small Business Server (SBS)
schedules, coordinating, 14
scheduling, with Microsoft Outlook, *102*
search engines, Microsoft Index Server as, 84–85
searching, for files, 5
security. *See also* firewalls; passwords
   active e-mail content, 357–58
   changing settings, 356–57
   on client/server networks, 28–29
   configuring Microsoft Outlook for, 354–55
   digital certificates, 355
   getting Microsoft Exchange certificate, 355–56
   Internet servers and, 71
   in Microsoft Exchange Server, 96
   with Microsoft Exchange Server, 348–50
   Microsoft Windows 2000 and, 109–11
   network operating system, 77–78
   planning for, 24
   printer sharing and, 309
   setting to use with all messages, 358–59
   setting up on Microsoft Windows–based server appliances, 239–41
   storing data files and, 291
sensitivity levels, of messages, 332
separator pages, 308–9
server-centric networks, *164*
servers. *See also specific types of servers*
   assigning IP addresses, 208–9
   checking users against account database, 77
   combination networks and, 32
   connecting to hubs, 143
   defined, 27
   FTP, 405
   importance of, 29, *30*
   isolating in computer rooms, 175–76
   mail, 322–24
   maintaining load distribution, 115
   multiple, 174
   storing e-mail on, 352
   Web, 83, 398
servers starting Microsoft NetMeeting and, 444
Set Up Computer Wizard, setting up and configuring workstations with, 89–90

share-level access, 262, 263–66
share-level access controls, 34, 109
shares, 261. *See also specific shared resources*
sharing. *See also* access controls; resources, shared
   accessing network resources and, 260–61
   adding services, 200–201
   computers, 215
   drives, 286–88
      hard disk, 261
      removable disk, 7–8
      with share-level access, 263–65
      with user-level access, 267–68
   facilitating, 271–75
   fax modems, 387–92
   files, 4–5
      adding service, 200–201
      on peer-to-peer networks, 25–26
      problems with, 61–62
   folders, 4–5
      access control and, 288–89
      adding service, 200–201
      availability, 261
      on peer-to-peer networks, 25–26
      problems with, 61–62
      with share-level access, 266
      with user-level access, 267–68
   formal vs. informal, 20
   Internet, 10–13
   ISP accounts, 371–74
   modems, 12–13, 371–75, 382–87
   My Documents folder, 266
   phone lines, 371–72
   printers, 8–12, 301–2, 309–16
   problems with, 61–63
shortcuts. *See* desktop shortcuts, facilitating sharing with
side-grading, 67
signal bounce, 153
small businesses, network system for, 63–64
S/MIME Internet security, 356
SMTP (Simple Mail Transfer Protocol), Microsoft Exchange Server handling mail from, 96
SNTP (Simple Network Time Protocol) standards, 70
software. *See also* applications, controlling; *specific software*
   installing Dial-Up Server, 434, *435*
   installing network, 185–87

470

Index

software, *continued*
   for Internet connection sharing, *385*
   recovering from failures, 115
   setting up Microsoft Windows–based server appliances workstations with, 241–42
   setting up networks and, 33
   sharing modems by using, 372–74
SOHOware, wireless networks by, 55
SOPs (standard operating procedures), identifying necessary, 22–23
SSL (Secure Sockets Layer), Internet servers as, 71
stackable hubs, 145
standard modem, advantages and disadvantages of, *373*
star bus topology, *143*
Start menu, accessing home page from, 401
star topology, 40
static addresses, 204, 234
static electricity, opening computer and, 129–30
Stop button, 398
storage. *See also* backing up
   analyzing current information, 20
   of e-mail, using Microsoft Outlook and Microsoft Exchange server, 351–53
   of e-mail drafts in Microsoft Outlook, 343
   of e-mail messages, 334
   of files, remotely, 293–94
   Microsoft Proxy Server and, 87
   network appliances for, 72–73
   peer-to-peer networks and, 27
   planning improved information, 21
   public, 97–98, 240
   server and, 28
   of shared data files, 290–92
STP (shielded twisted-pair) cable, 39
strippers, 150
subnet mask, 205
surge protectors, 424
switches, 146
switching hubs. *See* switches
Synchronization Manager, 112–14
Synchronize tool, 452
System Attendant, 96
system tray, 377

T

tape storage, backing up files with, 294
TaskPad, on Calendar folder, 361
T-connectors, 152–54

TCP/IP (Transmission Control Protocol/Internet Protocol), 196–97
   configuring, 204–8
   ensuring installation of, 374–75
TCP/IP networks, using Internet Connection Sharing with, 379
TCP/IP pocket print servers, 313–14
telecommuting, 70. *See also* remote computing
telephone cable coupler, 422
telephone lines. *See* phone lines
terminals, 179
terminators, 153
text, formatting web page, 411–12
Text tool, 451
ThickNet cable, 42
thin clients, 179–81
ThinNet coaxial cable, 41–43, *42*. *See also* coaxial cable
   connecting hubs with, 144
   using, 152–54
thin servers, 30–31
   adding, *64*
   assigning IP addresses and, 231–32
   balancing workload on client/server networks with, 174, *175*
   client/server network advantages over, 75
   connecting, 160–61
   as DHCP servers, 232
   Microsoft Windows–based server appliances, 161–63
   modem servers, 68–69
   multipurpose, 159
   NAS servers, 65–67
   network appliances, 72–73
   print servers, 67–68
   remote access servers, 69–70
   selecting, 159–60
   for small businesses, 63–64
   time servers, 70, *71*
   types of, 64–65
   universal serial servers, 72
threads, 97
three-to-one telephone adapter, 422
time bar, on Calendar folder, 360
time servers, 70, *71*
time slots, on Calendar folder, 360
To Do List, *248*
token ring networks, 146
tokens, 146, 349
tools, for installing NICs, 129
Tour icon, 398

Index

transactions, processing in client/server environment, 84
transceivers, 49–50
transformers, 59
troubleshooting, installation problems, 211–13
trusted domain, 169–70
trusting domain, 169–70
trust relationship, 169–70
twisted-pair cable
   connector for, 120
   Ethernet networks and, 38–41
   grades of, 149–50
   using, 149
two-to-one telephone adapter, 422
two-way trust, 170

U

UNC (universal naming convention) pathnames, 270
universal serial servers, 72
UPC (universal product code) scanners, 180
upgrading, vs. side-grading, 67
uplink ports, 142–43
USB connections, 54, 120
USB external interface, 107
USB network devices, 120–21
USB ports, 121
USB wireless systems, 51
user accounts, 77–78
   creating, 247–52
   creating for Microsoft Windows NT, 82
   creating from User Manager For Domains program, 252–54
   for Microsoft Windows–based server appliances, 163
   options for, 253
   types of SBS, 246–47
User Account Wizard, 247–52
user groups, 78
user-level access, 262–63, 267–68, 285
user-level access controls, 34
user-level permissions, 109–10
User Manager for Domains, 170
User Manager For Domains program, 252–54
users
   adding Postoffice, 327–28
   adding profiles for, 218–20
   assigning to Microsoft Windows–based server appliances, 236
   changing profile settings for, 220–21
   controlling access of, 78

users, *continued*
   creating profiles for, 217–18
   directory of mailbox, 95–96
   limiting authorized connection times of, 79
   PDC limits to, 169
Users group, 226
Use Shared Internet Connection option, 242
Utility Manager, 109
UTP (unshielded twisted-pair) cable, 39, 40

V–Z

VPN (virtual private network), 70, 442
WaveLAN Turbo wireless system, 55
WBTs (Windows–based terminals), 180–81
Web-based interface, controlling Microsoft Windows–based server appliances from, 162
Web-based interfaces, 83
Web browser. *See* browsers
WebGear, wireless networks by, 54
Web pages. *See also* home pages; links
   adding additional links to, 415
   converting it Microsoft Word files to, 416
   creating with Microsoft Access, 417–19
   creating with Microsoft Excel, 416–17
   creating with Microsoft PowerPoint, 419–20
   creating with Microsoft Word, 408–16
   favorite, adding to Favorite Links section, 414–15
   Internet servers and, 71
   Microsoft Excel, 417
   selecting layout of, 410
   selecting navigation methods, 410
   selecting themes for, 410–11, 412
   working with in Microsoft Word, 411–12
Web Page Wizard, 408–11
Web Publishing Wizard, 406–7
Web server, disabling temporarily, 398
Web-site locations, 83
Web sites, 393. *See also* home pages
   accessing, 398–99, 407
   accessing mailboxes through browser window, 96
   adding more pages to, 410
   creating with Microsoft FrontPage, 86
   creating with Microsoft Office, 408–20
   managing with IIS, 83
   managing with Internet Service Manager, 408
   publishing documents on, 403–4
   searching for files on, 84

Index

Web sites, *continued*
   tracking usage of, *85*
   using Personal Web Manager with, 397–99
Web Sites icon, 398
Whiteboard feature. *See* Microsoft NetMeeting, Whiteboard feature
Windows–based server appliances. *See* Microsoft Windows–based server appliances
Windows Messaging Inbox, *331,* 332
Windows Registry Editor, deleting profiles with, 224–25
wireless network connections, comparing with other network connections, *35*
wireless networks. *See* WLANs (wireless networks)
wizard, Home Page, 399–401
wizards
   Accessibility, 107, *108*
   Add Printer, *238,* 304–6
   Audio Tuning, 445
   Backup, 297–98
   Browser Connection Setup, 380–81
   Computer Setup, 241–42
   Enable Security, *240*

wizards, *continued*
   Home Page, 408
   Inbox Setup, 329–30
   Internet Connection, 236–37
   Internet Connection Sharing, 376–78
   Microsoft Windows–based server appliances and, 31
   Offline Files, 112
   Publishing, 403–4
   Set Up Computer, 89–90
   User Account, 247–52
   Web Page, 408–11
   Web Publishing, 406–7
WLANs (wireless networks), 48, 49–50
   advantages/disadvantages of, 50–53
   commercial-quality, 51–53
   configurations for connecting computers to, 50
   selecting, 54–55
word processing programs, tracking revisions on, 15
workgroups, managing, 13–15
workstations. *See* computers
Zone setting, 357–58

The manuscript for this book was prepared and submitted to Microsoft Press in electronic form. Text files were prepared using Microsoft Word 2000. Pages were composed by Microsoft Press using Adobe PageMaker 6.52 for Windows, with text in Garamond and display type in Frutiger. Composed pages were delivered to the printer as electronic prepress files.

Cover Graphic Designer
Patrick Lanfear

Cover Illustrator
Tom Draper Design

Interior Designer
James D. Kramer

Interior Graphic Artist
Michael Kloepfer

Principal Compositor
Barb Runyan

Principal Copy Editor
Kristen Weatherby

Principal Proofreader
Roger LeBlanc

Indexer
Leslie Leland Frank

Proof of Purchase

0-7356-0685-4

Do not send this card with your registration.
Use this card as proof of purchase if participating in a promotion or
rebate offer on *Small Business Solutions for Networking*. Card must be used in conjunction with
other proof(s) of payment such as your dated sales receipt—see offer details.

Small Business Solutions for Networking

_____
WHERE DID YOU PURCHASE THIS PRODUCT?

_____
CUSTOMER NAME

Microsoft®
mspress.microsoft.com

Microsoft Press, PO Box 97017, Redmond, WA 98073-9830

OWNER REGISTRATION CARD   *Register Today!*   0-7356-0685-4

Return the bottom portion of this card to register today.

Small Business Solutions for Networking

_____ _____ _____
FIRST NAME   **MIDDLE INITIAL**   **LAST NAME**

_____
INSTITUTION OR COMPANY NAME

_____
ADDRESS

_____

_____   _____ _____
CITY   **STATE**   **ZIP**

                                         ( )
_____   _____
E-MAIL ADDRESS   **PHONE NUMBER**

U.S. and Canada addresses only. Fill in information above and mail postage-free.
Please mail only the bottom half of this page.

start faster go farther

For information about Microsoft Press® products, visit our Web site at

mspress.microsoft.com

Microsoft®

BUSINESS REPLY MAIL
FIRST-CLASS MAIL   PERMIT NO. 108   REDMOND WA

POSTAGE WILL BE PAID BY ADDRESSEE

NO POSTAGE
NECESSARY
IF MAILED
IN THE
UNITED STATES

MICROSOFT PRESS
PO BOX 97017
REDMOND, WA 98073-9830